The Poetic World of Statius' *Silvae*

The Poetic World of Statius' *Silvae*

by
MICHAEL C. J. PUTNAM

Edited by
ANTONY AUGOUSTAKIS

with
CAROLE E. NEWLANDS

OXFORD
UNIVERSITY PRESS

Great Clarendon Street, Oxford, OX2 6DP,
United Kingdom

Oxford University Press is a department of the University of Oxford.
It furthers the University's objective of excellence in research, scholarship,
and education by publishing worldwide. Oxford is a registered trade mark of
Oxford University Press in the UK and in certain other countries

© Michael C. J. Putnam 2023
Preface and Introduction © Oxford University Press 2023

The moral rights of the authors have been asserted

All rights reserved. No part of this publication may be reproduced, stored in
a retrieval system, or transmitted, in any form or by any means, without the
prior permission in writing of Oxford University Press, or as expressly permitted
by law, by licence or under terms agreed with the appropriate reprographics
rights organization. Enquiries concerning reproduction outside the scope of the
above should be sent to the Rights Department, Oxford University Press, at the
address above

You must not circulate this work in any other form
and you must impose this same condition on any acquirer

Published in the United States of America by Oxford University Press
198 Madison Avenue, New York, NY 10016, United States of America

British Library Cataloguing in Publication Data
Data available

Library of Congress Control Number: 2023930587

ISBN 978-0-19-286927-2

DOI: 10.1093/oso/9780192869272.001.0001

Printed and bound by
CPI Group (UK) Ltd, Croydon, CR0 4YY

Links to third party websites are provided by Oxford in good faith and
for information only. Oxford disclaims any responsibility for the materials
contained in any third party website referenced in this work.

Preface

Michael C. J. Putnam has been an extraordinary scholar and teacher of Latin literature at Brown University for many decades, and Antony had the good luck of studying under him as his doctoral student. Michael is the foremost Virgilian scholar of our times. As a member of the Virgilian society and its editorial board, and also a member of the Accademia Nazionale Virgiliana, he has spent a good deal of time in Naples, the city crucial to the intellectual formation of both Virgil and Statius as poets. In an extraordinary set of articles, originally published in *Illinois Classical Studies*,[1] he turned his attention to the *Silvae* and to their intimate engagement with Augustan poetry, and with the poetry of Virgil in particular. Michael's deep knowledge and understanding of Virgilian poetry lend valuable insights into the reception of Virgil by Statius. He shows how seriously the later poet pays homage to his canonical predecessor, how thoroughly he interprets the complexities of Virgilian poetry, and how he often, by placing a Virgilian reference in a different social and cultural context, boldly turns Virgil to new and more positive purposes. These articles are partly detailed commentary on the individual *Silvae*, partly brilliant reflective essays. They are in short, like Statius' *Silvae, sui generis*.

It was important, in our view, that these essays by a foremost scholar of Latin poetry, be published as a set to draw attention to the major contributions that Statius' *Silvae* make to the study of ekphrasis and of material culture in the imperial age. Through Statius' close intertextual engagement with Virgil's poetry, a shift in moral and aesthetic attitudes to the Graeco-Roman world of empire can be charted.

In the process of putting this volume together, we decided that Carole was going to write the introductory chapter and Antony was going to edit the chapters and update them bibliographically. Both of us have also checked each other's work.

---

[1] 'Statius *Siluae* 2.3: The Garden of Atedius Melior: A Change for the Better', *ICS* 46.1 (2021): 241–85; 'A Labor of Love: Statius *Siluae* 3.1 (*Hercules Surrentinus Polli Felicis*)', *ICS* 45.1 (2020): 158–223; 'Statius *Siluae* 1.3: A Stream and Two Villas', *ICS* 44.1 (2019) 66–100; 'Statius *Siluae* 3.2: Reading Travel', *ICS* 42.1 (2017): 83–139.

vi PREFACE

Antony would also like to thank his current home at the Department of the Classics at the University of Illinois, the superb resources of the famously incomparable Classics Library, The College of Liberal Arts and Sciences and the University have provided generous research funds through a Langan Professorial Scholarship first and then a University Scholarship.

Carole would like to thank Antony and Michael for their enthusiasm and support of this project. It has been a privilege to work with them both. She would also like to thank the wider Flavian community for their friendship and encouragement over many years, and for their inspiring scholarship on Statius.

We would also like to extend a warm word of thanks to Charlotte Loveridge who supported this project from the beginning and her team for seeing it through completion.

Finally, on the occasion of his 90th birthday, we would like to dedicate this volume to Michael himself and extend our warmest thanks and best wishes for decades of friendship, mentoring, and generosity.

Antony Augoustakis and
Carole E. Newlands

August 2022

Contents

List of Abbreviations	ix
Introduction	1
1. A Stream and Two Villas (Statius' *Silvae* 1.3)	11
2. The Garden of Atedius Melior: A Change for the Better (Statius' *Silvae* 2.3)	45
3. A Labour of Love (Statius' *Silvae* 3.1)	89
4. Atedius Melior's Parrot (Statius' *Silvae* 2.4)	156
5. Domitian's Banquet (Statius' *Silvae* 4.2)	183
6. Reading Travel (Statius' *Silvae* 3.2)	215
Bibliography	275
General Index	283
Index Locorum	287

List of Abbreviations

Greek authors and works are abbreviated according to the system of the *OCD*[4], while Latin authors and works follow the system of the *OLD* with a few adjustments (e.g. Virg. instead of Verg.). Periodicals have been abbreviated based on *L' Année Philologique*. For Statius' *Silvae*, we follow Courtney's OCT edition unless otherwise indicated; translations are our own. For other Latin authors, we have followed these editions: Ennius, Jocelyn, Skutsch, and Vahlen; Horace, Shackleton Bailey; Propertius, Heyworth; Seneca, Zwierlein; Tibullus, Putnam; Virgil, Mynors.

Courtney	Courtney, E., ed. (1992). *P. Papini Stati: Silvae*. Oxford: Clarendon Press.
FGrHist	Jacoby, F. *et al.*, eds (1923–58, 1994–). *Die Fragmente der griechischen Historiker*. Leiden: Brill.
FPL[4]	Blänsdorf, J., ed. (2011). *Fragmenta poetarum latinorum post W. Morel et Büchner*. 4th ed. Berlin: Walter de Gruyter.
Heyworth	Heyworth, S. J., ed. (2007). *Sexti Properti Elegos*. Oxford: Oxford University Press.
Jocelyn	Jocelyn, H. D., ed. (1967). *The Tragedies of Ennius*. Cambridge: Cambridge University Press.
L&S	Lewis, C. T. and Short C., eds (1879). *A Latin Dictionary*. Oxford: Clarendon Press.
Liberman	Liberman, G., ed (2010). *Stace, Silves: Édition et commentaire critiques*. Paris: Calepinus.
Mynors	Mynors, R. A. B., ed. (1969). *P. Vergili Maronis Opera*. Oxford: Clarendon Press.
OCD[4]	Hornblower, S., Spawforth, A., and Eidinow, E., eds (2012). *The Oxford Classical Dictionary*. 4th ed. Oxford: Oxford University Press.
OLD	Glare, P. G. W., ed. (2012). *Oxford Latin Dictionary*. 2nd ed. Oxford: Oxford University Press.
Putnam	Putnam, M. C. J., ed. (1973). *Tibullus: A Commentary*. Norman, OK: University of Oklahoma Press.
Shackleton Bailey	Shackleton Bailey, D. R., ed. (2008). *Q. Horati Flacci Opera*. 4th ed. Berlin: Walter de Gruyter.
Skutsch	Skutsch, O., ed. (1985). *The Annals of Quintus Ennius*. Oxford: Clarendon Press.

X LIST OF ABBREVIATIONS

TLL — *Thesaurus Linguae Latinae* (1900–). Leipzig/Berlin: Teubner/Walter de Gruyter.

Vahlen — Vahlen, I., ed. (1928). *Ennianae poesis reliquiae*. 2nd ed. Leipzig: Teubner.

Zwierlein — Zwierlein, O., ed. (1986). *L. Annaei Senecae Tragoediae*. Oxford: Clarendon Press.

Introduction

In this volume Michael Putnam offers detailed studies of six of the twenty-seven *Silvae* that Statius published in his lifetime. Written between 2016 and 2022, his essays, in the form of penetrating critical commentary, make a major contribution to our understanding and appreciation of these innovative poems within the Latin literary canon. Putnam's studies demonstrate, moreover, the authority of Augustan poetry, including Virgil above all, to the shaping of the Flavian imagination and to the construction of a second 'Augustan' age under the emperor Domitian. Statius lacked the social standing of Virgil or Horace but raised in the rich cultural milieu of the Bay of Naples, where Virgil had studied Epicurean philosophy, he offered a sophisticated outsider's perspective upon imperial Rome. Putnam's essays reveal how Statius' superb mastery of the Latin poetic canon endows his imperial poetics with a rich aesthetic, moral, and intellectual authority, while his special bicultural origins in Naples allowed him to challenge as well as to appropriate his literary inheritance. These studies offer a privileged entry into the mind of this imperial poet and to a worldview that was as profoundly shaped by literature, in particular Augustan literature, as by the changed sociopolitical realities of his times.[1]

Putnam shows the impressive range of Statius' inner poetic thesaurus of Latin literature. The Republican poets Lucretius and Catullus, as well as the Neronian poets Seneca and Lucan, are formative influences. But the Augustan poets—first Virgil, Statius' '*non pareil* example and guide' (in Putnam's words), and then Horace, followed by the elegists Tibullus, Propertius, and Ovid—form the essential literary matrix for the Flavian poet. Putnam's insightful commentaries upon the multi-layered, allusive texture of the *Silvae* shed light on the formation of the Latin literary canon over the hundred years between Virgil's death and the age of Domitian, thus helping to delineate the expected reading knowledge of the educated Flavian community.

---

[1] For recent scholarship on Statius' bilingualism see the essays of Bessone (2022a) and Pittà (2022).

The Poetic World of Statius' Silvae. Michael C. J. Putnam, Edited by: Antony Augoustakis with Carole E. Newlands, Oxford University Press. © Oxford University Press 2023. DOI: 10.1093/oso/9780192869272.003.0001

2 THE POETIC WORLD OF STATIUS' *SILVAE*

There is nothing heavy-handed about Statian intertextuality. Putnam shows the delicate interplay of multiple allusions within the *Silvae* and their seamless interweaving of multiple genres that generate constantly shifting perspectives. Allusion is key to both the aesthetic and the intellectual world of the Flavian poet. For not only do the Augustan poets provide a highly stylized, complex poetic language, they also offer an important precedent in their attempts to craft a new semiotics to address the phenomenon of imperial governance. We see from Putnam's studies how the *Silvae* build upon the epic and lyric voices of Virgil and Horace to formulate both the distant relationship between poet and *princeps*, and close relationships between the author and his wealthy patrons and friends. The *Silvae* help to shape a new 'Augustan age' that acknowledges the multiple differences that separate it from that earlier period. Allusion provides an essential tool for the Flavian poet through which both continuities and changes in his socio-political world could be charted, reflected upon, and debated.

The new Augustan age constructed in the *Silvae* is, however, not focused upon the capital city of Rome. Unlike most of his Augustan literary predecessors, Statius did not stand close to the centre of imperial power. The *Silvae* present no intimate chats with Domitian such as Horace enjoyed with Augustus in *Satires* 1.6. Rather, when Statius on a singular occasion is invited to an imperial banquet, he is one of a thousand guests (*Silv.* 4.2). In the *Silvae* Statius frequently moves us off centre from the political world, more often than not surveying Rome from outside the city, and in particular from his home base of Naples with its Greco-Roman culture and attentive literary patronage. The *Silvae* offer ample celebration of personal friends, people who would otherwise be unknown to us. Several of them preferred to live apart from political life in Rome. Statius in the *Silvae* makes central to the Flavian age his own sociopolitical world centred upon friendship. In these poems the farms celebrated by Horace and Virgil as models of traditional patriotic values have been supplanted by villas, no longer vulnerable to military incursions or seizures by war veterans, but rather secure refuges of peace and prosperity whose harmony with a tamed nature accords with their soft power. The villas of the *Silvae* advertise a beneficent use of wealth in creating peaceful conditions conducive to artistic creativity and to the provision of reliable literary patronage when little of such patronage was to be found at court. As Statius writes to his Neapolitan patron Pollius Felix of his new, third book of *Silvae*, *securus itaque tertius hic Silvarum nostrarum liber ad te mittitur* ('consequently, this third book of our *Silvae* is delivered to you *in safety* [my italics]', *Silv.* 3 *praef.* 6–7).

INTRODUCTION 3

The peaceful enclaves of villas are also represented as energetic sites of artistic creativity and pleasure in the *Silvae*. The majority of Putnam's studies here focus upon a particular innovation of the *Silvae*, the application of ekphrasis to actual buildings such as villas.[2] Putnam shows how Statius looks back in particular to the two longest ekphraseis of the *Aeneid*, those describing the murals of the Temple of Juno in Carthage (*A.* 1.441–92) and the engraved images on the shield of Aeneas (*A.* 8.625–731), doing so in order to elevate the aesthetic achievements not of nobility, but of otherwise unknown contemporaries. For instance, on a Bay of Naples still ravaged by the Vesuvian eruption of 79 CE, the villa and temple built by Statius' friends, the married couple Pollius Felix and Polla, stand as a testament to human resilience and offer a recuperative symbol of cultural regeneration (*Silv.* 2.2 and 3.1). Similarly, the villa owner Manilius Vopiscus engages in another recuperative act, the rescue of literature itself from decay and neglect (*Silv.* 1 *praef.* 23–5). Putnam demonstrates that Statius' use of ekphrasis provides an effective strategy for inviting the reader to join the poet in entering these special places of artistic wonder and emotional refuge, thus sharing the synesthetic experiences that stimulate both the imagination and the mind. Ekphrasis, grounded in the Virgilian model but also adapted from it, enables the poet and his readers to form a personal community of mutual pleasure and ethical and intellectual rapport. Moreover, an engaging feature of these essays is how Putnam himself, in his personal addresses to his readers, invites us to share in his aesthetic and intellectual journey into the world of the *Silvae*.

Summaries will not do justice to Putnam's brilliant essays, but they will provide a preliminary idea of the intellectual and aesthetic scope of this volume. To that end, Antony Augoustakis and I as editors present them not in the chronological order in which they were first published in *Illinois Classical Studies*, but in an order that, in Statian manner, invites thematic interplay and intellectual engagement. It is important too to note that much criticism of the *Silvae* has focused on the poems involving Domitian, and thus Statius' other achievements in this unique genre have been overshadowed;[3] yet, of the *Silvae* published in Statius' lifetime, fewer than a quarter involve Domitian directly. We therefore start this volume of essays

---

[2] Putnam (1998) provides a major study of ekphrasis in Virgil's poetry. Studies of ekphrasis as an important feature of Statius' poetics have been recently published by Econimo (2020) and by Chinn (2022).

[3] Most recently, for instance, Gunderson (2021).

4 THE POETIC WORLD OF STATIUS' *SILVAE*

on the *Silvae* with Putnam's analysis of *Silv*. 1.3, 'A Stream and Two Villas', the poem which showcases Statius' pioneering achievement in ekphrasis.

Silv. 1.3 offers a panegyrical description of the private villa of Manilius Vopiscus at Tibur. Here Putnam demonstrates the importance of intertextuality to an understanding of Statius' *Silvae*; in *Silv*. 1.3 various poetic antecedents, Catullus, Horace, and Propertius, work smoothly alongside Virgilian models to new purposes, in particular to the innovative expansion of the possibilities of ekphrasis. *Silv*.1.3 is pioneering in that here ekphrasis departs from traditional fictional norms in describing a historic building, not an imagined one; it is pioneering also in its focus on the private villa of an otherwise unknown friend secluded in Tibur, rather than upon art works and buildings belonging to divinities and nobility. The construction of Vopiscus' villa from twin buildings facing one another across a river complements Statius' double emphasis in this poem on the importance of the act of seeing—*aspectu visusque* (*Silv*. 1.3.52)—as a necessary prelude to innovative ekphrastic display. Yet as Putnam demonstrates, the tradition of ekphrasis, particularly as deployed by Virgil, shaped Statius' representation in its transmission of ways of viewing and of responding to monumental architecture. Ekphrasis offers a synesthetic experience, appealing particularly to sight and sound and arousing strong emotions. But whereas in the *Aeneid* the murals on the Temple of Juno arouse grief in the primary viewer, Aeneas, and his magnificent shield arouses only his incomprehension, Vopiscus' villa brings delight, expressed through dazzling visual images and assonant sound. Moreover, Statius here brings social and moral values into ekphrasis. The ekphrasis of Vopiscus' villa is inclusive, not exclusive; it invites the reader to join the poet in discovering its pleasures. Reading ekphrasis with the poet's guidance enacts specifically the value of friendship, of Vopiscus to Statius, and of Statius to his readers. The ekphrasis of Vopiscus' villa thus marks Statius' changed sociocultural world. While the villa retains the ethical integrity of the Virgilian farm of the *Georgics*, its description pushes further the importance of technological mastery and endorses wealth as a means of creating a spiritual equilibrium that can temporarily be shared. Putnam's analysis of villa culture in this poem departs widely from the frequent modern critical focus on luxury and decadence in the Flavian Age. For Putnam, Vopiscus embodies the Epicurean ethical ideals of living in contentment and friendship without turmoil and pain. This study introduces the *Silvae* as innovative poetry that melds various genres and poetic voices, adapting an authoritative literary tradition to new experiences of time and place.

Putnam's second study, on *Silv.* 2.3, 'The Garden of Atedius Melior: A Change for the Better', moves to an estate within Rome itself, but, like Vopiscus' villa at Tibur, it too is a sequestered and peaceful site. It is owned by Atedius Melior, a friend of Statius who has withdrawn from public life. The poem starts from a simple occasion, the celebration of Melior's birthday, but as with the other *Silvae* in general, the poem swiftly assumes a more complex dimension. The narrative of *Silv.* 2.3, Statius' birthday gift for Melior, is prompted by the initial description of a curiously shaped tree that overshades a reflective pool in Melior's garden. We are led to expect an erotic myth on the model of Ovid's violent rape narratives. Instead, as Putnam shows, the immanent physicality and violence stimulated by Pan's desire for a nymph is checked during the course of Statius' narrative. Moreover, erotic desire is counterbalanced by the setting in which Statius places us, the peaceful, calm-filled environment beloved by Epicureans, and by Melior, a realm, in Putnam's words, 'of ethical enlightenment, combining straightforwardness of behaviour with enjoyment, and lacking the inner *tumultus* that regularly beset humankind' (p. 46).

The poem is richly intertextual. In the first few lines alone Putnam traces the presence of Ovid the elegist as well as of Virgil, Lucan, Martial and, more circumspectly, Horace, in his role as lyricist. A major model is again *Aeneid* 8. Melior's estate actualizes Evander's early history of Rome as a site of Fauns and nymphs. As Putnam brilliantly shows, through the narrative of Pan's desire for a nymph, Statius' short poem traces a larger, more significant story, the origins of Rome and the temporal development of civilization through the change in land use from wilderness to sacred groves to ploughlands and then to Melior's garden. Putnam argues that Melior's estate, situated on the Caelian hill but nonetheless secluded from the political life of the capital, represents the acme of civilization.

Silv. 2.3 thus offers an instance of an overall pattern that Putnam traces in Statius' deployment of poetic allusion, namely the transformation of a negative setting or incident to a more positive outcome. Such a pattern is particularly illustrated at the end of *Silv.* 2.3 through its modulation from epic models to pastoral poetry. Putnam argues that the compliment to Melior for putting his life in order, *digeris ordine vitam* (69), clearly echoes Meliboeus' ironic injunction to his vines at the end of Virgil's first *Eclogue, insere nunc, Meliboee, piros, pone ordine vites* ('Graft now your pears, Meliboeus, plant your vines in a row', *Ecl.* 1.73). But now in a time of imperial peace Melior puts his life in figurative order the way a farmer should place his vines in careful arrangement for their healthy growth. In this instance again, Putnam

6   THE POETIC WORLD OF STATIUS' *SILVAE*

argues, Statius turns a moment of great distress in Virgil, the shepherd-singer's abandonment of his beloved landscape, into a celebration of stable order and security, shored up by a horticultural language that now has a significant ethical dimension. Yet, as Putnam shows also later, pastoral echoes, however muted, introduce an unsettling note of temporality into the garden.

Putnam's third study, 'A Labour of Love', skilfully navigates the special complexities of *Silv.* 3.1, an ekphrastic narrative devoted to the restoration of a temple to Hercules on the estate of Statius' Neapolitan patrons, Pollius Felix and his wife Polla. The temple is simultaneously actual, metapoetic, and metaphysical. Putnam discusses *Silv.* 3.1 as a dynamic interplay of epic, lyric, comic, and pastoral modalities in which *Aeneid* 8 again looms large as a model of social, cultural, and ethical values that are here both appropriated and challenged. Statius flags Virgil's importance early on through the phrase *cernere erat* (*Silv.* 3.1.15), the same phrase that introduces the climactic description on the shield of Aeneas, the Battle of Actium (*A.* 8.676). This allusion claims the reader's attentiveness to the programmatic importance of *Silv.* 3.1 in Statius' collection and to new purposes for ekphrasis, removed now from the realm of war to that of peace, and from destructive violence to restoration and regeneration. As Putnam observes, ekphrasis extends beyond external observation to inward reflection. Moreover, Statius personalizes ekphrasis through his close relationships with his patron friends. The poem often moves from a high register into a lighter and more easeful mood through the frequent modulation of genres, from epic and pastoral to Horatian lyric and even Horatian satire. The remaking of an old temple of Hercules on Pollius' estate becomes in this poem a celebration of piety and of technological mastery over a harsh landscape in a physically unstable volcanic region. *Silv.* 3.1 is also a *tour de force* of the remaking of ekphrasis for a society that deeply valued friendship, peaceful security, and the creative arts.

With *Silv.* 2.4, 'Atedius Melior's Parrot', Putnam takes a novel approach. Rather than emphasizing its parodic features within the Roman elegiac tradition for the death of a beloved pet established by Catullus and Ovid, he focuses on the poem's fascination with the power of words, and on its confrontation of speech and silence. He also focuses on the creative role of ekphrasis, here on a miniature scale. The parrot's cage is not described in Ovid's elegy on the death of Corinna's parrot (*Am.* 2.6). But the central portion of *Silv.* 2.4 is occupied by such an ekphrasis as a signature of Statius' 'Silvan' poetics (11–15). The description of the cage is inspired, moreover, by an epic model, the glittering chariot of the Sun in Book 2 of Ovid's

Metamorphoses (105–10). As Putnam argues, the gorgeous cage of Melior's parrot is a vehicle through which the bird can make artful music. The cage also has a metapoetic dimension. Though small, like Statius' short poem, it is partly built upon the poetic past and can reach beyond its generic confines; it sings the history of song, as an expansion of poet upon poet. And indeed, the expansion is not confined to Catullus and Ovid. In a brilliant conclusion to this fourth study, Putnam notes that *Silv.* 2.4 ends with a gesture of friendship to Melior, *dilecte Melior* (*Silv.* 2.4.32), that serves as a direct reminder of Horace's address to his own special benefactor, *dilecte Maecenas* (*Carm.* 2.20.7) at the conclusion of his second collection of odes. In this strange and wonderful lyric meditation on poetic immortality, Horace imagines his metamorphosis into a swan, a bird that stands as a symbol of the perpetuity of his verse. Statius of course is writing about a parrot and in a lower stylistic register. The subtle allusion to Horace's fanciful metamorphosis may well serve as a reminder of its humorous dimension and its odd fusion of hubris and self-mockery; Statius will not presume so far, and indeed there may well be implied criticism of his predecessor's baroque self-imagining. At the same time, perhaps, as Putnam suggests, the later poet draws upon Horace to indicate more modestly a form of perpetuity for himself also through artistic reinvention.

The essay on *Silv.* 4.2, 'Domitian's Banquet', by contrast takes the reader to the grandeur of Domitian's court and to commemoration of an imperial banquet to which the poet was invited. The poem's dominant strains are epic; the poem, for instance, begins with allusion to Homer and Virgil, poets who memorably sang of royal feasts. The poem's register is further elevated by persistent epic allusions, in particular to Dido's banquet for Aeneas, and by a soaring ekphrasis of magnificent architecture that draws upon the description of Latinus' palace in *Aeneid* 7. Allusions also to Horace's lyric political poetry, especially here to *Carm.* 1.12, situate *Silv.* 4.2 as a hymn of praise to Domitian, the new 'Augustus', and to his architectural achievements.

Putnam's main focus in *Silv.* 4.2 is thus upon the multiplicity of grand allusions through which Statius pushes language to the extremes of praise as an indication of the ineffability of imperial power. Towards the conclusion of his essay, however, he notes again the despairing voice of Virgil's pastoral shepherd Meliboeus, which, as we saw, echoed at the end of *Silv.* 2.3. When Statius, in muted complaint, mentions that 'after a long time' (*longo post tempore, Silv.* 4.2.64) Domitian rewarded his poetry with a victory at the Alban games, he uses the same phrase as Meliboeus at the end of Virgil's

8   THE POETIC WORLD OF STATIUS' *SILVAE*

Eclogue 1 when, heading into exile, he wonders if, 'after a long time' (*longo post tempore, Ecl.* 1.67), he may ever see his beloved native land again. For Putnam, the promise of the young Octavian/Augustus implied in *Eclogue* 1 finds fruition in the Flavian emperor praised in *Silv.* 4.2. His analysis of this poem more broadly, however, shows how Statius' masterful interweaving of various genres in a single poem can surprise and complicate the challenges of imperial praise. As at the end of *Silv.* 2.3, the powerlessness of the pastoral world of Statius' great literary master, Virgil, in the face of Roman military might, provides a tragic code that subtly hints at the Flavian poet's precarity and perhaps too of the peaceful world he constructs in song.

Putnam's final study, 'Reading Travel', of *Silv.* 3.2, the *propemptikon* for Maecius Celer who is leaving Italy for military duty in Syria, tackles one of Statius' longest and most ambitious poems; correspondingly, it is Putnam's most ambitious essay and a fitting conclusion to this volume. Here Statius himself plays a prominent role as poet both of the *Silvae* and the *Thebaid*. *Silv.* 3.2 follows Celer's journey from the Bay of Naples to Syria and back through a series of generic and tonal changes that range through lyric, elegy, pastoral, and epic. Again, it is Virgil, both as writer of the *Aeneid* and as addressee of Horace's *propemptikon, Carm.* 1.3, who figures most prominently in the intellectual and emotional background of Statius' poem. As Putnam comments, Virgil is doubly present before us in *Silv.* 3.2—as a major poetic influence on Statius' own literary struggles and accomplishments, and as reimagined by Horace in *Carm.* 1.3, the lyric genius observing his own talented colleague engage in a sea voyage that metaphorically represents the struggles involved in his attempt to write a great Roman epic.

Unlike Horace, however, who in *Carm.* 1.3 creates a wide gap between the lyric poet left at home and the epic poet voyaging out into unknown waters, in *Silv.* 3.2 Statius creates parallel and complementary journeys between himself and Celer that form a testament to the strong bonds of affection that underpin this poem. While Celer embarks on a dangerous voyage, Statius is struggling at home on the Bay of Naples to bring his *Thebaid* to a successful close. In this study of *Silv.* 3.2, Putnam engages closely with the intersection between Virgilian allusion and the outsider's perspective on imperial ambition and mission. From the standpoint of the Bay of Naples, the poet emphasizes the ominous nature of Celer's voyage, suggesting moreover that, by cementing Roman power in Syria, Celer is bringing further violence to the province. The bonds of friendship, moreover, are stretched the greater the distance that Celer travels from Italy; the imperial mission is fulfilled in threatening circumstances that are also dehumanizing and that temporarily, at least, disrupt the homosocial world in which friendship and literature flourish. Indeed, in a daring confrontation with Virgil and Lucan here, Statius represents Celer's journey through Egypt as an allegorical tour through the mummified past, where the once vibrant, tragic figures of Cleopatra and her alter ego Dido have become idle objects of touristic curiosity. Statius thus boldly creates space for his own innovative epic of civil war, the *Thebaid*, and conceives of himself as a second Amphion, rebuilding the walls of Thebes through the medium of words.

Putnam demonstrates that *Silv.* 3.2 is a highly complex poem in which a variety of genres and themes—the dangers of seafaring, the violence of Roman imperialism, Egyptian tourism, the neutralization of a bloodied historic and literary past—are skilfully woven together in a double, courageous journey, the literal journey of Celer to his military post in Syria, and the metaphorical journey of Statius to the challenging conclusion of his epic poem. The poet's persona is also doubled, as both a successor to Virgil embarking on epic composition, and a successor to the lyric Horace warning of the dangers of physical overreach. *Silv.* 3.2 completes the partial arc of Horace's third ode through the twin achievements of his friend's successful return and his own completion of his *Thebaid*. *Silv.* 3.2 thus demonstrates the poet's confidence in his ability to confront the Augustans even as he owes them his allegiance, and to create his own form of immortality through a new imagining of the multiple possibilities of poetry, including epic, for the Flavian age.

With these meticulous, nuanced studies of the *Silvae*, Michael Putnam has made a strong case for the importance of the Augustan poets to the forging of the poetic imagination in the age of the new Augustus, Domitian. At the same time, he delineates the reading practices of an educated Roman in the late first century CE. Virgil and Horace, the first Roman poets to engage with the realities of imperial governance, emerge as crucial to the poetic construction of a new imperial age in their provision of a rich, reflective language that Statius can appropriate, manipulate, and challenge in terms of his own social setting and worldview. That view, in Putnam's *Silvae,* is generally positive; the tensions in Virgil's poetry, he argues, are often given a more sanguine turn in an age where the emperor has become an established institution. Some critics, of course, may argue that the tragic resonances of Virgilian pastoral and of the *Aeneid* and the *Thebaid* within these poems can likewise be heard, reinforcing the tensions that Putnam

10   THE POETIC WORLD OF STATIUS' *SILVAE*

himself detects in the *Silvae*, a title with pastoral overtones.[4] One point on which critics can agree, however, is that Putnam's essays on the *Silvae* enrich classical studies through their incisive revelation of the mind and craft of Statius. His profound meditations on these poems of the Flavian age invite us to sharpen our responses to the artistic and emotional complexity of these new forms of poetry with their blend of innovation and tradition. By offering us multiple perspectives from which to approach this demanding, elusive, and powerful poet, they provide a key to a fuller appreciation of Statius' experimentation with poetic language and genres and his bold transgression of long-standing cultural and social norms. By doing so, these essays expand and refine our understanding of the complex literary dynamics of the Flavian world.

I was first introduced to the *Silvae* when I was an undergraduate at the University of St. Andrews. The lecturer responsible for assigning the texts for the final lectures of my Honours course in Latin literature chose Statius' *Silvae* and T. S. Eliot's *Wasteland* as complementary works to explore in depth. Unforgettably he galvanized my class with his excitement at the brilliance and exuberance of Statius' verse: its allusive complexity, its bold experimentation. Like Eliot's verse of two thousand years later, this was poetry that challenged the mind and stimulated the imagination, and it provided a fresh and dynamic entry point to Roman literary tradition. Putnam's recent essays on the *Silvae* succeed in capturing that initial excitement and deepening and enriching it. His essays on the *Silvae* are the fitting tribute of a brilliant Latin literary critic to a brilliant Latin poet.

CAROLE E. NEWLANDS

---

[4] For instance, they may wonder about the frequent references that Putnam points out to Dido's banquet in Statius' own banquet poem, *Silv.* 4.2. See, for instance, Malamud (2007), and also Newlands (2022) on sound in the *Silvae*.

1

A Stream and Two Villas
(Statius' *Silvae* 1.3)

This chapter aims to examine closely *Silvae* 1.3, one of Statius' two great poems devoted to describing a villa and its owner, in this case Manilius Vopiscus. My particular interest lies not specifically with the history of the Roman villa, nor with its location, say, nor its architecture, interior design, or furnishings. I am not concerned with the familial background, social standing, or economic circumstances of its master. Such practical matters cannot help but be part of my discussion when aspects of them appear prominently in the poem's narrative. My chief goal is to survey the quality of the poem itself as a creative unity. I seek to trace some of its salient themes, its notable patterns of expression, the poet's brilliant word play as well as dense use of allusion, all of which help deepen the suggestiveness of the whole.[1] In particular, I trace the eroticism that permeates the poem and examine how sensuality helps confirm its central notions of doubling, concord, and reciprocity. Statius places complementary emphasis on the varied implications of travel to and from destinations of importance. Synaesthesia, as a prominent rhetorical figure, is salient for the way that it binds together several senses at once to lend expressive depth and unity to the poetry.

The Poem's Opening

> Cernere facundi Tibur glaciale Vopisci
> siquis et inserto geminos Aniene penates
> aut potuit sociae commercia noscere ripae

---

[1] For appreciations of *Silvae* 1.3 see, e.g., Cancik (1978) *passim*; Newlands (1988) throughout, (2002) 119–53, (2012) 57–8, and (2017), esp. 174–67; Dalby (2000) 35–6; Zeiner (2005), esp. 78–81 and 270–83; Rühl (2006) 257–64; Kreuz (2017) 479–544; Nelis and Nelis (2020) 187–8; Gunderson (2021) 254–5; Chinn (2022) 242–55. Newlands' impressive chapter has served as a crucial guide to interpretation, and the commentary on the *Silvae* by Vollmer (1898) has been a constantly informative source.

The Poetic World of Statius' Silvae. Michael C. J. Putnam, Edited by: Antony Augoustakis with Carole E. Newlands, Oxford University Press. © Michael C. J. Putnam 2023. DOI: 10.1093/oso/9780192869272.003.0002

12   THE POETIC WORLD OF STATIUS' *SILVAE*

> certantesque sibi dominum defendere villas,
> illum nec calido latravit Sirius astro
> nec gravis aspexit Nemeae frondentis alumnus:
> talis hiems tectis, frangunt sic improba solem
> frigora, Pisaeumque domus non aestuat annum.
> ipsa manu tenera tecum scripsisse Voluptas
>
> *   *   *   *   *
>
> tunc Venus Idaliis unxit fastigia sucis
> permulsitque comis blandumque reliquit honorem
> sedibus et volucres vetuit discedere natos.
>
> (Stat. *Silv.* 1.3.1–12)

If anyone has had the opportunity to behold the cool Tibur of eloquent Vopiscus and the twin homes, with the Anio introduced between, or to gain knowledge of the intercourse of the partner riverbank and the mansions vying to lay claim to their master for themselves, neither Sirius with his hot star barked at him (5) nor did the offspring of leafy Nemea glare at him oppressively. Such winter is in the dwellings, so relentlessly do chills break the sun, and the house does not swelter through Pisa's yearly season. Pleasure herself with her tender hand [is said] to have written down with you. Then Venus anointed the rooftops with juices from Idalium (10) and smoothed them with her hair and bestowed seductive esteem upon the dwelling and forbade her winged offspring to take their leave.

Like many great poets Statius in his opening lines regularly takes the opportunity to offer his readers clues to help us engage with the complex text that follows. *Silvae* 1.3 is no exception. Both the two proper names, *Tibur* and *Vopisci*, are intertwined with attributes that activate our senses. *Facundi*, alerting us to the characteristic eloquence of the poem's honouree, forewarns us that our sense of hearing, in this case specifically the ability to attend to the word on the page as if it were spoken, will often be called upon. The fluency of the poet, and its impact on readers and listeners alike, will ever complement the rhetorical ability of his host.

The word *glaciale* in turn orients us to the importance in what follows to physical responses to the environment and, in particular, to the sense of touch. It especially prepares us to recognize in Statius' refined verses the individual's varied reactions to a richly tactile milieu.[2]

---

[2] Cancik (1978) 117 finds Statius' use of *glaciale* 'die erste Hyperbole, der viele, zu viele folgen'. Newlands (1988) 106, sees the adjective as 'odd' because it suggests 'unpleasant cold'. But its only other use in the *Silvae* occurs at 4.4.15 to describe the woods at Nemi (*nemus glaciale*

A STREAM AND TWO VILLAS (STATIUS' *SILVAE* 1.3)   13

The availability of all the senses as aids to understanding is subsumed in the striking opening word, *cernere*.[3] We are asked at the start to have all our spiritual and physical faculties ready for the act of appreciating and evaluating what follows. Statius will call on our ability, literally, to make a wide variety of conceptual distinctions, based not least on our talent for visualizing mentally what is being depicted for us verbally through the medium of ekphrasis. For the poem is in fact one large appraisal in words of the estate, and person, of Manilius Vopiscus, a description that is in turn made up of a series of smaller sketches that together conjure up for our enjoyment the expansive scenario as a whole.[4] At the same time we are also witnessing, on the creative level, a grand demonstration of how a poet can brilliantly affiliate the sensory and the graphic for our reading pleasure.

The resonance of the name Vopiscus is also crucial for interpreting the text that follows. The word, as several ancient authors explain it, refers to the survivor of twins, one of whom has, for whatever reason, died before birth.[5] As his poem evolves, Statius builds on the implications, for Vopiscus and for us, of this meaning in manifold ways. One major theme will be centred around the presence of doubles, of dualities, in a diverse series of manifestations.[6] These can especially take the shape of lovers joined or separated, of bodies of water that either unify or divide, of journeys that foster harmony or present challenges, or simply of losses redeemed or compounded.

Dianae). This forms part of a list of places to which Romans retreat to escape the summer heat. *Tiburis lucos* (17) is added to the catalogue shortly. For a variety of approaches to the study of the sense of touch in antiquity, see Purves (2017). On the relationship of architecture and interior decoration with climate in Statius' villa poems, see Myers (2000) 115, referring to Cancik (1978) 118.

[3] On the nuances of *cernere* and its differences with *noscere*, see Hardie (1983) 177–8, where he aptly quotes Virg. *G.* 2.490–4. *Silv.* 1.3 combines Lucretian *voluptas*, and the Epicurean calm that it assumes, with Virgilian spirituality illustrated, for example, by the constant immanence of divinity in various aspects of nature whose vitality is ever before us. For *cernere* and Epicureanism, see Konstan (2008) 32–4. *Cernere* enters the tradition of ekphrastic writing at Virg. *A.* 8.676 (*cernere erat...*) taken up by Statius at *Silv.* 3.1.15. Cf. also *A.* 6.596 and Apollo *cernens* at 8.704, as well as Cicero's earlier use at the *De consulatu suo* 6.58 *FPL*[4]. See also Faber (2018) 4.

[4] In the preface to *Silvae* 1 (*praef.* 26), Statius tells of Vopiscus' boast that 'his Tiburtine villa was described by us in one day' (*...villam Tiburtinam suam descriptam a nobis uno die*). The poem renders the visible through the written word, sights for viewing become visions for imagining; on *descriptam* for ekphrasis, see Pittà (2021) 120. See Spencer (2010) 105, on the poem's conjunction of 'perception and speech' even in its opening line.

[5] For ancient authors on the meaning of the name, see Plin. *Nat.* 7.10.47; Quint. *Inst.* 1.4.25; Isid. *Etym.* 9.5.21. Lucius Afranius wrote a *togata* entitled *Vopiscus* (Nonius, 230M = 341L). Nisbet (1978) mentions the name in a list of puns by Statius on the names of people, especially of addressees of his poems. For the meagre evidence that we possess on Vopiscus himself, see Cancik (1978) 120–1, who finds the poem as a whole 'noticeably impersonal' (*auffällig unpersönlich*, 128); Hardie (1983) 68–9.

[6] On 'reciprocity and duality' as a founding principle for Vopiscus' estate, see Newlands (2002) 134 n. 65 and 145–8 for more detail.

14   THE POETIC WORLD OF STATIUS' *SILVAE*

One act of replacement for a crucial absence, or of implicit fulfilment after suffering deprivation, we find at the poem's outset. It lies in the building compound itself which consists of *geminos penates*, by metonymy standing for the duplicate houses whose very name, *penates*, in itself conjures up the twin youths holding spears who were guardian spirits of the Roman house and especially of its larder.[7] Even the insertion of the Anio River, which here makes its first appearance, cannot keep the two kindred dwellings truly apart.[8] For Vopiscus this double creation would seem right at the start an act of fulfilment that substitutes a visual memorial for a psychological absence, a palpable demonstration of replacing a past deprivation through a visual design that is also symbolic of a lost balance now restored.

The next lines offer our initiation into the erotic vocabulary that will also serve as a complementary pattern throughout the poem to that of emptiness and restoration. There is 'commerce' between the two domestic entities, and for the reader to 'know' of it has a parallel, for example, in Catullus' wish that Lesbia be true when she says that she 'knew' (*nosse*) Catullus alone.[9] The viewer of the two personified buildings thus gains immediate knowledge of the interchange each has with the other.[10]

And with line 4 Statius' expressiveness grows still more intense. The two humanized villas are in competition with each other to lay claim (*defendere*) to the *dominus*, the lord of the manor as, by innuendo, their master in the more physical sense, one who sees to their emotional gratification.[11]

---

[7] For ancient evidence, see, e.g., Dion. Hal. *Ant. Rom.* 1.68.2; Serv. *ad A.* 3.12. The two figures are to be seen on the west front of the *Ara Pacis Augustae*, where Aeneas is depicted at Lavinium as he sacrifices to the Penates, visible in their shrine at the upper left (see further *Ant. Rom.* 1.57.1).

[8] On the 'threading' of the Anio between the two buildings, see Newlands (2002) 132 and 305 on the river as 'not so much subjugated as cooperative with human needs'; see also Newlands (2012) 58.

[9] Catul. 72.1. Cf. also Ov. *Ars* 3.561 and, for further examples, *OLD* s.v. *nosco* 4 and 12. For *commercia*, see *OLD* s.v. 5b and Adams (1982) 203. For the amatory connotations of *socius*, see Pichon (1966) 264. Ovid (*Tr.* 5.10.35) uses the conjunction *sociae commercia* in connection with *linguae*. Cf. also Stat. *Theb.* 5.668 (*sociae commercia vittae*).

[10] With *ripae*, cf. also *ripas* (25) and *ripis* (44, 107). Here and elsewhere Statius' language recalls Hor. *Carm.* 4.2, in this case particularly 4.2.30–2: *circa nemus uvidique/Tiburis ripas operosa parvus/carmina fingo* ('around the woods and banks of well-watered Tibur in my small way I fashion well-crafted songs'). We will hear Horace, especially the lyric Horace, regularly in our ears as the poem unfolds; see Chinn (2022) 242–55.

[11] See *OLD* s.v. *defendere* 8: 'to defend one's right to (a possession), claim'. *Silv.* 1.3.4 is cited as the single example of a 'poetic' usage of the verb. For *dominus*, see *OLD* s.v. 4b and, as an *adpellatio amatoria*, Pichon (1966) 134. Newlands (2002) 148 traces an epic quality to the language.

A STREAM AND TWO VILLAS (STATIUS' *SILVAE* 1.3)   15

Vopiscus may have once lost a twin, but he now has created for himself a double domestic arrangement each part of which, if only in Statius' suggestive language, vies to fulfil his needs. (Unlike Statius' other 'villa' poem, *Silvae* 2.2, addressed to Pollius Felix and Polla, there is no mention here of wife and offspring. Their absence is replaced in part by the emotional bond between its lord and his domain, its houses and landscape, with all their expansive satisfactions.)

Statius now turns more directly to *illum*, the thus far unnamed, presumably generalized visitor venturing into this intriguing terrain, and centres his attention on expanding the implications of *glaciale*. Manifestations of heaven's challenges, even at their most ferocious, cannot do this onlooker physical harm with their contact. The metaphorical bark of the Dog Star Sirius, which is to say, in terms of climate, the threatening degree of summer heat, cannot menace him. And, if we are lucky enough to have access to Tiburtine mildness, we do not have to be a Hercules to withstand the torrid glare emanating from the sign of Leo, here specified as Nemean to serve as a reminder of one of the hero's notable antagonists. In fact, such is the unique setting of Vopiscus' houses (*tectis*) that we have winter (*hiems*) climate when it is the height of summer elsewhere.

Mention of Nemea also anticipates one further analogy phrased in an extraordinary manner: Vopiscus' home (*domus*) does not 'blaze as if it were during a Pisaean year'.[12] The Olympic games, counterpart to those held at Nemea, took place in August and September, which is to say while the season was still at its warmest. Through a bold form of figuration complementing a standard use of the accusative case, Statius replaces summertime, which is to say a single season, with the larger timespan of which it forms a quarter. The result is a form of heightening that further corroborates the specialness of the villa's weather. Even the heat of a Grecian summer expanded, as it were, into a whole year cannot interrupt the wintry coolness we experience at Tibur at a time when others are enduring the opposite.

The naming of Nemea and allusion to the Olympic competitions held near Pisa in the Peloponnese are separated by a phrase that looks back at another aspect of Statius' language: *frangunt sic improba solem/frigora*. The personified 'chills' that abound at Tibur in the season of high summer are

---

[12] Mention of the Olympic games held at Pisa prepares the reader for allusion to the River Alpheus at 68–9. The Alpheus and Greek Pisa are linked, explicitly or implicitly, on several occasions, e.g., Stat. *Silv.* 1.2.203–8 and *Theb.* 4.238–9; Virg. *G.* 3.180. At *A.* 10.179, Virgil in the phrase *Alpheae Pisae* alludes to the supposed Greek origin of Italian Pisa.

16   THE POETIC WORLD OF STATIUS' *SILVAE*

strong enough to 'break' the sun. In the language of the senses the *frigora* have sufficient, wanton power to shatter any potential emotional opposition to them on the part of the greatest source of natural heat.[13] On another level of nature, bouts of coolness associated with Tibur have the paradoxical ability to conquer any spiritual hardness the hot sun might exhibit toward them, of winning him over to them, of taming his negative instincts. It is as if he were a relative of the celestial canine Sirius or the Nemean lion, with his significant position in the Zodiac, or even a lover, capable of being seduced from one mode of behaviour to another.

As though to confirm the implications of his earlier language, Statius now brings the erotic component of his presentation 'stage front' through the presence of *Voluptas* (9). The reader tracing the poem's intellectual background thinks immediately of the opening hexameters of Lucretius' *De Rerum Natura* where *Voluptas* is synonymous with Venus as emblematic of the Epicurean principle of the moral enjoyment of pleasure.[14] Statius will ultimately lead us to the philosopher himself. Here he would have us also directly attend to the amatory aspects of his own poem as it evolves. The text is corrupt, but it is with an appropriately 'tender hand' (*manu tenera*) that *Voluptas* joins with 'you', Vopiscus himself, in scripting what may well have been the plan of the villa itself.[15] *Voluptas* possesses one of the standard features of an elegiac lover as, in all probability, she superintends the written design of what we are to experience.[16]

Her role as a counterpart of Venus is corroborated as the text resumes. Once the written sketches are put to use and the buildings are completed it is the goddess of love herself who, suggestively, performs a blessing and anoints their rooftops with juices brought from one of her primary places of

---

[13] For lines 7–8, see in particular Marshall (2011) 324. For the implicit eroticism of *frangere*, e.g., see Pichon (1966) 155. A reader of Horace might well think of the immediate physicality of *frangere* in *Carm.* 1.23.9–10: *atqui non ego te tigris ut aspera/Gaetulusve leo frangere persequor...* ('But I myself am not tracking you like a savage tiger or a Gaetulian lion to crunch you up'). As part of his metamorphosis Statius turns Horace's lion from breaker to broken!

[14] Though there is a gap between lines 9 and 10, the two hexameters are clearly meant to form an entity in imitation of Lucretius' enjambment of *voluptas* and *alma Venus*. Whatever implicit opposition might exist between the two, Vopiscus' domain is an Epicurean Eden but also a precinct where the creation of poetry is of paramount importance.

[15] See Pichon (1966) 277 for specific uses of *tener* and *manus* by the elegiac poets and Newlands (2002) 142 for the association of the former with elegiac poetry specifically. At *A.* 11.578, Virgil employs the phrase to portray Camilla as she learns military artistry at an early age. Statius will turn to the word again at lines 16, 31, 47, and 51.

[16] Cf. *Silv.* 3.1.117 as Pollius prepares to construct his temple to Hercules:...*cum scripta formatur imagine tela* ('...when the design is shaped after the plan has been sketched'); on *Silv.* 3.1, see also pp. 89–155 in this volume.

A STREAM AND TWO VILLAS (STATIUS' *SILVAE* 1.3) 17

worship, Idalium on the island of Cyprus, as if the turrets stood for the tresses of celebrants at a festivity. And Statius confirms the implicit sexuality of the image by suggesting that Venus also soothed the personified dwelling with her hair as if she were caressing someone beloved. It is suitable that the honour she grants is *blandus*, alluring, as she bestows it and as it will later serve in a display to gratify the visitor.[17] Venus and her sons, the *Cupidines* that Catullus twice links with *Veneres*,[18] which is to say with Venus in her multiple guises, remain as fitting permanent denizens in this enticing, inviting environment.

Landscape and Synaesthesia

> o longum memoranda dies! quae mente reporto
> gaudia, quam lassos per tot miracula visus!
> ingenium quam mite solo, quae forma beatis
> ante manus artemque locis! non largius usquam
> indulsit natura sibi. nemora alta citatis
> incubuere vadis; fallax responsat imago
> frondibus, et longas eadem fugit umbra per undas.
> ipse Anien (miranda fides), infraque superque
> saxeus, hic tumidam rabiem spumosaque[19] ponit
> murmura, ceu placidi veritus turbare Vopisci
> Pieriosque dies et habentes carmina somnos.
>
> (Stat. *Silv*. 1.3.13–23)

O day long to stay in memory! What joys do I carry back in my mind, how weary my eyes ranging through so many marvels! How gentle the

---

[17] For the erotic connotation of *blandus*, see Pichon (1966) 94–5. For *volucres* Vollmer refers to Stat. *Silv*. 1.2.61. On *unxit*, Newlands (2002) 137 comments: 'Venus' seductive treatment of the house as a human body suggests that the house is a metonymy for Vopiscus himself.' The conjunction *blandum...honorem* resembles the phrase *blandum amorem* that appears in the same position in the hexameter at Lucr. 1.19 and reinforces the connection Statius has just established with the poem's opening lines. The alteration of *amorem* to *honorem* adds a sense of privilege to the sensuality already present.

[18] Catul. 3.1 and 13.12.

[19] At line 21, I follow the reading of M instead of *spumeus...saxosa* which both Courtney and Liberman print. Among the reasons for preserving the manuscript's reading are the parallel with A. 10.212 (*spumea semifero sub pectore murmurat unda*), as well as the figuration with enjambment, based on assonance, that leads us from *tumidam rabiem* to *spumosa* and then to *murmura* at the start of the subsequent hexameter. Forms of *spumosus/spumeus/spumo* are often to be found adjacent to the word *murmur* as well as to variations of *tumidam*. For Courtney's defence of his reading, see Courtney (1987) 31.

18 THE POETIC WORLD OF STATIUS' *SILVAE*

intelligence of the ground, what shapeliness to the happy (15) landscape before hands' artifice! Never did nature so generously gratify herself! The lofty groves brood over the excited waters; the deceitful image answers the foliage back and this same shadow takes flight along the extending waves. The Anio itself—astonishing the belief!—rocky both below and above (20), here lays aside its swollen wrath and foaming roars as though it feared to incommode kindly Vopiscus' Pierian days and slumbers that contain songs.

We turn now from a summary overview of the domain itself, and of what is expected of the visitor in the process of its appreciation, to details of what he encounters. For the first, impressive time, the word 'I' enters the poem, taking the attention of a potential guest directly to the recorder of the event himself. The day is *memoranda*, worthy for Statius, newly arrived, to remember but also for Statius, the poet, in his own guise as creative writer, to immortalize in the verses in which we are taking pleasure and that will also stay at length in our memories. We are now drawn, as readers, to witness in our own imaginations what he has witnessed in fact. This experience assumes two forms—the joys that he takes back in his mind, presumably to enumerate, in his turn unforgettably, in the single day which the preface tells us was given over to the act of the poem's composition, and the sights, worthy of his amazement, that he absorbs and whose visual impact he conveys to us.

As at the start, Statius divides his material into both the spiritual and the tangible. First, we have the sensory pleasures, harboured in the speaker's mind, that are to be translated through the power of the writer's wit into the stuff of poetry. Then, as abstract is complemented by concrete and imagined by actual, our eyes are put to work, taking in the spectacles that the speaker discovers during his exhausting tour. These are the multitude of *miracula*, marvels that, in the poet's etymological play, are to be made worthy of our own admiration as we imagine them through his language. The totality is a further demonstration of Statius' skill at the writing of ekphrasis, as he conveys in words the awe that first strikes the visitor when he views the manifold beauty before him and that then presumably accompanies him in the subsequent act of turning astonishment at visual display, which delights the eye, into verbal art for our reading pleasure.[20]

---

[20] On the primacy of a sense of wonder as a characteristic of ekphrastic writing, see Marshall (2011) 322 n. 2. In *Silv.* 1.3 we find its manifestations here (*miracula*), at 20 (*miranda*), and at 37 and 57 (*mirer*).

A STREAM AND TWO VILLAS (STATIUS' *SILVAE* 1.3)   19

We begin with the landscape setting and, appropriately enough, with the ground itself. This, too, has both an inner self and an outer appearance that are consequential. As if the Tiburtine earth were human, it has inner intelligence and talent (*ingenium*) as well as external comeliness (*forma*). When man arrives with his forceful workmanship (*manus*), he adds his skill (*artem*) to modelling what is already innately ideal.[21] The resulting combination of *ars* and *ingenium* comes close to defining as exemplary the object portrayed as it also does the poetic artistry that formulates the description.[22] The perfection of what we see is complemented by the perfect combination of imagination and technical prowess that tells of it.

There remains a still further dimension to the humanization of the landscape, one that also anticipates an important aspect of the subsequent narrative, as it evolves. The soil of Tibur is both fertile and mild in that it also reflects the local climate. But it likewise could be said to serve suitably as a palpable manifestation of the gentleness and kindliness that characterize the human side of Vopiscus himself and his establishment.[23] The same holds true of the 'blessed spots' (*beatis locis*) soon to come into our purview through the poet's eloquence. These places are rich, in the superficial meaning of productive. Horace, for instance, draws attention to the vineyards as well as the orchards that flourished in the area.[24] But in a more metaphysical reading the landscape that Vopiscus inhabits and adapts is also both fortunate and happy, offering further external evidence of the taste as well as the spiritual and moral well-being of its talented owner. Personified nature now enters the picture, expansively self-gratified at the attractive aspects of her setting that were in place before manipulation by man's acts of acculturation.[25] Two of her primary figures, forests and floods, inanimate inhabitants of the land and their nearby stream, are presented to us as if they

---

[21] For a human example of this combination of attributes, see Gellius' vignette of Plato's Phaedo (*NA* 2.18.3): *is Phaedon servus fuit forma atque ingenio liberali* ('This Phaedo was a slave of noble appearance and intelligence'). Cf. also Ov. *Her.* 15.31–2 and *Fast.* 6.805–6.

[22] For the commonplace opposition of *ars* and *ingenium*, cf., e.g., Prop. 2.24.23 and Ov. *Tr.* 2.424. It is at the basis of Horace's *Ars* 408–11; see Brink (1985) on 295–6, 330. The word *artes* also appears here at 47 and 55.

[23] Forms of *mitis* are found again at 24 and 87. Statius has in mind Hor. *Carm.* 1.18.2, where the poet speaks of the *mite solum Tiburis*. For the erotic connotations of the word see Pichon (1966) 203–4.

[24] For detailed treatments of the influence of Horace on *Silv.* 1.3, see Hardie (1983) 155–71; Newlands (1988) *passim*. To her list of allusions, I would add especially *Carm.* 3.29 (see below, n. 70) and *Ep.* 1.4.

[25] For the erotic connotations of *indulsit*, see Pichon (1966) 167 on the meaning of *indulgentia* as *diligens obsequium*. Nature here seems rightly absorbed with self-satisfaction.

20   THE POETIC WORLD OF STATIUS' *SILVAE*

were lovers. The vertical, masculine trees brood over the excited, feminine waters.[26] The descending image answers back as if in suggestive agreement. But it is deceitful and, in the form of a shadow, takes flight down the lengthening, distancing, waves.[27] Statius again draws us near to the world of Roman elegy and, in particular, to the standard behaviour of a fickle *inamorata*, transient like the semblance vanishing in the ever-flowing waters.

This charming vignette is enhanced by the poem's first example of synaesthesia. Images are seen, not heard, yet the poet's verbal legerdemain merges or, better, replaces aural with visual. The aqueous likeness, given its own voice, sends a reply to the terrestrial messenger above which we now view in the synecdochic form of the foliage on the boughs of the impending trees. The deliberate confusion of multi-sensory apprehension adds brilliantly to our first look at the native loveliness of Vopiscus' *paesaggio*. We next turn to the figure that from the poem's initial lines we have seen as central to its evolution, and to the landscape through which it flows, the River Anio (Anien). Before detailing its behaviour Statius offers a pungent comment upon it: *miranda fides*. Even in this world of delights deserving of the speaker's, and our, wonder, trust in what we are about to learn has to be remarked upon. The poet's wit takes us from a *fallax imago*, a deceitful spectre within his storytelling, to an appeal that we readers place merited trust in the truth of his very words, in what we are about to learn, because it might otherwise seem so outlandish.

The river that is rocky above the domain's ground and again after it has passed through, with all that this implies about noise, suppresses its bursting frenzy and foamy rumble while within Vopiscus' territory. It does so in order not to trouble the owner's quietude and the poetic creativity that attends his days and sleep. What may test the reader's credibility is the manner in which the Anio miraculously changes its ways from earlier and later behaviour. But such is the powerful complementarity here between man and nature that the river takes on the characteristics of its extraordinary host. It suddenly lacks its ordinary unruliness and racket, and instead imitates, and supplements, the repose that accompanies Vopiscus' Pierian gifts.

Perhaps we are meant to witness an aspect of poetry's potential at work. Certainly we are beholding an instance where nature tames herself

---

[26] For the language and context, cf. *Silv.* 2.3.43–5, lines also concerned with an erotic connection between a tree and water; see also pp. 45–88 in this volume.

[27] For *fallax* and deceiving love or deceptive lover, cf. Catul. 30.4 and 64.151 (at 64.56, the adjective is applied to sleep that deceives in imitation of an absconding paramour).

A STREAM AND TWO VILLAS (STATIUS' *SILVAE* 1.3)   21

spontaneously rather than through any physical interventions imposed by our human engineering. Here at Tibur man and nature support each other. The force of Vopiscus' inner quietude, his emanations of spiritual serenity, as it were, are emulated in the behaviour of the river Anio as, for a spell, it suppresses its own innate ebullience in order to foster the humane qualities of the lord through whose estate it momentarily passes in its timeless course. Statius' lines resonate with language that Virgil, at the start of the *Aeneid*, draws on to describe Neptune smoothing the turgid waters after Juno's horrendous storm: *tumida aequora placat* (*A.* 1.142). Here it is Vopiscus who is *placidus* like the Anio who for this stretch of its flow suppresses any inherent *tumidam rabiem*—its characteristic swollen madness. No Neptune is needed here to teach the river the ways of peace, only the example of Vopiscus himself.

Once again Statius both acknowledges and enhances the rich ambivalence of the landscape by his own verbal play, in particular with another example of synaesthesia. The roars that we ordinarily hear are now also made visible through the adjective *spumosa*. The poet has us see the froth that accompanies the sound of the rushing stream. We picture what we take in with our ears, and vice versa. The adjective *saxeus* varies the same theme. Rocks per se do not imply sound but now once again the visual suggests that we listen, in this case, to the roar that the poet has us imagine arising when flowing water is challenged by barriers of stone in its path. No such friction, especially when treated negatively, devalues the decorum of the Anio as it passes serenely, inaudibly, through Vopiscus' realm.[28] Statius would have us likewise imagine that no negative moral obstacles stand in the way of a tranquil life for the *dominus* through whose territory the river makes its way.

The personification of the river adds to the suggestiveness of the setting. The Anio, like any maddened human, can be a victim of *rabies*, destructive rage. Here what holds it back is fear to trouble the spiritual serenity of Vopiscus and the creativity that permeates both his days and nights, days that are controlled by the Pierian Muses, sleeps, by metonymy for nights, that 'have' *carmina* as if owning them was what most mattered during the time of darkness, as if, in the case of Vopiscus, any implicit physical eroticism that nocturnal hours might bring were replaced by spiritual creativity in the form of the magic of songs. We now turn back to the domain itself:

---

[28] For further discussion of lines 20–4, especially of their generic background, see Newlands (2017) 175–6.

22 THE POETIC WORLD OF STATIUS' *SILVAE*

> litus utrumque domi nec te mitissimus amnis
> dividit; alternas servant praetoria ripas,
> non externa sibi fluviumue obstare queruntur.
> Sestiacos nunc fama sinus pelagusque natatum
> iactet et audaci uictos delphinas ephebo:
> hic aeterna quies, nullis hic iura procellis,
> numquam fervor aquis. datur hic transmittere visus
> et voces et paene manus. nec Chalcida fluctus
> expellunt reflui, nec dissociata profundo
> Bruttia Sicanium circumspicit ora Pelorum.[29]

(Stat. Silv. 1.3.24–33)

Either shore is part of home nor does the gentlest of rivers separate you; the mansions guard each of the banks (25), nor do they complain that they are foreign to each other or that the stream stands in the way. Now let Fame boast of the bays of Sestos and of the sea that was swum and of the dolphins overwhelmed by the bold youth. Here is everlasting peace. Here no storms have rights, the waters never seethe. Here it is granted to pass glances (30) and voices and nearly hands across. Nor do the tidal floods repel Chalcis away nor does the shore of Bruttium, kept apart by the deep, look around for Sicilian Pelorus.

Through his further attention to the river, Statius now helps us once again see unity between dualities. The Anio's two shores are equally at home, equally a part of the same continuum. And the river, now as mild as possible (*mitissimus*), like the earth through which it passes, serves to unify 'you', the personified habitations through which it glides.[30] The two grand mansions, given a life of their own, guard the banks and cannot complain that they are separated from each other because of the waters. Again, Statius lends a sense of elegy to his language, this time implying loyalty, not duplicity. In this magical terrain there is nothing adventitious (*externa*), not even a beautiful stream, that can separate (*dividit*) the two sympathetic entities.[31]

---

[29] At 24, for *tectum* (Courtney [1992]) I follow Liberman by reading *nec te* (M). At 26 I adopt the reading *fluviumve* (Politianus, followed by Liberman) in place of *fluviorum* (Courtney, following M). At 31–2, I accept Shackleton Bailey's change from *sic... sic* (Courtney and Liberman, following M) to *nec... nec*.

[30] The singular *te* in itself suggests the strong bond existing between the two mansions.

[31] With the language of 25–6, cf. Prop. 1.3.43–4: *interdum leviter mecum deserta querebar/ externo longas saepe in amore moras...* ('Meanwhile, abandoned, I complain gently to myself of your often long lingerings in someone else's love'). For *divido* and the separation of lovers, see

A STREAM AND TWO VILLAS (STATIUS' *SILVAE* 1.3)   23

To strengthen the erotic tone of the passage, Statius adds the first of several allusions he makes during the course of the poem to bodies of water that paradoxically both sunder and conjoin. The Anio, the poet strongly suggests, will not correspond to the Hellespont which served to part the lovers Hero and Leander, forcing the youth to entrust himself to the peril-ous waters in order to reach his amour.[32] For, while he defeated the dolphins as he swam from Abydos to Sestos on the opposite shore, ultimately his boldness led to death by drowning. There is nothing tragic about the intimacy between Vopiscus' homes, an intimacy here fostered rather than impeded by the soft water that flows between them. What is constant here is not any lasting remembrance of myth, nor even the implicit ever-endurance of death, but *quies*.[33] The water is ever tranquil, there are no storm blasts, such as figure in Virgil's retelling of the tale (*G.* 3.258–63). The stream never seethes here, in echo of any lovers' passion, but display of affection between the two sites does indeed take a physical form with parts now assumed by the humanized constituents of the property.

And once more the poet calls on several of the senses, in rising order of proximity, to further activate the scene. Sight gains the first place, especially given the importance of vision for the poem as a whole. Then we have hearing in the form of voices exchanged between the two segments of the dwelling. Sight and sound lead in place of climax to touch, to hands that can nearly bridge any separation between one segment of the pair and the other.[34]

The drafting hand (*manu*, 9) of *Voluptas* helps sketch the construction to come. The hands (*manus*, 16) of man the artificer are ready to enhance the already considerable beauty of the site itself. Now the hands of the inhabitants

---

Pichon (1966) 132 and for *externum* (139). Statius visualizes the two *praetoria* as elegiac part-ners that the stream cannot keep apart. With *alternas ripas*, cf. *alternas mensas* (64).

[32] For the sexual implication of *sinus*, see Adams (1982) 90–1, 228; Pichon (1966) 264. The best appreciation in Latin letters of the myth of Hero and Leander is the exchange of letters that Ovid imagines at *Her.* 18 and 19. For a detailed study of the legend and its history, see Montiglio (2018).

[33] *Quies* introduces another motif of the poem. Cf. *quiescam* (34) and the repetitions of *quies* at 41 and 91.

[34] The crossing of water is a theme of the poem. With *transmittere* cf. *transcurris* (67), and *transcurrere* (107), as well as *emissas* (37). With *paene manu*, cf. Ov. *Her.* 18.179 where Leander writes to Hero that he can almost touch her, his beloved, across the strait with his hand. Ovid repeats the word *paene* in the subsequent pentameter (180) to give emphasis to yearning as a central emotion. At 195 he speaks of his own *felix audacia*, a notion that Statius absorbs into line 26 where Leander is called an *audaci ephebo*. Further parallels between the two poems deserve separate elaboration.

24   THE POETIC WORLD OF STATIUS' *SILVAE*

themselves come close to touching, which is to say, to bridging what little distance might lie between them, caused by the intervening channel.[35]

To highlight his point Statius now offers us two further, contrasting examples of bodies of water quite unlike the peaceful flow of the Anio. The Hellespont served to dramatize the challenging setting that the lovers Hero and Leander had to surmount in order to meet. Statius' new parallels again stress the difference with Vopiscus' calm stream as he illustrates how nature, in these subsequent contrasts, herself now fights against potential unities within her jurisdiction. The Anio will not find a complement in the Euripus whose wild flow runs between the island of Euboea and Boeotia. Its masculine *fluctus reflui*, tidal currents, forcefully drive the feminine city of Chalcis away from contact with the neighbouring mainland. Nor will the Anio claim a similarity with the dangerous straits of Messina. Their perilous depths serve here not, as ordinarily, to threaten passing vessels but again, unlike the *sociae ripae* (3), the 'allying bank' of Vopiscus' stream, to part (*dissociata*) the mainland, in this case that of the Italian peninsula, from the island of Sicily.[36]

Once more the distinction between feminine and masculine is suggestively operative, here taking topographical form in the coast of Bruttium (*ora Bruttia*) and the promontory of Pelorus on the northeast tip of Sicily. Though entwined by the poet's brilliant, complex word order, the first cannot even gaze in search of her opposite number, much less touch him! Again the Anio, at least in this part of the river, offers no such difficulties of intercommunication, whatever senses might be involved.

> quid primum mediumve canam, quo fine quiescam?
> auratasne trabes an Mauros undique postes
> an picturata lucentia marmora vena
> mirer an emissas per cuncta cubilia nymphas?
> huc oculis, huc mente trahor. venerabile dicam
> lucorum senium? te, quae vada fluminis infra
> cernis, an ad silvas quae respicis, aula, tacentes,
> qua tibi tuta quies offensaque turbine nullo
> nox silet et nigros imitantia murmura[37] somnos?

---

[35] Like *domus*, the word *manus* is central to the poem's creative language. It appears at 9, 16, 31, 47, and 51.

[36] No nautical peril, which here is to say no social or moral threat, such as Scylla and Charybdis might present to travellers, lies in store for those journeying to Vopiscus' villa.

[37] At 42, I follow the reading of M (*nigros imitantia murmura*) instead of *pigros mutantia murmura* (Courtney); Liberman obelizes *imitantia*.

A STREAM AND TWO VILLAS (STATIUS' *SILVAE* 1.3)   25

an quae graminea suscepta crepidine fumant
balnea et impositum ripis algentibus ignem,
quaque vaporiferis iunctus fornacibus amnis
ridet anhelantes vicino flumine nymphas?

(Stat. Silv. 1.3.34–46)

What shall I sing of first, or in the middle, with what conclusion shall I fall
to rest? Shall I marvel at the gilded beams or everywhere the Moorish
doorposts (35) or marbles glistening with a vein of colour or Nymphs
released through all the bedchambers? I am drawn to here with my eyes,
to here with my mind. Shall I tell of the venerable old age of the groves? Of
you, who behold the flow of the stream below, or you, courtyard, who gaze
at the silent woods, (40) where your rest is safe and night, troubled by no
turmoil, and roars, that imitate black dreams, grow silent? Or the baths,
taken up on a grassy outcrop, that smoke, and fire placed on the ice-cold
banks where the stream, linked to the steaming furnaces, (45) laughs at
the Nymphs panting from the nearby river.

Statius now turns our attention again to himself, to the lyric poet at work,
and in particular to the act of structuring his language, to the start, middle,
and conclusion of the demarcated passage that follows as he sings and then
rests in quiet. The shaping of verses, based, first, on a series of five self-
interrogations, reflects the palpable world around him as it, too, takes shape.
We now enter the dwelling itself and, not unexpectedly, watch culture at
work on nature—beams that are gilded, Mauritanian citrus-wood made into
doorposts,[38] water channelled by man's ingenuity into all the bedrooms.[39]
In the instance of the glistening, decorative marbles, personified nature
herself helps to refine her product with a vein of colour that itself has been
coloured as if by a painter.

It may not be coincidental that Seneca, in a letter to Fabianus Papirius
(*Ep.* 100), compares the latter's writing style to a *domus recta*, a house that
is both suitable and proper, though it might lack 'variety of marbles and a
distribution of water flowing through the bedrooms' (*varietas marmorum et*

---

[38] For *auratas trabes,* see also Virg. *A.* 2.448; [Tib.] 3.3.16; Sen. *Thy.* 646. But Statius is most
likely thinking of Prop. 3.2.12, where mention of *auratas trabes* is followed by reference to
Phaeacas...pomaria silvas (cf. *Silv.* 1.3.81) and *Marcius liquor* (cf. 66–70).

[39] The double use of metonymy in *cubilia* (bed for bedchamber) and *nymphas* (water goddesses for the liquid itself) is noteworthy. With its suggestions of the erotic, the latter is the first
of several locutions that implicate the gods sensuously with Vopiscus' domain. Cf. the repetition of *nymphas* at 46.

26   THE POETIC WORLD OF STATIUS' *SILVAE*

concisura aquarum cubiculis interfluentium). The reflection of Seneca's words in the verses of Statius, as the poet's elaborate style mimics the surroundings of which his words tell, suggests that Statius, when his writing deals with a context as rich as that which Vopiscus provides, will knowingly rise beyond a simple manner of expression, fitting for an unpretentious dwelling, to a studied level suited to the actual objects, the sight of which captures his imagination. It will be, and is, as artful in its own way as the skilful material that it depicts.[40]

After these initial details, the poet-speaker again enters the narration. *Mirer*, for example, informs us once more of the important role of wonder in ekphrastic description. We marvel as the tourist-speaker himself marvels, and the awe that animates his verse inspires his readers in turn. Statius follows with a further reminder that we are enjoying a special example of poetic description: *huc oculis, huc mente trahor*—'I am drawn to here with my eyes, to here with my mind.' We are experiencing the power of verse that tells of the narrator's reliance on what he sees and of how this at the same time affects his mind as he readies himself to speak his thoughts in words (*dicam*). And the author's preparation for crafting an excellent example of ekphrasis, as he is lured visually now to one place, now to another, is conveyed to us in the course of our appreciation of the inventive words as they work on the inner eye of our imaginations.

Statius demonstrates his dexterity as we move for a moment from interior decoration to external setting and to the individual graces of the local landscape. The first item listed is the worshipful old age of the local groves which claims our attention with the adjective *venerabile*. They are appropriately worthy of religious respect but, in the poet's wordplay, they also have *venus* about them, a beauty that is characteristic of Vopiscus' estate, as we have seen from the poem's start. Nature is also humanized. Water, by metonymy, is replaced by *nymphae*, its inherent divinities who bring it animation, and the local trees, like men, have an old age. Personifications become still more immediate as the poet turns briefly to apostrophe as he addresses what are probably two courtyards of the villa: 'you' who gaze at the floods below and 'you' who gaze at the hushed woods that utter no sound, where for 'you' (the *aula*, but now presumably Vopiscus and all who delight in the milieu)

---

[40] For an earlier example of *exaedificatio*, the structuring of a building, as rhetorical metaphor, see Cic. *Or.* 2.63 and the comments of Woodman (1988) 83–6.

A STREAM AND TWO VILLAS (STATIUS' *SILVAE* 1.3)   27

the calm is troubled by no turbulence.[41] Statius compliments the first with the verb *cernis*. Like the villa's visitor-viewer, whom the poem's first word urges to examine carefully (*cernere*) what he beholds, the first courtyard has the talent to scrutinize the waters beneath. The other *aula*, also spoken to in the second person, already puts aspects of this ability doubly to work. It watches what is silent, using its eyes for an unforthcoming response to the ears. And Night is silent as are any roars that imitate black dreams. Here at Tibur we have no reason to fear nocturnal darkness (*nox*) which, according to an ancient etymology, is a time when harm may come our way (*noceo*).[42] Statius also indulges in another impressive example of synaesthesia in imagining how the inner blackness of nightmares takes aural shape as night's rumblings.[43] These worries are suppressed in Volpicius' peaceful world of Epicurean repose. The quiet of the poet, anticipated at line 29, that both begins this section and looks to its conclusion (*quiescam*, 34), does not coincide with the quiet of nature (*quies*, 41), as we might expect. Instead, man now again enters the picture, this time by the fact of his addition of baths to the landscape's inherent design. The pleasing river also serves a practical purpose. The presence of the baths introduces a series of antonyms that are also conjunctions as well as creatively paradoxical. Hot is linked with cold, dry with wet, and fire consorts with water. Statius peoples this elemental world and brings it further alive for us. The banks feel the chill of the stream passing by. The baths are 'taken up' by the ledge that houses them. The personified river laughs at his waters who are once again projected as the goddesses, now gasping, who are native *numina* of the stream. And here, too, there is a tinge of the erotic to the language. Fire is 'placed upon' the banks.[44] The river is 'joined' to the steaming furnaces. The nymphs

---

[41] For second-person apostrophe as a hallmark of ekphrasis, see Marshall (2011) 322 with nn. 4 and 336. Statius makes use of variants of the figure, as well at 39–40, 59–61, 66–7, and 105–10.

[42] See Maltby s.v. *nox* (415).

[43] For a trenchant parallel to *nigros somnos* and its context, Statius would have us think back to Tib. 2.1.87–90:...*iam Nox iungit equos, currumque sequuntur/matris lascivo sidera fulva choro,/postque uenit tacitus furvis circumdatus alis/Somnus et incerto Somnia nigra pede* ('...now Night is yoking her horses and the tawny stars in mischievous band follow their mother's chariot, and after her comes Sleep, wrapped in swarthy wings, and black Dreams on unsteady foot'). Tibullus is first imitated by Ovid at *Fast.* 4.662: *nox venit et secum somnia nigra trahit* ('night comes and draws with her black dreams'). For Statius, therefore, the earlier tone of elegy continues now into our experience of nightfall and a double silence.

[44] For the implication of copulation suggested by *impositum* and *iunctus*, here between a series of opposites (as well as hot and cold, dry and wet, fire/land and water, we have natural and artificial, human and divine, male and female), see Adams (1982) 207 and Pichon (1966) 171 for less graphic forms of eroticism.

28   THE POETIC WORLD OF STATIUS' *SILVAE*

pant almost like lovers of the neighbouring stream that has been warmed by
the heat that the nearby baths exude, as if *flumine* designated both location
and agent.[45]

Artifacts and Wealth

> Vidi artes veterumque manus variisque metalla
> viva modis. labor est auri memorare figuras
> aut ebur aut dignas digitis contingere gemmas,
> quicquid et argento primum vel in aere minori
> lusit et enormes manus expertura colossos.
>
> (Stat. *Silv.* 1.3.47–51)

I saw artistry and handwork of the ancients and metals alive in differing
ways. It is an effort to recall to mind the shapes of gold or the ivory or the
gems worthy to touch fingers, and whatever, first in silver or in smaller
bronze (50), the hand toyed with, about to make trial of huge colossi.

Statius now moves our vision away from landscape setting to pursue his
own direct inspection (*vidi*) of the artifacts in Vopiscus' possession. His
lines are a virtuoso display of verbal skill at work, running from general to
particular, to aid us in envisioning with our eyes the museum-like presentation of what art can accomplish. *Artes*, for instance, is a form of metonymy
where all artistry anticipates a detailed listing of exemplars. *Manus* exemplifies both metonymy and synecdoche. We look especially at the hands of the
artisans, specified as belonging to those working in the past, at the same
moment as we visualize the resulting objects created once upon a time.
Metalla takes our imaginations by figuration from source to product, from
mines to the ores that came from them and thence to the resultant figures.
Viva in turn proposes the paradox that the artisan has the Orphic power to
animate the inanimate, to bring metals alive for artistic purposes.

And in this connection the poetic artist has his own form of intellectual
labor, to fashion in words something that stays in our memory. We once more
share in the renewal of the tradition of ekphrasis wherein the stimulation of
poetic figuration enables us to review *figuras* that now share in the tangible
artistic medium of sculpture. The verbal and the visual are in harmony.

---

[45] On *anhelo* and variants in an erotic context, see Adams (1982) 195 and Pichon (1966) 86
on *anhelitus*.

A STREAM AND TWO VILLAS (STATIUS' *SILVAE* 1.3)   29

There follows a list of the types of material used—gold, ivory, precious stones, silver, bronze—as well as of the images fabricated, ranging in size from rings, that take the focus of our eyes from the hands of the maker to the gems touching the fingers of the wearer, to small bronze figurines to *colossi* large enough to 'stretch the norm'. The brief passage is given a wholeness by the repetition of *manus*. We end as we began with a reminder of the artisan and his ability to shape.

But the crafty poet is still moulding our thoughts. We watch him at work from the start as we admire his own *labor* in elegantly cataloguing the contents of Vopiscus' museum for us to appreciate. Statius allows the verb *lusit* to have particular salience. Forms of *ludere* are rarely employed to illustrate the 'play' of fine artists as they go about their work. By contrast, the verb is used regularly by authors to describe the 'amusement' that complements the creative process. We find it put to service in connection with the writing of epigram, elegy, and satire as well as of pastoral and lyric verse.[46] The artisan-poet, therefore, as our own wordsmith would have it, engenders his own gratification as he focuses on the artisan-sculptor at work, using a verb that brings the variety of poetry into play to outline the different aspects of the fine artist pursuing his métier, be it in the medium he employs or in the resultant potpourri of items for our delectation.

> dum vagor aspectu visusque per omnia duco
> calcabam necopinus opes. nam splendor ab alto
> defluus et nitidum referentes aera testae
> monstravere solum, varias ubi picta per artes
> gaudet humus superatque novis asarota figuris.
> expavere gradus.
>
> (Stat. *Silv.* 1.3.52–7)

While I wander in my viewing and I cast my sight everywhere, I was unexpectedly treading on wealth. For radiance pouring down from on high and tiles reflecting the gleaming air showed off the ground where the earth, painted by manifold skills (55), rejoices and with original shapes surpasses 'unswept pavements'. My steps were astonished.

Statius' double emphasis on the act of seeing—*aspectu visusque*—as a necessary preface to an ekphrastic display now introduces a superb example of *enargeia*

---

[46] For examples where lyric is concerned, see commentators on Catul. 50.2 and Hor. *Carm.* 1.32.2 and 4.9.9; for pastoral, Virg. *Ecl.* 1.10, 6.1 and G. 4.565; for satire, Hor. *Sat.* 1.10.37; for elegy, Ov. *Fast.* 2.6; for epigram, Mart. 12.94.8.

30   THE POETIC WORLD OF STATIUS' *SILVAE*

with the nature/culture dichotomy at the forefront. We have before us explicit or implicit allusions to a cluster of Empedoclean elements: the air on high, with radiance flowing down on us, and earth that shimmers sufficiently to return the resplendent glow from above.[47] We absorb the paradox that light behaves like water (*defluus*) and that earth through human artifice now astonishingly glistens like the bright sun.

We also acknowledge human creative involvement in this project; the earth is beautified with a floor covered with a mosaic pavement. Nature rejoices in the resultant picture and boasts that its inventive shapes (*novis figuris*) surpass even *asarota*, the depictions in *tessellae* of the leavings on the floor after a dinner party. Statius' choice of an unusual Greek delineation involving an abstruse foreign pedigree serves both to praise Vopiscus' breadth of aesthetic knowledge and to exemplify tangibly his goal to take advantage of the exotic as well as the local to embellish his handsome villa.[48]

> quid nunc ingentia mirer
>
> *   *   *   *   *
>
> aut quid partitis distantia tecta trichoris?
> quid te, quae mediis servata penatibus arbor
> tecta per et postes liquidas emergis in auras,
> quo non sub domino saevas passura bipennes?
> et nunc ignaro forsan vel lubrica Nais
> vel non abruptos tibi debet Hamadryas annos.
>
> (Stat. *Silv.* 1.3.57–63)

Why should I now marvel at huge or why at structures separated with divided apartments? Why at you, tree, saved in the midst of the dwelling, who rise up through roofs and over doorposts into the clear breezes (60), not about to suffer the cruel axes under this master? And now, though you are unaware, perhaps either a supple Naiad or Hamadryad owes you unbroken years.

The dialogue between nature and culture continues, as Statius expands and further delineates nature's personification. We have just watched the earth rejoicing in her new adornment as she surpasses intriguing foreign art with her novel decor. We now are asked to cast a careful eye on a tree that the

---

[47] *Nitidum* can be read with either *aëra* or *solum* and resonates with both. For the latter, cf. *ingenium … mite solo* (15).

[48] See Plin. *Nat.* 36.60.184 on the innovation of Sosus who at Pergamum designed a chamber called 'the unswept room' because it contained a depiction in mosaic of banquet leftovers.

A STREAM AND TWO VILLAS (STATIUS' *SILVAE* 1.3)

poet humanizes by his apostrophe. Statius greets the tree as a 'you' who ascends into the breezes. These are *liquidas*, clear but also sharing the trait of fluidity like the *splendor defluus* that we have just seen coming down from on high to illuminate the fresh mosaic.[49] This tree is also a participant in the villa's refinement, situated as it is in the middle of one of the houses and making its way skyward past doorways and through roofs.

But Statius expands the personification by giving the tree a distinctive life of its own. It has been saved by a *dominus* (61) who, behaving differently from putative harsher masters, unwittingly spares it from the threat of the felling axe. The poet deepens his use of the pathetic fallacy by suggesting that the tree is actually the sacred precinct of a Naiad or Hamadryad who owes her very existence to Vopiscus' humane care. The interconnection is further confirmed by Statius' use of the second person (*tibi*, 63) to call attention again to the nymph just as *te* referred us four lines previously to the rescued tree (59). The implicit intimacy between master and a supposedly inanimate piece of his property, now brought vividly alive, finds an earlier parallel at line four where we have been observers as each of the personified villas vies with the other in laying claim to the attentions of their *dominus*.[50]

Here the personification gains special force because the object in question may be the province of a semi-immortal female divinity of the natural world who might, under other circumstances, have suffered an irreparable loss because of her ties to a particular part of the landscape. The undercurrent of eroticism in the earlier behaviour of the competitive villas is continued in the suggestion of the obeisance that the goddess owes the *dominus* who saved her. The presence of the numinous, here and in what follows, is a crucial adornment of Vopiscus' realm, lending it a complimentary touch of prestige as well as of geniality.

> quid referam alternas gemino super aggere mensas
> albentesque lacus altosque in gurgite fontes,
> teque, per obliquum penitus quae laberis amnem,
> Marcia, et audaci transcurris flumina plumbo,
> ne solum Ioniis sub fluctibus Elidis amnem
> dulcis ad Aetnaeos deducat semita portus?
>
> (Stat. *Silv.* 1.3.64–9)

---

[49] Statius imagines a paradox for us whereby water becomes air through a double metaphor (*liquidas, emergis*).

[50] Cf. *Silv.* 2.2.81–2, as well as the larger context of *Silv.* 2.3; on which poem, see also pp. 45–88 in this volume.

32   THE POETIC WORLD OF STATIUS' *SILVAE*

Why should I tell of successive tables upon the twin embankment and light-coloured pools and springs deep in the current, (65) and you, Marcia, who glide slantwise deeply through the stream and run through the river in bold lead, so that a sweet pathway does not conduct only Elis' stream under Ionian waters to haven at Etna?

The next in this vivid series of vignettes also takes us momentarily back to the poem's opening through the word *gemino*, the river's twin banks. The reminder of the double dwellings (*geminos penates*, 2) through which the Anio has been thrust prepares us for the re-entry of the river into Statius' continuing ekphrasis as we now admire its white pools and deep springs.[51] Then suddenly the poem's cast of characters is again expanded. By another apostrophe on the poet's part the *aqua Marcia*, one of Rome's famous system of aqueducts, that followed the Anio, and largely its south bank, for much of its initial course as it approached Tibur, is enlivened before us.[52] Through the writer's genius her personified self glides from the main aqueduct in a separate lead pipe, deeply under the river's ordinary path toward its domestic destination. Its boldness, carefully paralleled with the boldness of Leander seeking his beloved across the treacherous Hellespont, is equally personified.[53]

The implicit eroticism that Statius has already suggested in outlining the relationship between Vopiscus and several aspects of his domain is now brilliantly extended and enriched. We move from the house and its charms and from the wood nymph, whose tree the owner has saved, to the surrounding landscape and to the personification of one of Rome's major suppliers of water as she flows in an oblique branch beneath the Anio toward

---

[51] *Alternas mensas* also serves as a reminder of *alternas ripas* (25) as well as *litus utrumque* (24). *Albentes* anticipates the appearance of *Albula* (75). Statius may also have us hear Horace's mention of the *domus Albuneae resonantis* (*Carm.* 1.7.12), not least because of the ode's subsequent lines: *et praeceps Anio ac Tiburni lucus et uda/mobilibus pomaria rivis* ('and the plunging Anio and the grove of Tiburnus and the orchards drenched by rushing streams', 1.7.13–14). On Horace's mentions of the Anio in relation to Statius' description, see Newlands (2017) 174–5.

[52] For the Acqua Marcia, see also *Silv.* 1.5.26–7 (*...Marsas nives et frigora ducens/Marcia*) where it is the aqueduct that brings coolness. It had its origins on the Anio, roughly twenty kilometres northeast of Tibur. See also commentators on [Tib.] 3.6.58, Prop. 3.22.24, Mart. 9.18.6. For a recent discussion, see Evans (1993), esp. 455, for a professional look at 'Vopiscus' special tap of the Marcia'. *Plumbo* (67) receives emphasis both for its personification and as an example of metonymy.

[53] Newlands (1988) 101 sees *audaci* as adding a note of violence. I prefer to emphasize the idea of boldness, both here and at line 28, as human courage is pitted against the challenges posed by nature. More generally, on hazardous waters and the Roman quest for empire, see Rimell (2018) throughout.

A STREAM AND TWO VILLAS (STATIUS' *SILVAE* 1.3)   33

Vopiscus and his abode. As in the case of the *asarota* mosaic pavement, where earth creates the setting for man's artifice, culture and nature again combine, with water now being the particular element involved. Rome's genius for engineering created the city's unique network of aqueducts, channelling an abundance of water toward the metropolis to satisfy its varied needs, lending it charm as well as sustenance. Vopiscus' particular skill taps this extraordinary man-made source so that a small tributary, now of his own construction, crosses under the river. By the ingenuity of humankind, nature's quality is twice-over harnessed to our service, be it for a single dwelling or an urban expanse.

Here Statius calls particular attention to the sensual innuendos by drawing an analogy between Marcia, approaching Vopiscus and his dwelling, and the 'sweet path' that Arethusa, turned into a stream, followed from Elis under the Ionian Sea to her Sicilian port no great distance south of Mt. Etna. It was, of course, the same route that the river Alpheus, assuming his natural shape, took in pursuit of her. As Ovid's Arethusa pointedly puts it (*Met.* 5.638), he could then 'mingle himself with me' (*se mihi misceat*). Their final destination was the fountain, on the island of Ortygia in the harbour of Syracuse, which bears her name. In his brief retelling of the story of this *dulcis semita*, the pathway of sweet water, flowing unsullied through the salt sea, that also speaks to love's own enjoyable, untainted rewards, Statius leaves it to our imaginations to appreciate the series of double-entendres that lead the aqueous lovers *ad Aetnaeos portus*, to their adventure's dramatic conclusion on Sicily's east coast.[54]

> illic ipse antris Anien et fonte relicto
> nocte sub arcana glaucos exutus amictus
> huc illuc fragili prosternit pectora musco
> aut ingens in stagna cadit vitreasque natatu
> plaudit aquas; illa recubat Tiburnus in umbra,
> illic sulpureos cupit Albula mergere crines.
>
> (Stat. *Silv.* 1.3.70–5)

---

[54] Statius' language shows familiarity with Virg. *A.* 3.694–6 and more generally with *Ecl.* 10.1–5 and its implicit definition of pastoral. The bittersweetness of love is a concept that goes back to Sappho. For the potentially obscene suggestiveness of *semita,* see Adams (1982) 89 and for *portus,* see Pichon (1966) 236. For its erotic significance in the tale of Hero and Leander, cf. Ov. *Her.* 18.198. Martelli (2009) 154 n. 2 takes *semita* to refer to Arethusa herself. *Deducat* is a word often connected with poetic composition; for its Callimachean connotations, see most recently Martelli (2009) 154–6.

34 THE POETIC WORLD OF STATIUS' *SILVAE*

There the Anio himself, having left behind his grotto (70) and spring in the secrecy of night, stripped of his grey-green garb, now here, now there, spreads his chest with delicate moss or in his vastness falls into the pools and splashes the glassy waters as he swims. Tiburnus reclines in that shade, there Albula yearns to plunge her sulphurous hair (75).

The next episode in this extraordinary verse continuum introduces us to the river-god Anio (Anien) and his neighbour companions, the city's eponymous hero Tiburnus and the goddess Albula. It is both opened and bounded by the adverb *illic* (70), repeated at line 75. Statius asks us to look 'there' from wherever we are, having just admired 'you', Marcia, as she crossed the stream. But a further deictic, *ipse*, quickly changes distance to immediacy. The generalized *altos fontes*, that we heard of at line 65, now become the particular *fonte* that is the god's own. And, if we give the pronominal adjective its full force, we meet the god himself in his own person, conjured up by the poet naked before our eyes. In the privacy of secret night, with his cloak shed, he moves the stream's moss with his chest and with his huge body makes the water resound.[55]

If *illic* both lures our vision to the event and delimits the story it tells, its cognates *huc* and *illuc* draw us into the particulars as we follow the bulky river-god pushing the delicate moss about, now here, now there, as he swims. Statius' use of the adjective *vitreus* then presents the opportunity to imagine the results of the energy released by the god's physical presence upon the stream's previous calm. We end the scene by observing Tibur's founder reclining appropriately in that very shade (*illa umbra*),[56] and the repetition of *illic* points our line of vision, still there, to the goddess of the sulphur springs west of the city as she yearns to bathe her hair in her own beneficial waters.[57]

> haec domus Egeriae nemoralem abiungere Phoeben
> et Dryadum viduare choris algentia possit
> Taygeta et silvis accersere Pana Lycaeis.

---

[55] Statius' Anio has a noble epic heritage. The only other two uses together in Latin of forms of *glaucus* and *amictus* occur at *A.* 8.33 (of the river god Tiber) and 12.885 (of the river goddess Juturna).

[56] The phrase *recubat in umbra* has a rich poetic pedigree. Among other references back in literature, it takes us to Virg. *Ecl.* 1.4 (*recubans...in umbra*) and Prop. 3.3.1 (*recubans Heliconis in umbra*) as well as Calp. *Ecl.* 4.37. So both pastoral and elegy are again drawn into Statius' creative network.

[57] With *mergere* (75) cf. *emergis* (60). One nymph emerges, the other immerses.

A STREAM AND TWO VILLAS (STATIUS' *SILVAE* 1.3) 35

> quod ni templa darent alias Tirynthia sortes,
> et Praenestinae poterant migrare sorores.
>
> (Stat. *Silv.* 1.3.76–80)

This house could separate woodland Phoebe from Egeria and bereave chill Taygetus of its choirs of Dryads and summon Pan from the woods of Lycaeus. And if the Tirynthian shrine did not give other oracles, the sisters of Praeneste might have made the move (80).

Statius announces his poem's next segment with another deictic that takes us from there to here, and to a series of summary appraisals. *Haec domus*, this house, this domain, and its distinction, are once again at the centre of our purview.[58] We begin with four places for comparison, two Italian and two Greek. The first and fourth are in Latium, the *domus Egeriae*, which is to say Aricia with its sacred grove, southwest of Tibur, and Praeneste to its southeast. In between we find ourselves at Mt. Taygetus, looming over Sparta, or in the woods of Arcadia. Such is the magnetic quality of Vopiscus' estate that it can lure gods away from their own native haunts and even places of worship.[59] Statius gives Diana (Phoebe) the epithet *nemoralis* as a reminder of a standard cult-title, *Nemorensis*, attached to her worship at Aricia. The attraction of Vopiscus and his *nemora* (17) is strong enough to entice the goddess of the sylvan world away from one of her own special shrines to the eminence of a Tiburtine villa. For the same reason Taygetus would lose its choruses of Dryads and Pan would depart from his home-land, also in the Peloponnese. The fortune-telling sisters of Praeneste would likewise have transferred their loyalty did not the temple of Hercules at Tibur apparently already offer services similar to theirs.

There is an irony latent in Statius' catalogue, to be found especially in the words *abiungere* and *viduare*. Such is the potency of Vopiscus' realm that it can separate Diana from Egeria and bereave Taygetus of his nymphs. It can even summon Pan away from his woodlands. In a poem that puts such a strong focus on pairings and their disjunction, on unities and losses, the poet's stress here is for an instant double-edged. Such is the excellence of this Tiburtine community that it can also cause disruption. The compliment is enormous. It is not every locale that can claim the alliance of gods

---

[58] We find forms of *domus* at 8, 24, 76, and 84; of *dominus* at 4 and 61.

[59] In this poem where unities are a special topic the act of separation (*abiungere*) has particular force. Cf. *iunctus* (45).

36   THE POETIC WORLD OF STATIUS' *SILVAE*

whose allegiance regularly belongs elsewhere. But is there an implicit cost, we might ask?

> quid bifera Alcinoi laudem pomaria vosque,
> qui numquam vacui prodistis in aethera, rami?
> cedant Telegoni, cedant Laurentia Turni
> iugera Lucrinaeque domus litusque cruenti
> Antiphatae, cedant vitreae iuga perfida Circes
> Dulichiis ululata lupis, arcesque superbae
> Anxuris et sedes Phrygio quas mitis alumno
> debet anus, cedant quae te iam solibus artis
> Antia nimbosa revocabunt litora bruma.
> (Stat. *Silv.* 1.3.81–9)

Why should I praise the twice-bearing orchards of Alcinous, and you, boughs, that never stretched empty toward the heavens? Let the fields of Telegonus yield, let the Laurentian fields of Turnus yield and Lucrine dwellings and the shore of bloody Antiphates, let the treacherous ridges of glassy Circe (85), with the howls of Dulichian wolves, yield, and the proud citadels of Anxur and the dwelling that the gentle old woman owes to her Phrygian nursling, let the shores of Antium yield which will call you back when the suns narrow in the cloudy time of winter.

We turn now to a catalogue of prominent locations that serve as touchstones for evaluating the distinctiveness of Vopiscus' estate. We begin with a reference to the orchards of Alcinous on Phaeacia.[60] But the plurality of places is to be found in neighbouring Italy. One town, Tusculum, is well inland and another, Ardea, is some few miles from the Mediterranean shore. But for the majority the tour takes us on a haphazard, topographically varied itinerary along the Italian littoral, north down the coast, from Antium, nearly due south of Rome, to Baiae, on the Bay of Naples, with stops at Anxur, Caieta, and Formiae along the way. The tone of the poet's encomium changes markedly

---

[60] On the orchards of Tibur, see Hor. *Carm.* 1.7.14 (quoted above, n. 51) and *Prop.* 4.7.81–6, lines on the death of Cynthia that Statius clearly valued: *ramosis Anio qua pomifer incubat arvis,/et numquam Herculeo numine pallet ebur,/.../.../HIC SITA TIBVRTINA IACET AVREA CYNTHIA TERRA:/ACCESSIT RIPAE LAVS, ANIENE, TVAE* ('where the apple-bearing Anio broods over bough-filled fields and under the protection of Hercules ivory never yellows...HERE LIES GOLDEN CYNTHIA IN TIBUR'S GROUND: ANIO, PRAISE HAS REACHED YOUR BANK'). Statius may also wish us to hear echoes of Virg. *G.* 2.87: *poma...et Alcinoi silvae* and 4.119: *biferi...rosaria Paesti*. On the connection with Homer's Alcinous, see Marshall (2009) *passim*.

A STREAM AND TWO VILLAS (STATIUS' *SILVAE* 1.3)   37

from what has preceded. We begin with a question and then another apostrophe which brings us directly 'there' for a moment: why praise the fruit-trees of Alcinous and you, their ever-productive branches, if only to put on display how much better are your Tiburtine colleagues! The energy in the list that follows derives in part from the fourfold repetition of the word *cedant* which gives the poet's petitions the powerful property of a litany. Our eye may dart from place to place, each with its various significant associations, but our thoughts remain concentrated on Vopiscus and the superiority of his surroundings by comparison with the ample variety of offerings to be found elsewhere. Let other abodes of importance pale is the poet's prayer, when thought of alongside that of Vopiscus! The compliment to Statius' host is enormous. The common link between the majority of the places mentioned is their connection with epic. The orchards of Alcinous take us particularly to Books 7 and 8 of the *Odyssey*. Homer's masterpiece is also the setting where we find Antiphates, king of the cannibalistic Laestrygonians who appear in the poem's tenth book and have associations with Formiae. Circe, from whom the promontory Circeii derives its name, dominates the same book.[61] She is the mother by Odysseus of Telegonus, the supposed founder of Tusculum and therefore to be associated with post-Homeric saga. The *Aeneid* enters the parade via mention of Turnus who hailed from Ardea peopled by the Laurentes. Caieta, Aeneas' aged nurse, and her eponymous port, play a prominent structural part as a bond between Books 6 and 7 of Virgil's epic and thus between the poem's first and second halves. Circe reappears on several occasions in the latter book as events of the poem's second half take their start, and Baiae makes a brief entrance in the poem at line 710 of Book 9.[62]

The quadruple use of the verb *cedere* also serves as a reminder of one of the most well-known distichs in the poetry of Propertius: *cedite Romani scriptores; cedite Grai:/nescioquid maius nascitur Iliade* ('Yield, Roman writers; yield Greek! Something greater than the *Iliad* is coming into being!' 2.34.65–6). The couplet, with its striking repetition of *cedite* that commands Greek and Roman writers to give way before a work of superior excellence, announces the arrival of the *Aeneid* on the literary scene, a masterpiece that will surpass in brilliance even the *Iliad*, *fons et origo* of classical literature

---

[61] Newlands (1988) 104 points out how the transference of *perfida* from the goddess to the ridges of her promontory gives it particular force. Her treachery permeates the terrain. Nothing of the sort, we presume, exists in Vopiscus' spiritual or moral landscape.

[62] Baiae also appears, along with *arduos Sabinos*, Praeneste, and Tibur *supinum*, in a list of places of inspiration for Horace (*Carm.* 3.4.21–4).

38   THE POETIC WORLD OF STATIUS' *SILVAE*

and model for its future distinction. The lines became rightly famous in antiquity when the production and the greatness of Virgil's poem was the subject of discussion.[63] One of Statius' purposes in calling it to our attention here is to reinforce still further the presence of epic tonality at the service of a great variety of locations in these lines as they praise the outstanding quality of Vopiscus' estate. A powerful means that the poet has at his disposal is, at least for a moment, to turn from his usual modality of lyric expressiveness to that of the supreme poetic genre. Vopiscus' property outdoes the example of Alcinous in Homer's *Odyssey* and of Ardea, Baiae, and Caieta in the *Aeneid*. And the other references in Statius' catalogue drawn from epic serve only to add authority to the discussion of his domain.

The two places in Statius' list without direct associations with epic, Antium and Anxur, are primarily known as major destinations for the worship of Fortuna and Jupiter, respectively.[64] The majesty of religion is thus added to the special dignity gained from the procession of locations affiliated with the prestige of epic narrative to further underscore the eminence of Vopiscus' estate and its grand exposition in supposedly occasional verse. Antium secures particular prominence not only from its position as the conclusion of the catalogue but as the place that serves as the point of re-entry of *te* (89), you, the *dominus* himself, back into the narrative. Even Vopiscus ventures away from the beauties of Tibur to the comfort of the Latian shore when the sun narrows and the winter clouds over.

The Owner

> scilicet hic illi meditantur pondera mores,
> hic premitur fecunda quies virtusque serena
> fronte gravis sanusque nitor luxuque carentes
> deliciae, quas ipse suis digressus Athenis
> mallet deserto senior Gargettius horto.
> haec per et Aegaeas hiemes Hyadumque nivosum

---

[63] See commentators on Suet. *Vita Verg.* 30 from which Donatus' *vita* was drawn.

[64] We might question the presence of *superbae* (86) and therefore the intimations of pride in an analogy meant to praise Vopiscus' person as well as residence. But Statius may be thinking back to Virg. *A.* 7.799–800, where the poet lists the fields over which 'Jupiter Anxur keeps watch' (*Iuppiter Anxurus...praesidet*), part of a catalogue of Italian warriors, which Statius knew well. (Reference to Anxur follows immediately upon mention of the *iugum Circaeum*.) If so, the reference is merely to the loftiness of his famous temple rather than to any haughtiness on the part of the king of the gods.

A STREAM AND TWO VILLAS (STATIUS' *SILVAE* 1.3)   39

sidus et Oleniis dignum petiisse sub astris,
si Maleae credenda ratis Siculosque per aestus
sit via; cur oculis sordet vicina voluptas?

(Stat. Silv. 1.3.90–8)

Here for sure that way of living ponders weighty themes (90), here a fruitful calm is enshrouded and august courage with serene brow and sensible elegance and pleasure without extravagance, which the old man himself from Gargettus, leaving his garden behind after departing from his Athens, would prefer. It is worth having gone in search of this through Aegean storms and the Hyades' snowy constellation (95) and beneath the Olenian stars, though the ship must be entrusted to Malea and the route lie through Sicilian surge. Why does pleasure near to hand seem mean to our eyes?

After this series of complimentary comparisons, which introduce us to nearby Italian locales often by way of reference to the work of Homer and Virgil, we turn back to the estate of Vopiscus and now in particular to the owner himself. In the previous catalogue, however honorific—at the start Statius singles out Alcinous and his orchards for praise—the poet reminds us, along with 'proud' Jupiter and 'gentle' Caieta, also of 'bloody' Antiphates, the cannibal, and of the glittering witch Circe who on her 'treacherous' hillside turned Odysseus' men into wolves. And Horace had long since recalled for his reader that Telegonus had killed his father.[65] What follows seems purely laudatory.

Two adjacent deictics forming a paradoxical duo, *hic* and *illi*, bring us back to our Tiburtine villa and its *dominus. Hic* draws us directly to the place itself and *illi* to those *mores* that we have previously taken for granted and now will enjoy being explicitly recounted. Our touchstone can be words drawn from Statius' other 'villa' poem offered to Pollius Felix about his estate at Surrentum: *hic praeceps minus audet hiems, nulloque tumultu/stagna modesta iacent dominique imitantia mores* ('Here the rushing storm lessens its boldness and the pools lie disciplined without agitation and simulate the manners of their master', Stat. *Silv.* 2.2.28–9).[66] At Tibur as well master and domain complement each other. Personification adds force to the enumeration of attributes. The *mores* themselves have the power to contemplate weighty matters, and the accompanying *quies*, and its colleagues, *virtus, nitor,* and

---

[65] See n. 70, below.
[66] There is a close resemblance between these lines and *Silv.* 1.3.41–2.

40   THE POETIC WORLD OF STATIUS' *SILVAE*

deliciae, are stable, masked in silence, guarded from ostentation. All are qualified with positive accolades. The calm is creative and the courage self-assured yet weighty like the *pondera* which Vopiscus' manners reflect upon. The elegance is reasoned and the accompanying delights neither too opulent nor too overweening. If *deliciae* hints discretely at erotic pleasures—an innuendo we have seen from the poem's start—along with the happiness that is the consequence of good living, they are exploited without over-indulgence.[67] The whole would be sufficiently attractive to lure the elderly Gargettian, the philosopher Epicurus, not only from his famous enclosed garden and its quietude but also from its larger setting in Athens itself, honoured centre of civilization. His putative journey, first amid the storms of the Aegean, then around Cape Malea and through the swirls of Charybdis, which has already been called vicariously to our attention at lines 32–3, is not only venturesome but also the climax of the poem's several references to travel that energize its progress.[68] We have watched bold Leander swim the Hellespont to meet his beloved Hero, then the *aqua Marcia* cross the Anio in her equally bold pipe to gratify Vopiscus and his estate. She in turn claims analogy with the water nymph Arethusa eagerly pursued by the river god Alpheus on their underwater route to the shores of Sicily.

Reference to *Aegaeas hiemes* serves to remind the reader of one of Horace's most impressive odes, *Carm.* 3.29, whose next-to-last line (63) tells of his two- oared skiff making its way unscathed 'through the Aegean's turbulence' (*per Aegaeos tumultus*).[69] Horace's great poem about life's vicissitudes is much on Statius' mind as he writes.[70] Here we need only note how the lyricist's self-control, his inner security, is a match for any external threats, however

---

[67] For *deliciae*, see Pichon (1966) 125; for *luxus*, commentators, beginning with Servius on Virg. *G.* 3.135–7 and *A.* 4.193, are helpful. Here the word means something like self-indulgence that suggests surfeit. Valerius Maximus (4.7. *praef.*) speaks in negative terms of the *consortione deliciarum et luxuriae* ('conjunction of pleasure and extravagance') that rots a friendship.

[68] Mention of sea-storms in a context involving Epicurus serves as a reminder of their association with inner spiritual turbulence. Statius has in mind Lucretius' treatment of such imagery at the start of *De Rerum Natura* 2 as he writes the closing lines of *Silv.* 2.2, esp. 131–2.

[69] Horace juxtaposes *otium* and *patenti...Aegaeo* at *Carm.* 2.16.1–2.

[70] Among other parallels we note the mentions of Tibur at *Carm.* 3.29.6 and of Telegonus at l.8 while references to Procyon (18) and Leo (19) anticipate Statius' bows to Sirius (5) and the lion constellation (6). The earlier poem is an invitation to Maecenas to visit the author near Tibur at a hot season of the year. The second finds Statius in the act of marvelling at a Tiburtine villa at a similar time. The landscape Horace describes has similarities to that of Vopiscus, with shade (*umbras*, 21), a stream (*rivum*, 22), and a silent bank (*ripa taciturna*, 24). More generally, and perhaps suggestive to Statius, is how Horace's analogy between our lives and a river's flow speaks to the notion of changeability, of the alterations between the hectic and the halcyon that punctuate the average person's existence.

A STREAM AND TWO VILLAS (STATIUS' *SILVAE* 1.3)   41

violent, that his *curriculum vitae* can bring his way. Epicurus' journey, as imagined by Statius, is equally real and symbolic, again at once literal and figurative. We are to envision a factual itinerary from Greece to Italy, from an Athenian pleasance to a consequential establishment in the hills east of Rome.

But for the founder of Epicureanism any such putative schedule is richly symbolic. It would take him away from his spiritual retreat into the realm of inner human trials and external tribulations from which his philosophy seeks to shield the thoughtful individual. But this temporary exposure to life's sea of troubles would have its reward in his arrival at Tibur where he would find a recreation, however idiosyncratic and distinct from Epicurus' Athenian abode, of his own *hortus conclusus*, emblem at once of a physical escape from the hurly-burly of existence and of the spiritual assurance and equilibrium that comes from inner peace of mind.

There is an immediate difference between Statius' exposition of the putative voyage that makes Vopiscus' haven a worthy destination toward which to imagine Epicurus journeying and the other water crossings we have noted dot ting the poem. Statius makes this clear in the line that follows the details of the philosopher's possible travel. It is put as a brief question: 'Why does pleasure near to hand seem mean to our eyes?' (*cur oculis sordet vicina voluptas?*). The earlier journeys, of Leander to Hero, of Marcia, as a modern version of Alpheus, to Vopiscus, centre directly, or by suggestion in the case of the latter, on eroticism as an element of importance in the poet's parallels. Here the key word is *voluptas* (ἡδονή) which we have seen earlier (9) personified as helper, with Venus to follow, in the probable designing of Vopiscus' dwelling. In both cases the word denotes not so much carnal pleasure as the Epicurean moral ideal of living happily in the absence of turmoil and pain. Any implications of sexual attraction that surfaced in the earlier exempla are now sublimated as we attain a higher level of desire through the contemplation of philosophical values. These are to be discovered, and appreciated, in Epicurus' Athenian abode and in its reincarnation on the banks of the Anio. One need in fact not travel at all, or especially not behave like the restless, unsatisfied Roman lord, as described by Lucretius (3.1060–75), who roams about from place to place, at the mercy of his own inner ennui. Whatever joys that are necessary to satisfy the needs of the practicing Epicurean are right to hand.

> hic tua Tiburtes Faunos chelys et iuvat ipsum
> Alciden dictumque lyra maiore Catillum,

42   THE POETIC WORLD OF STATIUS' *SILVAE*

> seu tibi Pindaricis animus contendere plectris
> siue chelyn tollas heroa ad robora siue
> liuentem saturam nigra rubigine turbes
> seu †tua non alia† splendescat epistula cura.
>
> (Stat. *Silv.* 1.3.99–104)

Here your lyre brings pleasure to the Fauni of Tibur and to Alcides himself and to Catillus, named by a greater harp (100), whether it is your mind to strive with the quills of Pindar or you lift your lyre to the strength of heroes or roil up spiteful satire with its black rust or your letter sparkles with no different skill.

And now, with the last in a row of uses of *hic* that takes us from line 90 to 91 and 99, with the variation *haec* at 95, we turn to Vopiscus, the intellectual, and to his varied poetry. We remember that in the preface to *Silvae* 1 (*praef.* 24–5) Statius characterizes Vopiscus as 'the most learned of men and one who especially lays claim to literature now nearly vanishing from neglect' (*vir eruditissimus et qui praecipue vindicat a situ litteras iam paene fugientes*).[71] The language is strong. Statius may be thinking of the analogy between a finished volume and a slave fleeing the control of his master. But *situs* is a powerful overlord, implying both the impact of erosion, as time passes, that can come from neglect but also the ability of Vopiscus to wrench literature away from the clutches of decay.[72] The compliment is deep, implying that Vopiscus in his own way helps the world of letters surmount the ravages of time. This may simply mean that Vopiscus keeps past writing alive by using his own erudition through an interest in readings, preservation of manuscripts, and the like.[73]

But Statius may also be implying that Vopiscus keeps literature and its traditions from vanishing by practicing the art of poetry so brilliantly himself. Certainly the lines that follow suggest both the value and the extent of his oeuvre. He brings pleasure to the living and the dead, to local divinities of the natural world, like *Fauni*, to Hercules, man become god with a nearby place of worship, and Catillus, one of the traditional founders of Tibur. Four genres speak to Vopiscus' proficiency. All are specifically connected with 'you', the creator (*tua chelys, tibi, tollas, turbes, tua epistula*), and each has

---

[71] See Pittà (2021) 118–19.

[72] Lovers of Horace will think of his striking play on the word *situs* at *Carm.* 3.30.2.

[73] *Fugientes* might also be viewed metapoetically as applying to the analogy of books to runaway slaves. See, e.g., Cic. *Att.* 4.8a.3; Hor. *Ep.* 1.20 (with Oliensis [1995] 212); Mart. 1.3.12; Pliny *Ep.* 2.10.3 (with Whitton [2013] 150). Does Vopiscus save fugitive poetry?

A STREAM AND TWO VILLAS (STATIUS' *SILVAE* 1.3) 43

distinguishing characteristics. To emulate Pindar is to have *animus* and to 'contend', in the manner of the athletes celebrated in his epinician odes. To commemorate heroes on the tortoise-shell lyre is to dwell on their strength. Satire needs to be roiling as it goes its colourful way, black when involving envy, red when something blighted is the subject.[74] By contrast the epistle, as composed by Vopiscus, gleams with the special concern for literary excellence that he lavishes on it.

Only the initial mention of Catillus, *dictum...lyra maiore*, is open to some debate, since the hero is named by both Virgil (*A.* 7.672) and Horace (*Carm.* 1.18.2). Statius decides the matter for us in two ways. First, the synecdoche *chelys* is specified at line 102 as the instrument to be linked with epic. More directly, it is hard to dissociate *lyra* from lyric poetry and hence with Horace, Rome's greatest practitioner of the genre, who would be a clear candidate for the compliment.[75] For all his generous gestures to Vopiscus, Statius does not allow his writings to outshine those of the Augustan master, especially when they are dealing with the same subject.

> digne Midae Croesique bonis et Perside gaza,
> macte bonis animi, cuius stagnantia rura
> debuit et flauis Hermus transcurrere ripis
> et limo splendente Tagus, sic docta frequentes
> otia, sic omni detertus pectora nube
> finem Nestoreae precor egrediare senectae.
>
> <div align="right">(Stat. <i>Silv.</i> 1.3.105–10)</div>

O worthy of the wealth of Midas and of Croesus and of the treasure of Persia (105), be blessed in the resources of your mind. The Hermus with its yellow banks should have passed across your pool-filled acreage and the Tagus with its gleaming silt. So may you celebrate learning's leisure, thus, freed in your heart from every cloud, I pray that you surpass the limit of Nestor's old age (110).

The poem draws to a close with two further apostrophes to Vopiscus, both concerned with *bona*. In the first Statius addresses his host as worthy of the enormous amount of the world's goods that has come his way. His external

---

[74] For the colour of envy, see Ov. *Met.* 2.776 and Stat. *Silv.* 4.8.16–17. The verb *turbes* in connection with satire picks up the negative associations of *turbare* (22) and *turbine* (41). Unlike the peaceful Anio, whose passage enhances its Tiburtine environment, satire is a metaphorical river whose agitated course stirs up blackness.

[75] For a defense of *lyra* as referring to epic and specifically Virgil, see Harrison (1995) 121.

44   THE POETIC WORLD OF STATIUS' *SILVAE*

domain is such that it deserves to be further enhanced by the riches contained in the gold-replete flow of the rivers Hermus, whose tributary, the Pactolus, was associated with King Midas, and Tagus. In the last of the several appearances of particular bodies of water that we have been tracing through the poem, nature is at the service of humans. In this case it would amplify the surface beauties of Vopiscus' estate, beauties that its possessor knows how both to manage properly and to relish, within the reasoned framework of a true Epicurean. In particular the brightness of the Tagus reflects the shimmering elegance (*nitor*, 92) of what a visitor experiences at the Tiburtine villa.

Vopiscus should also rejoice in his *bona animi*, the mental assets that he brings as complement to the physical charm of his surroundings.[76] Here too the river Tagus plays a part, echoing in its gleaming mud (*limo splendente*) the verbal brightness (*splendescat*, 104) of the owner's poetic accomplishment.[77] These goods of the spirit find appropriate venue in the *docta otia* that are regular accompaniments to Vopiscus' style of living.[78] Just as stretches of leisure are an habitual part of his routine, so is the learning that here is their essential partner. Leisure allows for the relaxed delight in the superficial graces of the Tiburtine domain. Learning deepens its excellence by adding its owner's superiority of mind, and the distinction of the literature that is its result, to the ingredients crucial to the well-being of the whole.

We end with the positive omen of a cloudless heart for Vopiscus, echoing the scintillating clarity of his world, and with a prayer that he attain Nestor's proverbial length of days, a final reminder of Homer's potent presence in the poem and thus of the enriching presence of allusions to earlier literature that lends it grace.

We glean from the poem as a whole Statius' impressive understanding of Vopiscus' spiritual and physical world, and of the importance to it of creating unities when separation or absence might have been the rule. The presence of beauty, be it in nature, in the display of visual art, or in the practice of writing well, is also crucial in forging the harmony that lends singularity to the whole.[79]

---

[76] Statius is at pains throughout his poem to show that Vopiscus' riches, in spite of Epicurus' opposition to luxury, do not stand in the way of his appreciation of the crucial value of spiritual quality. The poet seems to imply that, for Vopiscus at least, economic worth is only a means to help one live an exemplary moral existence.

[77] Cf. the *splendor* (53) that nature adds to the exotic but man-made *asarota* mosaic.

[78] On *otium* in the poetry of Statius, see Myers (2005).

[79] Newlands (2012) 58 observes that 'technology and nature are engaged in productive cooperation, a mirror or a social world woven together by reciprocal ties of friendship and a common love of literature'.

2

The Garden of Atedius Melior

A Change for the Better (Statius' *Silvae* 2.3)

Statius' birthday poem, a gift for his friend and patron Atedius Melior, focuses on the history of a plane tree situated on the brink of a pool in the latter's garden on Rome's Caelian Hill.[1] Celebration of an *arbor* finds an apt place in a larger collection devoted to *Silvae*. Reference to the tree's particular setting and strange shape, which looks as if part of it grew from a fresh stem lodged in the water's depths, leads to the work's central narrative. This is devoted to a mythic tale, apparently of the author's invention, wherein Pan pursues the nymph Pholoe, on the spot where Melior now dwells, but is thwarted in his erotic intentions by the intervention of the goddess Diana. The deprived god then proceeds to dedicate to Pholoe, as a form of remembrance of love lost, a *platanus* that he plants on the side of the nearby waters into which she has plunged to escape his advances. The tree, in Statius' brilliant portrayal, serves as a surrogate suitor, evincing the god's warmth and finally receiving a gesture of affection from the naiad in return. In a fitting conclusion the poet returns to Melior, mention of whom had been made in the first hexameter, in the form of a eulogy of his quality of mind and character. May he live for many a year, prays the speaker, leaving the reader to meditate on the power of Statius' verse to ensure his subject's permanence!

In the trajectory of his presentation, we will find Statius touching on many other topics besides the immortalizing power of poetry, or, more generally, time and its passing, birth, of course, and youth but also death.[2]

---

[1] I am greatly in debt to the detailed commentaries by Newlands (2011a) and Van Dam (1984) with which I have been in constant dialogue. For what we know of the biography of Atedius Melior, see White (1975) 272–5.

[2] For the many examples of oppositions and antitheses that permeate the poem, see Vessey (1981), esp. 49 and n. 16. He mentions brightness and shadow, height and depth, the visible and the hidden. To these we might add, among others, noise and silence, war and peace, public and private, past and present, permanence and evanescence, nature and culture, motion and stillness, devotion and abhorrence, sterility and fecundity.

The Poetic World of Statius' Silvae. Michael C. J. Putnam, Edited by: Antony Augoustakis with Carole E. Newlands, Oxford University Press. © Michael C. J. Putnam 2023. DOI: 10.1093/oso/9780192869272.003.0003

46   THE POETIC WORLD OF STATIUS' *SILVAE*

The nature of eroticism, in its varied nuances, will be ever before our minds. The physicality and violence that desire stimulates, prominent in the central myth, are checked during its course. But they are also counterbalanced by the setting in which Statius places us, the peaceful, calm-filled environment, beloved by Epicureans, of Melior, a realm of ethical enlightenment, combining straightforwardness of behaviour with enjoyment, and lacking the inner *tumultus* that regularly beset humankind. We also enter a world of origins not only of myth but of history, of the evolution of civilization and, in particular, of events occurring during its initial years on the site of what was to become mighty Rome.

We will also be following closely Statius' utilization of earlier or contemporary Latin poetry as a critical tool for delving into, as well as for bringing clarity to, the richness of meaning that permeates his work in its complexity. By absorbing previous texts into his, he extends their special intensity of meaning to his own novel imaginative effort. The result can display the power of previous writing reinvigorated by the present poet's unique artistry or of one context shedding light on another through parallels that serve to complement, to differentiate or, on occasion, to succeed in both supplementing a poem's intent as well as confirming its uniqueness. And specific allusions often bring with them the effectiveness of the larger genre in which they originally appeared as a further resource to help in evaluating the tone and sense of a given passage.

The Poem's Opening

As critics have long illustrated, the influence of Ovid, author of the *Metamorphoses*, master narrator of tales of pursuit and its consequences, is at the forefront of the influences on Statius.[3] But in the first few lines alone we trace the presence of Ovid the elegist as well as of Virgil, Lucan, Martial and, more circumspectly, Horace, in his role as lyricist. First let us look at the lines themselves:

> Stat quae perspicuas nitidi Melioris opacet
> arbor aquas complexa lacus; quae robore ab imo

---

[3] On *Silvae* 2.3 and Ovid, see, e.g., Newlands (2011a) 157–8 as well as Vessey (1981) 46; Dewar (2002), esp. 398–403; Hardie (2006), an essay to which the present paper is indebted for its Horatian insights as well.

THE GARDEN OF ATEDIUS MELIOR (STATIUS' *SILVAE* 2.3)   47

[in]curvata[4] vadis redit inde cacumine recto
ardua, ceu mediis iterum nascatur ab undis
atque habitet vitreum tacitis radicibus amnem.
quid Phoebum tam parva rogem? vos dicite causas,
Naides, et faciles (satis est) date carmina, Fauni.

(Stat. *Silv.* 2.3.1–7)

There stands a tree which shades the crystalline waters of glowing Melior, embracing the pool. Bending toward the shallows from the base of its trunk, it returns thence aloft, with crest straight, is if it were born again from the middle of the waves and dwells in the glassy stream with silent roots (5). Why should I ask Phoebus for such insignificance? You, Naiads, tell the circumstances, and, favouring Fauni, grant the poetry. It is sufficient.

Throughout the opening septet of hexameters our eye is on the tree lodged on Melior's property and on the idea of birth and rebirth that is part of its history. But other notions add breadth to the passage. First is the idea of translucency and its complement, clarity. We will learn over the course of the poem that these are among the particular virtues of Melior. But the symbiosis between owner and setting is suggested already here at the start through the adjective *nitidi*. The epithet validates the connection through meanings that embrace both the literal and the figurative. Melior 'gleams' like the pellucid, glassy waters of his garden. But his inner bearing is equally elegant, outstanding for honesty, openness, and poise.

The initial lines also tell us that the erotic will have a large presence, both direct and by innuendo, in what follows. *Complexa* sets the tone, and anticipates the *amplexus* (56), the embraces that the tree will later attempt to offer, at first without any success, to the water-nymph beneath. In the present context it leads directly into the suggestiveness of male sexuality that we find in *robur, incurvata, cacumine recto*, and *ardua*, and which the poem will elaborate in the behaviour of Pan and his proxy, the *platanus*.[5]

At the end of the description of the tree *tacitis* stands out as an unexpected epithet, of which Statius is a master. It has the effect of personifying *radicibus*, roots that in other circumstances might tell their own version of the tale to follow. Here the word offers a salient variation of synaesthesia

---

[4] For [in]*curvata* (followed by Liberman), Courtney reads [*cur*] *curvata* and treats the initial five lines as a question.

[5] Statius keeps his reader waiting until line 39 to learn the type of tree involved. For sexual implications of *incurvata*, see Adams (1982) 191–2; of *cacumine*, 72; of *radicibus*, 24, 27, 219. *Arduus* is also linked by Priscian to *ardeo* (Adams [1982] 49). Cf. Pan's *ardenti pectore* (19–20).

48   THE POETIC WORLD OF STATIUS' *SILVAE*

where the seen is unexpectedly replaced by the heard, thus bringing both senses into play. In Melior's world of quiet, the roots that might ordinarily be hard to view beneath the water's shimmering surface also share in the calm of the general ambience.

Finally, to round out the initial paragraph, Statius tells us of his indirect request to Apollo for inspiration but immediately apostrophizes the Naiades and Fauni to relate the *causae*, and grant the poetry to explain them, for what follows.[6] We will return to the appropriateness of the Naiads and Fauns as stimuli for the imagination, not least because the protagonists in the tale that follows, Pholoe and Pan, are drawn from their number. But first let us look at some of the intensive allusiveness that invigorates these lines and prepares us for what lies ahead.

An initial paragraph of seven verses in length, traditional for ancient epic from the *Iliad* on, forewarns the reader that earlier practitioners of the genre will play parts in what follows. Such is already the case with the opening hexameters where Virgil makes a prominent appearance. The phrase *opacet arbor*, enjambed between the first two lines, is a clear reminder of perhaps the most famous part of a tree in ancient literature. In the Sibyl's words:...*latet arbore opaca/aureus et foliis et lento vimine ramus*...('There lurks on a shady tree a bough, golden both in its leaves and supple stem', Virg. *A.* 6.136–7). We are at the crucial moment where the hero Aeneas is preparing to enter the Underworld and to learn at length from his father about Roman leaders from the early years of the city to the reign of Augustus Caesar. The golden bough, a gift to Proserpina, serves as a form of passport, first, literally, for a living human into the realm of the dead, then, intellectually, for the founder of the empire to come to know the magnificence that lies in its future. Statius' shading tree serves a parallel purpose. Here it is the poet who is suggesting to his readers, appropriately at the poem's start, that a highly symbolic moment in Virgil's *Aeneid* and therefore, implicitly, that aspects of the whole poem itself, will act as one of the several guides towards an appreciation of both the plot and the presentation of what follows.

---

[6] Alliteration links *faciles* and *Fauni* in line 7. As *faciles* the rustic deities are 'doers' (from *facio*) and therefore should be particularly supportive of a wordsmith, a 'maker' of poems. But the word *Faunus* itself is linked with *fari*, to speak, e.g. by Serv. *ad A.* 7. 47: *dicti sunt Faunus et Fauna a vaticinando*, id *est fando* ('Faunus and Fauna draw their names from *vaticinor* [to prophesy, to sing with inspiration], that is to say from *fari* [to speak]'). The *faciles Fauni* are thus appropriately associated with the *carmina*, the enchanting words that follow as a result of the poet's prayer. *Fauni* and *Dryades* are among the divinities that Virgil invokes at the commencement of the *Georgics* (*G.* 1.10–11); on the extensive dialogue between the poem and the *Georgics* (as well as Virgil and Ovid), see Baumann (2019) 22–65.

THE GARDEN OF ATEDIUS MELIOR (STATIUS' *SILVAE* 2.3) 49

The striking initial monosyllable, *stat*, leads us to another epic and to another tree by allusion to which Statius will lead us to a further appreciation of his artistry. Near the opening of his *Bellum Civile*, Lucan compares one of his chief protagonists, Pompey (Gnaeus Pompeius Magnus), still mighty but with diminished powers, to an ancient, venerated oak tree:

> ... Stat magni nominis umbra
> qualis frugifero quercus sublimis in agro
> exuvias veteres populi sacrataque gestans
> dona ducum nec iam validis radicibus haerens
> pondere fixa suo est, nudosque per aera ramos
> effundens trunco, non frondibus, efficit umbram...
>
> (Luc. 1.135–40)

He stands a shadow of his great name, like an oak tree, lofty in a fertile field, bearing a nation's ancient trophies and the dedicated gifts of leaders and that, clinging now with roots no longer strong, is secured by its weight, and, sending forth bare branches through the sky, it fashions shade from its trunk, not from foliage...

The force of these powerful lines permeates the opening verses of *Silvae* 2.3 and beyond. But I want to call particular attention to its play on the name *Magnus* in the simile's opening line that focuses on the statesman's cognomen. Both passages combine the conspicuous repetition of the initial word *stat* with a subsequent, extended description of a tree, whether metaphorical or literal. The close parallelism suggests that Lucan's play on nomenclature may also be present in this same initial word, *stat*. As a form of inaugural *sphragis*, Statius places a version of his own name at the very start of his creation. The qualities that make Melior worthy of his surname ('Better'), and of the comparisons that follow naturally from it, will be discovered in suitable places throughout the poem. But the poet himself, I suggest, firmly puts his personal stamp on his handiwork right from the beginning.[7]

The only other earlier classical Latin poem that begins with the word *stat* is the opening elegy in Ovid's third book of the *Amores*: *Stat vetus et multos*

---

[7] For the name Statius, see Schulze (1904) 37, 237, 469. For its particular association with slaves, see Dupont (1992) 58; Fitzgerald (2000) 23; Cheesman (2009) 516. As the poem progresses the verb *sto* is to be found again at *stant* (16) and *persta* (73). If we put trust in the etymology of Serv. *ad A.* 1.126 (*stagnum dicitur aqua stans* ['water standing still is called *stagnum*']), we hear it echoed in *stagnis* (33), *stagna* (38), and *stagnis* (54).

50 THE POETIC WORLD OF STATIUS' *SILVAE*

incaedua silva per annos... ('There stands a wood, ancient and unfelled over many years...', *Am.* 3.1.1). Since Ovid of the *Metamorphoses* will be such a vital presence in abetting Statius' imagination in what follows, an initial bow to Ovid the love-poet may come at first as a surprise. But two reasons tell in its favour. First of all, the tone and content of his elegies, as well as of those of Propertius and Tibullus, is far from foreign to the core narrative of what follows in which the meaning of eroticism, its challenges as well as its rewards, is ever in the reader's thoughts. Secondly, Ovid's opus is not concerned with sexual matters, at least explicitly, but with poetic genres, since its central topic is a debate between the personified figures of Elegy and Tragedy for control of the poet's future inspiration.

The connection with *Silvae* 2.3 may not be as distant as it first seems. This is especially true given the fact that, as we have seen and will soon see further, Statius makes reference, in the initiating hexameters of his 'occasional' poem, to at least four different poetic genres, knowledge of which will encourage us in our search for the meaning of his own accomplishment. To be more specific, it is also probably not accidental that the word *silva* is the prominent subject at the start of a poem on the mind of an author in the midst of penning a variegated collection with the general title of *Silvae*.

The adjective *nitidus*, whose richness of meaning we have already touched upon, will help lead us into a genre that we have yet to touch upon, epigram. In number 54 of his fourth book of epigrams, Martial addresses a certain Collinus, who has won the oak-leaf crown at Domitian's annual poetry context. In the course of the poem, his qualities are compared to those of other outstanding individuals, with a characteristic twist, at the end, by the master of the fitting apothegm. 'Though you be more splendid than elegant Melior'(*lautior et nitido sis Meliore licet*, 4.54.8), says Martial, still you will not escape the doom prepared for you by the three sister Fates. Further verbal parallels connect the two poems, and other epigrams, especially 9.61, on a *platanus* planted in Corduba by Julius Caesar, which reads like a partial summary of *Silvae* 2.3, offer continued proof of the interaction between the two contemporary authors, the chronology of whose works remains ever a subject of debate.[8] Whatever the actuality of influences, the common usage of *nitidus* suggests an interest on Statius' part in the concision of epigram, a briskness that will be most apparent in the portrait of Melior which helps round out his work.

---

[8] On Martial 9.61 and *Silvae* 2.3, see Newlands (2011b) throughout and Hardie (2006) 215–17.

THE GARDEN OF ATEDIUS MELIOR (STATIUS' *SILVAE* 2.3)   51

That representation, as we will see, also bears the mark of one of Horace's masterpieces, the *Carmen Saeculare*, which here, too, has a form of the word *silva* in its opening line.[9] So we can anticipate also the influence of yet another genre, the lyric, with its intense immediacy and, in the case of the *Carmen Saeculare*, its deep political and ethical significance, as the poem progresses.

Pan, Pholoe, and the Plane Tree

But as we leave, for a moment, the sanctuary of Melior's *locus amoenus* and the poet's plea for inspiration, it is Virgil, in particular through the *Aeneid*, who guides us in the transition from introduction to main narrative. We must bear in mind the preceding double apostrophe to *Naides* and *Fauni* as we turn to the central narrative itself:

> nympharum tenerae fugiebant Pana catervae;
> ille quidem it cunctas tamquam velit, it tamen unam
> in Pholoen. silvis haec fluminibusque sequentis
> nunc hirtos gressus, nunc improba cornua vitat.
> iamque et belligerum Iani nemus atraque Caci
> rura Quirinalesque fuga suspensa per agros
> Caelica tecta subit; ibi demum victa labore,
> fessa metu, qua nunc placidi Melioris aperti
> stant sine fraude lares, flavos collegit amictus
> artius et niveae posuit se margine ripae.
>
> (Stat. *Silv.* 2.3.8–17)

The delicate throngs of nymphs were in flight from Pan. He indeed strides as if he covets everyone; yet he strides toward Pholoe alone. She, through woods and streams (10), dodges now the hairy feet, now the wanton horns, of her pursuer. And already, skimming in her flight past the war-waging grove of Janus and the black countryside of Cacus and the fields of Quirinus, she entered the dwellings of the Caelian. There at last, overcome

---

[9] The full line (*Saec.* 1) reads as follows: *Phoebe silvarumque potens Diana,...* ('Phoebus and Diana, mistress of forests...'). Near his poem's start Statius appeals to Apollo as Phoebus (6) for inspiration, and Diana is a protagonist of the tale that follows. Pholoe's unique designation as *Phoebeia Nais* (60) confirms her connection with Diana but also acts as a reminder of Apollo.

52   THE POETIC WORLD OF STATIUS' *SILVAE*

by distress, exhausted from fear, where now the unclosed dwelling of calm Melior stands (15), deceit free, she gathered her flaxen-coloured garments quite tightly and placed herself on the edge of the snowy embankment.

As the poem moves from *Fauni*, as purveyors of poetry, to Pan tracking bands of *nymphae*, Statius would have us turn our attention to a pivotal moment in Book 8 of the *Aeneid* where Evander, the aged Arcadian king, walking through Rome with his guest, Aeneas, begins his disquisition on the early history of the site of the future city:

> 'haec nemora indigenae Fauni Nymphaeque tenebant
> gensque virum truncis et duro robore nata,
> quis neque mos neque cultus erat...'
>
> (Virg. *A.* 8.314–16)

'Native Fauns and Nymphs inhabited these woods, and a race of men sprung from tree-trunks and hard oak, who had neither custom nor civility...'

Statius brings alive Evander's matter-of-fact history by creating for us a numinous world of once-upon-a time, with epiphanic, omnipresent divinities. We are again near the same spot as Aeneas and his tutor were but, through the brilliance of language, the poet creates a setting where a myth, of his own design, fosters a sense of the real and the immediate. Evander, we recall, has encouraged his own form of civilization, especially through the worship of Hercules and a type of heroic humility that accompanies it.[10] We will hear the language of his final exhortation to his visitor echoed in Statius' concluding portrait of Melior:

> 'haec' inquit 'limina victor
> Alcides subiit, haec illum regia cepit.
> aude, hospes, contemnere opes et te quoque dignum
> finge deo, rebusque veni non asper egenis.'
>
> (Virg. *A.* 8.362–5)

'These doorways', he says, 'the victor Alcides deigned to enter, this mansion was big enough for him. Have the daring, my guest, to despise wealth and, too, make yourself worthy to be a god and come not disdainful of our meagre resources'.

---

[10] For Evander's role in the development of culture on the site of Rome, see Papaioannou (2003); Kondratieff (2014); Casali (2020), esp. 149–59.

THE GARDEN OF ATEDIUS MELIOR (STATIUS' *SILVAE* 2.3)   53

This is also the world that we enter as we embark on the saga of Pan and Pholoe.[11] Statius brings its opening line to our attention with the first in a series of examples of hypallage that have the effect of enlivening both sides of the transfer.[12] The abstract *catervae* are *tenerae* because their constituents, the nymphs, are tender. The personification humanizes the throngs along with their members. We then turn to Pan whose energetic quest is vivified for us by the initial deictic, *ille*, and the repeated *i* sounds that follow in *it*, *velit*, and the repeated *it*. As we turn to Pholoe in line 10, *ille* yields to *haec* as Statius concentrates our attention directly on the nymph and her movement. Statius underscores the immediacy of the moment at line 10, through the repetition of *nunc* and with a double use of personification. The *gressus* of Pan, itself a form of metonymy where the god's footprints stand for the feet that make them, are hirsute because, as we learn later at line 36, the god himself is shaggy, and Pan's horns, in another example of the same figure, are not *improba* in and of themselves but only because they are the appendage of a creature who is at the moment serving as an example of unprincipled behaviour.

The route the chase follows, detailed in lines 10–16, criss-crosses the hills of Rome, from the Capitoline, on the north height of which lay Janus' grove, south to the Aventine, lair of Cacus, north to the Quirinal and finally south-east to the Caelian and the property of Melior. Details catch the eye. The phrase *belligerum Iani nemus* offers us another striking example of hypallage where the personified grove of the god absorbs his martial quality to become equally warlike. And the area associated with Cacus is both literally and figuratively *atra*, darkened by the monster's trademark flames but also implicitly malicious and threatening like the villain himself.

But two other evolutions are also in progress. The first, of a more general sort, is of civilization itself. We find ourselves at the start among the woods and streams (*silvis...fluminibusque*, 10) that would originally have covered large segments of the landscape.[13] This designation is soon particularized in

---

[11] The echo of *subiit* (*A.* 8.363) in *subit* (14), both at the same position in the hexameter, may be purposeful.

[12] For Roman comments on the term, see Cic. *Orat.* 27.93 where he makes little difference between hypallage, exchange of words, and metonymy, exchange of nouns in particular; Quint. *Inst.* 8.6.23–7. See Lausberg (1998) 305–6, 685–6, and 677 referring to *TLG* s.v. *hypallage*. The transfer, and that of *belligerum* (12), is noted by Newlands (2011a) 161, 162.

[13] The realm of *flumina...silvasque* is one to which 'Virgil' would retreat if he were not given the inspiration to sing of nature's larger works and ways (*G.* 2.486). It is the world of Pan and the 'sister Nymphs' (*Nymphas...sorores*, *G.* 2.494). The evolution that follows in Statius is glossed at *G.* 2.207–8 where the 'angry ploughman' (*iratus arator*) does away first with woods (*silvam*) and then groves (*nemora*) that stand in the way of his agricultural pursuits (*G.* 2.207–8).

54   THE POETIC WORLD OF STATIUS' *SILVAE*

a grove (*nemus*), sequestered from the larger forest and sacred to the god Janus. We then move to the countryside in general (*rura*) which is in turn made specific in *agri*, open fields carved out of the original woodland, that are skilfully worked for agricultural benefit. From there the poet places us amid the *tecta*, the rooftops that serve as synecdoche for the homes that mankind learns to create for itself as it grows in sophistication, with the world of cave-dwelling now in the past. These abodes are then individualized, now with metonymy as the prominent figure, in the *lares* (16), the household gods of Melior's remarkable property to come. In brief, we have a succinct temporal survey of the development of culture from wilderness, into hallowed grove, into plough-lands after deforestation. We then find ourselves among primitive habitations on the early Caelian which anticipate the sophisticated, modern establishment of Atedius Melior where the original woods and streams have experienced a grand, refining metamorphosis into a beautiful pool and a singular tree which embellish its owner's handsome estate.

There is a second evolution within these lines that centres on the proper names involved and on a single characteristic. Statius sets both theme and tone with the phrase *belligerum Iani nemus* (12), the first item listed as the chase begins. Janus' grove, probably located on the northern summit of the Capitolium,[14] Rome's central hill, is warlike because, as Virgil puts it (*A.* 7.610), the god never leaves the threshold, which he tends, of the 'twin gates of War' (*geminae Belli portae*), his shrine always open at times of conflict, which is to say rarely closed during the history of martial Rome. We next have Cacus, of the evil name, whose contest with Hercules on the Aventine forms a centrepiece of the eighth book of the *Aeneid*. The hero further confirms his reputation as someone who rids the world of monsters by doing away with the villain of the place, as good seems to triumph over bad. But Virgil is at pains in one respect to point out a parallelism between the two antagonists: both are given to irrational violence in their struggle. At line 205 we hear of 'the mind of Cacus, wild with fury' (*furiis Caci mens effera*). Then, Virgil tells us how 'the indignation of Alcides blazed forth in fury with black gall' (*Alcidae furiis exarserat atro/felle dolor, A.* 8.219–20), using the same adjective, *atro*, with which Statius had described the countryside ravaged by Cacus, the miscreant (*atra*, 12). He corroborates the frenzy of

---

[14] For the location of the *nemus*, see Heyworth (2011). For the temple in the city below, see *A.* 1.293–6. It stood on the Argiletum, near the Basilica Aemilia, on the edge of the Forum Romanum.

THE GARDEN OF ATEDIUS MELIOR (STATIUS' *SILVAE* 2.3)   55

Hercules further at 8.228 where we observe the hero 'furious with wrath' (*furens animis*).

We find ourselves next passing through *Quirinales agri*, the fields on the Quirinal hill. The name Quirinus, from which *Quirinalis* derives, is on occasion also associated with Janus.[15] But primarily it is the appellation given to the deified Romulus who had particular associations with the god Mars.[16] He is, of course, the founding king of Rome, but to Horace, for example, he is the killer of his brother, Remus, and thus sets the archetypal pattern for the extensive period of civil warring to come for city and its domain.[17] Finally we reach the dwellings on the Caelian Hill (*Caelica tecta*, 14).[18] According to the learned Varro the name derives from Caeles (Caelius) Vibenna, an Etruscan nobleman who came to the aid of Romulus or Tarquinius Priscus in their various conflicts, with Titus Tatius or the Sabines.[19]

Statius, particularly by singling out Janus' warlike grove and the fields blackened by Cacus, in the itinerary, to stand for the Capitoline and Aventine Hills, suggests that we also trace a pattern of ferocity and warlike behaviour that courses through the history of Rome and resonates still in

[15] See, e.g., Hor. *Carm.* 4.15.9; Suet. *Aug.* 22.

[16] For detailed references in Hor. *Carm.* 3.3.15–16, see Nisbet and Rudd (2004) 43.

[17] Cf. the particularly bitter lines at Hor. *Epod.* 7.17–20.

[18] At line 14, I follow the reading of *M* (*tecta*) as I do also at 16 (*flavos*), 17 (*niveae*), 38 (*Bromium*), 39 (*visu*), 53 (*animata*), and 71 (*comere*). (Pederzani also accepts these readings with the exception of adopting the change to *tesca* here, which Van Dam (1984) 38 and Newlands (2011a) 46 also print, as well as Liberman in his critical edition.) My own interpretation of Statius' poem, therefore, regularly supports the wording of our unique early witness as authoritative. A strong intertextual reason for keeping *tecta* is to be found at Ovid. *Met.* 6.667–79, where the metamorphosized Philomela and Procne escape from their pursuer: *corpora Cecropidum pennis pendere putares:/pendebant pennis. quarum petit altera silvas,/altera tecta subit* ('You would think that the bodies of the Cecropides were poised on wings. They were poised on wings! One of them seeks the woods, the other enters the dwellings'). Statius echoes the phrase *tecta subit* at the same position in the hexameter, and *suspensa*, in the preceding line (13), draws on Ovid's *pendere...pendebant*. The word reminds us of Virgil's Camilla, *suspensa* in her fleetness of foot (*A.* 7.810). I assume the presence of *tecta* as anticipating Melior's own mansion to come. Statius takes us on an intellectual journey via the move from *silvis* (10) to *tecta*. Ovid has his bird-sisters make choices, one for *silvas* and the world of nature, the other for *tecta* and the realm of humankind.

[19] *L.* 5.46. See also Paul. *Fest.* p. 38L s.v. *Caelius Mons*. For the Caelian and Vibenna's friendship with Tarquinius Priscus, see Tac. *Ann.* 4.64–5. Thanks to Pliny (*Nat.* 36.7.48), we know in some detail of one house on the Caelian, that of Mamurra (first century BCE), creature of Julius Caesar and target of Catullus (poems 29 and 57 mention him by name). Further dwellings on the Caelian are discussed by Mann (1926). For the addition of the *Caelius mons* to the original city, see Cic. *Rep.* 2.18.33 and Liv. 1.30.1. Incidentally, there is no direct mention of the Palatine Hill in Statius nor of the Caelian in Virgil. Statius is staking out new territory as well as inventing a myth to go with it. His is the only preserved use of the adjective *Caelicus*.

56 THE POETIC WORLD OF STATIUS' *SILVAE*

the nomenclature of the city's central topography.[20] Then the poet performs one of his most impressive metamorphoses. As Pholoe collapses, in exhaustion and fright, on the Caelian, we suddenly move, for a moment, from then to now, from Rome's mythic origins to a present-day mansion on the same site, a mansion whose owner, Atedius Melior, whom we met in the poem's opening lines, is now distinguished with the epithet *placidus*. Suitably, because of his name, Melior is a 'better' emblem for Rome than its past warriors and the brutality that peppers their stories. We now have in him an example of negative energy purged in favour of an ethic based on internal and external peace.[21] And the moral evolution which he himself exemplifies finds further proof in his self-extension, his house's personified *lares*. They stand both *aperti* (15), patent and clear, like the waters of his pond, for all to appreciate, and *sine fraude* (16), harbouring no hidden deceit that might befall an unwary acquaintance, of the sort, for instance, that might bring about a brother's murder.[22] No evil Cacus lurks here.[23] Melior's character, like its external appendages, is conspicuous in the way that it seems frank and genuine, fraught with no shadowy danger to anyone drawing near his dwelling (or passing through life in company with the owner).

Statius turns forthwith to the nymph herself and vivifies the moment with a series of colour words. We have heard shortly before of the fields blackened (*atra*) by the monster Cacus. Statius offers us a contrast now in comely Pholoe's golden (*flavos*, 16) garments and in the snow-white (*niveae*, 17) edge of the pool on which she places herself.[24] The second is a form of anticipated hypallage. We will soon hear of her snowy limbs (*niveos artus*, 32) that she tries to hide from the pursuing Pan. It is appropriate that the water's margin on which she lies would take on the brilliant sheen of her own body. The nymph's

[20] For associations of the adjective *ater* with evil and malice, see Mankin (1995) 142 on Hor. *Epod.* 6.15 (*atro dente*). Cacus literally blackens the fields with his destructive flames which also figuratively represent his inner wickedness.

[21] Through the invention of the story of Pan's pursuit of Pholoe, Statius illustrates his own example of the eradication of violence, this time on the Caelian, through the intervention of Diana, a new, non-savage Hercules. We find no deadly strangling, just the awakening through touch (*tetigisse*, 30) of an arrow's feathers.

[22] Cassiodorus defines *fraus* as *fracta fides* (see Maltby [1991] s.v. *fraus* [243]). The reference to *fides* anticipates, first, Diana's *fidas...comites* (23–4) and then the apostrophe to Melior himself as *incorrupte fidem* (68).

[23] The anguish (*labore*, 14) and terror (*metu*, 15) that Pholoe has experienced stem from the heritage of the places that she has just rushed through as well as from the proximity of Pan.

[24] For both adjectives I accept the readings of *M* (see n. 18, above). Courtney (1990) 46 reads *fluxos* for the first and obelizes the second.

THE GARDEN OF ATEDIUS MELIOR (STATIUS' *SILVAE* 2.3) 57

bright beauty is assimilated to the bank on which she rests. What we presume to be green is whitened by her corporeal radiance.[25]

I suggest that the same holds true, by analogy, for her clothing as well. Virgil, for instance, styles the Nereid Lycorias as *flava* (G. 4.339) and a few lines later he tells us of Arethusa's *flavum caput* (352).[26] The transfer would again be from a characteristic of the naiad herself, her presumed blonde hair, to something associated with her, in this case her bright yellow raiment.

The chase continues:

> insequitur velox pecorum deus et sua credit
> conubia; ardenti iamiam suspiria librat
> pectore, iam praedae leuis imminet. ecce citatos
> advertit Diana gradus, dum per iuga septem
> errat Aventinaeque legit vestigia cervae.
> paenituit vidisse deam, conversaque fidas
> ad comites: 'numquamne avidis arcebo rapinis
> hoc petulans foedumque pecus, semperque pudici
> decrescet mihi turba chori?' sic deinde locuta
> depromit pharetra telum breve, quod neque flexis
> cornibus aut solito torquet stridore, sed una
> emisit contenta manu laevumque soporem
> Naiados aversa fertur tetigisse sagitta.

> (Stat. *Silv.* 2.3.18–30)

The swift god of flocks continues his pursuit and believes that marriage is his; now, even now, he brandishes sighs in his burning heart, now looms nimbly over his prey. But look: Diana turns thither her quickened (20) steps while she roams through the seven ridges and tracks the traces of a deer from the Aventine. What she saw grieved the goddess, and she turned toward her faithful retinue: 'Will I never prevent this insolent and foul flock from its greedy pillaging, and will the throng of my chaste company (25) always diminish?' So speaking she then draws from her quiver a short shaft, which she speeds neither with bow horns bent nor

---

[25] The several parallels between Statius' language here and Ovid's description of Priapus' approach to the sleeping Lotis (*Fast.* 1.423–30) deserve separate treatment. The poet's description of her as *niveae nymphae* (427) helps confirm Statius' usages here.

[26] For details on blonde hair see Pease (1935) 471–3, on A. 4.590 (Dido's *flaventis…comas*). *Flavus* or *flavens* in connection with clothing is virtually unexampled.

At *Buc. Eins.* 1.46 we find mention of a *flaventi vitta*.

58   THE POETIC WORLD OF STATIUS' *SILVAE*

with the usual whir, but, content, launched it with a single hand, and is said to have touched the naiad's baleful sleep with arrow reversed (30).

As the racing god nears his prey, and nimbly looms over her, he believes that their 'union' is in the offing. Statius stresses the immediacy of the moment by the repetitions of *iamiam* (19) and *iam* (20) within two lines. But, in a tour de force of the imagination, the poet now makes impressive use of a primary rhetorical device, metaphor. He concretizes the sighs (*suspiria*, 19) of the fervent lover by having him 'brandish' (*librat*, 19) them as if they were some sort of metaphysical weapon with which he might finally subdue his fleeing victim.[27] His last resort for gaining possession is not any bodily strength but merely the quietly audible manifestations of his inner feelings that might work their magic without any tangible harm.

But even that possible hope is dashed by the sudden arrival of Diana, announced by the interjection *ecce*.[28] Her 'quickened steps' (*citatos...gradus*, 20–1) serve as a reminder of Pan's 'hairy feet' (*hirtos gressus*, 11) only to underscore the difference between the two sets. He is a metaphorical stalker, bent on rape.[29] Diana is literally following the traces of a doe (*cervae*, 22), as is her wont, a doe from the Aventine which, in Rome to come, will be home to her chief place of worship.[30] But she is also a goddess renowned for her chastity, and her sudden mission is now to save a member of her 'chaste company' (*pudici...chori*, 25–6) from debasement. At the same time as he raises Diana's position from huntress into an exemplar of moral innocence,

---

[27] For instances of *libro* in this sense, see *L&S* s.v. IIc; *OLD* s.v. 3.

[28] We might note, as we follow Statius' account of Diana's intervention into Pholoe's misadventure, that when we first meet Dido in Virgil's *Aeneid* she is likened to Diana (*A.* 1.499), a chaste, quasi-divine ruler presiding over a flourishing domain. After she has become the prey of Cupid and fallen in love with Aeneas, she herself, also in simile, becomes akin to a 'doe after an arrow has been hurled at her' (*coniecta cerva sagitta*, *A.* 4.69). The godlike human has become the animal victim because of her yielding to passion, and death soon follows. In Statius' splendid variation, the virginal goddess-huntress turns from tracking a *cerva* to rescuing a potential victim of another divinity's lust, with a *sagitta* (30) turned to a saving use. Once again, Statius reorients a Virgilian text from negative to positive, here from prospective hurt, that proves mortal, to avoidance of wildness that leads ultimately to gentle, accepted affection. Statius also reverses aspects of Ovid's presentation of the Actaeon myth, in Book 3 of the *Metamorphoses*, which deserve more detailed treatment. Here, Diana is troubled by what she saw (*vidisse*, 3.23) and reacts with restraint. Ovid, by contrast, has the goddess respond to being seen (*visae sine veste Dianae*, 3.185). She does so not with the arrows (*sagittas*, 3.188) that she would ordinarily have employed but with a splash of water that turns the huntsman into a stag (*cervus*, 3.194).

[29] Pan's feet become, by metonymy, the steps that they take and together they stand for the creature himself whose skin, we soon learn, is *hirtae* (36) as well.

[30] See Liv. 1.45.1–7 for the establishment of the goddess' first temple by Servius Tullius. It was restored by Lucius Cornificius in 33 BCE.

THE GARDEN OF ATEDIUS MELIOR (STATIUS' *SILVAE* 2.3) 59

Statius also lowers the stature of Pan from 'god of flocks' (*pecorum deus*, 18) to 'an insolent and foul flock' (*petulans foedumque pecus*, 25), from a divinity, one of whose roles is to be a protector of herds, to a member of the drove itself, a god become animal, in the words of Diana, because of his heinous advances toward a virtuous nymph. The plurality implicit in *pecus* may refer to *Fauni* in general just as 'lustful acts of rape' (*avidis rapinis*, 24) looks to a group of perpetrators. Then again—and equally likely—it could simply serve to emphasize the enormity of Pan's viciousness, in the eyes of Pholoe's divine protectress.

Statius follows her words with one of the most inventive episodes in the poem. The goddess extracts a short arrow from her quiver, then propels it by hand, feather side first, against the 'pernicious slumber' of the nymph. The figuration here is as incisive as it is evocative, but first a word on Diana's gesture. She forgoes her standard role as a huntress. The felling of an animal is not her purpose but rather the sequestering of a devotee from unwanted erotic overtures, and her arrow is not utilized with point toward a potential victim but reversed in a creative gesture. And the performance takes place without the energizing bow, horns bent, aimed toward its quarry and, appropriately here, without the shriek that would ordinarily accompany the speeding of an arrow.[31] No unnecessary noise, especially as an accessory to needless violence, should enter the domain, past or present, associated with *placidus* Melior.

Two examples of verbal nuance deserve further comment. The first is the paranomasia inherent in the participle *contenta* (30). Diana is 'stretched' (from *contendo*) because she is metaphorically playing the role of the bow, speeding a weapon on its way. But she is also 'content' in a double sense: she is restrained (the verb is *contineo*) from using the godlike physical potential available to her, and at the same time she is also satisfied that this can be the case without any harm coming to her devotee. She is not following Pholoe as if she were animal booty but saving her from being the semi-divine quarry of a rapacious god.

The phrase *laeuum soporem* (30) also catches the attention. Diana directs the fletched end of her arrow not at some potential prey but at a mere personification, an aspect of sleep that means harm. But the word *sopor* is also a type of metonymy where sleep replaces, or in this case controls the destiny of, the person reposing. Diana's non-deadly weapon is directed toward

---

[31] Diana's abstention from the use of the bendable horns of her bow (*flexis cornibus*, 27–8) contrasts with the evil intent implicit in Pan's *cornua* (11).

60 THE POETIC WORLD OF STATIUS' SILVAE

saving the possible victim of a malign slumber that readies her for rape. In having the goddess touch her *sopor* rather than the nymph herself, the poet divorces Diana from any destructive use of her arsenal. This distancing is furthered rhetorically by Statius' use of the word *fertur* (31) as he tells the tale. By having the narrator back away for a moment from the actual story to imply that it is based on tradition, or some sort of hearsay, Statius accomplishes the secondary effect of lessening any potentially physical vehemence on the goddess' part and enhancing the gentleness of her gesture, directed not at Pholoe herself but at the sleep that has her in its hostile grip.

The nymph awakens:

> illa diem pariter surgens hostemque proteruum
> vidit et in fontem, niueos ne panderet artus,
> sic tota cum veste ruit, stagnisque sub altis
> Pana sequi credens ima latus implicat alga.
> quid faceret subito deceptus praedo? nec altis
> credere corpus aquis hirtae sibi conscius audet
> pellis et a tenero nandi rudis. omnia questus,
> immitem Bromium, stagna invida et invida tela.
> primaevam visu platanum, cui longa propago
> innumeraeque manus et iturus in aethera vertex
> deposuit iuxta vivamque aggessit harenam
> optatisque adspergit aquis et talia mandat...
>
> (Stat. *Silv.* 2.3.31–42)

Rising up, she saw, at the same time, the daylight and her impudent enemy and, lest she display her snow-white limbs, just as she was she plunged into the spring with all her clothing, and, believing that Pan is following, in the depths of the pond wraps her side in weeds at the bottom. Suddenly duped, what was the brigand to do? He dares not trust his body to the deep waters (35), fully aware of his hairy hide and from his youth untrained in swimming. He complained of everything—of pitiless Bromius, malevolent pond, and malevolent arrows. He put in place at the edge a plane tree, in youthful prime to the sight, with lengthy stem, countless twigs and a crest about to make its way heavenward (40), and heaped living sand against it and sprinkles it with water for which it yearned and commands it thus...

Illa (31) turns our attention now to the nymph herself and to her sight that, in a variation of zeugma, takes both tangible and emotional forms. We watch her watching as she sees, at once, the light of day and baleful Pan whose

THE GARDEN OF ATEDIUS MELIOR (STATIUS' *SILVAE* 2.3)   61

protervitas expands immediate sight into insight, when she appreciates the danger he presents. Our visualizing continues on as we view her snowy limbs, an event that Statius emphasizes through his use of *panderet* (32).[32] As commentators note,[33] this is the only occasion where the human body is the object of the verb *pando*. And a punning alliteration may also play a part in its dynamism. After all, it is the god Pan from whom she is shielding her beauty. And, as the picture continues, her *niveos… artus* (32) are particularized in the *latus* which she now enfolds in weeds and which receives strong figuration. *Latus* (34) is a synecdoche that is also a metonymy. It stands as part for the whole attractive *corpus* of Pholoe. But it also calls particular attention to an area of the lower body involved with sexual activity, the locus at once of desire and of its satisfaction, an area that the naiad would especially want to hide from her wanton stalker to whom Statius now turns.[34]

He first utters reproaches,[35] initially against his patron god Bromius/ Bacchus, who should be his sustainer but here has turned out to be harsh, like some vintages of his cherished wine.[36] He also inveighs against the waters where Pholoe has found a place of refuge and against the weapons that Diana used to forewarn her of his proximity. Once again Statius uses two of his favourite devices to hold our attention. Both *stagna* and *tela* (33) are personified, as if they had a life of their own. In particular, they have the power to use their sight to discommode someone with whom they come in contact. From Pan's point of view they have cast an evil eye on his prospects with Pholoe.

The emphasis on seeing now takes dramatic form in another vivid act of personification as Statius asks us to observe closely the sturdy plane tree, *primaevam visu* (40), in the flower of youthful growth, as is clear for all to see—a tree with countless 'hands' (*manus*, 40) and a lofty 'head'

---

[32] The suggestiveness may continue with the further help of alliteration, at the mention of Pan's sacred trees, the pines (*pinus*, 52). See Bailey (2017) 1250 on 587 (…*Pan/pinea*) and Ov. *Met.* 1.699 (*Pan…pinu*) and 14.638 (*pinu…Panes*).

[33] See Van Dam (1984) 310; Newlands (2011a) 167.

[34] See, e.g., Adams (1982) 49; Pichon (1966) 185; Vessey (1976).

[35] The disparaging word Statius uses here to qualify Pan is *praedo* (35). It echoes *praeda* (20) by means of which the poet also has us enter the thoughts of the would-be rapist god as he ponders his prey, Pholoe. As noted by Newlands (2011a) 168, the noun is used by three speakers in the *Aeneid* to label Aeneas and put a negative connotation on his aspirations toward Lavinia (7.362, 10.774, and 11.484). Here the poet himself takes the role of critic as the reader enters the mind of Pan 'suddenly duped' (*subito deceptus*) in his nefarious act of pillage.

[36] Courtney and Newlands (2011a) 168 read *Brimo* in place of *M*'s *bromium* (which Liberman prints), Diana (through a rare epithet) instead of Bacchus. For *immitis*, see *OLD* s.v. 1 and Nisbet and Hubbard (1978) 84 on Hor. *Carm.* 2.5.10 (*immitis uvae*), a poem in which *Pholoe fugax* figures (in line 17).

62 THE POETIC WORLD OF STATIUS' *SILVAE*

(*vertex*).[37] And this stress on sight makes us imagine all the more closely its extensive stem, numberless small branches and crest shooting skyward, as if the tree were one powerful family in and of itself. Pan attends to his planting by banking it with fertile sand[38] and with water that it desires, as a lover should.

A word is in order here on the plane tree and its suitability, in the present context, to function as a symbolic gesture on the part of Pan. The *platanus* is known for two characteristics that often go together, the abundance of shade that it produces, which the word *opacet* at line 1 already illustrates, and its sterility. For further instances of the first we need look only to our familiar Latin poets. At *G.* 4.146, for example, Virgil tells of the Corycian *senex*, the old man who, in a gesture markedly parallel to Pan's here, has the strength to transplant full-grown trees to embellish his sparse acreage, among them 'a plane tree purveying shade to drinkers' (*ministrantem platanum potantibus umbras*, *G.* 4.145). And we note how the plural *umbras* associated with a single tree suggests the abundance of protection offered by the plane against the elements.[39] More indirectly, Horace, at *Carm.* 2.11.13, tells of the 'lofty plane' (*alta platano*) under which the speaker and his symposiast

[37] As Van Dam (1984) 314–15 and Liberman, I follow the reading of *M visu* instead of adopting the frequent change to *nisu* (as Courtney does). Among the occurrences of *primaevus* in the *Aeneid* we might mention 'young men in the flower of youth' (*primaevo flore iuventus*, 7.162), 'Clausus with his physique in youthful trim' (*primaevo corpore Clausus*, 10.345), and, with adjective directly modifying the person to be admired, 'Helenor in the fullness of youth' (*primaevus Helenor*, 10.545). Pan's tree is already stalwart, like a young warrior fit for battle. With the growing plane tree, 'about to send its crest heavenward' (*iturus in aethera vertex*, 40), we can compare the aged oak that 'stretches with its crest to the breezes of heaven' (*vertice ad auras/aetherias...tendit*, Virg. *A.* 4.445–6) to which Aeneas is likened. In this case the tree is no longer youthful and beginning to aim to the sky, but it is still 'rugged with the strength of years' (*annoso validam cum robore*, 441). For *manus* as the 'twigs' of a tree, *OLD* (s.v. 2b) cites only *Silv.* 2.3.40; the *TLL* viii.366.32–4 also cites [Sen.] *Her. O.* 1625.
[38] With *vivam harenam*, cf. Virg. *G.* 1.70 (*sterilem harenam*), sandy earth around which nothing will grow, and the litotes *male pinguis harena* (unfertile sand) at *G.* 1.105. By clear contrast, Pan's attachment to both tree and nymph is 'living', on-going like the nourishing soil around it.
[39] Petronius (*Sat.* 131.8) offers another parallel example of the emphatic poetic plural in connection with our tree when he tells how 'the waving plane-tree had extended its summer shade' (*mobilis aestivas platanus diffuderat umbras*). There it forms part of the *locus amoenus* where Encolpius and Circe have their erotic rendezvous. For the plane tree in general, see Plin. *Nat.* 12.6–13. For other references to the connection between plane trees and shade, see Cic. *Div.* 2.63, Mart. 9.61.16, and, by implication, Catul. 64.290 and *Culex* 123–4. The younger Pliny (*Ep.* 1.3.1) mentions a *platanon opacissimus* ('the shadiest grove of plane trees'). In ancient literature the plane tree is probably best remembered as the centerpiece for the setting of Plato's *Phaedrus*. See *Phaedr.* 229a–b and 236e, where Phaedrus himself swears an oath on the tree, as well as the direct mention of the same scene by Cicero (*Or.* 1.7). One of the central subjects of the dialogue is the meaning of love, a topic complementary to the main narrative of *Silv.* 2.3.

THE GARDEN OF ATEDIUS MELIOR (STATIUS' *SILVAE* 2.3)   63

friend, Quinctius, find ample cover as they quench the fire of their Falernian, appropriately for the setting, with water from a nearby stream.

Both poets also offer examples of the barrenness associated with the plane tree. Virgil tells of planes that are unfruitful unless grafting makes them productive (*et steriles platani malos gessere valentis*, 'and the barren plane-trees have borne stout apples', Virg. *G*. 2.70), and at *Carm*. 2.15.4 Horace speaks of the 'bachelor plane-tree' (*platanus caelebs*) that 'will over-run the elms' (*evincet ulmos*) in this world of social decadence. The point is multifaceted. In the luxury gardens of the poet's Rome, towering planes, with their abundant shade providing comfort for a variety of pleasurable moments, are replacing the utilitarian elms that offered the most common stem on which to grow vines. More generally, it remains to be said that, agreeable though its protection was against the sun's heat, the deep shade that the tree's broad leaves provided also restricted the growth of anything planted against or adjacent to it.

In sum, though the plane tree is on regular occasion associated with beauty of setting, Statius performs one of his major acts of metamorphosis by making it the particular tree that Pan offers to the water-dwelling nymph, to serve as a token of his devotion and even as a surrogate lover.[40] As we shall see, the tree therefore plays a positive role in the description that follows. There is no implication that the tree's shade has a negative effect. Far from it! And Horace's *platanus caelebs* has been transformed into a living exemplar of the unremitting suitor, ever seeking a response from his beloved. The god begins with an imperative:

> 'vive diu nostri pignus memorabile voti,
> arbor, et haec durae latebrosa cubilia nymphae
> tu saltem declinis ama, preme frondibus undam.
> illa quidem meruit, sed ne, precor, igne supremo
> aestuet aut dura feriatur grandine; tantum
> spargere tu laticem et foliis turbare memento.
> tunc ego teque diu recolam dominamque benignae
> sedis et inlaesa tutabor utramque senecta,

---

[40] *Deposuit*, a usual word for planting, acts also as a reminder of Pholoe who, at line 17, *niveae posuit se margine ripae*. The position *margine ripae* is now replaced by the simple *iuxta*, which is to say near where the god is standing. The tree on the pool's border substitutes for the nymph, who is now in the waters below, and becomes the symbol of Pan's affection for her.

64   THE POETIC WORLD OF STATIUS' *SILVAE*

> ut Iovis, ut Phoebi frondes, ut discolor umbra
> populus et nostrae stupeant tua germina pinus'.
>
> > (Stat. *Silv.* 2.3.43–52)

'O tree, live long, pledge, worthy of remembrance, of our desire, and do you at least, as you lean over, love this hidden bed of the harsh nymph, press the water with your foliage (45). Indeed, she has deserved it, but, I pray, let her not swelter with heat from the heavens or be struck by harsh hail; only do you remember to sprinkle and agitate the liquid with your leaves. Then will I long reflect upon both you and the mistress of the kindly dwelling and I will guard each of you in an unscathed old age (50), so that Jupiter's foliage, so that Phoebus', so that the poplar, with its contrasting shade, and our pines may be in awe of your sprouting.'

The final scene is a second love story, now with an animated plane tree serving as replacement wooer. This time all implications of energy misused are gone and touch is at first either delicate or disallowed. It is appropriate that Pan begin his directive to the tree with an apostrophe dealing with extent of time: *vive diu* ('live on and on', 43) commands the lover. As long as the symbol of the god's affection endures, so long, the implication is, will the emotion itself continue to thrive and be understood. The power of memory and especially of memorialization through the art of poetry is a central theme for Statius, here and as the narrative progresses.[41]

But, through the poet's enriching use of allusion, the phrase has still more to tell us. The two-word conjunction is found only twice elsewhere in classical Latin poetry. Tibullus' use, at 1.6.63, concerns us directly.[42] There the speaker addresses the mother of his *inamorata*, Delia, and prays for her longevity in thanks for her help in fostering his liaison with her daughter. It is a striking allusion that once again illustrates how informative Statius' interaction with earlier poetry is in guiding our reading of his own words. Coming at the very start of the god's instructions to his deputy lover, who can gain proximity to Pholoe in a way never allowed to him, the phrase directs the reader to expect that the poem will now take a particularly elegiac turn in both content and tone. We watch a small erotic drama unfold which plays out bitter-sweetly as the naiad's hate turns to love and at least the tree's

---

[41] For a discussion of the importance of memory in *Silv.* 2.3, see Kreuz (2017) 355–91.
[42] The other occurrence is at pseudo-Virgilian *Elegiae in Maecenatem* 2.171.

THE GARDEN OF ATEDIUS MELIOR (STATIUS' *SILVAE* 2.3) 65

branches, a synecdoche for the *platanus* that represents the forlorn god himself, are invited into her aqueous abode.[43]

The strong erotic element, suggested by *voti*, continues on immediately. The nymph is unresponsive (*durae*, 47) but also hidden away like her bed (*cubilia*, 44) which gains particular emphasis as a synecdoche for her dwelling in general and from the poetic plural to which Statius calls particular attention for its sexual inferences on the part of Pan. There is a further irony in *latebrosa* (44) because Pholoe seems to be escaping from an admirer's advances rather than receiving him in an out-of-the-way spot for the sake of a covert dalliance. The amorous element now takes blatant form in the emphatic *tu...ama* (45) where the nonessential use of the pronoun adds force to the god's command to the tree to behave as he wishes that he could have done and to play directly the part *inamorato*.

The implications of *declineis* (45), which is at once literal and figurative, further the point. Taken as a descriptor of the tree, as it droops, leaning forward over the water, the adjective makes one of its very rare appearances.[44] For help in divining the word's metaphorical implication let us turn to Horace's use of its kindred verb *declino* at *Carm.* 1.33.5–7. The lyricist, addressing his elegist colleague, Tibullus, takes as topic examples of lovers' aberrations, when the object of one individual's fondness vexatiously fixes his or her attentions on someone else. Albius treasures Glycera, who in her turn adores a person younger. Then:

> insignem tenui fronte Lycorida
> Cyri torret amor, Cyrus in asperam
> declinat Pholoen....

> (Hor. *Carm.* 1.33.5–7)

Love of Cyrus scorches Lycoris, beautiful for her low forehead, Cyrus bends toward pitiless Pholoe...

Horace employs the cognate verb *declinat* (7) with the meaning to deflect one's concentration from one fancy to another.[45] Statius' adjective, *declinis*,

---

[43] On Statius' erotic gaze in 2.3, see Chinn (2022) 282–91, who discusses how the Horatian background of the poem can be read against the Ovidian intertexts, ultimately prevailing as the 'correct' way to read Melior's tree; cf. Morzadec (2003) and (2009) 321–4, 333–6.

[44] *OLD* s.v.1b quotes this as its only example of *declinis* with the meaning 'bending down, drooping' and *TLL* v.1.190.57–70 notes only two other classical usages of the adjective in relation to terrestrial phenomena.

[45] For the erotic connotations of the cognate *inclino*, see Adams (1982) 192–3.

66   THE POETIC WORLD OF STATIUS' *SILVAE*

changes the nuances somewhat but keeps the same duality. A tree, that would ordinarily grow toward heaven, bends downwards because it is fulfilling its role as lover, in this case directing its caring regard toward the beloved hidden below. Through the later poet's suggestiveness, there is no implication that the *arbor* is shifting from one object of affection to another. Rather, Pan and his tree guide their desire toward Pholoe alone. It cannot be coincidental that the same feminine name is common between the two poems.[46] Statius fulfils his regular role of turning a predecessor's tacit negativity, in this case aimed toward erotic duplicity or infidelity, to something more positive. The correction here takes the implicit form of undeviating loyalty as god-tree 'inclines' toward Pholoe alone. And Statius makes use of a lyric poem that also involves one of Rome's premier elegists to make his point, bringing to bear two genres closely associated with amorous matters to enhance his own presentation.

Pan finishes his row of imperatives with *preme* (45), again a verb with strong sexual overtones.[47] He then pauses for a moment of reflection as he considers it the tree's task to ward off the harshness of the elements in the form of the sun's fire or the hardness of hail (*dura...grandine*, 47), which reasserts the hardness of the nymph herself. This novel platanus-lover, in a minor form of metamorphosis, instead of offering a shade that could repress what is beneath it, serves as protector, furnishing a secure covering that keeps at bay any external menace from extremes of hot or cold, dry, or wet. The god also asks for a further important act of memory on the tree's part: 'Remember to sprinkle and ruffle the liquid with your leaves' (*spargere tu laticem et foliis turbare memento*, 48). Statius is thinking of Mopsus' commanding song, in Virgil's fifth *Eclogue*, where the shepherds are mourning the passing of their hero Daphnis: *spargite humum foliis, inducite fontibus umbras* ('Strew the ground with petals, draw shade over the springs', *Ecl.* 5.40). *Folia* here are flower petals to be scattered ritually on the grave of the dead shepherd.[48] But Statius offers another of his extraordinary variations on the text of his great predecessor. Virgil's flower petals now become the leaves of the tree which spreads them on the top of the waters beneath

---

[46]   Besides *Carm.* 1.33.7 and 9 the name Pholoe is also to be found at Hor. *Carm.* 2.5.17 and 3.15.7 and at Tib. 1.8.69. A Cretan slave girl, given as a prize at Virg. *A.* 5.285, bears the same name. In this context, it is worth noting that Pholoe is also the name of a mountain on the western border of Pan's Arcadia. It is mentioned among others by Ovid (*Fast.* 2.273) and may also serve as a reminder of Virgil's *Arcades* (*A.* 8.51) and their king, Evander, *rex Arcas* (*A.* 8.102).

[47]   For an example, see Prop. 1.13.22 as well as Adams (1982) 182 and Pichon (1966) 239.

[48]   For *folia* as petals, see *OLD* s.v. 3.

THE GARDEN OF ATEDIUS MELIOR (STATIUS' *SILVAE* 2.3) 67

which lies its, and Pan's, beloved.[49] But, as critics rightly note, they also serve as remembrance of the garlands and their residue which yearning lovers leave as offerings on the threshold of their resistant mistresses. We are thus reminded of one of the standard plots in elegiac poetry, the *paraklausithuron*, serenade before an unyielding doorway.[50] This in turn continues the pattern of reference to elegy that we have already noted and which, as we will also see, remains a constant in what follows.

Thus Statius again takes a sombre moment in Virgil, the death of a salient figure in the pastoral world, and turns it to more inspiring ends, thereby deepening still further the personification of the tree. Perhaps a residue of bitterness remains from the allusion to *Eclogue* 5 as the tree longs for its absent would-be paramour. But Statius also imagines Pan's stand-in as specifically playing the barred lover and strewing the water above Pholoe with flower petals the way a locked-out elegiac lover's offerings would shed their leaves on his aloof lady's threshold. In Statius' inventive transformation of his mentor's theme, the plane tree, through the single metonymic gesture of scattering its leaves as if they were flower petals, is both mourning a lost love, itself a form of elegy, and gesturing his affection for the apparently unobtainable, in the manner of an elegiac lover's complaint.

The erotic motif continues on by means of the word *turbare*.[51] We think, for instance, of the narrator's comment, as Turnus watches Lavinia: *illum turbat amor figitque in virgine vultus*... ('Love agitates him and he fixes his gaze on the maiden...', Virg. *A.* 12.70). In Virgil it is love itself that sends the suitor into turmoil. Here it is the masculine tree, symbol of Pan's devotion, which creates the commotion as further evidential proof of the fervour of his emotion, to be apprehended by Pholoe, nymph of water, the feminine element, in her habitat below. And here, unlike *tumultus* with a negative charge, the agitation has a promising, not a pernicious purpose.

The subsequent verb, *recolam*, given emphasis through the presence of *ego*, confirms and continues earlier themes.[52] Just as he had heaped 'living

---

[49] The word *latex* appears only here in the *Silvae*. Servius (*ad A.*1.686), connects it with the verb *latere* ('to lurk'), an etymology that ties it closely with *latebrosa* (44). The water itself shares in the act of hiding the naiad concealed below its surface.

[50] See Van Dam (1984) 318 and Newlands (2011a) 171, 175. The standard survey of the sub-genre is by Copley (1956).

[51] See again Van Dam (1984) 318: '... a play on erotic disturbances'.

[52] Virgil employs the verb *recolo* only once, at *A.* 6.681, as the narrator has us watch Anchises going over in his thoughts the figures of Roman greats about to be reborn—further evidence that this particular book of the epic was much on Statius' mind as he wrote these lines. Through the verb's tangential metapoetic meaning of rethink, Pan invites us also to

68   THE POETIC WORLD OF STATIUS' *SILVAE*

sand' (*vivam harenam*, 41) around the newly replanted tree to foster its flourishing, so now Pan promises to cultivate afresh his representative as the future evolves. And just as he had asked the tree, itself part of a *pignus memorabile* (43), to 'remember' (*memento*) his orders in time to come, so now he pledges to continue to keep both the *platanus* and his beloved nymph in his mind. In the process she, too, and her setting suffer favourable change from the 'hidden bed of the harsh nymph' into 'mistress of a kindly dwelling' (*dominamque... benignae sedis*, 49–50). Hard-heartedness has given way to kindliness, and she who had been aloof can at least for a moment be contemplated as a mistress, if not his, at least of a dwelling that might echo, in a form of hypallage, a new gentleness on her part.[53]

The elegiac theme we have been tracing continues in the word *dominam*, standard designation of the male lover's mistress. But the theme of time's passage also gains renewed prominence. Not only will the god bear his proxy in mind 'over a lengthy period' (*diu*), he will also protect both tree lover and now kindly beloved into a trouble-free old age just as the tree itself shelters those beneath it from threatening weather. Time may pass but the stress now is on growth (*germina*)[54] and on the beauty of the *platanus*, stand-in for Pan. Its foliage, that we have just watched being used to 'press' the water under which Pholoe lives, will now surpass that already honoured for decorating trees associated with Jupiter, Apollo, Hercules, and Pan himself whose pine is here on a level with oaks, laurel, and poplar.

One detail stands out in the way that Statius has the god present his arboreal list. The adjective that we are prone to link with Hercules' poplar tree, because of our reading of Virgil, is *bicolor*, 'of two colours' (*A*. 8.276). The duality in question stems from the leaves of the poplar which, because they are bright on one side and dark on the other, claim associations with life and death and, in the particular case of Hercules, with exploits concerned with the Underworld as well as the realm above.[55] In its place Statius turns

---

reconsider the meaning of the plane tree, especially in relation to other trees that Statius has invited us to recollect during his poem's path.

[53] *Benignus*, as rightly understood by Paul. *Fest*. p. 30L, is formed of a combination of *bonus* and the root for birth in *gigno*. Statius may be suggesting *in parvo*, through the word's etymology, the process by which Pholoe, initially *dura* toward her tree love, becomes implicitly *bona* and in the end summons its branches into her watery domain. As often in the poem, the idea of coming into being and of evolution support each other. Virgil's unique use of the adjective occurs at *A*. 1.304 describing Dido's 'kindly attitude' (*mentem... benignam*) toward the arriving Trojans.

[54] The noun's etymology (**gen-men*) again stems from the same root as *gigno*.

[55] For details, see Serv. *ad A*. 8.276 and Serv. *ad Ecl*. 7.61.

THE GARDEN OF ATEDIUS MELIOR (STATIUS' *SILVAE* 2.3) 69

again, as often, to Virgil but this time to quite a different tree, on which Venus' doves perch:...*discolor unde auri per ramos aura refulsit* ('...whence the contrasting sheen of gold shimmered through the branches', *A.* 6.204). Though we are dealing with the synecdoche of a tree and not with a full specimen itself, Statius' adoption of the earlier poet's *discolor* (51), a rare enough word in itself, in place of the expected *bicolor*, puts particular stress on his choice of the epithet here. In the midst of Pan's eulogy of the *platanus*, especially by comparison with other noteworthy examples, Statius would have us turn again for a moment, as he had at the poem's start, to the sixth book of the *Aeneid* with our focus on the 'golden bough' As we noted earlier, this branch serves as a warrant for the poem's hero to leave the sphere of the living and enter the abode of the dead and, while there, to learn of the many *vitae* still to come whose individual histories will brighten the glorious future of Rome.

Pan's Herculean poplar thus looks not only to matters of life and death but also to present and future time. In the immediate context, and with its vicarious association with Virgil's *ramus*, we ponder birth and generation through the *germina* of his tree, and matters of longevity and old age along with the god's prayer for tree and nymph as he looks to their life spans. We also yet again bear in mind the immortality of the poetry that puts these heady thoughts before us and the potent traditions from which this possibility springs.

Statius now turns to the tree's reaction to the god's requests:

> sic ait. illa dei veteres animata calores
> uberibus stagnis obliquo pendula trunco
> incubat atque umbris scrutatur amantibus undas.
> sperat et amplexus, sed aquarum spiritus arcet
> nec patitur tactus. tandem eluctata sub auras
> libratur fundo rursusque enode cacumen
> ingeniosa levat, veluti descendat in imos
> stirpe lacus alia. iam nec Phoebeia Nais
> odit et exclusos invitat gurgite ramos.
>
> (Stat. *Silv.* 2.3.53–61)

So he speaks. It, enlivened by the god's warmth of old, hanging with angled trunk, looms over the abundant shallows and examines the waves with loving shade (55). It hopes also for embraces, but an emanation from the waters stands in the way and does not suffer touch. At last as it

70   THE POETIC WORLD OF STATIUS' *SILVAE*

struggles skyward it is balanced on its base and in cleverness raises again its knotless crest, as if it descends into the bottom of the pool on a different stem. Now Phoebe's Naiad no longer (60) hates it and invites the branches once denied entry in her stream.

The tree, enlivened by the god's spirit, becomes the personification of his intense affection (*calores*, 53). The *stagnis* (54), that hitherto had been either deep (*altis*, 33) or grudging (*invida*, 38), are now abundant but also implicitly rich and fertile. The suggestiveness is taken up in both *pendula* (54) and *incubat* (55) which serves as a reminder of *cubilia* (44) and a supplement to *calores* (53) where in both instances the plural draws further attention to the erotic implications.[56]

But it is the phrase *umbris...amantibus* (55) that particularly catches the reader's attention, the amorous shades that the plane tree casts on the waters that enclose its beloved. The immediate, tangible result of the god's command *ama* (45) to his alter ego, they are personified, and project, especially through the use of the plural, the constancy, and keenness, of the god's emotion, as transmitted by his representative. It is also well to remember some aspects of the complex history of the word *umbra* that Statius would have inherited from Virgil. The first *Eclogue*, for instance, begins and ends with mentions of *umbra* as the shade, in which the soon-to-be-exiled Meliboeus sees the lucky shepherd Tityrus lying, yields, during the course of the poem, to the ominous shades of nightfall that, in conclusion, enclose both singers in its grasp (*Ecl.* 1.4 and 83). By contrast, as the collection draws to an end, the poem's speaker three times announces the evils of shade, thus preparing us for the *Georgics* to come (Virg. *Ecl.* 10.75–6). The latter, Virgil's didactic masterpiece, more often than not, dwells on the harmfulness of shade which inhibits the development of whatever lies near it and demands the constant vigilance of the farmer to necessary acts of pruning and the like. But here, too, Virgil surprises for, though shade often acts as a repressive element in the countryman's existence, it also serves as a sustaining refuge from the insistent trials of working the land or from the more universal horrors of human existence. We think, for instance, of the speaker's prayer in Virgil's second book of the *Georgics*: *o qui me gelidis convallibus Haemi/sistat et ingenti ramorum protegat umbra!* ('O for someone to place me in the cool glens of Haemus and shield me with the branches' mighty shade', G. 2.488–9).

---

[56] For *pendula* in an obscene sense, see Adams (1982) 57. For *cubo*, see Adams (1982) 177 and Pichon (1966) 117 (s.v. *cubile*).

THE GARDEN OF ATEDIUS MELIOR (STATIUS' *SILVAE* 2.3)   71

Or, in a more practical vein, we find our Virgil urging the shepherd to escape the noonday heat in a 'shady dell' (*umbrosam vallem, G.* 3.331) or:...*sicubi nigrum/ilicibus crebris sacra nemus accubet umbra...* ('...where a grove, dark with many holm oaks, reclines in its holy shade...', *G.* 3.333–4). This positive approach to the beauties of shade carries over into the present situation and the mention of the protection it brings to what lies below. It also reinforces a point that I made earlier. Instead of the plane tree keeping sustenance away from plants that might be literally dependent upon it, Pan's proxy offers shade that not only acts as safeguard from imminent outside dangers but also brings abiding affection with it, emblematic of the god's own fidelity.

This leads us back to the extraordinary phrase itself, *umbris amantibus.* The figuration is multifaceted. By metonymy shade stands for the leaves of the tree that proffers it, leaves which in turn stand for the tree itself. This in its own metonymic way embodies Pan's emotion and therefore the god himself. The figuration is also part of the larger personification, which the poet's use of the plural noun, as we noted, further heightens. It takes a plethora of *umbrae* for the shade to express the power of Pan's protective caring for the nymph in hiding in the *stagna* which it enshrouds. And the verb which the phrase encloses, *scrutatur*, adds to its effectiveness. It is already paradoxical that an evanescent, impalpable entity labelled shade passes as an aspect of a living creature, especially one living the part of a passionate individual. We now observe the tree itself turn from brooding over the waves to probing them with shades which become a species of eyes, presumably in expectation of a reaction from the depths of the *lacus.*

The personification continues in the tree-lover's hopes for an embrace. This is met by a rebuff from the *spiritus aquarum*, the life's breath of the waters, as if they, too, were personified and served as representatives of the emotions of the nymph whom they enclose. For a moment, at least, the tree's desire for physical contact with the lake's surface, as if it stood for Pholoe herself, is kept at bay. The *platanus* responds accordingly by turning back up toward the air above, the way that it would naturally evolve, as if, but only in appearance, it had grown from a new stem at the bottom of the pond. At Pan's very act of planting, we remember, the tree starts from its position at the water's edge, with countless branches and 'a crest about to make its way heavenward' (*iturus in aethera vertex*).[57]

---

[57] The counterpart of *vertex* here is *enode cacumen*. It is worth noting, as Statius expands the agricultural aspects of his description, that Virgil employs the adjective *enodis* only at *G.* 2.78

72   THE POETIC WORLD OF STATIUS' *SILVAE*

Here the word *ingeniosa* (59), describing the cleverness of the tree, comes into particular focus.[58] With a similar etymological play to that of *germina* (52), Statius would have us ponder the *ingenium* of the tree itself, the disposition with which it was born, its innate talent, as if it were a sensate being. The tree has the power intuitively to imagine that it might seem to be two different entities, the one rising upward, the other apparently going down into the water and starting from another, different stem. That inborn 'wit' furthers the personification of the actual tree, as if it first attempted, artfully, to fulfil Pan's desire and be together with Pholoe, but then followed its own instinct and soared toward the sky. The word also urges us to ponder Statius' own creative gifts, author of a brilliant poem about a tree that is a lover's offering but that also forms part of a collection of *Silvae*.[59]

The conclusion of the narrative segment of the poem offers the final, perhaps most moving, of the several metamorphoses with which Statius leavens his work. We have seen, for instance, how rusticity leads to civilization in the development of Rome, reaching its acme in the estate of Melior on the Caelian. We have traced the mutation of the plane tree, ordinarily unwed and subverting the proper nature of plants near it with its shade, into a symbol of a lover's fondness whose foliage wards off threatening weather and whose shade proves fostering instead of uncongenial. We now turn to the nymph Pholoe in her watery hideaway:... *iam nec Phoebeia Nais/odit et exclusos invitat gurgite ramos* (60–1). These lines form one of the extraordinary nexus of the poem. As commentators point out, the use of the adjective *Phoebeia,* as reference to Diana instead of Apollo, is unique in Latin.[60] But the reversal of our expectations is for a purpose. By emphasizing the nymph's association with the virgin goddess of the wild, the word not only recalls Diana's strongly adverse reaction to Pan's pursuit of Pholoe earlier in the poem, it also apparently confirms the latter's chastity as she ensconces herself in her aqueous shelter. The act of figuration by which Statius verbally embraces the name is, therefore, all the more surprising: *nec.../odit* (60–1). The litotes puts stress on the fact that the nymph, in not hating, in fact very

---

(*enodes trunci*), just as *enode* here is the single example in Statius. Virgil's unique use of *germen*, whose plural (*germina*) appears here at 52, we find at 2.76. And we have forms of *cacumen* at 2.29 and 307. Georgic language—of plant-life and its growth, of enriched soil, fertile pools, and the need for water itself—appropriately haunts these lines as does the teaching presence of the great poet himself; see Baumann (2019) 22–65, who studies the georgic language of the poem.

[58] At *G.* 2.20–1, Virgil makes brief mention of the greening of every type (*genus omne*) of forest trees, shrubs, and groves.

[59] See further the incisive comment of Newlands (2011a) 175.

[60] See Van Dam (1984) 326 and Newlands (2011a) 175.

THE GARDEN OF ATEDIUS MELIOR (STATIUS' *SILVAE* 2.3)   73

much loves the tree and in so doing would seem to acknowledge positively what it stands for. In other words, she responds in kind to Pan's command to his substitute to 'make love' (*ama*, 45) and to the plane tree's subsequent gesture of looming over the waters 'with loving shades' (*umbris...amantibus*, 55). Pholoe, though remaining *pudica*, professes her burgeoning attachment.

The resulting brief acknowledgement of acceptance is reified verbally over the reader's time as we move from *exclusos* to *invitat* (61), from *ex-* to *in-*, as the branches, which by synecdoche stand for the tree as a whole which in turn metaphorically substitutes for Pan and his erotic devotion, are summoned to enter Pholoe's hideaway.[61] The point is enhanced by the nuance of the word *exclusos* which, in the parlance of the elegists, regularly refers to lovers who are kept apart from their mistresses, whether actual or only desired, by the house-door which often simply stands for hardness on the part of the unresponsive beloved herself. The word thus brings to a climax the earlier references we have traced to the *paraklausithuron* and to the genre of elegy as a whole. We are in fact observing a rare example of the subgenre where the plot ends somewhat happily. The courter seems to get past any obstacles, usually the door itself, so as at least to be invited to enter the abode of the beloved, which is to say to secure her affection, if only momentarily.

Finally, two words are here worth special comment. The first is *ramos* (61). On two earlier occasions, the first being the poem's opening line, we have made reference to Virgil's *aureus ramus*, the famous golden bough that serves as Aeneas' laissez-passer into the realm of death and life, past and future. Here the plural noun, in synecdoche, helps accent a transition far less heady but somewhat more immediate than Virgil's, from loathing to loving, from implicit rejection to apparent acceptance as the tree-suitor nears the naiad's dwelling. Likewise, the word *gurgite* (61), its only appearance in the poem, seems specifically well-chosen to enhance its context, just as *laticem* does at line 48. Though etymologists, both ancient and modern, connect it with the word *voro*, to 'swallow greedily',[62] it is doubtful that Statius would wish to add a negative tinge to this moment of approbation, as we bid our farewell to *placidus* Melior's special tree. Nevertheless, it could be said that the poet hints at a further touch of emotionality, even of intensity,

---

[61] Presumably *tactus* (57), but of an innocent variety, approvable by Diana, are now allowed!

[62] See Maltby (1991) s.v. *gurges* (265); Ernout and Meillet, s.v. *gurges*. Of the poem's many turns on words for water, *vadis* (3), *amnem* (5), and *fontem* (32), besides *laticem* and *gurgite*, make single appearances.

74 THE POETIC WORLD OF STATIUS' *SILVAE*

as Pholoe asks the branches, as lover, into her domain via a medium that could be said to absorb eagerly whatever came in contact with it.[63]

Atedius Melior

Having finished his expansive *aition*, Statius himself enters the poem again to tell us about its genesis and purpose as well as to inform us in detail about its dedicatee whom we have hitherto only seen characterized directly through the highly suggestive adjectives *nitidi* (1) and *placidi* (15):

> haec tibi parva quidem genitali luce paramus
> dona, sed ingenti forsan victura sub aevo.
> tu cuius placido posuere in pectore sedem
> blandus honos hilarisque tamen cum pondere virtus,
> cui nec pigra quies nec iniqua potentia nec spes
> improba, sed medius per honesta et dulcia limes,
> incorrupte fidem nullosque experte tumultus
> et secrete palam quod digeris ordine vitam,
> idem auri facilis contemptor et optimus idem
> comere divitias opibusque immittere lucem...
>
> (Stat. *Silv.* 2.3.62–71)

This gift we are readying for you on the day of your birth, small, to be sure, but perhaps destined to endure for a vast length of time. In your calm breast esteem that charms, and integrity, light-hearted but with authority, have established their abode (65). Your repose lacks sloth, nor is your forcefulness unjust nor your ambition perverse, but a middle path through the estimable and the gracious, blameless in your good faith and

---

[63] As Newlands (2011a) 175 observes, *gurgite* can be taken either as ablative of separation (with *exclusos*) or instrumental ablative. The poet may be teasing us into pondering both possibilities; see also Hardie (2006) 211. Statius may be thinking here of two lines from Ovid. The first, a pentameter, occurs at *Am.* 1.8.78: *audiat exclusi verba receptus amans...* ('Let the lover you have received hear the words of the one barred...'). The second is from Ov. *Rem.* 35–6: *et modo blanditias, rigido modo iurgia postidicat et exclusus flebile cantet amans* ('And let the barred lover utter now flattery, now reproaches, to the unyielding doorpost and sing a lament'). The two lines ending in *amans* may offer a hint that we should allow the word *amo* to resonate from within Statius' concluding word for line 61, *ramos*. If so, his hexameter takes us on a version of Catullus' brilliantly paradoxical *odi et amo* poem (85) where we move away from the combination of hatred and loving to the triumph of the second over the first. As so often, Statius turns a negative setting in an earlier masterwork, in Catullus' case that of the suffering lover, to a happier outcome.

THE GARDEN OF ATEDIUS MELIOR (STATIUS' *SILVAE* 2.3)   75

experiencing no turmoil, and special because you openly arrange your
life's pattern, likewise an easy despiser of gold and likewise the best at (70)
shaping your wealth and a allowing light in on your resources...

The word *parva* (62) returns us to line 6 and to the poet's mock-humble
request to Apollo for inspiration as he begins his central tale. Likewise, *par-
amus* (62) takes us back to that same moment and to the only previous
appearance of the speaker's 'I' in the poem (*rogem*, 62), now given emphasis
by the plural 'we', in the process of rounding out the work as a whole. The
two deictics, *haec tibi*, call attention both to the preceding narrative itself,
that we now have before us as an apparently completed entity, as well as to
'you', Melior, its recipient, on the occasion of his birthday.[64] And words,
such as *germina* (52) and *ingeniosa* (59), that in the preceding lines have
pointed to the idea of growth and generation, now deserve particular consideration as Statius has us attend to the poem's special moment, the *genitali
luce* where the metonymy 'light' stands for the day itself and its generative
potential, and reminds us of *nitidi Melioris*, of Melior, shimmeringly elegant
of manner and mind.

The affirmative effect of first and second person pronouns and verb, subsequent to an essentially third-person accounting of a myth, is strengthened
by the use of *haec*. Statius' very poem is the small gift that he, the poet as 'I',
is in the act of bringing into being. Poem and dedicatee complement each
other, celebrating, in one case, a new birth or, in the other, a marker of life's
renewal. The rhetoric corroborates the lyric subjectivity of the moment as
we prepare to enter the inner *sedes* (64) of Melior's being, something far
different from the external dwelling (*sedes*, 50) of the nymph Pholoe. In
sum, we are witnessing the creation of both poem and addressee whose
quality of mind and ethos are also in the process of being eternalized.

The language Statius uses to characterize the poem's future is particularly
suggestive (... *ingenti forsan victura sub aeuo*, 63). The combination of *ingenti*
and *sub* reminds us, for instance, of Virgil, announcing a time: ... *Parnasia
laurus/parva sub ingenti matris se subicit umbra* ('... when the small laurel
of Parnassus springs up from under the mighty shade of its mother',
G. 2.18–19).[65] The result in Statius, with *sub* used temporally, as it seldom is,

---

[64] As we have seen, the two words also initiate the hexameter at Virg. *Ecl.* 5.74, confirming
the deification of Daphnis.
[65] *Parva* is clearly echoed in *parva dona* (62–3). Statius' *victura* is anticipated by *vivam* (41)
and *vive* (43), and is reinforced by *vitam* (69), while *aevo* recalls Pan's *platanus* in the prime of

76 THE POETIC WORLD OF STATIUS' *SILVAE*

instead of spatially, is to personify *aevum* as if were an individual able to foster the gift-poem over time like a mother tree nurturing its sapling (and we recall that Pan's plane tree is characterized as *primaevam*, 39). The point is complemented by the extremely rare employment of *ingens* in a temporal sense.[66] This attribute, too, brings with it a type of personification that suggests space as well as time, a lifespan of special endurance where the passage of time and the extent of space somehow enhance each other. Through its central letters, *-gen-*, the adjective also stands as a further reminder that birth and the development that follows upon it is a central theme of the poem, reaching an initial climax here as poem and birthday prove mutually sustaining.

The phrase *haec tibi* (62) also serves a further purpose. It stands as an additional reminder of Virgil's fifth *Eclogue* where the shepherd Menalcas sings of the ceremonies that will now celebrate the deification of the pastoral hero Daphnis: *haec tibi semper erunt, et cum sollemnia vota/reddemus Nymphis, et cum lustrabimus agros* ('These rites will forever be yours, both when we will offer our yearly prayers to the nymphs, and when we will purify our fields', *Ecl.* 5.74–5). There may be a subtle hint here that Atedius Melior will attain a form of permanence because of his glorification in the poetry of Statius. But the poet may have a more specific purpose. We have seen earlier how Statius, at line 48, alludes to *Eclogue* 5 in connection with the death of Daphnis and how the poet there turns an apparently negative occasion into something positive as the tree-lover displays affection for his dear naiad below. The same can be said for the reference here as Statius takes Virgil's celebration of the posthumous deification of Daphnis and makes of it an occasion for the recollection of life's initiation and renewal on his friend's birthday.

The poem concludes with two eulogies, for Melior and Blaesus. It is only fitting that the most expansive praise be devoted to the first, and it is equally appropriate that the premier characteristic singled out by Statius is one that we already gleaned at lines 15–16. There we learned of the 'flawless, accessible dwelling of calm Melior' (*placidi Melioris aperti/ ... sine fraude lares*), his consequential estate on the Caelian Hill. Here, as literal home becomes

---

life. No new growth will be 'blighted' under the god's loving present. So also Statius' gift to Melior is destined to survive under the protection of a time frame that promotes endurance.

[66] See Newlands (2011a) 175–6; Van Dam (1984) 328. Statius may be suggesting, through assonance, a punning relationship with *genitali* in the previous line which hints further at the link between birth, longevity, and poem. Virgil seems to play on the connection at *A.* 12.708 (*ingentis genitos*) and Statius at *Silv.* 4.2.26 (*ingenti genio*).

THE GARDEN OF ATEDIUS MELIOR (STATIUS' *SILVAE* 2.3)   77

metaphoric, we learn of his 'calm heart' (*placido pectore*) in which virtues of a wide variety make their domicile. We have marvelled at a poem where unwonted violence is suppressed and the loveless become tender-hearted lovers.[67] It seems especially suitable that the tone of implicit quietude that results should be the initial trait of his dedicatee that Statius isolates for praise.

The phrase *posuere... sedem* (64) has a series of parallels which could cast further light on Statius' intent. I select a moment from Statius' great epic, the *Thebaid*, published before the *Silvae* and possibly also in the poet's own mind as he initiated his praise of Melior. Near the poem's conclusion we find ourselves in Athens where, in its midst:... *mitis posuit Clementia sedem* ('... gentle Clemency had established her abode', *Theb.* 12.482). At the centre of Theseus' famous city is to be found a temple devoted essentially to peace at which those thankful for its advent into their troubled lives, or craving its presence when their situation is in turmoil from war or other manifest-ations of brute force, come for solace. According to Statius' figuration, Melior himself is thus a human version of the metropolis with a shrine to human harmony established at its core. But the heart of his patron, as the poet would have it, is in itself a still more capacious sanctuary of which for-giveness and moderation are only the initial objects of appreciation. And, if we keep the conclusion of the *Thebaid* still in mind, Melior becomes tan-gentially a modern-day equivalent of the great king who secures concord between battling parties.

Lines 65–71 continue the catalogue of the ethical virtues that have taken up residence in Melior's tranquil breast. They constitute the qualities that combine to display his 'mind-set and behaviour patterns' (*animi morumque*, 72). The attributes personalize, humanize, make subjective, the impressive abstractions that they modify. In doing so they also help enhance the moral values, the superlative spiritual disposition, by which he lives his life and, in the process, exemplifies the best in present-day Roman civilization. The respect (*honos*, 64) that has been bestowed upon Melior is charming (*blan-dus*, 64) in that he uses its implicit effectiveness to delight and not cajole, or worse. His excellence, his prowess (*virtus*, 65), is carried with both cheerful-ness and substance which is to say that his moral sturdiness possesses ease along with authority. Though he is known for his innate quietude it is never

---

[67] We note the difference between Melior's *placido pectore* and Pan brandishing his sighs for Pholoe 'with burning heart' (*ardenti... pectore*, 19–20). There is no negative weaponry in the moral arsenal of kindly Melior.

78   THE POETIC WORLD OF STATIUS' *SILVAE*

accompanied by sloth—a riff on Cicero's *cum dignitate otium* ('leisure combined with worthiness').[68] Though he has power it is never exercised unjustly (*nec iniqua potentia*) and whatever hope he cherishes is never wrongheaded.

Statius concludes this segment of his catalogue of Melior's qualities, and their challenging restrictions, by means of a topographical metaphor. The latter's life-journey has followed a pathway between two separate, differing spiritual territories which he has been able to straddle and then amalgamate. The first we might call the land of uprightness (*honesta*). The second would be the realm of enjoyment and pleasure. *Limes* stands for a boundary line between the two spheres. We think, for instance, of the reminder to the lucky Tityrus, on the part of Virgil's shepherd Meliboeus, that he will continue to enjoy the buzzing of bees from the 'hedge on your neighbour's border' (*uicino ab limite saepes*, *Ecl.* 1.53).[69] Still more à propos is Virgil's description, at *A.* 12.897–8, of a huge, ancient stone, of sufficient prestige to act as a *limes*, in this case a single marker, that would 'keep any controversy from the fields' (*litem... discerneret arvis*). There will be no arguing over ownership.

In the case of Melior, the *limes* of his *curriculum vitae* is a metaphorical route through life that postulates an internal ability to integrate qualities that might, if embodied in a less fortunate man, be at odds with each other.[70] It would be easy enough to find evidence, in the actions of an ordinary human being, of power used in an unbalanced way, for instance, or of relaxation that has slipped into indolence. The nouns that Statius utilizes by way of summary are *honesta* and *dulcia*. The poet intimates that we could readily come upon examples in the lives of other prominent characters where personal gratification would corrupt the ordinarily honourable, or even of the opposite, where the seemingly admirable assumes an unwonted stiltedness because the world of personal happiness has been forced to play a secondary role in the person's makeup. Melior, in Statius' insightful portrait, is able to balance both capacities in a life that draws sustenance from accomplishments that serve the world around him and at the same time make his own personal existence a pleasant one. This *limes*, instead of playing the impartial role of settling possible disputes, acts as a conduit that merges the enterprising and the satisfying into a creative whole as Melior follows life's trajectory.

---

[68] Cic. *Fam.* 1.9.21, varied at *Sest.* 98 and *Or.* 1.1.

[69] Virgil uses the word *limes* with the meaning of pathway also at *G.* 1.126; *A.* 2.697 and 6.900, where the reading is debatable.

[70] We are also, after all, drawing near to the poem's conclusion and *limes* might thus suggest a 'bound' of closure to what is in large measure a paean to calm and contentedness.

THE GARDEN OF ATEDIUS MELIOR (STATIUS' *SILVAE* 2.3)   79

Statius follows with three apostrophes. The first, *incorrupte fidem* (68), is a clear bow, as commentators note, to Horace *Carm.* 1.24.7, where *incorrupta Fides*, sister of *Iustitia*, in company with *Pudor* and *Veritas*, define the character of Quintilius whose passing is the subject of the poet's lyric dirge.[71] As often, Statius takes a bittersweet context in past Latin poetry, here the death of a friend, and gives it an uplifting turn. Something similar could be said for an earlier appearance of *Fides* in one of Horace's odes where one of the attributes of a person given too liberally to the joys of wine is escorted by 'trust, lavish with what is secret, more clearly transparent than glass' (*arcani Fides prodiga, perlucidior vitro, Carm.* 1.18.6).

Again, Statius turns Horace's intent to the better. Melior, *incorruptus*, is gifted with *Fides* but instead of embodying a trust that betrays others, as is the case with Horace's drunkard, he displays a fidelity that is patent, manifest, sincere. The poet would have us recall again Melior's 'wide-open dwelling, lacking deceit' (*aperti/... sine fraude lares*, 15–16). But we also have another example of circularity back to the clear, glass-like waters of the poem's opening that emblematize the many-sided perspicuity of Melior's inner being through the translucence of his external world. Once more, Statius takes a nearly satirical moment in the earlier lyricist and turns it into a compliment for Melior, 'better' than his earlier poetic analogies.

The second apostrophe, *nullos experte tumultus* ('you who undergo no turmoil', 68), underscores wise Melior's adherence to Epicureanism and its respect for inner calmness and dispassion. We recall Horace's advice to his friend Grosphus that no riches or political power can rid the tormented person of spiritual troubles:

> non enim gazae neque consularis
> summovet lictor miseros tumultus
> mentis et curas laqueata circum
>   tecta volantis.
>
> (Hor. *Carm.* 2.16.9–12)

For neither wealth nor the consul's lictor wards off wretched disorders of the mind and the worries that fly around coffered ceilings.

Horace glosses the metaphor inherent in *tumultus* at *Carm.* 3.29.63, where he speaks of the two-oared skiff that will take him safely through 'the Aegean storms' (*Aegaeos tumultus*), which is to say that his inner quietude

---

[71] See Newlands (2011a) 177; Van Dam (1984) 331–2.

80   THE POETIC WORLD OF STATIUS' *SILVAE*

and lack of overweening ambition for externals will carry him without harm through life's disquieting vicissitudes.[72] Both passages help us engage both literally and figuratively with Melior. No spiritual disorders of destructive emotionality, toward whatever end they are oriented, will disrupt the *quies* of Melior's existence. Once more our thoughts return to the poem's opening and to the analogy that Statius suggests between the *perspicuas... aquas* (1–2) and *uitreum amnem* of Melior's garden pool and the lack of any inner agitation on the part of its owner. Neither he nor the externals that represent his spiritual self suffer from the agitations that afflict others less fortunate in their personality or ethos. The final apostrophe opens with a paradox: *et secrete palam quod digeris ordine vitam* ('and [you are] set apart because you openly arrange your life's pattern', 69).

Melior is *secretus* because he both enjoys a private life and is distinct from others for having its details open to public view. The metaphor is drawn from agriculture and here, as often, Virgil offers us a parallel.[73] We witness a georgic moment within a pastoral environment as the soon to be exiled shepherd-farmer Meliboeus addresses himself with bitter irony: *insere nunc, Meliboee, piros, pone ordine vites* ('Graft now your pears, Meliboeus, plant your vines in a row', *Ecl.* 1.73). The echo of *ordine vites* in *ordine vitam* is clear.[74] Melior puts his life in figurative order the way a farmer places his vines in careful arrangement both for the sake of the regularity of the plants' expansion and for the seemliness of the meticulous design.[75] The horticultural language recalls Statius' use of *limes* at line 67. Just as the pathway of Melior's ethics holds a happy mean between duty and contentment, so also his life itself has a suitably structured pattern. It is as if it were a type of vineyard with which the farmer has taken exacting pains to form an impressive arrangement, for the sake of the vines themselves, which here is to say Melior's inner being, but also for an onlooker to admire. This is the aspect that the adverb *palam* (69) helps conjure up in the depiction of Melior's quality as seen publicly by an outsider. He may be special, yet his very apartness, his seclusion, is available for all to peruse.

---

[72] For larger *tumultus* afflicting mankind, cf., for Virgil, the *caecos tumultus* (*G.* 1.464) that denote civil war to come, the 'great shock' (*magno tumultu*, *A.* 6.857) of the Second Punic War, and the *tumultu* (*A.* 8.4) that presages the beginning of war in Latium upon Aeneas' arrival.

[73] As noted also by Newlands (2011a) 177–8.   [74] Baumann (2019) 38 n. 57.

[75] For forms of *digero* in Virgil used in connection with the proper disposition of plants see *G.* 2.54 and 267. We find *ordinibus* for ranks of vines at *G.* 2.277 with the word *limite* in the subsequent hexameter.

THE GARDEN OF ATEDIUS MELIOR (STATIUS' *SILVAE* 2.3)   81

In this instance again Statius turns a moment of great distress in Virgil, in the present case as a shepherd-singer prepares to abandon his beloved landscape, into something creative. The 'vine' of Melior's existence can sustain its orderly mode as an example that he has 'planted out' for everyone to admire, like a good landsman of the spirit.

The agricultural language, that began, implicitly, with *sedem posuere*, and continued more pointedly with *limes* and *digeris ordine*, is reaffirmed in the final item in Statius' eulogy of his patron who is: *idem auri facilis contemptor et optimus idem/comere divitias opibusque immittere lucem* ('...likewise an easy despiser of gold and likewise the best at shaping your wealth and at allowing light in on your resources, 2.3.70–1). Statius begins with a recollection of the *faciles Fauni* to whom he initially prays for a smooth flow of inspiration as if Melior's birthday, or indeed as if the man himself, had supplied stimulus for the engendering of the poem honouring him. Initiation of the work suggests its crafting and here the word *comere* comes into play, continuing the line of horticultural metaphors which we have been tracing.[76] In another paradoxical juxtaposition, Melior is an 'easy' scorner of gold while himself being the possessor of wealth.[77] But it is wealth that he knows how to arrange in comely fashion, how to prune so as to appear without guile to the curious outsider. The compliment receives particular stress because Statius here turns Melior's name from the comparative form to the superlative, *optimus*, for the only time in the poem. Caring for his resources is what he is supremely good at.

The metaphor is not common, but we find it, for instance, in a letter of Fronto where he speaks of 'myrtle and boxwood and other shrubs suitable for clipping, which are accustomed to being most assiduously and carefully pruned, watered, and trimmed...' (*myrtum buxumque ceteraque tonsilia arbusta atque virgulta summa diligentia et studio radi rigari comi solita...*, *Ep.* 1.204.25–6). The vegetation on either side of the pathway flanked by *dulcia* and *honesta* deserves to be kept in seemly order to reflect the quality of the man embracing both ethical realms. For a person despising the evils

---

[76] I accept the reading of *M* that is regularly changed by editors to *promere* (e.g. Courtney and Liberman).

[77] At 70–1, Statius is in dialogue with the end of the second book of the *Georgics*, a diatribe against modern society's decadents. One man brings ruin on a city so that he can drink from a jewel: *condit opes alius defossoque incubat auro* ('another hides his wealth and broods over his buried gold', *G.* 2.507). As we have often seen, Statius again takes a worrisome moment in his predecessor's work and ameliorates it. Melior, unlike Virgil's hoarder, exemplifies the well-off individual who despises gold for its own sake, whose wealth is on display for all to see and is presumably available for the benefit of the world around him.

82 THE POETIC WORLD OF STATIUS' *SILVAE*

that gold can cause, there is all the more reason for keeping the manifestations of his own wealth, on display to all, as tasteful and apposite as possible both to view and to appreciate.

Last in the poet's list of *laudes* is the unusual combination *immittere lucem* to depict the way Melior displays his affluence to the onlooker. Since the phrase appears nowhere else in Latin literature, we might here turn to examples of its opposite, and once again Virgil can serve as guide. The didactic poet calls to our attention a sucker which would flourish, if separated from its original tree trunk and placed in an open field. Otherwise:

> nunc altae frondes et rami matris opacant
> crescentique adimunt fetus uruntque ferentem.
>
> <div align="right">(Virg. <i>G.</i> 2.55–6)</div>

As it is, the lofty foliage and branches of the mother overshadow it and take away fruit from it as it grows and blast it as it bears.

Shade can have both positive and negative effects, as we have seen as Statius' poem progresses. As we saw at line 1, shade provides shelter for those taking pleasure in the brilliant waters of Melior's garden. And, as lines 46–7 called to our attention, the plane tree, which serves as manifestation of Pan's devotion to Pholoe, wards off any harmful manifestations of the elements—hail due to cold, and the sun's celestial fieriness—from the naiad harboured below. We also took note, however, of the plane's vitiating feature of stunting the growth of anything planted beneath it because of the very thickness of the shadow that it casts.

Statius thus, at the conclusion of his praise of Melior, makes a final use, here implicit, of an agricultural metaphor to put before us graphically how his friend treats his wealth with due propriety. Now we have light let in on Melior's *vitem/vitam* so that it can flourish and be on view to all. He 'illuminates' the extent of his possession of the world's goods for two reasons. As a reliable 'financial' farmer, he has the intelligence to 'elucidate' his holdings so as to allow them to increase naturally, with no implication of wrongdoing in the process. The notion of illumination also follows directly from the portrait that the poet has painted of Melior from the start, as the clarity of his ornamental pool finds a corresponding parallel in the 'open household' (*aperti… lares*) in which he thrives. He is both practical and transparent in the way he treats his holdings, for his own advantage but presumably also for the benefit of those, even poets, who have the good fortune to share in his situation, both prosperous, materially, and candid, ethically.

THE GARDEN OF ATEDIUS MELIOR (STATIUS' *SILVAE* 2.3) 83

By way of summary, and of a further, tacit complement to Melior, let us turn again to Horace's *Carmen Saeculare* and to the lyric poet's summary of the multivalent quality of the age of Augustus as seen in the glorious hymn written for the celebration of the renewed *Ludi Saeculares* in June of 17 BCE:

> iam Fides et Pax et Honos Pudorque
> priscus et neglecta redire Virtus
> audet, apparetque beata pleno
> Copia cornu.

(Hor. *Saec.* 57–60)

Now Trust and Peace and Honour and old-fashioned Modesty and disregarded Virtue have courage to return, and blessed Plenty, with full horn, is in evidence.

Statius has found an open *exemplum* of *Fides*, *Honos*, and *Virtus* in the person of Melior, and *Pax* gains a ready partner in *Quies*.[78] His adherence to *Pudor* is suggested by fact that he scorns *spes improba*, ambition in any way tainted by misconduct. To accompany these manifestations of ethical excellence it could also be said that *Copia*, with her horn of plenty, has also richly endowed him with possessions. Melior thus embodies, in the age of Domitian, what the supreme lyricist of the Augustan age proclaims were among the qualities of greatness that, in his presentation, sparked the spiritual renewal of Rome as the millennium drew to a close. That he was economically prosperous further supports the parallel that Statius' language suggests.[79]

Statius concludes with a prayer that his youthful cluster of present distinctions may continue into a long old age for Melior, similar to that of his parents. The fates have prayed for this as has the glorious memory of his friend Blaesus which survives through his bearing witness as well as through the poetry of Statius, now in the process of immortalizing both:

---

[78] Another Horatian text important for comparison here is the whole of *Carm.* 4.9 where the poet assures immortality to Lollius through his *laudatio* of the latter's quality. Lollius, for instance, exhibits the excellence of a consul '…as often as, being a good and faithful judge, he has put the honorable before the pragmatic…' (…*quotiens bonus atque fidus/iudex honestum praetulit utili*…, *Carm.* 4.9.40–1). Lollius shuns *fraus* (37) as does Melior, and equally disdains wealth ill-used (38).

[79] We should note here that the phrase *sine fraude* is here applied by Horace to Aeneas, escaping 'without injury' from the flames of Troy (*Saec.* 41). Statius had employed it, we remember, at 16, to describe the household gods of Melior, manifest to all, without any hidden deceit. Aeneas' physical lack of hurt in the midst of danger is matched by the scatheless morality manifest to the knowing viewer in Melior's dwelling, external evidence of his inner righteousness.

84   THE POETIC WORLD OF STATIUS' *SILVAE*

> hac longum florens animi morumque iuventa
> Iliacos aequare senes et vincere persta
> quos pater Elysio, genetrix quos detulit annos.
> hoc illi duras exoravere sorores,
> hoc, quae te sub teste situm fugitura tacentem
> ardua magnanimi revirescet gloria Blaesi.
>
> (Stat. *Silv.* 2.72–7)

Flourishing for a long time in this youth of mind and behaviour, stand firm in equalling the Ilian ancients and in surpassing the years which your father, which your mother, took down to Elysium. This they have entreated from the unbending sisters (75), this the lofty renown of high-souled Blaesus which will grow green again, about to escape the silence of neglect, with you as witness.

The horticultural image that we have been following recurs pointedly in the word *florens* as the poet prays for continued youthfulness for Melior. Paradoxically, it is a youthfulness that will surpass even that of the most ancient of ancients, Priam and Tithonus, as well as the length of years given to his mother and father. But Melior is different. Priam, though long-lived, died a tragic death, and Tithonus, according to his myth, though he was allotted timeless years, wasted away in body until he resembled a cicada. As Statius would have it, Melior, by contrast, will survive to a ripe old age, but will also magically continue to possess *hac iuventa*, this very youth that we can see about him as he celebrates his birthday. He may be compared to two *senes* of storied note, but he will have no share in the *senectus*, however preternaturally extensive, that came their way.[80]

Here again Horace and his *Carmen Saeculare* will help us appreciate the larger picture that Statius is creating. We looked earlier at how Melior embodies some of the noble characteristics that the lyricist sees pervading the Roman world under the enlightened leadership of Augustus. Some stanzas earlier in the poem Horace has his choristers pray to the denizens of heaven on behalf of his contemporary Rome. The gods had ensured that Aeneas escape unharmed from the flames of Troy and that the exiles from the

---

[80] We note that the Fates are called *duras sorores* (75), gaining the same attribute that Statius ascribes to Pholoe (*durae*, 44), before her dwelling suffers metamorphosis into *benigna*, and to the hard hail (*dura grandine*, 47) that the plane tree will ward off from the nymph's abode. The prayer to the three sisters, that they depart from their ordinary sternness in the case of Melior, asks for a similar transformation.

THE GARDEN OF ATEDIUS MELIOR (STATIUS' *SILVAE* 2.3)   85

ruined city arrive safely on the Etruscan shore. Now is the time for them to
bless their modern descendants:

> di, probos mores docili iuventae
> di, senectuti placidae quietem,
> Romulae genti date remque prolemque
>> et decus omne.

(Hor. Saec. 45–8)

Gods, grant righteous habits to our educable youth, gods [grant] peace to
our calm old age, [grant] to the race of Romulus both resources and
offspring and every grace.

We quickly enter the world of Melior by means of his defining adjective
placidus, since *quies*, we remember, is one of the salient qualities that characterize his personal quality. But Statius would seem to be directly calling
our attention to Horace's phrase *probos mores docili iuventae* when he distinguishes Melior's present career as thriving for a long while 'in this youth
of mind and behaviour' (*hac... animi morumque iuventa*). As in the case of
the earlier list of Horatian abstractions that we found applicable to the life of
Melior, as Statius delineates it for us, so also here we turn from general to
individual. Horace's universal prayer, that the gods bestow proper *mores* on
the Roman young, is particularized in Statius' pronouncement that Melior
will always remain an exemplification both of freshness of attitude and of
the decorous conduct that befits it.

The compliment to Melior is enormous and akin to the several instances
of extraordinary evolution in the poem such as the development of Rome
from rustic woods and streams into the elegance of Melior's domain on the
Caelian, or of the plane tree from a darkening plant that blights what is
attached to it into a surrogate of Pan, courting an underwater beloved in
his stead. In this case the aspect of temporality is especially dramatic. What
happens here is not so much a metamorphosis as an extraordinary, even
unique, type of conjunction. Statius wishes for his patron the years of the
two Trojan ancients (*senes*), which is to say a remarkably extensive old age.
But this is also miraculously accompanied by an already on-going youthfulness. In Melior's case, the notion of time implicit in his singular *senectus* is
not so much changed into a form of eternity, as in the case of Tithonus who
lives on and on but is subject to aging, as it is companioned by *iuventa*, in
which he remains *florens*, ever blossoming, like Pan's *primaevam platanum*,
in the prime of a continuous young manhood.

86   THE POETIC WORLD OF STATIUS' *SILVAE*

One detail stands out in Statius' mention of Melior's parents. Though his father receives the designation *pater*, his mother is singled out by the word *genetrix*, the title that Lucretius gives Venus in the opening line of *De Rerum Natura* and which Virgil four times bestows on the goddess as the mother of Aeneas (*A.* 1.590, 4.227, 8.383, 12.412). The gesture does particular honour to the woman, now in Elysium. It also calls our attention one final time to the notion of generation and production that surfaces now and then throughout the poem, appropriately for a work Statius designates as in preparation for Melior's birthday to which, we recall, he gives the metonymic title *genitali luce*, 'creative light'. Melior himself, he whom we have seen to 'let light in' on his world, stands, along with the 'innately gifted' (*ingeniosa*) plane tree, as a figure also granted life by the poet in words that we still contemplate with pleasure.

Much the same notion is varied in the poem's final two hexameters that centre on Melior's friend Blaesus whose *gloria* joins the prayers of the dedicatee's parents in asking for a long, youthful, old age for their son. The last, beautifully structured golden hexameter line ends with the name Blaesus which receives the epic epithet *magnanimi*, but the subject of the sentence is *gloria* which is enlivened through both accompanying adjective, *ardua*, and verb, *revirescet. Ardua* serves a special purpose by acting as a reminder of the *arbor* of Melior which is equally *ardua* (4). We thus have a forceful example of ring-composition where the actual *platanus* of Melior's garden, eye-catching and an inspiration for the poem, becomes the metaphorical tree of Blaesus' honour, fostered by Melior, and given special prominence by Statius.[81]

The central verb, *revirescet*, also carries the essence of a major theme of the poem, namely the implicit link between mankind's behaviour and the agricultural world that surrounds us. This we found particularly true of the life of Melior, in the *limes* through which he makes his ethical way, in the pattern by which it is laid out (*ordine*) and the trimming necessary to keep it in shape (*comere*), and in its openness to the light (*lucem*) necessary for its fruition. Here once more Virgil will help us to an understanding of Statius' meaning. Virgil's only use of the verb *revirescere* occurs at *G.* 2.313, where he describes the effects of a ruinous forest fire on the trees that remain: *hoc ubi, non a stirpe valent caesaeque reverti/possunt atque ima similes*

---

[81]   For details, see Van Dam (1984) 334–5 and, for Blaesus' life in general, and specifically for Melior's share in keeping his memory alive, see Van Dam (1984) 334–5 and 191–3; Janan (2020) 201–6.

THE GARDEN OF ATEDIUS MELIOR (STATIUS' *SILVAE* 2.3)   87

revirescere terra... ('When this happens, [the trees] have no strength in their stem and, when cut down, cannot start again and from the depths of the soil once more grow green as they had been...', *G.* 2.312–13). The equivalent to Virgil's destructive blaze in the career of Blaesus is death itself and the obliteration of memory that often comes in its wake. But here once more Statius turns the gloomy aspects of a passage in his great predecessor to more joyful ends. Blaesus will not suffer any form of the permanent damage that would ensue for Virgil's trees in the wake of a catastrophe that takes the possibility of renewal away from them. Because of Melior's practical care and the far-ranging efforts of Statius' imagination, there will be an enduring form of continuity for him after his passing. We begin the poem with mention of Melior and his brilliance in the opening line, but we end pondering the *gloria* of Blaesus and it is the man himself who literally has the last word that we take with us.

This sense of renewal that we deeply apprehend as we conclude the poem and ponder its import, both specific and general, has already been qualified, in a positive sense, in the preceding, penultimate hexameter. We note the extraordinary phrase *situm tacentem*, where the personification gives a special thrust to the word *situs*, the annihilating power of negligence with its concomitant decay. At the conclusion of his great *sphragis* to his first collection of *Carmina*, Horace boasts *dicar*, I shall be spoken, recited, sung, back where I was born, picking up the earlier prediction *non omnis moriar*, I will not completely die. Though his human remains may lose life, his words will continue on undying.[82] Statius implies the same possibility for Blaesus' reputation but he puts the matter in the form of a double negative. In place of the lyricist's *dicar* Statius promises that his friend's honour will stay fresh because it flees the silence of neglect through the poet's own speaking words and their promise of perpetuity. Statius avoids Horace's direct mention of death but allows us to infer its presence through the word *situs*, the potential evanescence in the offing for our tangible remains.[83]

The word *tacentem* itself joins *ardua* in taking us back to the poem's opening, here to the word *tacitis* (5), to bring matters full circle and help unite the whole. The juxtaposition deserves comment. The 'quiet roots' of Melior's tree, as we saw, are a synecdoche for the residence of the master himself (*placidus*), with his own inner peacefulness reflected in the tranquillity of his surroundings. At the end of the poem, we witness a negative form of

---

[82] *Carm.* 3.30.10 and 6. The poem was much on Statius' mind as he wrote his own lines.

[83] For *situs* and death, see the comments of Nisbet and Rudd (2004) 369 on Hor. *Carm.* 3.30.2.

88 THE POETIC WORLD OF STATIUS' *SILVAE*

silence, the silence of *situs*, which dooms its victims to a form of oblivion. But the silence in this case is broken not by the sounds of *tumultus* that afflict the ordinary mortal as he experiences life's buffets but by the good deeds of Blaesus, to which Melior bears witness, and by the poetry of Statius whose spoken words, like Horace's on his own behalf, will ensure that his subject's excellent accomplishments will live on as they deserve.

The word *fugitura* also takes us back into the body of the poem. We first meet the verb *fugio* at line 8 where we find the throngs of nymphs fleeing the advances of Pan. The topic continues at line 13, with verb changed to noun (*fuga*), as Statius turns specifically to the situation of Pholoe, taking flight from the approaching god. In each instance we are witnessing an escape from the brutality of unwanted violence, a condition out of place in the calm ambience of *placidus* Melior. When we reach the poem's conclusion, we find the personified *gloria* of Blaesus also in a position of flight, not from immediate hurt but from something more intangible, namely the clutches of time and the corrosion that accompanies it. But here the ultimate outcome is a happy one. As befits the conclusion of a *genethliakon* in which longevity is a key theme, we end on a positive note, with continuity now taken for granted.

Early in *Silvae* 2.3 Statius calls on Apollo, the Naides, and the Fauni, for inspiration to tell the *causae*, the origins, of the various narrative strands to come, in particular the tale of Pholoe and Pan. By the time the poem reaches its finale, we, its readers are grateful for the quality and variety of the verse itself that their stimulus called into being. Whether we ponder the longevity of Pan's affectionate tree, the extent of Melior's paradigmatic life span, or the ever-freshness of Blaesus' epic *gloria*, we do so in terms of the abiding quality of the poetry through which such topics are exalted. We attend, in sum, to a work of literature that constructs a myth dedicated to enlivening a distinctive context. This combination of novel story and special setting has much to tell us about the larger symbiosis of life and art, of our transient human existence and of the imagination that retains the power to keep significant details steadily before us.

3

A Labour of Love (Statius' *Silvae* 3.1)

Silvae 3.1 consists of one substantial *aition* devoted ostensibly to the genesis and erection of a new temple to Hercules on the part of Pollius Felix on the shore of his estate at Surrentum. Its progress also takes the form of a meditation on several themes. Statius focuses specific attention on the conversion of Hercules from god of dauntless adventures into an aesthetic civilizer of a still brutish, undisciplined landscape, as well as on the humanity of his votary, Pollius, and the latter's wife, Polla. In the process we as readers enjoy a paean to the harnessing of extraordinary energy for the betterment of the earth and its denizens.

While we share in the rituals of athletics, religion, and verse-making, Statius at the same time grants us the opportunity to ponder larger issues such as the passage of time, as we deal with matters physical and spiritual, with questions of loss and endurance, evanescence, and permanence, of life and death, mortality and eternity. Eroticism in several nuanced guises is also a prominent topic.

The Poem's Opening and Hercules

As aids to our reading pleasure the poet has us regularly recall earlier Latin verse in a variety of genres, especially, but not exclusively, epic, lyric, and elegy. Not surprisingly, Virgil, and then Horace, loom largest among the poet's intellectual mentors, allusion to whom enriches the poem's course.[1] Hercules' monument suggests a type of tangible perpetuity. Its metaphysical complement is the poetry of Statius and the perhaps even more cogent memorialization that it tacitly promises through the resources of the imagination:

---

[1] I am indebted to the commentaries of Vollmer (1898) and Laguna Mariscal (1992), and in particular to the critical writings of Newlands (1991). More recent studies of *Silv.* 3.1 include Rühl (2006) 302–6; Newlands (2012) 149–56; Bessone (2022b). On Pollius in *Silv.* 2.2 (forming a diptych with this poem), see Rosati (2019).

The Poetic World of Statius' Silvae. Michael C. J. Putnam, Edited by: Antony Augoustakis with Carole E. Newlands, Oxford University Press. © Michael C. J. Putnam 2023. DOI: 10.1093/oso/9780192869272.003.0004

90 THE POETIC WORLD OF STATIUS' *SILVAE*

> Intermissa tibi renovat, Tirynthie, sacra
> Pollius et causas designat desidis anni
> quod coleris maiore tholo nec litora pauper
> nuda tenes tectumque vagis habitabile nautis
> sed nitidos postes Graisque effulta metallis
> culmina, ceu taedis iterum lustratus honesti
> ignis ab Oetaea conscenderis aethera flamma.
>
> (Stat. *Silv.* 3.1.1–7)

Pollius renews the interrupted rites for you, O Tirynthian, and outlines the reasons for the sluggish year, that you are worshipped under a grander dome, nor in poverty do you possess empty shores and a dwelling that houses roving sailors, but gleaming doorposts and roofs supported by Greek marbles (5) as though, purified once more by the torches of revering fire, you ascended to the heavens from Oeta's flame.

Statius appropriately begins his narrative of the history of a new place of worship for Hercules on the southern coast of the Bay of Naples with an apostrophe to the god himself, bringing to life before us one of the two main protagonists in the subsequent tale. The other major figure is the deity's mortal patron, Pollius Felix, who likewise receives rhetorical stress through the enjambment of his name at the beginning of the poem's second verse, a rhetorical figure that also keeps the reader waiting until he finds a subject for the initial line's verb. The complementary character of their relationship will prove a core to the poem's evolution, as Hercules becomes specifically Surrentine and a special part of his devotee's world.

But it is particularly to the god that Statius would have us attend. A primary means he employs for this purpose is simply the deployment of seven hexameters to form the poem's initial self-contained paragraph. This arrangement is a signpost for the opening of epic, a tradition initiated by the *Iliad* of Homer, whose opening septet of lines begins and ends with a mention of the poem's central hero, Achilles, whose inclination to destructive wrath leads to his particular strife with Agamemnon. This model is echoed at the start of Virgil's *Aeneid*, the influence of which will pervade Statius' composition. The first seven verses that form its exordium take us from *Troiae* to *Romae* which is to say through the course of the epic's storyline from the downfall of the hero's natal city to the prelude in Italy of the foundation of what will ultimately prove to be one of the world's centres of power. Virgil awards none of the prominence that Homer gives Achilles at the opening of the *Iliad* to Aeneas who is not named until the poem's

A LABOUR OF LOVE (STATIUS' *SILVAE* 3.1) 91

ninety-second line. At his epic's start he is simply a *virum* as if his individuality, his intrepid persona, were subsumed by, and absorbed into, the august sweep of Rome's evolution.

Statius offers us a carefully parallel disposition of verses but for a different purpose. Instead of tracing the advance of empire from east to west, from loss to renewal, with no immediate mention of the epic's main character, our poet, like Homer, has us concentrate on the curriculum of one remarkable individual, allusions to whose varied acts of valour pepper the subsequent narrative. The opening apostrophe, *Tirynthie*, not only rivets our attention directly on Hercules at the start, just as the *Iliad* concentrates on Achilles, but also reminds us of Tiryns, his place of origin, and therefore of the initiation of an extraordinary career. Then, at the conclusion of this powerful grouping, we find ourselves on Mt. Oeta, bearing witness to the pyre whose flames waft the dying hero heavenward.[2] We thus follow his *vita* from birth to death but we also watch the extraordinary turn his particular biography takes as we move from the Argolid to the ether, from earth to heaven, while contemplating the *curriculum vitae* of a human who sheds his mortality and undergoes apotheosis to become part of the community of gods.

This distinguished metamorphosis, traced over the prefatory hexameters, embraces a series of smaller but cumulative changes to which we will turn in a moment. But first we should follow out some suggestions of the opening verses. The word *renovat*, for instance, alerts us to the fact that this is to be a poem about renewal and refreshment not only of the rites of Hercules but of the whole Surrentine setting.[3] (It also intimates the inventiveness of the

---

[2] Mention of Oeta leads us back to two earlier references to the mountain in Latin literature. The first occurs in the second epithalamium of Catullus where the chorus of youths announces that the Evening Star (*Noctifer*) is displaying his 'Oetaean fires' (*Oetaeos...ignes*, 62.7) to mark the time when a wedding ceremony can commence. We find the second in Virgil (*Ecl.* 8.30) where once more the Evening Star (now called *Hesperus*), departing from Oeta, serves as herald of the proper time for nuptials to start. Statius thus adds pastoral to his opening mix of genres and reinforces the presence of lyric. In terms of the career of Hercules it also adumbrates in particular his wedding that will take place, after his deification, to Hebe who is mentioned shortly later (26–7). At 1.13.23–4, Propertius more briskly conjoins 'Hercules' burning love for the goddess Hebe' (*caelestem flagrans amor Herculis Heben*) with *Oetaeis rogis* ('the pyre on Oeta'). So we can also at the start add elegy to the poem's rich generic blend. The allusions also point, more generally, to Hercules' domestication into a patron god who now enjoys peace and the refinements of art once his life of valiant deeds is past. For the 'history' of the god's deification from the flames on Mt. Oeta, see Cic. *N. D.* 3.41.10 (with Pease *ad loc.*).

[3] *Renovat*, in relation to Hercules, is also the first of many reminders of the eighth book of Virgil's *Aeneid* that dot Statius' text. At *A.* 8.189, Evander describes to Aeneas the due repetition of annual rites to Hercules on the Aventine (*meritos novamus honores*). For newness as a theme see also *novos* (66), *renovabo* (174), *nova* (177). It is complemented by the theme of birth (*nascentibus*, 28; *nascentes*, 163).

92 THE POETIC WORLD OF STATIUS' *SILVAE*

language that tells the tale.) We note, too, the alliterative connection between the words *designat* and *desidis*, which is to say between Pollius and the personified year (*annus*) that has now presumably cast off its sloth and reached a productive terminus, capped by the ceremonies that lie ahead. The verb *designat* summarizes the reasons why the *sacra* of Hercules have been kept in abeyance, but it also suggests the future role of Statius' patron as one of the planners of the impending aesthetic activities, drafting the outline of the great edifice soon to be constructed as well as calculating the refinement necessary to make the associated landscape seemly.[4] Taken together the two words introduce us to the visual and temporal spheres that will figure prominently in the text as it unfolds.

Embraced by the larger evolution of Hercules are a series of smaller transformations that anticipate the narrative to come. *Maiore* prepares us to expect a more distinguished edifice than the one that had previously sufficed as the god's place of veneration. He who had been poor (*pauper*) before will be graced with beautiful imports, and the naked seaside will see a building with doorposts arrayed in brightness and rooftops supported by stone quarried in Greece. Through the poet's positioning *vagis nautis*, sailors who come and go, give way to *Grais metallis*, suggesting the noble stability of attractive marbles. There the metonymy, as quarries stand for the marbles cut from them, calls attention to the visual manifestation of Pollius' love for things Greek to which Statius will later come back.[5]

During this rhetorical period of compressed intensity, as we move from the rites offered to Hercules by man to that same hero's moment of deification, the reader's eye climbs first from seashore, and its combination of land and water, to a temple's heights, then to Mt. Oeta with its ritual fire and, finally, from there to the ether of the gods' heaven—an itinerary followed by our inner eye that expertly manipulates the four elements to complement Hercules' own route skyward.

The poem's opening paragraph thus encapsulates a chronicle of superhuman effort and creativity that we are about to discover, a tale primarily centred on the building of a temple and on the concomitant celebrations at its completion. But its first word, *intermissa*, also plays an equally important role in aiding interpretation, one likewise centred on matters of genre as

---

[4] Virgil's two uses of the verb *designare* are connected with the delineation of a new city (*A.* 5.755 and 7.157). Ovid (*Met.* 6.103) is the first to give it the meaning depict, in connection with Arachne's tapestry.

[5] The word *Grais* also helps make the transition from the shore at Surrentum back to Greece and Mt. Oeta.

A LABOUR OF LOVE (STATIUS' *SILVAE* 3.1) 93

well as of tone. Since this is also the initial word of the opening poem of Horace's fourth book of *Carmina*, commencing with the announcement of Venus' 'battles' which the aging poet now has to forego, Statius asks us to take advantage of our knowledge of the ode to open up a new angle of approach from which further to enlarge our present reading experience.[6]

This additional approach to interpretation takes two forms, the general and the particular. First the general: the opening hexameters forewarned us that we were about to enter a poetic world with similarities to epic, that we would soon gain pleasure from an 'occasional' poem that resonated with aspects of a more expansive, supposedly more prestigious, genre devoted to grandiose accomplishment in whatever form. We are about to experience a spacious style of writing, and Statius does not disappoint. But reference to Horace also prepares us to appreciate a narrative that is also permeated by elements of lyric, broadly considered. This is to say that we will be entering a world where culture is brought to nature, where its inhabitants respect architectural grace, music, and poetry, and thrive on peace as a core value. We will share in the specifics of a life where personal warmth, especially as focused on a consequential moment in the life of a person of eminence, will also be of importance as leavening within the account of remarkable events that form the poem's larger perspective.

Some specifics overlap between the two poems. Statius' repetition of *intermissa* takes us from Horace's metaphorical *bella* to the real *sacra* of Hercules that were suspended for a period of time. But our expectation of *bella* also serves to suggest that a major project in what follows is Hercules' renunciation of the martial physicality that pervades his career in favour of the human, even amatory, aspects of his saga. Horace's powerful ode also deals with the life of an accomplished lawyer, Paullus Fabius Maximus, whom the poet imagines building a temple, on this occasion to Venus, around which are held appropriate festivities.[7] But it also comments movingly on one of the genre's major topics, the encroachment of temporality. We enter the bittersweet domain of sexuality, lost and for a brief moment

---

[6] For Statius' penchant for references to Horace in his opening lines, see Vollmer (1898) 386 and Laguna Mariscal (1992) 128. Newlands (2002) 160 n. 21, remarks that Statius' other poem that deals with Pollius' estate, *Silv.* 2.2, also starts with an allusion to Horace, on that occasion to *Carm.* 2.6.18–20.

[7] It is not coincidental that the adjective *facundus*, applied to Pollius by Statius at line 65, is employed by Horace to describe his own tongue which now loses its charm in the face of Ligurinus' enervating influence (*facunda... lingua*, *Carm.* 4.1.35–6). It is well to remember an ancient etymology of *facundus* as *fatu iucundus* ('delightful at speaking'). See Maltby (1991) s.v. *facundus* (220).

94 THE POETIC WORLD OF STATIUS' *SILVAE*

regained, in the speaker's dreams of a beloved youth, handsome but now beyond possessing. We thus also share in lyric's equally universal complement to desire, its mutations and ultimate disappearance, and to beauty with its similar challenges, namely the infinite power of time over our existence.

We watch the aging poet coping with the losses that life's passage brings about, as it advances from its dayspring to its evening. Through Statius we will meditate on the same topic as we follow the career of Hercules from his birth as a human to his final position as a divinity beyond the reach of mortality's clutches, and in the process we will be treated to a précis of his prominent erotic feats. We will also admire the affection that passes among Pollius, Polla, and their family, and ponder, as well, their patron god's attempt to keep senescence at bay complemented by his pledge of permanence for his temple, an Horatian *monumentum aere perennius* in the making.[8] What Hercules promises to secure perhaps poetic genius will fully assure.

The apostrophe in each opening line deserves a further word.[9] We move from Horace's appeal to Venus, appropriate for a poem on yearning, its initiation and vanishing, to *Tirynthie*, the formidable key figure of the poem called to our attention through his place of origin. This is the first of only two appearances of the vocative form of *Tirynthius* in Latin.[10] It is also remarkable how close a resemblance the word bears to *Ligurine*, the object of Horace's affection, when he is finally addressed at line 33 of *Carm.* 4.1. Both are four syllables long and both share in virtually the same vowel sounds. The reminiscence is calculated. Statius may be advising us that heroic deeds will now replace amatory longing in the poem that follows. But he may also be gently forewarning his readers that there is also a Venusian presence, an element of varied sexuality, in his own poem that must be reckoned with:[11]

---

[8] We remember that Horace continues with the boast that his poetic memorial is 'loftier than the royal structure of the pyramids' (*regali...situ pyramidum altius*, *Carm.* 3.30.2) with its play on another word *situs* with the meaning of decay. Unlike the pyramids, Hercules' monument may well be completely saved from time's implicit ravages by the magic power of words.

[9] For apostrophe as a lyric gesture, see Smith (2007).

[10] The second appearance is at Stat. *Silv.* 4.6.90. The first uses of the toponym *Tirynthius* are at Virg. *A.* 7.662 and 8.228 where the accompanying language is a clear influence here on Statius who uses the adjective again at 125 and 136. With *Silv.* 3.1.5 (*postes...effulta*), cf. *A.* 8.227 (*fultos...postis*), in the story of Hercules and Cacus. *Effulta* is apparently a Virgilian coinage (*A.* 7.94), reused by Statius in a similar context at *Theb.* 1.145.

[11] For a different way of appreciating Statius' reference to Horace here see Newlands (1991) 440–1, (2002). See above, n. 6.

A LABOUR OF LOVE (STATIUS' *SILVAE* 3.1)   95

> vix oculis animoque fides. tune ille reclusi
> liminis et parvae custos inglorius arae?
> unde haec aula recens fulgorque inopinus agresti
> Alcidae? sunt fata deum, sunt fata locorum.
>
> (Stat. Silv. 3.1.8–11)

Scarcely do eyes and mind have trust! Are you that lowly guardian of a doorless threshold and a little altar? Whence this newly made residence and unexpected brightness for rustic (10) Alcides? Gods have destinies, places have destinies.

Just as Virgil uses the word *vix* to initiate the actual plot line of the *Aeneid* (1.34), so Statius takes advantage of its sense of immediacy to lead us dynamically into his own narrative. In Virgil we are drawn briskly into events that will dramatically change the course of the hero's fated journey. Statius, by contrast, insists that his reader pause and absorb with sudden amazement what history has lately accomplished. The suppression of verbs in lines 8–10 asks for our concentration on the physical details of the poet's presentation, and the combination of eye and mind, in which we can scarcely put our trust because of the miracle it seems to put before us, will in its own way also be crucial for an appreciation of what follows.

Put more generally, the notion of external observation leading to reflective understanding, which in turn is preserved in writing of quality, could serve as a definition of ekphrasis, a rhetorical device to which Statius will have regular recourse in the verses to come. On more than one occasion, for instance, we will be asked to remember Aeneas, enthralled before the murals in Dido's temple to Juno or in ignorance staring at vignettes excerpted from Rome's chronology as detailed on Vulcan's expressive shield.

Statius now conveys the wonderment that often accompanies ekphrastic moments by means of two interrogative statements that could equally well serve as exclamations. The flow of events is, as often, a crucial ingredient in such descriptions, taking the reader from then to now. Statius here effects the transition by turning from the implicit distance of the demonstrative pronoun (*ille*) to the intimate immediacy of the personal pronoun (*tu*).[12] The former Hercules, with nothing to boast about, had been locally honoured with a shrine apparently without doors and containing only a small altar. The change, from a past that we are required to imagine to a

---

[12] Virgil achieves much the same effect at *A.* 1.617 where Dido addresses Aeneas (*tune...ille*). Cf. also *A.* 9.481 and Stat. *Theb.* 7.500 (Jocasta to Polynices).

96 THE POETIC WORLD OF STATIUS' *SILVAE*

present vividly before our eyes, is first accomplished through another pronoun, *haec*, used as a deictic. We now directly see the metamorphosis of his place of worship from something serving only an unsophisticated individual into an aristocratic *aula*, just as 'you', Hercules, esteem it with us, too. The bumpkin, grandson of the mortal Alcaeus,[13] is now honoured with brilliance suitable to his divine status. It is not long since we have heard of *nitidos postes* and Greek marbles, and the small altar (*parva ara*) has already been superseded by a larger dome (*maiore tholo*).

Interrogatives turn directly to exclamation at line 11 as the speaker connects the intertwined destinies of gods and of places. The saying is generalized, but our poem is concerned with a particular divinity and a particular location. We have seen details of how Pollius' Surrentine beach now sports a dynamic, newly magnified place of worship for Hercules. We will now have the opportunity to value the poet's elegant version of when and how this dramatic turn of events took place:

> o velox pietas! steriles hic nuper harenas
> ad sparsum pelago montis latus hirtaque dumis
> saxa nec ulla pati faciles vestigia terras
> cernere erat. quaenam subito fortuna rigentes
> ditavit scopulos? Tyrione haec moenia plectro
> an Getica venere lyra? stupet ipse labores
> annus et angusti bis seno limite menses
> longaevum mirantur opus. deus attulit arces
> erexitque suas, atque obluctantia saxa
> summovit nitens et magno pectore montem
> reppulit: immitem credas iussisse novercam.
>
> (Stat. Silv. 3.1.12–22)

O swift piety! Here recently there were to behold barren sands, at a mountainside splashed by the sea, and rocks shaggy with thickets and terrain unready to endure any footprints. What good luck suddenly enriched stiff (15) crags? Did these walls come into place by means of Tyrian quill or Getic lyre? The year itself is amazed at the efforts, and the months, confined by their twice-six course, marvel at the timeless work. A god brought and raised his towers, and through struggle removed the opposing boulders (20) and with his mighty chest pushed back the mountain. You might believe that his pitiless stepmother had given the order.

---

[13] Hercules is also called Alcides at 51, 83, and 162, perhaps as a reminder of his human side.

A LABOUR OF LOVE (STATIUS' *SILVAE* 3.1)   97

The opening seven lines of the poem advise us that elements of epic will suffuse the account that follows. The exclamation *o velox pietas* suggests that we think specifically of the *Aeneid* and the distinguishing characteristic of its eponymous protagonist. This, as we will see, is appropriate for Pollius as he expands Hercules' place of veneration. It is also vicariously suitable for the great hero god himself who, as the poet would have it, strongly assists in the endeavour.[14]

Statius has in store in the next sentence a more exact reference to Virgil's masterpiece: *cernere erat*. He holds the words in abeyance until the end of the period and gives them further emphasis through enjambment. He would have us recall line 676 of *Aeneid* 8. There the phrase, equally enjambed, helps introduce us to the battle of Actium as it is portrayed on Aeneas' shield whose decoration, as we mentioned, illustrates events in the history of Rome from the birth of Romulus and Remus to the triumph celebrated by Octavian after his great victory. Statius thus places us, as we become modern exemplars of Aeneas for a moment, centrally in one of the most famous specimens of ekphrasis in Latin letters.[15] The result is twofold. In the reader's mind it raises the importance of the present narrative, as it evolves, to epic stature. Pollius' and in particular Hercules' taming of a piece of property, in preparation for the magnification of his temple, will be a labour worthy of incorporation in the annals of the grandest of verse.

The allusion also has the effect of asking us to employ our inner eyes to conjure up what is being depicted in words. This consists here in imagining the landscape as it existed until recently. Virgil helps our visualization when, in his didactic mode, he urges his husbandman to tend a certain type of soil in September:...*sterilem exiguus ne deserat umor harenam* ('...lest the slim moisture abandon the barren sand', *G.* 1.70). If the farmer does not turn the soil to keep the water in, we presume that it will become too light and therefore infertile. Pollius and Hercules will accomplish something more remarkable, the implication is. They will persist until what lately had been useless, sandy, and dashed by seawater, will now appear to the viewer both refined and generative.

---

[14] We hear of Aeneas' *pietas* already at *A.* 1.10 (...*insignem pietate uirum*), a phrase echoed at 6.403. We will see Pollius emerge as a type of Aeneas, as well as of his father, Anchises, as the poem progresses.

[15] One major difference between this aspect of *Silv.* 3.1 and *A.* 8 is that here we are made to appear actually privy to the 'history' of what we see evolving before us. Aeneas, by contrast, is uninitiated into the future and therefore 'ignorant of the matters' (*rerum...ignarus*, 730) in whose depiction (*imagine*) he rejoices.

98   THE POETIC WORLD OF STATIUS' *SILVAE*

The land had recently also consisted of *hirtaque dumis/saxa* (3.1.13–14). Again, critics are correct to turn to Virgil for a parallel, in this case to the *Aeneid* where Evander takes Aeneas on a tour of the site of future Rome.[16] After showing him the Argiletum, 'from here he leads [him] to the Tarpeian house and to the Capitolium, golden now, once bristling with thickets of trees' (*hinc ad Tarpeiam sedem et Capitolia ducit/aurea nunc, olim siluestribus horrida dumis*, *A.* 8.347–8). The Capitolium, in the past cloaked with thickets, is now golden, in reality and figuratively, as we apprehend it in our thoughts as emblematic of the magnificent age of Augustus. Pollius and Hercules will bring about a similar metamorphosis at Surrentum as they not only give arrangement to the rocks, rough with underbrush, but also embellish them with a resplendent edifice.

But Statius adds still further nuance to his description through the attribute *hirta* that in effect personifies the rocks we are examining, shaggy, as if their attachments were a type of beard that belonged to a human face. In a unique metaphoric use of the adjective,[17] Horace applies the adjective, now negated, to the innate talent of Julius Florus:...*non tibi parvum/ingenium, non incultum est et turpiter hirtum*...('...your intelligence is not small, not untrained and unpleasantly shaggy...', Hor. *Ep.* 1.3.21–2). Following Horace's lead, Statius suggests that not only do Pollius and Hercules adorn the terrain, they also cultivate it, both literally and metaphorically, as if it were a mind in need of guidance. They bring civilization to it.

Finally, in the list of the land's attributes for us to envision in time gone by, we are to imagine 'ground that was not open to tolerating any footsteps' (*nec ulla pati faciles vestigia terras*). Statius here glances at the eulogy of the farmer's world with which Virgil concludes the second book of the *Georgics*:...*extrema per illos/Iustitia excedens terris vestigia fecit* ('...through their midst Justice placed her final footprints as she withdrew from the earth', *G.* 2.473–4). Hercules' education of the land reverses its former intractability and makes it now amenable to receiving human steps. Again, we are to engage our inner eye in imagining terrain that had never been trodden but on which people could now walk. If the poet would have us think directly of the passage from Virgil, then he is complimenting the new caretakers, human and divine, by suggesting a parallel between them and the goddess of justice who would find a ready welcome in the precinct of a

---

[16] Bessone (2022b) treats at length the close relationship that *Silv.* 3.1 has with the eighth book of the *Aeneid*.

[17] See Mayer (1994) 129.

A LABOUR OF LOVE (STATIUS' *SILVAE* 3.1)   99

man who, as we soon learn, loves peace and the Muses' songs. The two interrogative sentences that follow, expressions of astonishment at what the poet would have us behold through his verbal wizardry, are as much summaries as queries. The crags that had once been unyielding (*rigentes*) are now suddenly decorated by the favour of fortune. We will later contemplate again the *rigidas rupes* (167), the rugged rocks whose implicit primitivism, in words Statius gives to Hercules, has been tamed by the instruction of Pollius. Here the act of teaching is treated metaphorically as a skill that in several senses brightens its surroundings, like the Capitolium that becomes gilded through the cleverness of man. With its past barrenness in mind as a touchstone, we now see before us a transformed landscape, both fertile and handsomely decorated. The deictic *haec*, attached to *moenia*, especially invites us to picture closely the magnificence of the altered tract of ground with its splendid temple to Hercules, as if it were the metaphoric equivalent of the walls of Thebes. The enormous compliment adumbrates a parallel of Hercules and Pollius with Amphion or Orpheus. The former are the contemporary equivalents of the two famous singers of myth who through their music-making, their imagination's extraordinary power expressed in sound, could not only captivate dolphins and charm the world of the dead but also make inanimate nature do their inventive bidding, as art moves the ordinarily unmovable.[18]

At line 17, Statius modulates our concentration away from space toward time through the personification of the year, already mentioned at line 2, that it took the work to be accomplished, and of the twelve individual months that made up its span.[19] He heightens the figuration by further recourse to ekphrasis, once again with a bow to Virgil. The word *stupet*, in association with *mirantur* that follows in line 19, as the year looks in amazement at what has been achieved during its course, takes us to *Aeneid* 1 and to Aeneas as he bides his time while anticipating the arrival of Dido: *haec dum Dardanio Aeneae miranda videntur,/dum stupet obtutuque haeret defixus in uno…* ('While these seem worthy of wonder to Dardanian Aeneas, while he is amazed and clings transfixed in a single gaze', *A.* 1.494–5).[20] The hero has been mesmerized by the scenes of Troy's collapse that decorate

---

[18] Statius would have us also acknowledge the astonishing suddenness of the event (*subito*, 15). Cf. also *subiti* (49) and *subitis* (71).

[19] The word *labores* (17) announces a motif, appropriate for a poem in which Hercules is central, that continues with 116 and 123 (*labor*), and 166 (*labores*).

[20] See also the discussion of *Silv.* 4.2 and these allusions to *Aeneid* 1, in pp. 192–8 in this volume.

100   THE POETIC WORLD OF STATIUS' *SILVAE*

the temple to Juno that the Carthaginian ruler has been constructing. Statius thus proposes that his reader re-imagine the first great example of ekphrasis in the epic, its longest except for the shield of Aeneas. The allusion is confirmed by reference back to parallel language in the verses that serve as prelude to the same description. Aeneas awaits the monarch's advent:…*dum quae fortuna sit urbi/artificumque manus inter se operumque laborem/miratur*…('…while he marvels at the city's good-fortune and the handiwork of the group of artisans and the effort of their accomplishments…', *A.* 1.454–6). In the first reference, *stupet* is linked with *miranda*. In the second *operum* and *miratur* are nearly adjacent. Statius draws on both associations as he reminds us, first, of the introduction and then of the conclusion of the Virgilian description. It is a god who has brought all this about. Like Amphion and the *moenia* of Thebes—and later, at line 115, we hear more directly of the *Amphioniae arces*—he has wondrously carried towers and put them in place. And, as we have already heard and will soon learn in greater detail, he has won the challenge against humanized rocks, which contend against him, and hyperbolically thrust back the defiant mountain by means of his own burly chest.[21]

The conclusion of this brief look at the changes in the visual prospect before us comes with an extraordinary line:…*immitem credas iussisse novercam* (22). The results, incorporated in what we have been contemplating, are parallel to aspects of those stemming from the god's twelve labours, imposed on him by Eurystheus because of the unforgiving jealousy of his stepmother, the goddess Juno. The reluctant natural world has been shaped for the better, its wildness subdued to receive the majestic eminence to be placed upon it.

The word *credas* has special relevance on several levels. It draws the reader, become viewer, into the conversation and asks 'you' to turn the observed into the understood, what is physically eyed into what is valued inwardly. It also serves a marked figurative purpose. The phrase *cernere erat* (15) had taken us to *A.* 8.676 and specifically to the battle of Actium as crafted by Vulcan on the famous shield.[22] The word *credas* takes us fifteen

---

[21] With *nitens* (21), cf. Virg. *A.* 8.237 where Hercules is also straining (*nitens*) against a rock that is part of a mountain (191, 221, 231).

[22] Cf. also *A.* 6.596 where the phrase initiates a list of the damned, commencing with Tityus. For further analysis, see Newlands (2013) 70–1, though I would argue against the suggestion that 'the image of the barren landscape is not present before our eyes'. A comparison on our part of visions of the topographical setting both before and after the intervention of Hercules and Pollius seems essential to the poet's point. A major aspect of the hero's epic

A LABOUR OF LOVE (STATIUS' *SILVAE* 3.1)   101

lines later, to verse 691 of the same book, as the depiction of the scene continues. Again 'you', the reader, are asked to turn witnessing into believing, with the poet now relying on analogy to make his point. As designed by the god of fire, the ships opposing each other are so huge that they seem like Cyclades, or like mountains, clashing. We, in the know, are with uninformed Aeneas, watching an artist's rendering of an episode that demands of us that we adjust our vision into accepting what we see, whatever its apparent peculiarities, as truth.

The resulting recourse to ekphrasis as a means of claiming the reader's vigilance is especially potent. The segment of our poem from lines 15 to 22 is bracketed by means of references to *Aeneid* 8. In between we have a series of allusions to *Aeneid* 1. All the citations are concerned with depictions of works of art, the two lengthiest in the epic, thus presented chiastically with one double set of references poised within another. We visualize on the page a quadruple bow to the greatest examples of this noted type of rhetorical usage in Virgil's poem. The effect on Statius' part is further to rivet our attention on his own delineation of an undisciplined plot of earth after it has taken exquisite form under the tutelage of a designing god and his mortal colleague:

> ergo age, seu patrios liber iam legibus Argos
> incolis et mersum tumulis Eurysthea calcas,
> sive tui solium Iouis et virtute parata
> astra tenes haustumque tibi succincta beati
> nectaris excluso melior Phryge porrigit Hebe,
> huc ades et genium templis nascentibus infer.
> non te Lerna nocens nec pauperis arva Molorchi
> nec formidatus Nemees ager antraque poscunt
> Thracia nec Pharii polluta altaria regis,
> sed felix simplexque domus fraudumque malarum
> inscia et hospitibus superis dignissima sedes.
>
> (Stat. *Silv*. 3.1.23–33)

Come, therefore, whether, free now from its laws, you dwell in the Argos of your fathers and trample on Eurystheus, sunk in his tomb, whether you reside at the throne of your Jupiter and among the stars, won by your courage (25), and Hebe, her tunic gathered up, better than the relegated

---

accomplishment is the enrichment (*ditavit*, 16) of an impoverished milieu by gracing it with beauty, as much a spiritual as a physical improvement.

102   THE POETIC WORLD OF STATIUS' *SILVAE*

Phrygian, proffers to you a draught of blessed nectar: be present here and bring your guardian spirit to your temple as it comes into being. Neither injurious Lerna demands you nor the lands of penniless Molorchus nor the terrifying field of Nemea nor the caves (30) of Thrace nor the defiled altars of the Pharian king, but a home both happy and innocent, and ignorant of evil deceits, and a dwelling most worthy of guests from heaven.

The poem's opening seven lines took us on an arc through the earthly life of Hercules by means of reference to his birth (*Tirynthie*) and then to his assumption of immortality (*Oetaea*). At line 23, as we ponder the hero's present location, we follow a parallel trajectory. He might be at Argos, the neighbour—and here equivalent—of Tiryns, where he would be free from the extraordinary constraints imposed by Eurystheus whose tomb he can scorn. He could also be enjoying his role as god, now possessing the stars at the throne of Jupiter because of his supernatural *virtus*.[23] In particular, he will be proffered a drink of blissful nectar by Hebe who will become his spouse.

Statius calls attention to the celestial setting by the curious phrase *excluso Phryge*. Ganymede is usually considered the successor of Hebe as cupbearer to the gods.[24] By relegating the Trojan lover of Jupiter from the honorific role and replacing him with the goddess of youth, the poet eliminates any hint of pederasty in the behaviour of Hercules. No Ligurinus, in whatever guise, will be part of the god's everlasting life. But, as we have seen, Horace's imagined *inamorato* also symbolizes the poet-speaker's young years that have been slipping away and, more particularly, the comeliness of early love that is now out of reach of the aging, time-ridden speaker. Statius replaces Ganymede/Ligurinus with Hebe, the glamorous goddess who personifies Iuventas itself. Unlike the human Horace, Hercules not only gains immortality as a god. By marrying Hebe, he also lays specific claim to everlasting youth.

It is a moment of birth for the new temple as well, and Statius honours the event, and his poetic past, with a specific allusion, this time to Tibullus.[25] The only other occurrence in classical Latin of the phrase *huc ades et genium*

---

[23] Virgil's only use of the form *solium* is also in connection with the throne of Jupiter (*Iovis...solium*, *A.* 12.849) which is attended by the Furies. As so often Statius replaces a gloomy with a favourable context.

[24] Cf. Servius' comment *ad A.* 1.28 (*remota Hebe*).

[25] The first of eight appearances of forms of the word *templum* occurs at line 28 (the others are at 46, 49, 82, 106, 109, 138, 180, and we have the metonymy, *tholo*, at 3). The repetition speaks to both continuity and stability. For the phrase *huc ades*, cf. Virg. *Ecl.* 2.45, 7.9, 9.39 and 43, all contexts where lovers are in the act of summoning their partners.

A LABOUR OF LOVE (STATIUS' *SILVAE* 3.1)   103

is to be found at line 49 of the seventh poem in the first book of the elegist's corpus. There the god Osiris, the Egyptian Bacchus with power over the living and the dead, is invited to join the birthday celebration of the poet's patron, Messalla. The compliment to the latter is enormous but so is the allusion on the part of Statius to Tibullus' cletic hymn, inviting the immortal to a ceremony of celebration. The homage does rich honour to Hercules by calling attention to the expansive range of his divine power and, therefore, all the more to the importance of his attendance at the dedication of his shrine as it comes into being.

This is not the occasion for the poet to dwell on the challenging events that tested the hero's mettle during his enterprising past. Nevertheless, Statius takes time to recall for us some salient points in his biography, not least to help form a contrast with his reception by Pollius. *Lerna nocens*, for instance, leads us to the Argolid and Hercules' challenging second labour. Molorchus and then *formidatus Nemees ager* are direct reminders of the slaying of Nemea's lion. With *antra Thracia* our eye moves north and east, to the flesh-eating horses of Diomedes, and with mention of the *Pharii…altaria regis* we are in Egypt with Busiris who offered up strangers as human sacrifices.[26] We will come upon nothing similar in the ambience described in *Silv.* 3.1. The *antra* that we meet either house the creative forges of Vulcan on Lemnos (131) or serve as dwellings of the verdant Nereides who prepare to watch the incipient games (144). And the poem's *altaria* (184) are devoted not to nefarious murders but to the worship of Hercules whose career was partially spent purging the world of the likes of Diomedes and Busiris.

Instead we find ourselves in the appropriately *felix* home of Pollius Felix. Nothing sinister lurks here: *sed felix simplexque domus fraudumque malarum/inscia et hospitibus superis dignissima sedes* (Stat. *Silv.* 3.1.32–3). The career of Hercules has certainly been neither fully *felix*, which is to say blessed by fortune, nor *simplex*, straightforward and, in a moral sense, guileless. In fact, it abounds in the ambiguities of valorous deeds, whether in fact or as told in story. Nor could it be said to be ignorant of 'evil deceits'. Here Horace can help us to a further understanding. Statius is thinking of one of the lyricist's greatest odes, *Carm.* 1.3, which is addressed to his friend

---

[26] The combination of direct mention of Eurystheus (24) and Molorchus (29) along with indirect reference to Busiris (31) takes the reader back to the opening of Virg. *G.* 3, lines 4, 5, and 19, where all are mentioned in connection with Virgil's imagined temple of poetry to be written on behalf of Caesar Augustus.

104   THE POETIC WORLD OF STATIUS' *SILVAE*

Virgil as he embarks on a treacherous sea voyage which many critics, correctly in my view, consider metaphoric for the challenges the poet faced as he wrote the *Aeneid*, a poem, as we regularly see, of special importance to Statius. The lyric focuses on the destruction wreaked upon humankind by immoral overreachers, a category which later in the poem includes Hercules himself when we hear of *Herculeus labor* (36), the perverse effort it took on the future god's part to rifle the Underworld and return alive. At lines 27–31, Horace looks particularly at Prometheus who, against the wishes of the immortals, stole fire from its home in the heavens (*aetheria domo*) for man's use:

> audax Iapeti genus
>   ignem fraude mala gentibus intulit;
> post ignem aetheria domo
>   subductum macies et nova febrium
> terris incubuit cohors…
>
> (Hor. *Carm.* 1.3.27–31)

The bold offspring of Iapetus by evil deceit brought fire to humankind; after fire was brought down from its home in heaven gauntness and a novel band of fevers brooded over the earth…

We will return to the ode in more detail. Here the comparison with Horace underscores the absence in this setting of any form of criminal treachery of the sort practiced by the Titan. In the earthly home of happy Pollius there is no room for any similar, unworthy behaviour or, the implication remains, specifically for the presence of a Hercules who had on occasion been given to such conduct.[27] He, too, is now to be guileless in his demeanour as he begins to share in a dwelling that is worthiest of all for visits from the gods:

> pone truces arcus agmenque immite pharetrae
> et regum multo perfusum sanguine robur
> instratumque umeris dimitte rigentibus hostem.
> hic tibi Sidonio celsum pulvinar acantho
> texitur et signis crescit torus asper eburnis.
> pacatus mitisque veni, nec turbidus ira

---

[27] Forms of the word *domus*, like its synonym *tectum*, mark the poem, appearing at 63, 79, 96, 183, as well as 32. Ancient etymologies also connected the verb *domo*, which appears at 168, with *domus*. Cf. also *indomitus* (122). For further detail, see Maltby (1991) 195.

A LABOUR OF LOVE (STATIUS' *SILVAE* 3.1) 105

nec famulare timens, sed quem te Maenalis Auge
confectum thiasis et multo fratre madentem
detinuit qualemque vagae post crimina noctis
Thespius obstupuit, totiens socer. hic tibi festa
gymnas et insontes iuvenum sine caestibus irae
annua veloci peragunt certamina lustro.   45
hic templis inscriptus avo gaudente sacerdos
parvus adhuc similisque tui cum prima novercae
monstra manu premeres atque exanimata doleres.

(Stat. *Silv.* 3.1.34–48)

Put aside your fierce bows and the pitiless array in your quiver and your cudgel deeply drenched in the blood of kings (35) and doff the enemy spread on your stiff shoulders. Here for you a lofty couch is interwoven with Sidonian acanthus and a bolster expands, rough with ivory figures. Come, calm and mild, not swollen with anger or fearful in slavish fashion, but you, wearied with revelry and drunk with your brother's abundance, whom Maenalian Auge (40) held, and such as Thespius was astonished at, so many times a father-in-law, after your many capers during a wandering night (45). Here your festival games and the harmless angers of gloveless youths carry out annual contests as five years rush by. Here in your temple a priest is enrolled, to his grandfather's joy, still a child, and like you when you crushed with your hand your stepmother's first serpents and grieved at their demise.

The speaker now commands the god to be appropriately dressed and accoutred for the place and the occasion. This means ridding himself of his *truces arcus*, bows personified as fierce because such was their wielder when they were used in combat.[28] The 'pitiless array of your quiver' (*agmen immite pharetrae*) must also go. Metaphorically his arrows have the equivalent capability of a troop of soldiers. They, too, are without mercy, like their possessor who, we soon are told, must now become *mitis* (39), their opposite, in order to fit with Pollius' irenic setting.[29] No instruments of deadly combat are welcome in the world of Surrentum. Such patently impressive moments are to be put aside.

---

[28] Cf. *Ilias* 561: *pone truces animos infestaque tela coerce* ('Put aside your fierce anger and control your furious weapons'). The scene is drawn from *Iliad* 6 where Diomedes speaks to Glaucus, an epic setting where one hero asks the other for an end to combat.

[29] With *pacatus mitisque*, cf. Hor. *Saec.* 33 where the now-unwarlike Apollo is described as *condito mitis placidusque telo* ('gentle and calm, with weapon put away').

106   THE POETIC WORLD OF STATIUS' *SILVAE*

This holds true for other standard parts of Hercules' weaponry, the cudgel, slathered with blood,[30] and the lion's skin to which Statius devotes an extraordinary hexameter: *instratumque umeris dimitte rigentibus hostem* (36). The line is built as a chiasmus centred around the command *dimitte*. The initial and final words of this verse receive special attention. The first is unexampled elsewhere, and the concluding *hostem* is a striking combination of metonymy and synecdoche by means of which the enemy replaces the lion which is in turn particularized by its skin which acts as an impenetrable safeguard for the hero.[31] The word *rigentibus*, an emendation to which we will return in a moment, is the second of three appearances of the verb *rigeo* in the poem.[32] Statius uses it first at 15 (*rigentes scopulos*) to describe the stiff rocks that have now been ennobled by the god's new monument, and then again at 110 (*solidus riget umbo maligni/montis*) where Hercules faces the inflexible, spiteful shield of the mountain that needs to be pacified and given welcoming shape to receive his magnificent place of honour. In the case of *rigentibus*, the god's shoulders have the appearance of inflexibility in Pollius' environment because he is still wearing one part of his armour in the form of the lion-pelt. Statius teases his readers with the irony that Hercules, the great tamer of monsters, has himself to suffer a form of pacification when making an appearance in the serene atmosphere of Surrentum. His martial character needs to be mollified, and its symbols— bows and quiver, club and hide—dispensed with before he can be deemed fitting as a steady resident.

Statius now turns to details of the setting that Pollius has prepared for the reception of Hercules: a *pulvinar*, appropriate for a divinity, and a cushion to ornament the couch's decoration: *hic tibi Sidonio celsum pulvinar acantho/texitur et signis crescit torus asper eburnis* (37–8). One is already lofty, the other grows before our eyes, as we absorb the configuration and colour of each. The word *Sidonio* has a particular resonance. The weaving on the couch is of acanthus leaves coloured purple with the dye for which Sidon was famous. But the adjective would remind any Virgilian of Sidonian Dido. Though on several occasions the poet of the *Aeneid* attaches the geographical attribute to the sovereign of Carthage as a reminder of her heritage,

---

[30] The initial use of *robur* as metonymy for Hercules' cudgel is by Virgil at *A*. 8.221.

[31] For the lion-skin as an instrument for inciting fear, cf. Virg. *A*. 7.669 where we find Aventinus, son of Hercules:...*horridus Herculeoque umeros innexus amictu* ('...grim and with his shoulders garbed in the cloak of Hercules').

[32] The emendation is by Gevartius (1616) in place of *gerentibus*, the reading of *M* (obelized by Liberman).

A LABOUR OF LOVE (STATIUS' *SILVAE* 3.1) 107

Statius has a particular passage in mind. He places us during Aeneas' arrival at Dido's palace at the moment when he is preparing to offer to his hostess guest-gifts, remnants from Troy, to be brought from his ships:

> ... pallam signis auroque rigentem
> et circumtextum croceo velamen acantho,
> ornatus Argivae Helenae, quos illa Mycenis,
> Pergama cum peteret inconcessosque hymenaeos,
> extulerat...

> (Virg. *A.* 1.648–52)

> ... a mantle stiff with figures and gold and a veil embroidered roundabout with yellow acanthus, the treasures of Helen of Argos which she had taken from Mycenae when she sought Pergamum and forbidden marriage...

The echo of *rigentem* in *rigentibus* acts as an introduction of one scene to the other, and the alteration from *croceo* to *Sidonio* reaffirms the link with Dido. The connection between the two passages is strengthened by several other parallels, among them the repetition of *signis* and of *acantho*, the latter at the line ending.[33] By means of the correspondences Statius draws us into a noble setting where visitors, especially if they are one of the immortals, are solemnly entertained and gifts exchanged. More specifically, Pollius would be a type of Aeneas, offering an elaborate *pulvinar* and *torus* to his divine visitor just as Aeneas bestows the *palla* and *velamen* of Helen on Dido. Hercules would thus find a partial analogue in the Carthaginian ruler, the receiver of suitable trappings from a visitor who, in the case of the god, will take up a semblance of enduring residency.[34] But there is a major difference. Aeneas, with pointed irony on Virgil's part, offers Dido symbols of an ill-fated journey and of a wedding that was not duly sanctioned. As so often in Statius' allusions to Virgil, the earlier author's troubling context is altered so that the new placement for his words remains inspiriting. No parallel to Helen's illicit liaison with Paris, and the resultant war between nations, will enter into the calm, gentle atmosphere of Pollius' family and his peninsular domain.[35]

---

[33] On the word *texitur*, see Bessone (2022b), who points to another allusion to Virg. *Ecl.* 10.71–3 (*texit... crescit*).

[34] Hercules is also parallel to Dido in that he brings elegance and order to the Surrentine landscape and helps build a temple to himself just as the ruler of Carthage is erecting an edifice dedicated to Juno.

[35] Put another way, Pollius is akin to a Dido, already gifted, preparing for an Aeneas-like hero who brings only good to his new residence.

108   THE POETIC WORLD OF STATIUS' *SILVAE*

As the poet further commands in line 39, the god is to arrive at peace (*pacatum*) and gentle (*mitis*), as we have seen. He is not to be in his vindictive mode, 'swollen with anger' (*turbidus ira*), akin to the Hercules of *Aeneid* 8 who is 'burning with anger' (*fervidus ira*, 230) as he pursues the wicked Cacus.[36] Instead, in Pollius' tranquil circumstances, Hercules, the stalwart hero with a reputation for physical prowess, manifests a more sensitive side as Hercules, the friend and lover. In this role he is not to feel the terror of enslavement, as in his relationship with Omphale. Rather, Statius would have us dwell on his liaison with Auge and on the astonishment of Thespius at the drunken gallant's elaborate manifestation of his virility.[37] In Pollius' world the wrathful battler is suitably replaced by the erotic adventurer whose amatory exploits would be more at home in elegy's lighter mode than in the seriousness of epic.[38]

Anger still has a place in this celebratory world but with a crucial alteration in tone. Statius carefully echoes *ira* (39) in *irae* (44) but we are now dealing with moments of indignation that are *insontes*, occasions for the guiltless competitiveness that is standard in athletic rivalry. But the poet appends one proviso: these events are to be *sine caestibus*, without the deadly boxing gloves weighted with metal that figure, for example, in the match between the Trojan Dares and the Sicilian Entellus in *Aeneid* 5. There, at line 410, the latter reminds his audience of the 'gloves and arms of Hercules himself' (*caestus ipsius et Herculis arma*), equipment with which the hero, returning home with the cattle of Geryon, had once killed Aeneas' half-brother Eryx. With knowledge of this past history Aeneas has the contestants fight with *caestus aequos* (424) and neither antagonist is done to death. Nevertheless, at the end of the episode Entellus, the victor, demonstrates the fatal force of a *caestus* (479) by using it to kill the bull offered to him as a prize. The implication remains, therefore, that, if he were to have

---

[36] The parallel is noted by Laguna Mariscal (1992) 143.

[37] *Multo fratre madentem* (41) anticipates *bacchatus* (163), with a change in metonymy from wine to the god of wine. Hercules, besotted with the help of his brother and ready for love's enterprises, gives way to the inebriated poet, inspired through wine to sing of his hero's new glory. The phrase resonates with the language of Catullus 101.9 where the poet's words of sorrow are 'dripping wet with a brother's tears' (*fraterno multum manantia fletu*). Catullus' elegiac sadness suffers metamorphosis into a different brother's revelry.

[38] The phrase *vagae noctis* is adopted from the first epithalamium of Catullus (*uaga nocte*, 61.110–11), where love's joys are the subject (for the second marriage hymn, see n. 2 above). Statius offers us a startling example of hypallage. In Catullus night roves through the sky in her chariot. Here it is Hercules, not the night, who does the figurative 'wandering', though *nox* could be said literally to abet his amorous exploits.

A LABOUR OF LOVE (STATIUS' *SILVAE* 3.1) 109

followed the model of Hercules, Dares might have been the human victim. Instead an animal serves as his surrogate.

Statius thus takes us back to the boxing bout of the *Aeneid* but with careful changes. As a general procedure, boxing contestants for the new games in honour of Hercules will don only harmless gloves. There will be no gauntlets in use with deadly potential. More specifically, Hercules will be in attendance, as a viewer and perhaps participant, but not one remembered for a past exhibition of his expertise which in this instance does not deserve emulation. Once again, with Virgil in mind, the poet turns negative to positive. The Hercules, who is ready to enjoy his incipient festivity, will leave behind his reputation as a boxer who brutally killed his opponent and instead, as a model of pacificity, will share in games where the young will utilize their energies only in sportive recreation, in contests that will return every five years.

As climax of this segment of the poem Statius employs the deictic *hic* for the third time in ten lines to place us directly at the new temple and to introduce Pollius' small grandson at the moment when, to the delight of his grandfather, he is inscribed as Hercules' priest, with all the cultural and moral prestige that such a position implies: *hic templis inscriptus avo gaudente sacerdos parvus adhuc/similisque tui cum prima novercae/monstra manu premeres atque exanimata doleres* (46–8). Once more the hero himself figures in the narrative as the poet draws a complimentary parallel between the new officiant and the baby Hercules, already coping with monsters as he would throughout his career. More specifically, through the word *manu* Statius allots the *parvus* a claim to the valour of the mythic hero, valour that is appropriately celebrated in the athletic games now offered in his honour.[39] Here again Statius has a particular passage from Virgil in mind to help in appreciating his own words. Not unexpectedly he returns to *Aeneid* 8.

After Evander tells the story of Hercules on the Aventine, the choruses of Salii sing the praises of his glorious deeds beginning, as follows: ... *ut prima novercae/monstra manu geminosque premens eliserit anguis* ... ('... when by crushing he strangled with his hand twin snakes, the first monsters of his stepmother ...', *A.* 8.288–9). The close parallel with Virgil points up Statius' omission of the phrase *geminos eliserit anguis* as if to downplay, in a setting devoted to the present gentleness of Hercules, the sheer physical violence of the child as he squeezed to death the twin serpents. Statius, however, adds

---

[39] *Manu* anticipates several further appearances of the word (118, 155, 157).

110   THE POETIC WORLD OF STATIUS' *SILVAE*

one signal detail to his Virgilian model, the phrase *exanimata doleres*. The later poet appends a touch of sympathy to the behaviour of the incipient warrior. His sadness for the victims, even of a necessary act of killing, serves, in Statius' telling of the event, to set an ethical standard already to be pondered by Pollius' young descendant. The portrayal is also suitable for the early life of the grand Hercules who now appears 'with his weapons set aside' (*positis armis*, 125). The enraged combatant of *Aeneid* 8, and of Seneca's *Hercules Furens*, whose behaviour might seem a bad precedent for the young and out of place in the world of *placidus* Pollius, is now purposefully missing.

The Temple of Hercules

> sed quaenam subiti, veneranda, exordia templi
> dic age, Calliope; socius tibi grande sonabit
> Alcides tensoque modos imitabitur arcu.
>
> (Stat. Silv. 3.1.49–51)

But, august Calliope, come and tell of the beginnings of this sudden temple; Alcides, your cohort, will make impressive sound (50) and imitate your music's measures on his stretched bowstring.

Statius' apostrophe to Calliope opens a new phase of his poem. For the next hundred lines or so we will be rewarded with an extended narrative, in the manner of epic, detailing for us the origin of the temple of Hercules and then its actual building. It is appropriate that the 'most important' of the Muses, according to Hesiod,[40] be addressed at this salient juncture in the poem's progress. But, as usual, allusions to Virgil, in this case to three diverse apostrophes, complicate and expand our intellectual horizon.

Let us turn first to Virgil's only direct address to Calliope herself. It occurs at *A.* 9.525 as the poet calls on the Muse, and by implication her sister goddesses, to grant him inspiration as he catalogues the slaughter that Turnus will inflict upon the enemy ranks: *vos, o Calliope, precor, aspirate canenti/ quas ibi tum ferro strages, quae funera Turnus/ediderit…* ('O Calliope, I pray, you [Muses] inspire me while I sing what slaughter then Turnus brought to pass there, what deaths, with his sword', *A.* 9.525–7). Statius would presumably have us turn the reference into its reverse and expect the following saga

---

[40] See Hes. *Theog.* 79. Calliope, we remember, is particularly associated with epic.

A LABOUR OF LOVE (STATIUS' *SILVAE* 3.1)   111

to have a promising meaning with superhuman energy being expended on a majestic endeavour of a worthwhile sort.[41]

The second Virgilian apostrophe which Statius suggests we ponder occurs at the start of the epic's second half as the poet, at first surprisingly, calls on Erato while he outlines the situation in Latium as the Trojans land on its shores. She is the muse associated with lyric poetry and, as her name suggests, matters of the heart (*A*. 7.37), and Statius, as we have seen, already in his poem's first word presages the importance of lyric elements in what follows. The many-levelled eroticism of the poem appears most poignantly at line 104 when Statius has Hercules announce to Pollius: *litus quod pandis amo* ('I love the shore that you open out').

Virgil continues with language that now directly affects Statius' own:...*et primae revocabo exordia pugnae/tu vatem, tu, diva, mone* ('...and I will recall the beginnings of the first strife. Do you, goddess, you advise your poet', *A*. 7.40–1). In Statius' case his subject will not be the start of the first battle but *subiti...exordia templi* (49), the initiation of a graceful temple whose construction was extraordinarily expeditious. As so often with his alterations of his model text, Statius turns war to peace, violence to usefulness.

The third Virgilian apostrophe at work in Statius' invocation centres on the word *veneranda*. The only other occasion in Latin literature where the word occurs in the vocative, and therefore its first use as such, is to be found at *G*. 3.294, where the poet addresses Pales in language similar to that of Statius: *nunc, veneranda Pales, magno nunc ore sonandum* ('Now, worshipful Pales, now we must sing with a great voice'). Reference to a transitional moment in *Georgics* 3 reminds us that we should also be prepared to enter a didactic mode. This will soon take direct form as the poet's voice has us watch and admire Hercules' taming of an intractable plot as he prepares the ground to receive his imposing place of worship.

In sum, by alluding to the three Virgilian apostrophes, Statius suggests to the reader that his dazzling composition will, in its course, contain, and sometimes even merge, elements of epic, lyric, and didactic poetry. In particular, he will have us admire how the martial elements in epic give place to the extensive preparations for a glorious temple and how Hercules,

---

[41] For instance, the iron weapon (*ferro*) used by Turnus for massacre on the battlefield becomes the iron tool (*ferro*, 124) that the new Hercules uses against the rocks that impede his advance. Put more generally, the apostrophe that often introduces the *aristeia* of a warrior in action becomes now an invocation that prefaces the detailing of a new form of heroic endeavour.

112 THE POETIC WORLD OF STATIUS' *SILVAE*

the warrior, becomes Hercules, known for his erotic prowess, who is also the lover of landscape and refiner of its coarseness for cultural ends. For the purposes of Statius' poem, the civilizer must also sustain his own form of civilizing.

Statius reinforces a major part of his point in his apostrophe's remarkable final line. Hercules himself will 'sound' mightily along with Calliope.[42] The bow, that at line 34 we saw was a ferocious part of his weaponry (*truces arcus*), will now be put to use echoing the rhythms of a muse whose influence is acknowledged by poets as diverse as Lucretius, Horace, and Propertius. Hercules' bow will be stretched not to fell some antagonist but to favour the art of melody as it takes on the capabilities of a musical instrument.[43] Instead of performing a destructive function Hercules' bow will now be used as a lyre, to serve a metaphysical purpose, to foster the imagination and the beauty that it helps design, and the hero himself will become a singer of tales instead of their subject.[44]

> tempus erat caeli cum torrentissimus axis
> incumbit terris ictusque Hyperione multo
> acer anhelantes incendit Sirius agros.
>
> (Stat. *Silv.* 3.1.52–4)

It was the time when the axis of heaven, at its hottest, broods over the earth and harsh Sirius, stricken by Hyperion's intensity, sets the panting fields afire.

The saga begins on an appropriately epic tone. Virgil's only use of the phrase *tempus erat* occurs at *A.* 2.268 as Aeneas begins to tell Dido of his dream of Hector. There, in the subsequent line, Virgil attaches a superlative adjective to the calm of night (*quies…gratissima*). Statius' figuration, by contrast, would have us concentrate first on the excruciating power of heaven's pole

---

[42] Statius echoes the phrase *grande sonabit* at 130 (*grande sonat*) where Hercules-Vulcan is at work transforming the terrain.

[43] See commentators on Hor. *Carm.* 1.1.34 (*tendere barbiton*) and *OLD* s.v. *tendo* 5b. Statius may also be suggesting a variation of Hor. *Carm.* 2.10.18–20:…*quondam cithara tacentem/ suscitat Musam neque semper arcum/tendit Apollo* ('…on occasion Apollo rouses the silent Muse with his lyre nor does he always stretch the bow'). Statius expands on Horace by turning the bow from weapon of attack to instrument for the projection of the imagination's capability. Cf. also Prop. 4.6.69–70, where the elegist suggests a similar change in Apollo to that which Statius implies for Hercules.

[44] A plausible connection between these lines and Hom. *Od.* 21.406–8 is noted by Laguna (1992) 147, where Odysseus, about to kill the suitors, is compared to a lyre player stretching a new string onto his instrument. Statius responds with a series of brilliant reversals, as Homer's simile becomes part of the later poet's narrative.

A LABOUR OF LOVE (STATIUS' *SILVAE* 3.1)   113

to burn the earth (*torrentissimus axis*). The date is 13 August when Sirius is in the ascendant. The Dog Star is first itself assailed by the sun which gains emphasis from a triple metonymy as the Titan Hyperion stands for his son, then for the heavenly body itself and finally for the heat that emanates from it. Sirius in turn has the force to set aflame the personified fields which pant in response:

> iamque dies aderat profugis cum regibus aptum
> fumat Aricinum Triviae nemus et face multa
> conscius Hippolyti splendet lacus; ipsa coronat
> emeritos Diana canes et spicula terget
> et tutas sinit ire feras, omnisque pudicis
> Itala terra focis Hecateidas excolit idus.   60
> ast ego, Dardaniae quamuis sub collibus Albae
> rus proprium magnique ducis mihi munere currens
> unda domi curas mulcere aestusque levare
> sufficerent, notas Sirenum nomine rupes
> facundique larem Polli non hospes habebam,   65
> adsidue moresque viri pacemque novosque
> Pieridum flores intactaque carmina discens.
>
> (Stat. *Silv.* 3.1.55–67)

And now the day was at hand when Trivia's Arician grove, fit for run-away kings (55), gives off smoke and the lake, privy to Hippolytus, glows with many a torch. Diana herself crowns her veteran hounds and polishes her arrows and allows wild creatures safe passage, and the whole land of Italy celebrates the ides of Hecate at chaste hearths (60). But I, although my own property, under the hills of Dardan Alba, and, a gift to me from a mighty ruler, its running water were enough to soothe the annoyances and lighten the swelter at home, was residing, no stranger, at the rocks known by the Sirens' name and at the dwelling of eloquent Pollius (65), diligently devoting my mind to the man's character and his quietude as well as to new flowers of the Pierides and virginal songs.

Statius now moves from summer season to the exact date on which the momentous event occurred. August 13 is the festival day of Diana Nemorensis that is annually celebrated at her temple on the northern edge of modern Lago di Nemi. The poet could have been there, he continues, because he had a dwelling with a stream under the hills of Alba, courtesy of the emperor Domitian whose own palatial villa was on the western side of

114   THE POETIC WORLD OF STATIUS' *SILVAE*

the neighbouring Lago di Albano.[45] Instead he finds himself at Surrentum, sharing the feast with Pollius, his friend and host.

The section commences with a nine-line *aition* telling of the event that takes place near Aricia and its nearby gleaming lake. As we learn of the goddess, we are reminded of her other names, Trivia and Hecate, and of how she frees her hounds from hunting on a day when Italy, its homes suitably purified, offers her worship. For the first six verses Statius draws on the summary of the tale of Hippolytus that Virgil gives us as he introduces the Greek hero's son, Virbius, as part of the catalogue of Latian soldiers that brings the seventh book of the *Aeneid* to a conclusion (761–82). The preceding apostrophe to Calliope had recalled Virgil's address to Erato near the opening of the same book. Now we return, as poet remembers poet, to its finale as the fighters prepare to do battle. But once again Statius turns Virgil's potential destructiveness, with its assumption of war's turmoil in the offing, to an auspicious conclusion. We are experiencing a moment when Diana polishes, instead of employs, her weaponry,[46] and entering a world where peace and the imagination's workings are paramount.

There is a further dimension to these lines and as often with Statius genre helps point us in its direction. The only other occurrence of the phrase *iamque dies aderat...cum* in Latin is to be found at Horace's *Sermones* 1.5 (20), during the course of the poet's famous journey to Brundisium, as 'Horace' awakens on the second morning of the trip. The companions have left Rome and spent the first night at Aricia. Now they are between Forum Appii (3) and Lucus Feronia (24), aboard a skiff on the canal that for some ten miles parallels the Via Appia. After that they will head south, to Anxur and Formiae as they aim ultimately for Italy's southeast coast.

Like the scene Horace paints through his diary of the wayfarers on their actual route, Statius has his reader's eye move from Aricia, where Diana is prominently honoured, to Alba Longa where he might have gone to stay at his own home, and then back to Surrentum where the poet is in fact lodged with his patron. But the particular reminiscence of the earlier poet is for a

---

[45] The phrase *ast ego* appears twice in Virgil (*A.* 1.46 and 7.308), on each occasion the goddess Juno is speaking. Statius' persona brings a better mood. As noted by Laguna Mariscal (1992) 151, the phrase *aestus...levare* (63) echoes *A.* 7.495 (*aestus levaret*). The seventh book of the *Aeneid* is a particularly strong influence on Statius here. Cf. also *A.* 7.655–69 and *Silv.* 3.1.36, *A.* 7.761–82 and *Silv.* 3.1.55–60.

[46] At 58 (*spicula terget*), Statius is thinking back to Virg. *A.* 7.626 where all the warriors of Ausonia are readying their armor for battle and 'polish their bright javelins' (*spicula lucida tergent*). Here, too, as we have regularly observed, Statius takes an ominous scene in Virgil and turns it to a pacific end. The Latin preparations for conflict are carefully replaced by Diana's foregoing even of the use of her arrows against creatures of the wild.

A LABOUR OF LOVE (STATIUS' *SILVAE* 3.1) 115

purpose. Through it Statius adds a touch of satire's picturesque, even picaresque, quality to the poem's prominent focus on Surrentum, Hercules, and his incipient monument. The change of genres, in the allusiveness of these lines, from epic (*Aeneid* 7) to satire (Horace's initial book), again helps maintain a light and easeful mood and tone. It also keeps on display Statius' casual genius as a writer with many facets of technique at his command.

As we move from season, to date, to place, the poet's virtuosity reaches a point of climax in the brief hexameters that outline his stay as a regular visitor to the house of eloquent Pollius' (*facundi larem Polli*, 65). We are in the realm of the Sirens,[47] but now in particular in a setting where the master combines high moral stance with devotion not only to rhetorical fluency but also to innovative poetry and song, to words and music: *adsidue moresque uiri pacemque novosque/Pieridum flores intactaque carmina discens* (66–7). Statius glorifies the moment by arranging dialogues with Virgil and Lucretius. The first takes a double form. We find ourselves initially in the first book of the *Aeneid* where Jupiter outlines for Venus the future of her son:...*populosque feroces/contundet moresque viris et moenia ponet.* ('He will beat down fierce tribes and will establish customs and fortifications for the people', *A.* 1.263–4). Aeneas will not only crush ferocious opponents and build city walls, he will establish proper standards of conduct for those under his sway. By analogy Pollius will be a new Aeneas not because he is a successful man-at-arms and politician but because his Epicurean ethics set an example to be absorbed and emulated by those touched by his presence.

A. 6.852 is perhaps still closer to our passage. At the conclusion of what could be considered the greatest preceptive passage in the poem, Anchises tells his son, who now stands for all Romans to come:

> 'tu regere imperio populos, Romane, memento
> (hae tibi erunt artes), pacique imponere morem,
> parcere subiectis et debellare superbos'.
>
> (Virg. *A.* 6.851–3)

'Do you, Roman, remember to rule races with might (these will be your arts), and to establish a custom for peace, to spare the humbled and war down the haughty'.

---

[47] The phrase *notas Sirenum nomine rupes* remains curious because the Sirens themselves are usually associated with *scopuli* (e.g. Virg. *A.* 5.864; Ov. *Met.* 14.88; Apul. *Met.* 5.12.21). Statius' use of *rupes* transfers us from islands, that are a hazard to navigation, to the mainland near Surrentum and, in particular, to the living rock which will soon be given refined shape by the energy of Hercules (for *rupes* see also 124 and 167).

116   THE POETIC WORLD OF STATIUS' *SILVAE*

Pollius in his turn, through the medium of the Virgilian reminiscence, becomes a type of Anchises, the patriarch, lecturing his future descendants in general on their behaviour, and, again, of Aeneas, moulding the character of the Italians that he will subdue. The compliment to Statius' patron is enormous. Pollius Felix incorporates the standards that Virgil, through his mouthpiece Anchises, would see as models for all to imitate.

But the tribute goes yet deeper. For illustration we must turn to Lucretius. In *De Rerum Natura*, in the following lines that also open the poem's fourth book, Lucretius proclaims his own individuality:

> ... avia Pieridum peragro loca nullius ante
> trita solo. iuvat integros accedere fontis
> atque haurire, iuvatque novos decerpere flores...
>
> (Lucr. 1.926–8)

> I roam through pathless ways never trodden before by anyone's foot. It delights me to approach and drink from virginal fountains, and it delights me to pluck new flowers...

In words that would inspire many a later writer, Lucretius boasts of his role as a teacher of Epicurean philosophy who expands the tradition of didactic literature in verse that is as fresh as it is magnetic.[48] Through the compliment offered by Statius' allusion, Pollius becomes also a type of Lucretius, expounding his chosen way of life not only by example but also by producing new poetry, presumably with a particular emphasis on serenity and calm.

We will return in a moment to *Aeneid* 6 and Roman creativity as reflected in the person of Pollius. What Statius has already accomplished is to have us see his friend's verse, from which his poet-guest claims to learn, as combining epic and didactic elements absorbed from the tradition of Virgil and Lucretius. In the case of the former, didactic themes run through both Anchises' lecture to Aeneas and Jupiter's exposition of the future to his daughter. The bow to Lucretius presupposes that Pollius not only adheres to the norms of his philosophical model but also possesses the wit to write

---

[48] These verses are also cited by Laguna Mariscal (1992) 153. Elsewhere (*Silv.* 1.2.238) Statius speaks of Hymen's *intactum carmen* for L. Arruntius Stella who also wrote light verse. Are Pollius' poems intentionally chaste like his domestic life? For *intacta*, see commentators on Catul. 62.45 and 56, as well as 11.23–4 (*flos tactus*). For further detail on both *intactus* and variations of *integer,* see Pichon (1966) 174.

A LABOUR OF LOVE (STATIUS' *SILVAE* 3.1) 117

original verse, with quality of mind complementing and enhancing quality of life. He serves as an instructive paragon for an ethical lifestyle as well as for civility in the broadest sense:

> forte diem Triviae dum litore ducimus udo
> angustasque fores adsuetaque tecta gravati
> frondibus et patula defendimus arbore soles,
> delituit caelum et subitis lux candida cessit
> nubibus ac tenuis graviore favonius austro
> immaduit, qualem Libyae Saturnia nimbum
> attulit, Iliaco dum dives Elissa marito
> donatur testesque ululant per devia nymphae.
>
> (Stat. Silv. 3.1.68–75)

By chance, as we, vexed by our narrow doorways and familiar setting, were passing Trivia's day by the damp shore and warding off the intense sun with leaves and a tree's spread (70), the heavens darkened and the bright light yielded to sudden clouds, and the slender breeze grew dank with the weight of the south wind—such a cloudburst as Saturnia brought to Libya when rich Elissa is bestowed on her Ilian groom and the nymphs as witnesses howl through the byways (75).

At 68 *diem* picks up *dies* (55) as we begin a new section of the saga in which Statius recounts the adventures of the feast day itself.[49] Instead of honouring the occasion inside a building on the estate, we find ourselves in the open, on the seaside below.[50] *Litore* recalls the intensive use of *litora* at line 3 which hinted at the importance of the 'naked shore' in the story to come.[51] Though we are celebrating Diana, Hercules will gradually move centre stage.

The plural (*soles*) emphasizes the force of the sun's heat and, as events proceed, the elements become a prime mover in their evolution. Allusion also plays a crucial part in deepening the reader's understanding. By directly referring to the fourth book of the *Aeneid*, in particular to lines 160–72, Statius gifts us with an unusual intertext which here offers not an indirect

---

[49] The phrase *forte die* initiates the hexameter at *A.* 8.102 where a festival to Hercules is occurring. The only other occasion where the words *udo* and *litore* occur together is at Hor. *Carm.* 1.32.7–8 as part of a direct reference to the poet Alcaeus.

[50] Since the adjective *patula* (70) appears in the same position in the hexameter at Virg. *Ecl.* 1.1, Statius may be adding a pastoral touch to his description. Cf. also the uses of forms of *defendere* at *Ecl* 7.6 and 47.

[51] See also *litoris* (100) and *litus* (104).

118   THE POETIC WORLD OF STATIUS' *SILVAE*

reference that enhances our appreciation, but an explicit parallel between particular events. This in turn suggests that the actual circumstances and the *dramatis personae* of the two plots themselves are somehow directly analogous, a suggestion abetted by the fact that Statius narrates the complementary moment in the present tense. In the *Aeneid* Virgil projects not an ordinary storm but a very specific one that results in dire consequences for one of the protagonists. Statius makes his readers ask what can be parallel between Dido and Aeneas, their hunting interrupted by a rainstorm, consummating their liaison in a Libyan cave, and a festivity in honour of virginal Diana aborted by a downpour that forces all the participants, along with servants and their paraphernalia, into a small hut dedicated to the worship of hero become god.[52]

One answer lies in the chief instigator of the event in the *Aeneid*, namely Saturnia, which is to say Juno, daughter of Saturn. This is the name by which she is introduced in the *Aeneid* (1.23) as Virgil first calls attention to her malevolent emotionality toward the Trojans as a prime cause of their misfortunes throughout the epic. Statius turns matters around. Juno has already made two appearances in *Silv.* 3.1 as Hercules' stepmother, the *noverca* who had helped initiate his notorious labours (22) and who had earlier in his career sent serpents to strangle him as an infant (47). The poet now has us remember that, in the *Aeneid*, the goddess' evil intent, in the scene from Book 4, ultimately causes Aeneas' departure to Italy with the grand history that follows. Here she is the covert cause of a new but now inventive task that comes the way of a willing Hercules—the training of a rugged locale to be suitable to receive a magnificent temple of which he is the dedicatee.

We also witness, however, perhaps the most salient moment, of several scattered throughout the poem, where Statius takes a threatening situation or setting in the *Aeneid* and brings it to a fortunate termination. In this example the earlier poet's epic storm is the initiation of circumstances that lead to the death of Dido. Here only good comes of the weather's impetuosity as the landscape is transformed and the spiritual and aesthetic lives of its inhabitants improved accordingly.

---

[52] Vollmer (1898) 388 speaks of 'die absichtliche Komik des Vergil parodierenden Vergleiches'. My contrary suggestion is that Statius' analogy offers a corrective parallel with a serious intention. Virgil shows us an ill-starred union that leads finally to the doom of one of the principals. Statius has us enjoy watching a happily married couple who are in the process of fulfilling a propitious destiny, with a sign from above to direct their way.

A LABOUR OF LOVE (STATIUS' *SILVAE* 3.1)   119

diffugimus, festasque dapes redimitaque vina
abripiunt famuli; nec quo convivia migrent,
quamvis innumerae gaudentia rura superne
insedere domus et multo culmine dives
mons nitet; instantes sed proxima quaerere nimbi
suadebant laesique fides reditura sereni.

(Stat. Silv. 3.1.76–81)

We take flight, and the servants snatch up the festival's banquet and the wreathed wine; and there is no place where our dinner party might make its way although countless dwellings sit atop the rejoicing countryside and the rich mountain gleams with many a rooftop. But the looming storm-clouds (80) and our trust, soon to return, in the damaged calm were urging us to seek what was nearest by.

The same transformation of Virgil holds true for the episode as it continues to evolve. *Diffugimus* serves as a striking reminder of line 212 of the *Aeneid's* second book where the word also initiates the hexameter. There the Trojans flee the sight of Laocoön and sons being strangled by gigantic serpents. But the moment paves the way for the destruction of Troy and the departure of its inhabitants for unknown destinations. Statius offers a far smaller, domestic version of such high drama, now, however with a happy outcome.[53]

There is violence in the process (*abripiunt*) and the movement of all concerned is like the departure of a whole people from its base (*migrent*), whether necessitated by the elements, as here, or under some greater duress. But once again Statius gives his bow to Virgil, initiating a deeply troubling event, a fruitful result. We watch a minuscule version of departure into exile as the troop of celebrants heads, not toward the exquisite, spacious, housing gleaming on the mountain above,[54] but in the direction of a humbler abode

---

[53] In Statius' text 'we' takes us from *ducimus* (68) to *defendimus* (70) to *diffugimus* (76). As the reader looks back to Virgil, 'we' share in a change in the plot of *Aeneid* 2 ultimately for the better. The same could be said for the poet's reworking of *Aeneid* 4 as well. In the *Aeneid*, Dido and Aeneas escape into a cave with a disastrous 'marriage' as a result. In *Silv.* 3.1 we have a joyous throng crammed into a tiny space, but what follows is a form of inspiring affection. Hercules embraces Pollius in his thoughts with befitting accomplishments to follow.

[54] The phrase *innumerae gaudentia rura superne/domus* (78–9) looks back, in sound and sense, to Hor. *S.* 1.10.44–5: *molle atque facetum/Vergilio adnuerunt gaudentes rure Camenae* ('The Muses who rejoice in the countryside have granted to Virgil smoothness and elegance'). The reference pays a gentle, double compliment to two of Statius' great poetic guides and further confirms both satire and pastoral in the background of *Silv.* 3.1.

120   THE POETIC WORLD OF STATIUS' *SILVAE*

nearer by, in the trust that the storm's ferocity will lessen. But this gently parodic moment is a flight toward productivity, toward the further domestication and adornment of the nearby landscape for the benefit of all its inhabitants.

> stabat dicta sacri tenuis casa nomine templi
> et magnum Alciden humili lare parva premebat,
> fluctivagos nautas scrutatoresque profundi
> vix operire capax. huc omnis turba coimus,
> huc epulae ditesque tori coetusque ministrum
> stipantur nitidaeque cohors gratissima Pollae.
> non cepere fores angustaque deficit aedes.
>
> (Stat. Silv. 3.1.82–8)

There stood a modest hut called by the name of a holy temple and in its smallness it confined mighty Alcides in a lowly abode, scarcely roomy enough to enclose wave-roving sailors and investigators of the deep. Hither we enter, the whole throng (85), hither the foodstuffs and rich bolsters and the bevy of servants are crammed and the most gracious attendants of shining Polla. The doors cannot embrace the crowd and the narrow shrine falters.

Statius now carefully calls our attention to the original place of worship for our hero-god. It can be called a temple in title only. The key word here is *casa*. Virgil has the shepherd Corydon invite Alexis to come live with him in his *humilis casas* (*Ecl.* 2.29). Lowly huts are typical of country living. More pertinent still is Lucretius' mention of *casas* as an adjunct to skins and fire as a feature in the early development of mankind (Lucr. 5.1011). Huts, the implication is, were only a stage in the evolution of human housing as civilization evolved. More refined arrangements were still in the offing. The same holds true for Hercules and his place of worship. The *tenuis casa* will soon see something grander in its place, as culture takes its own special step forward on the estate of Pollius Felix.

The opening of the poem had already hinted at this change for the better. At line 4 Statius forewarns us that, for a while at least, we will be dealing with 'a dwelling lived in by wandering sailors' (*tectum vagis habitabile nautis*), and at line 9 he offers a reminder of what once had been a 'tiny altar' (*parva ara*). Both altar and its hitherto 'tiny dwelling' (*casa parva*) will now

A LABOUR OF LOVE (STATIUS' *SILVAE* 3.1)   121

give way to something worthy of the 'grand descendant of Alcaeus' (*magnum Alciden*), limited will become appropriately expansive.[55]

Statius' use of *magnus* not only contrasts with the double use of *parva*, it also recalls the adjective's appearance, in comparative form, at the poem's start, to describe by synecdoche the glorious temple (*maiore tholo*, 3) that now has arisen in place of the miniscule altar and shack.[56] The grammatical progression from *magnum* to *maiore* is a linguistic reflection of the graphic change from *tectum* to *templum*, meagre shelter to grand monument, from a place which once welcomed 'wave-wandering sailors' (*fluctivagos nautas*) and is now incapable of receiving those who will soon accomplish its replacement by a worthier edifice.[57]

> erubuit risitque deus dilectaque Polli
> corda subit blandisque virum complectitur ulnis.
>
> <div align="right">(Stat. <i>Silv.</i> 3.1.89–90)</div>

The god blushed and smiled and enters the beloved heart of Pollius and embraces the man with coaxing arms (90).

We now reach one of the emotional pivots of the poem. Hercules blushed out of chagrin for his *angusta aedes*, his 'narrow shrine' whose size was insufficient to hold the festive group. But he also accordingly felt shame for Pollius' lack of care in offering him an unworthy sanctuary. His response, a smile instead of a frown, serves as the energizing gesture for the events that follow.[58] Statius further confirms the deep affection between the two protagonists. Hercules not only invades a heart already beloved. The poet emphasizes the virtual physicality of the event by moving, within two lines,

---

[55] For *angusta aedes* (88), see Rimell (2015) 29, who refers to Janus' words at Ov. *Fast.* 1.201 describing the originally 'cramped temple' (*angusta aede*) of Jupiter on the Capitolium. She interprets this space, in which the god had scarcely room to stand up, as symbolizing the necessary start of Rome's enlargement of its empire. Statius is accomplishing something parallel by having us visualize, over the course of his poem, the growth of the influence of Hercules. We have witnessed a similar move, on a smaller scale, from *angusta aedes* to a *maiore tholo* as the god's shrine takes impressive shape before our eyes—an epic accomplishment for an epic hero within a lyric frame.

[56] Virgil's only use of the word *tholus* (*A.* 9.408) employs the same figuration.

[57] The mention of Polla (*nitidae...cohors gratissima Pollae*, 87) is a tasteful reminder of *Silv.* 2.2.10 (*nitidae iuuenilis gratia Pollae*), but it also links Polla with the glistening doorposts of the future temple (*nitidos*, 5) and with the mountain whose rich display gleams down upon the celebrants from above (*nitet*, 80).

[58] *Risit* is picked up by *ridet* at 105 and 151.

122   THE POETIC WORLD OF STATIUS' *SILVAE*

from past to present tenses as well as by calling to our attention the distinction between the two figures, as god (*deus*) appears to grasp mortal (*virum*) in seductive embrace.

Of the several parallels in earlier literature, perhaps the closest occurs in the *Metamorphoses* of Ovid at the moment where the shade of murdered Orpheus re-enters the Underworld and finds the wraith of his adored Eurydice. This he immediately 'embraces with eager arms' (*cupidis... amplectitur ulnis*, *Met.* 11.63) as the two commence a new existence, forever together amid the dead. The comparison serves to intensify the compliment to Pollius. The spirit of Hercules can pass into the heart of his beloved who, unlike the ghost of Eurydice, is still in the world of the living. The result is that, under the spell of an Orpheus-like divinity, he is stimulated to embark on a bravura project, which, we remember, at line 17 had already elicited a comparison with some magical feat by the Thracian bard.[59] This new endeavour both honours its specific recipient and adds quality to the surroundings at large:

> 'tune' inquit 'largitor opum, qui mente profusa
> tecta Dicaearchi pariter iuvenemque replesti
> Parthenopen? nostro qui tot fastigia monti,
> tot virides lucos, tot saxa imitantia vultus
> aeraque, tot scripto viventes lumine ceras
> fixisti?'

(Stat. Silv. 3.1.91–6)

'Are you,' he says, 'the donor of resources who through your prodigality filled the houses of Dicaearchus and young Parthenope as well, who attached so many towers onto our mountain, so many green groves, so many stones and bronzes that resemble faces, so many waxes alive with engraved (95) light?'

At virtually the mid-point of the poem, Statius now introduces the epiphanic god who speaks directly to the mind of his human disciple.[60] He begins by enumerating aspects of Pollius' largesse bestowed on Naples, but then

---

[59] With line 90 we could also compare, again for both sound and sense, Virg. *A.* 12.433 where Aeneas 'embraces Ascanius with his weaponry poured around [him]' (*Ascanium fusis circum complectitur armis*). A speech follows closely in each instance.

[60] On speeches by mythological figures in the *Silvae*, see Newlands (2002) 60, referring to Coleman (1999).

A LABOUR OF LOVE (STATIUS' *SILVAE* 3.1)   123

narrows his sights to Surrentum and the mountain which its owner has furbished with greenery and a variety of sculptures.

Lines 94–6 have a resonance of particular salience to the way in which Statius commends his patron. In our earlier discussion of line 66 we noted the importance of Anchises' disquisition near the end of *Aeneid* 6 for the poet's way of praising Pollius' unpretentious manner. There the reference was to the patriarch's command that future Romans impose a custom for peace in their political affairs. Here Statius expands the eulogy in a special way. Before lecturing his descendants on their behaviour when holding the power that will come their way, Anchises alludes obliquely to the unnamed Greeks and their skill, among other achievements, in oratory and in different types of sculpture:

> excudent alii spirantia mollius aera
> (credo equidem), vivos ducent de marmore vultus,
> orabunt causas melius...
>
> (Virg. A. 6.847–9)

Others will more softly hammer out breathing bronzes (indeed I believe it), will draw living faces from marble, will plead cases better...

We have already been made aware of Pollius' *facundia*, his rhetorical expertise, a talent that Anchises lists third among the artistic aptitudes for which the Greeks were noteworthy. Now, by a direct allusion, Statius draws a further parallel between him and the Hellenic world, if not in the creation of sculpture out of stone and bronze (to which he adds encaustic figures), at least in their appreciation, as he embellishes his setting. Though a Roman, he delights in the charm of things Greek. He therefore surpasses what Anchises asks of any Roman—to make peace a central virtue—by being a dedicated Hellenophile as well, a superb orator who also allows Greek aesthetics to play a conspicuous part in his lifestyle.

The compliment to Pollius is enormous, especially as it is divided between two segments of the poem so that we are reminded of one when we reach the other. We are dealing with matters internal and external. The first looks to the value of one's spiritual being, to the imagination that delights in poetic inspiration and to the moral temperament that provides calm and rationality to one's domain. The second details an artist's inclination to augment his surroundings with visual spectacles whose fineness delights the onlooker. The Greek and Roman segments of Pollius' life therefore find reflection in a dual excellence where physical and spiritual, outer and inner,

124 THE POETIC WORLD OF STATIUS' *SILVAE*

the imaginative and the practical, visual artistry and moral superiority, interact and are mutually supportive. And Virgil, as often in the poetry of Statius, is the touchstone that reveals the intricacies of the latter's art:

> '...quid enim ista domus, quid terra, priusquam
> te gauderet, erant? longo tu tramite nudos
> texisti scopulos, fueratque ubi semita tantum
> nunc tibi distinctis stat porticus alta columnis
> ne sorderet iter. curvi tu litoris ora
> clausisti calidas gemina testudine nymphas.
> vix opera enumerem: mihi pauper et indigus uni
> Pollius? et tales hilaris tamen intro penates
> et litus quod pandis amo. sed proxima sedem
> despicit et tacite ridet mea limina Iuno.
> da templum dignasque tuis conatibus aras,
> quas puppes velis nolint transire secundis,
> quo pater aetherius mensisque accita deorum
> turba et ab excelso veniat soror hospita templo.
> nec te quod solidus contra riget umbo maligni
> montis et immenso non umquam exesus ab aevo
> terreat: ipse adero et conamina tanta iuvabo
> asperaque inuitae perfringam viscera terrae.
> incipe et Herculeis fidens hortatibus aude.
> non Amphioniae steterint velocius arces
> Pergameusve labor.' dixit mentemque reliquit.
>
> (Stat. Silv. 3.1.96–116)

'For what was that house, what that terrain, before it rejoiced in you? You covered the naked crags with a lengthy roadway, and where there had been only a pathway, now for you stands a lofty portico with varied columns so that the passage not be a bore. On the edge of the curved shore (100) you enclosed the warm nymphs within twin roofs. I could scarcely list the accomplishments. Is Pollius penurious and needy to me alone? Yet nevertheless, I cheerfully enter such a house and I love the shore that you open out. But Juno next door looks down on my abode and silently scoffs at my threshold (105). Grant me a temple and altars, worthy of your achievements, which ships under fair sails will not wish to pass by, to which the heavenly father might come and the assembly of gods, summoned to the banquet, and my sister, as a guest, from her lofty temple. Do not be frightened that the dense mass of a baleful mountain (110), never eaten away by

A LABOUR OF LOVE (STATIUS' *SILVAE* 3.1)   125

the enormity of time, stiffens against you. I myself will be at hand and will lend aid to your endeavours and will shatter the harsh entrails of the reluctant earth. Begin, and take courage, trusting in the urgings of Hercules. Neither the towers of Amphion (115) nor the effort at Pergamum will have found their place more swiftly'. He spoke and departed from his thoughts.

Hercules continues with his praise of Pollius' setting as Statius has him personify the house and land which takes pleasure in what has happened to it.[61] To enliven the god's words the poet leads us on a brief tour with its own linguistic thread, based on the verb *eo*, from *tramite* to *semita* and finally *iter*, from the long footpath, whose humanized rocks have become suitably clothed, to the once-upon-a-time trail that is now nicely decorated, to the whole course itself which we have just traversed.[62]

The lofty portico that graces the road stands out for its *distinctis columnis* that exert their charm in several ways. Their separateness has our eye follow the route step by step as we move along. But the adjective in particular suggests that we prize the objects themselves not only for their shape as handsome markers but also for their diverse coloration. We know from elsewhere the satisfaction that Pollius took in assorted Greek marbles.[63] By dwelling here on the individual vividness of the columns Statius would be further expanding on his patron's love of things Hellenic that he suggested in the preceding lines.

As visual objects the columns serve further to enhance their surroundings. They would stand out against the green of the groves, the white and brown of sculpture in stone and bronze, and the varied luminosity of the wax images. Moreover, to follow out the poet's play on *sorderet*, they would keep the road from being mentally tedious by assuring aesthetic enjoyment on the part of its travellers. For those delighting in what they saw, the columns would turn the route, from being drab and dark, as the etymology of *sordeo* would have it, to bright and cheery like the rejoicing earth on which they have found their resting place.[64]

---

[61] For an insightful discussion of these lines, see Newlands (2002) 294 and n. 36.

[62] Both Varro (*L.* 5.35) and Isidore (*Orig.* 15.16.9) connect *semita* with *itus* and therefore *eo*, and Isidore (*Orig.* 15.16.10) links *trames* with *iter* and thus again with *eo*.

[63] Cf. *Silv.* 2.2.85–93 on the marbles in Pollius' villa at Surrentum.

[64] Statius' language at 98–100 bears a similarity to Prop. 2.32.11–12: *scilicet umbrosis sordet Pompeia columnis/porticus, aulaeis nobilis Attalicis* ('Certainly the Portico of Pompey with its shady columns, renowned for its hangings like Attalus', seems ignoble'). Statius inherits the play on the word *sordet* from the Augustan elegist. On the surface Propertius is saying that the beauty of the portico seems of small account to Cynthia as she pursues her affairs away from

126   THE POETIC WORLD OF STATIUS' *SILVAE*

At line 97 Hercules calls Pollius' attention to the fact that he has covered rocks in the area, that had previously been *nudos*—a reminder of the *litora nuda* (3–4) that are still the lot of the god. At line 100 he again returns for a moment to the poem's opening lines, to the Surrentine *litus* (100), this time to remind his patron that he has built a handsome, adjacent bathhouse for heated waters (under the guise of nymphs). Line 3 had seen him *pauper*. At line 102 he recalls for Pollius, and us, that this is how he still remains, as the poem's action, with its mid-point deliberately echoing its opening lines, now progresses toward a dynamic change in the god's situation.

Hercules reaffirms his affection for Pollius (*amo*) and his gratitude for the part of the shore (*litus*, once again) that the proprietor has made available to him. But he also indirectly suggests a further reason why his patron should feel ashamed. This is the first and only time in the poem that Juno, the *noverca* of lines 22, 47, and 137 and Hercules' nemesis, is directly named. Statius stresses the moment with a play on the word *despicit*. The goddess literally looks down upon his 'dwelling' from her nearby temple because her building is loftier than his. But she also figuratively disdains it just as she had scorned him during his mortal existence. Her smile, one of several in the poem, is of self-satisfaction at her apparent superiority. As Hercules would have it, Juno sees no comparison between the ancient divinity and the new initiate. But Pollius should know better and will presumably behave accordingly.

Pollius will redeem himself by the fabrication of a worthy place of worship. Statius brings the results to our attention in a small cycle, taking us from *templum* (106) to *templo* (109). He implies the building's universality by taking us first from its potential position on land and extending our imagined gaze seaward. Through a combination of synecdoche and metonymy, as we move from their sterns to the personified ships to the voyagers aboard them, the poet has us admire the view of the future monument from out on the water. We then enter another elemental sphere as we cast our eye heavenward to Jupiter, *pater aetherius*, who will join other gods in visiting the new terrestrial edifice. Just as Hercules ascends to heaven (*aethera*, 7) at his deification, so Jupiter *aetherius*, in his turn, will descend from above, accompanied by a group of divinities, to honour his son, the hero become god. Finally, we have another descent from nearer by. Father is now replaced

---

Rome. But there may be a more literal sense where the monument might actually appear dark, dingy, and therefore unprepossessing.

A LABOUR OF LOVE (STATIUS' *SILVAE* 3.1)   127

by sister, Minerva, who will come down from her famous promontory home to the local seaside, a guest at her brother's new, well-deserved residence.

So much for the planning stage. The god now gives a strong hint of the physical effort that lies ahead. Statius seems to invent the meaning of 'projected piece of land' for the word *umbo*.[65] But he also asks the reader to remember its original sense as the boss of a shield, often standing for the piece of armour itself. This is the inherent metaphor that energizes the poet's language. The mountain that the builders must confront is like the shield of a human army, one that Statius qualifies as *malignus*. The mountain's stone, which has not been eaten away by the natural processes of time, will be particularly inimical to any attempts to bring it to submission.[66] Its ranks are tight-packed (*solidus*) and its spirit ill-disposed. As Statius soon rephrases his depiction, the land, now personified as reluctant, has innards that are *aspera*, rough in texture, harsh in spirit, metaphorically, as it faces any attempt at conquest.[67]

But inimical nature is challenged by powerful antagonists. Hercules will be at hand to help subdue any opposition. The god also honours Pollius himself with significant analogies. The *labor* to come will be accomplished faster than the walls of Thebes took shape as guided by Amphion or those of Troy through the efforts of Apollo and Neptune. Hercules, of course, being a god, is akin to the latter pair. But, since we have already admired Pollius' imaginative life of the mind, a further parallel with the singer-magician of Thebes, and perhaps even with the god of the bow and lyre, is also a judicious compliment to the mortal Pollius as he joins forces with his divinized colleague:

> nec mora cum scripta formatur imagine tela.
> innumerae coiere manus; his caedere silvas
> et levare trabes, illis immergere curae
> fundamenta solo. coquitur pars umida terrae

---

[65] The *OLD* (s.v. 2b) refers to Stat. *Theb.* 6.257 and *Ach.* 1.408. as well as *Silv.* 3.1.110.

[66] With *umbo…montis…exesus*, cf. Virg. *A.* 8.418–19: *exesa/antra Aetnaea*, quoted below, and *G.* 4.418–19: *est specus ingens/exesi latere in montis…* ('There is a huge cave in the side of a mountain that has been eaten away…'). Statius, as we continue to observe, is particularly fond of this segment of the *Georgics*.

[67] Virgil's only use of the verb *perfringere* occurs at *A.* 10.279 (*perfringere dextra*) as Turnus exhorts his troops to 'break through' the enemy with their right hand, which is to say crush them by means of the sword. Virgil is also the first author to use the word *viscera* metaphorically for the insides of a mountain (*A.* 3.575) where the larger context was also on Statius' mind.

128 THE POETIC WORLD OF STATIUS' *SILVAE*

> protectura hiemes atque exclusura pruinas
> indomitusque silex curva fornace liquescit.
> praecipuus sed enim labor est exscindere dextra
> oppositas rupes et saxa negantia ferro.
> hic pater ipse loci positis Tirynthius armis
> insudat validaque solum deforme bipenni,
> cum grave nocturna caelum subtexitur umbra,
> ipse fodit, ditesque Caprae viridesque resultant
> Taurubulae, et terris ingens redit aequoris echo.
>
> (Stat. *Silv.* 3.1.117–29)

No delay, when the outline is given shape from the written design. Countless hands came together—the task of these to fell the trees and to smooth the beams, of those to pour the foundations in the ground. The damp part of the earth is baked (120) to ward off the cold and keep out frost, and the untamed flint is melted in a curved furnace. But the most special effort is indeed to hew out by hand with iron the hostile cliffs and contradicting rocks. Here the Tirynthian himself, father of the place, his weapons put aside (125), begins to sweat and, himself, digs out the shapeless ground with his mighty axe, when the brooding sky is interwoven with the darkness of night, and rich Caprae and green Taurubulae resound, and the mighty echo of the sea returns to land.

Before the enterprise begins in earnest there must be a visible layout, and Statius draws our attention to its presence with an astonishing line: *nec mora cum scripta formatur imagine tela* (117). The hexameter is built around a double enallage.[68] We expect that the *imago* ('imagined design') should be given *forma* ('actual shape') by means of the *tela* ('tangible plan'). Instead the *tela* receives *forma* from the *imago* inscribed on it. We are thus urged by the poet's careful but unusual deployment of words to ponder the different stages of this creation and their interdependence. The mental conception is followed by the act of writing it down which leads in turn to its actual realization.[69]

As a result, the concluding word, *tela*, gains special significance. This is its unique instance in Latin with the meaning of plan or design. Nevertheless, as in the case of *umbo* (110), the singularity of the poet's invention also asks

---

[68] As noted by Laguna Mariscal (1992) 168.

[69] Writing suggests a form of permanence. Cf. *inscriptus* (46) of the newly installed young *sacerdos* and *scripto lumine* (95), waxen images with light 'written' on them.

A LABOUR OF LOVE (STATIUS' *SILVAE* 3.1)   129

that we attend to the word's latent metaphor. *Tela* is derived, via *texla, from *texo*, to weave.[70] Thus here the object to be structured, in this case the landscape of Pollius' estate, takes on shape (*forma*), that is, gains an appearance of aesthetic distinction, from a written design. This is first plotted out, then put into effect by tremendous exertion. But etymology also implies that the landscape's 'craftsmen' are akin to weavers. Like those who fashion fabric from wool, the labourers are also disciplining nature to generate art which furthermore here takes its original form from writing, which is to say from another impulse that marks a creative endeavour. Just as writing interlaces words to frame them into a rigorous yet attractive pattern, so here physical toil, putting into effect a written design, will give harmonious proportion to the surface setting for a grand temple to come.

The tasks are many. They involve smoothing the rough, drying the wet, softening the hard. Again, one novel usage stands out. Line 121 contains the only preserved example of the word *protectura* in the sense of 'serve as safeguard against, ward off'. The personified land, after man's mediation, can now on its own defend itself against elemental cold, and bar heavy frost from its domain. (In the cases of *hiemes* and *pruinas* the plural stresses the potency of each noun.) The hardest of stones, flint, once untamed like any wild creature, human or otherwise, is now turned to liquid by man's efforts.

Statius calls attention to the line (...*indomitusque silex curva furnace liquescit*, 122) by suggesting that we remember its source of inspiration. We are, as often in the poem, in *Aeneid* 8 as Vulcan's assistants prepare to forge the shield of Aeneas. Bronze flows in streams as does gold:...*vulnificusque chalybs vasta fornace liquescit* ('...and the wound-making steel is melted in the enormous furnace', A. 8.446). Virgil's huge furnace takes more shapely form as Statius makes his rounded. But the gist remains the same. We are about to witness another example of the creation of beauty as god goes to work for man. But Virgil's gorgeous shield, encapsulating Roman history in its decoration, that was destined for the greater glory of a hero preparing to do battle at the start of Rome's illustrious chronicle, now yields place to the topographical setting of a notable building. Artisanship of the highest quality is still the goal but now it is the earth that needs to be disciplined by man's exacting training, not other human beings who must face submission or worse through the horrors of war. On the shield it is the *indomiti Dahae* (A. 8.728) who need subduing through Roman might.

---

[70] For the theme of weaving, see also *texitur* (38) and *subtexitur* (127). Both man and the inanimate world weave in artistic fashion.

130   THE POETIC WORLD OF STATIUS' *SILVAE*

In Statius it is only inert nature that, even at its hardest, now has to suffer acculturation, for its own betterment.[71]

Statius enlarges on the notion in the following lines: *praecipuus sed enim labor est exscindere dextra/oppositas rupes et saxa negantia ferro* (123–4). The especially difficult obstruction in the way of the toilers is the stones that offer resistance and the personified rocks that say 'no' to the iron tools.[72] A bow to Virgil again illuminates Statius' language. Here the poet is thinking of words spoken by Turnus (*A.* 9.137), as he proclaims that it is his role 'to exterminate a guilty race with the sword' (*ferro sceleratam exscindere gentem*).[73] Our poet, by contrast, asks that we consider the fact that the iron sword has now given way to a crowbar or its like, and that a criminal race is replaced by the inanimate landscape whose resistance must be overcome so that man, instead of destroying his human opponents, can beautify his setting.[74]

Two deictics (*hic, ipse*) and the honorific *pater* mark the appearance of the god himself on the scene (125).[75] Statius adds a special proviso: *positis armis*. Hercules is to arrive without the usual weapons of an extraordinary hero, and his de-arming is a focal theme of the poem. The poet has already commanded that he 'put aside his fierce bows' (*pone truces arcus*, 34), and we have witnessed how one of these has grown taut, not for the sake of shooting deadly arrows but to serve him as he joins Calliope in making string music (*tenso arcu*, 51). There is to be no physical battling now, only the fashioning of attractive sound to uplift the spirit.

Statius expands his point in the next line with the phrase *valida bipenni* (126). Once again Virgil's usage helps us construe the poet's suggestiveness. The Augustan poet employs *valida* with *bipennis* twice, first at *G.* 4.331 (*validam bipennem*), where Aristaeus imagines his mother hacking down his vines, and then at *A.* 11.651, where a *bipennis* forms part of the arsenal

---

[71] With Statius' context cf., e.g., *A.* 6.471 where Virgil likens Dido, unresponsive to Aeneas, to *dura silex*. The melting of *silex* would be as much a marvel as the thawing of the queen's icy rigidity.

[72] Cf. *A.* 10.427–8 for *oppositum* of an opposing enemy (*Abantem/oppositum*). The implicit personification of the mountain at Virg. *G.* 3.213 (*montem oppositum*) and 373 (*oppositum montem*) helps serve a similar purpose.

[73] Cf. also Virg. *A.* 2.177 (*exscindi Pergama*), on the possible capture of Troy. At 4.425 Dido remarks that she did not conspire to destroy the Trojans (*Troianam exscindere gentem*), and at 6.553, the gods are unable to destroy in battle the gate that leads to Tartarus (*exscindere bello*, where *M* reads *ferro*).

[74] See commentators on, e.g., Virg. *A.* 2.463 (*adgressi ferro*) and 12.695 (*decernere ferro*).

[75] The demonstratives *ipse*, in its various forms, and *hic*, by itself, are among the most important deictics in the poem, with eight instances each.

A LABOUR OF LOVE (STATIUS' *SILVAE* 3.1)   131

of Camilla. Without the adjective, a *bipennis* makes two notable appearances in *Aeneid* 2. We find it at line 479, where a two-bladed axe is the instrument by which Pyrrhus bashes his way through the hard doors of Priam's palace, and at 627, where, in simile, the destroyers of Troy are compared to farmers using *crebris bipennibus* (627), which is to say, by metonymy, frequent blows of the axe, to chop down a mountain ash, symbol of the toppling city.

As Hercules goes about the duty of giving *forma* to ground which it lacks (*solum deforme*), as he begins the effort of digging, he must start by putting his regular armour aside.[76] Statius has him then take a *valida bipennis* as the instrument to help him go about his mission. The poet thus performs a type of verbal metamorphosis in order to have his hero undergo his own career change so as to accomplish his new objective properly. He takes an implement which in the fourth *Georgic* might be employed for the annihilation of plants and in the *Aeneid* is a forceful device as war follows its devastating path and turns it to a powerful but inspired purpose as the god proceeds with his inventive assignment. The poet first has Hercules dispense with his regular *arma* but then immediately depicts him at work with an axe, not for ruinous purposes but instead to give a necessary pattern to an amorphous plot of earth.

The noise of his activity involves land and sea as well as the heavens through the reverberation. We hear as well as visualize the god at work.[77] Statius has us imagine the time of night with a particularly impressive hexameter: *cum grave nocturna caelum subtexitur umbra* (127). Statius may be thinking of Virgil's only use of the verb *subtexere* that occurs at *A.* 3.582 where Aeneas is describing to Dido how, as the giant Enceladus moves under Mt. Etna, all of Sicily groans and 'veils the sky with smoke' (*caelum subtexere fumo*).[78] The plume emanating from the volcano, which also soon appears in Statius' text, is replaced by the shade of night. But the repeated verb has a particular resonance here. As we follow out the metaphor of weaving, with darkness imagined as composing a cloth to cover the heavens,

---

[76] Hercules is readying a piece of soil (*solo*, 120) so that it can properly receive the foundations for the building to come. What is *deforme* will now become part of the monument when, we are reminded (l.117), 'the outline is given shape from the written design' (*scripta formatur imagine tela*). The god is employing manual virtuosity to prepare for a further example of artistry to come.

[77] Virgil uses the form *resultant* three times, each as the conclusion of a hexameter (*A.* 5.150, 8.305, and 10.330). The example of *A.* 8.305 is of special importance to readers of *Silv.* 3.1 as marking the conclusion of the celebration for Hercules to which Statius often calls our attention.

[78] See also Laguna Mariscal (1992) 171.

132   THE POETIC WORLD OF STATIUS' *SILVAE*

we think in general of nature in her own way also at the work of crafting in the sky at the same time as Hercules is remaking the earth. In particular, Statius has us hark back to the etymology of *tela* (117), the woven pattern that the initial workmen are adopting. The inventiveness in the heavens now complements that of the hero as he pursues his own vocation for design:

> non tam grande sonat motis incudibus Aetne
> cum Brontes Steropesque ferit, nec maior ab antris
> Lemniacis fragor est ubi flammeus aegida caelat
> Mulciber et castis exornat Pallada donis.
> decrescunt scopuli, et rosea sub luce reversi
> artifices mirantur opus. vix annus anhelat
> alter, et ingenti diues Tirynthius arce
> despectat fluctus et iunctae tecta novercae
> provocat et dignis invitat Pallada templis.
>
> (Stat. *Silv*. 3.1.130–8)

Not so grandly sounds Etna, as the anvils shake (130) when Brontes and Steropes strike, nor is there a greater crashing from the caves of Lemnos when fiery Mulciber chisels an aegis and adorns Pallas with chaste gifts. The crags lessen, and the artisans, returned at roseate dawn, marvel at the work. Hardly is a second-year panting (135), and the transfigured Tirynthian looks down at the waters from his huge tower and challenges the nearby dwelling of his stepmother and attracts Pallas to a worthy temple.

Statius now graces his text with a simile which serves several purposes. The analogy is based on sound: the resonance of Hercules reworking the earth is like that emanating from Etna when the Cyclopes Brontes and Steropes are at work at their anvils or from Lemnos when Vulcan, the Soother, is busy emblazoning a skin-shield for Athena. We are involved with a world of distinguished accomplishments, in the ornamenting of which in poetry ekphrasis plays a major role.

At line 122 we have already had a reminder of the eighth book of the *Aeneid*, specifically of Vulcan's smithy beneath Sicily's great mountain. The opening verses of the simile take us directly to *Aeneid* 8 and the volcano:

> ...quam subter specus et Cyclopum exesa caminis
> antra Aetnaea tonant, ualidique incudibus ictus
> auditi referunt gemitus.
>
> (Virg. *A*. 8.418–20)

A LABOUR OF LOVE (STATIUS' *SILVAE* 3.1)   133

...under which the cavern and the caves of Etna, eaten out by the forges of the Cyclopes, thunder, and the strong blows, heard from the anvils, send back their groans.

The reminiscence is extended by the mention of Brontes and Steropes drawn from 8.425 where they are named along with their colleague Pyracmon. The combination of passages serves to strengthen the analogy between the divinized Hercules, hewing rocks, and Vulcan in action as the divinity who moulds with fire. And since the subsequent portion of *Aeneid* 8 is devoted to the manufacture and furbishing of the shield of Aeneas, Statius would have us find a parallel between the two immortal workmen, the one securing a proper environment for his future shrine, the other anticipating both Aeneas going into battle and the subsequent destiny of Rome. The analogy is sustained in Vulcan's creation of an aegis for Athena, goddess of war but also, appropriately here, patroness of crafts and craftsmen.[79]

In the cases of both Aeneas and Athena the parallel deals with preparations for war. Vulcan's helpers and then the god himself are forging the pieces of weaponry for employment in battle. By his use of simile, however, Statius turns reality into metaphor, and in so doing again changes potentially violent activity to more promising ends. Hercules is doing battle not against men but with inanimate nature. He has a creative, not injurious, purpose in mind. Bellicose energy is redirected toward the improvement of nature on behalf of human life and its ennobling.

As the rocks shrink and night gives way to dawn, the human workmen return to gaze in wonder at the nocturnal activity of the unseen god.[80] Statius, too, expands his reader's horizon, once again with the help of Virgil. The phrase *artifices mirantur opus* calls our attention back to line 19 where the personified year and its months 'marvel at the enduring work' (*longaevum mirantur opus*) which has come into being during the course of that span of time.[81] But the poet's words also clearly recall *A.* 1.455–6, lines mentioned earlier. There we find Aeneas, awaiting the arrival of Dido, as he looks at the

---

[79] With lines 132–3, cf. Virg. *A.* 8.435–6 where the aegis forms part of the *arma* of Athena.

[80] The word *decrescunt* (134) is rare and not used by Virgil. It has particular poignancy here as referring to both size and strength. The rocks lose their power (to oppose the might of Hercules) at the same time as they gradually disappear. Versions of the word *scopulus* occur also at 16, 98, and 145.

[81] We have seen *annus* personified also at 2 (*desidis*) and 17–18 (*stupet*). The verb *anhelat* may serve as a reminder of Virgil's only use of the form, at *A.* 8.421 in connection with the fire in Vulcan's furnaces. The year gasps for breath because it has been working hard, the way that the god of fire would, paralleling Hercules as he crafts the landscape.

134   THE POETIC WORLD OF STATIUS' *SILVAE*

details of her temple to Juno:...*artificumque manus inter se operumque laborem miratur* ('...and marvels at the handiwork of the group of artisans and the effort of their accomplishments'). What follows, we remember, is the first lengthy description of a work of art in the epic. Aeneas in amazement views details of the saga of Troy as depicted presumably in murals on the temple walls. Statius' allusion thus serves several purposes. It draws a direct parallel between the workmen preparing the ground to receive Hercules' temple and Dido's artisans, along with the astonishing tale they have depicted. The Carthaginian queen again finds a parallel in Pollius whose workers are also in the act of admiration, in this instance of the nocturnal exertions of the god himself as he invisibly lends them a hand. Statius thus pointedly introduces the world of Virgilian epic again into his poem as he tells of Hercules' new labour and also reminds us once more of the importance of ekphrasis as a technical tool for strengthening his narrative flow.

Just as, at line 17, the personified year, along with its months, was astonished at what had happened over its extent, so now it pants (*anhelat*) after all that has occurred. The result is that a freshly glorified Hercules, from the height of his new edifice, can gaze down (*despectat*) on the waves below. He can now also challenge the nearby shrine of his infamous stepmother, a further reminder of Juno, she who had previously looked from above in contempt (*despicit*, 105) on his humble abode. Presumably Hercules' downward glance also embraces her nearby building with which his own now vies. He can also summon neighbouring Minerva to a temple now worthy of him—and her:

> iam placidae dant signa tubae, iam fortibus ardens
> fumat harena sacris. hos nec Pisaeus honores
> Iuppiter aut Cirrhae pater aspernetur opacae.
> nil his triste locis; cedat lacrimabilis Isthmos,
> cedat atrox Nemee: litat hic felicior infans.
> ipsae pumiceis virides Nereides antris
> exsiliunt ultro, scopulis umentibus haerent,
> nec pudet occulte nudas spectare palaestras.
> spectat et Icario nemorosus palmite Gaurus
> silvaque quae fixam pelago Nesida coronat
> et placidus Limon omenque Euploea carinis
> et Lucrina Venus, Phrygioque e vertice Graias
> addisces, Misene, tubas, ridetque benigna

A LABOUR OF LOVE (STATIUS' *SILVAE* 3.1)   135

> Parthenope gentile sacrum nudosque virorum
> certatus et parva suae simulacra coronae.
>
> (Stat. *Silv.* 3.1.139–53)

Now the peaceful trumpets give their signals, now the burning sand smokes with rites of strength. Neither Jupiter of Pisa (140) nor the father of shady Cirrha would scorn these acts of esteem. There is nothing sad in this place. Let tearful Isthmos yield, let cruel Nemea yield. Here a happier child offers sacrifice. Of their own accord the green Nereides themselves leap out from their pumice grottoes, they cling to the dripping crags (145), nor are they ashamed from their hiding-place to watch the naked wrestling. Gaurus, with its forest of Icarian vine-shoots, also watches and the woods which wreathe Nesis, fixed in the sea, and peaceful Limon and Euploea, good omen for ships, and Lucrine Venus, and from your Phrygian peak (150), Misenus, you will learn of Greek trumpets, and kindly Parthenope will smile at her people's rite and the men's naked competitions and the small images of her crown.

The repetition of the word *iam* declares the poet's eagerness for the start of a new subject in a new present. The temple, of which we hear no further detail, has been expeditiously finished. Now is the time to celebrate its completion with athletic games in the great Greek tradition. Statius highlights their introduction with variations on themes that punctuate the poem as a whole. Two words, for instance, stand out in the initial phrase, *placidae* and *tubae*. The competitions that follow are to be graced by trumpets which serve as the harbinger of peaceful endeavours that give pleasure to participants and audience alike, not to announce the imminence of battle with its dire consequences. *Placidae* is an apt descriptor. Statius will use it again shortly to qualify Pollius' villa near Puteoli (*placidus Limon*, 149) and at line 179 he lauds Polla as *placidae*. We think back also to the master himself and to the *pacem* (66) which the poet enjoys when he visits the domain at Surrentum. The trumpets, here, complement a calm world of orderly contests, not of mortal challenge.

The next phrase varies the theme: *iam fortibus ardens/fumat harena sacris* on the final word of the sentence. The games are to be considered holy moments to honour a solemn dedication. The fervour of the sand on which the events will take place and the very strength of the rituals themselves reflect, through metonymy, the eagerness and bravery of the contenders who are performing.

136   THE POETIC WORLD OF STATIUS' *SILVAE*

Fumat, enjambed from the previous hexameter, is itself a masterful transfer. At line 56 Statius uses the word to depict the grove of Diana as it smokes, probably with incense, on her festival day. Here we find smoke metaphorically enlivening the burning sand on which will occur the heated athletic challenges that grace the holy ceremony. Thus, through the poet's magic, vigorous, competitive man, his scenic surroundings, and the religious solemnity of the occasion all merge in a unity that does honour to the event itself.

Statius now names the four famous sets of Hellenic games in the background, two indirectly—*Pisaeus Iuppiter* standing for the Olympic games at Pisa in Elis, *Cirrhae pater opacae* for Apollo and the games at Delphi on the slopes of Mt. Parnassus—and two directly, Isthmos and Nemea. The latter are contrasted with Pollius' imminent presentations. The Isthmian games were associated with the death of the child Melicertes (Palaemon), Ino's son, and those at Nemea with the tragic loss of the infant Archemorus (Opheltes).

No similar sadness, mourning or dread will be found in this special new setting for games (*his locis*), paying particular homage to Hercules (*hos honores*). In fact, the bereavements in the two Greek myths are directly counterbalanced in the new dispensation by the presence of the young grandson of Pollius. We have earlier seen him inscribed as a priest (*sacerdos*, 46), to the delight of his grandfather. Now he actually performs the ceremony, youthful though he is (*litat hic felicior infans*). Statius not only conceives of him as luckier than Melicertes and Archemorus. He stresses the point by giving him a heightened version of his grandfather's epithet *felix*. The incipient games are blessed accordingly.

Statius now surveys the landscape, positioning for us remarkable people and places that will share in viewing the performances, an act that the poet stresses by the reiteration of the verb *specto* in adjacent hexameters.[82] He begins with the Nereides, to be found, presumably, on the shore at Surrentum itself.[83] He then orients our vision directly across to the northern side of the Bay of Naples, first to Mt. Gaurus, to the north of Puteoli (mod. Pozzuoli), near the western end of that edge of the bay, then to the

---

[82] Statius here singles out the theme of viewing that is central to the poem. Cf. *spectare* (146, 175) as well as *despicit* (105) and *despectat* (137).

[83] Statius is fond of the adjective *viridis* (144) which here nicely characterizes the sea nymphs (see also lines 94, 128, 161, 174). The majority of critics (e.g. Courtney, Liberman) prefer the alteration, in the same line, of *puniceis* (the reading of M) to *pumiceis*, and there are parallels to justify the change in Virgil, Ovid, Martial, and Silius as well as Statius himself. The juxtaposition of two words of colour, however, especially given the presence of *atrox* in the preceding hexameter, would add an appropriately intense vividness to the description.

A LABOUR OF LOVE (STATIUS' *SILVAE* 3.1) 137

island of Nesis, east, in the waters off Puteoli. He then turns our gaze farther east, to Limon, at Pausilypum (modern Posillipo). Still farther east we near Euploea, she who is kindly to sailors, which is to say, by metonymy, Venus and, by extension, the metropolis of Neapolis. (The temple in her honour was located in modern Pizzofalcone, an area just to the west of the port centre.) Statius has us then turn back, to the northern rim of the bay, toward another temple of Venus at Baiae, on the shore of Lacus Lucrinus, to the west of Puteoli, then to Misenum, on a promontory south of Baiae. We journey back to Naples again, now bearing, once more by metonymy, the name of Parthenope, a Siren, and her presumed burial spot. Our inner eye is thus kept active, twice scanning the bay's rim, from west to east, and each time concluding at Neapolis.[84]

Individual characteristics stand out. First, we have the green Nereides with their spontaneity and their glee in viewing the naked wrestling places (*nudas palaestras*) which is to say the gymnasts themselves.[85] A wood of vines distinguishes Gaurus and a forest crowns Nesis. Limon is appropriately *placidus* as the dwelling of Pollius. The goddess of love, again aptly, puts in two appearances. Through apostrophe Statius singles out Misenus, who stands for both the place and the person whose name it bears.[86] The adjective *Phrygio*, attached to the town's eminence, reminds us that he had been a fighter for Troy and, in particular, the trumpeter of Hector. Recalled to life by the poet's sleight of hand, he is to add *Graias tubas*, as well as Trojan, to his learning, not because, with loyalty shifted, he will serve again as herald of mortal conflict but because he is now summoning athletes to the games ahead, modelled on a premier Greek institution.[87]

Just as Trojan is replaced by Greek, so war gives way to peaceful competition and the deadly strife of battle is replaced by the salutary energy of athletic encounters. At line 139, Statius had called attention to the *placidae tubae* that were to signal the start of the events. He now strengthens his point. The celebration of Hercules in the peaceful realm of Pollius is to be graced not by a clarion call to arms but by trumpets that resemble those employed to help organize the great Hellenic competitions. Once again, we

---

[84] For a more general survey of Statius' interest in the topography of Campania, see Esposito (2019) who focuses especially on *Silv.* 3.5, 4.3, and 5.3.

[85] The metonymy calls attention to both parts of the figuration that finds a parallel at 152 (*nudos certatus*). The clothing of the naked is a subject at 4 (*litora*) and 97 (*scopulos*).

[86] The second-person address is also a telling reminder of his appearance at Virg. *A.* 6.149–235. The *tuba* of Misenus is mentioned at 233.

[87] And we remember that the Hellenophile Pollius employs *Grais metallis* (5) in the fabrication of his temple for the Greek hero-god.

138 THE POETIC WORLD OF STATIUS' *SILVAE*

are asked to attend to an example of human forcefulness being used for constructive rather than injurious purposes.[88] In the catalogue's place of honour is Parthenope, a kindly rather than baneful Siren. Her smile sanctions a rite that also belongs to her. Like the Nereides she enjoys watching the naked competitors and Statius adopts similar figuration to enliven her conduct. Just as the metonymy *nudas palaestras* (146) centred our attention on both wrestlers and wrestling floor, so the metonymy in *nudos virorum certatus* (152–3) asks us even more specifically to watch both the contests and the naked contenders. And, as further connection with Misenus, we remember that these competitions are athletic, not martial, in nature and that the *corona* awarded is not for military valour but for prowess in sports:

> quin age et ipse libens proprii certaminis actus
> invicta dignare manu; seu nubila disco
> findere seu volucres Zephyros praecedere telo
> seu tibi dulce manu Libycas nodare palaestras,
> indulge sacris et, si tibi poma supersunt
> Hesperidum, gremio venerabilis ingere Pollae,
> nam capit et tantum non degenerabit honorem.
> quodsi dulce decus viridesque resumeret annos
> (da veniam, Alcide) fors hic et pensa tulisses.
>
> (Stat. *Silv.* 3.1.154–62)

Indeed come and willingly yourself, with your invincible hand, consider worthy the activities of your own competition. Whether it is your pleasure to split the clouds (155) with a discus or surpass the speeding Zephyrs with your javelin or knot Libyan wrestling with your hand, look favourably on your rites, and, if you still have apples of the Hesperides, heap them in the lap of august Polla, for she delights in them and will not demean so great an accolade (160). But if she were to regain her sweet grace and youthful years—grant me pardon, Alcides—you might by chance here also have carried her weights of wool.

Statius now turns again directly to the god himself and asks him to deign to become a participant in the games, whether the contest be devoted to

---

[88] Virgil employs the *tuba* in both senses, to signal war (*A.* 2.313, 6.233, 7.628, 8.526, 9.503, and 11.424) and to usher in games (*A.* 5.113 and 139). At *A.* 11.192 a *tuba* also announces a funeral.

A LABOUR OF LOVE (STATIUS' *SILVAE* 3.1) 139

discus- or javelin-throwing or to wrestling.[89] The repeated use of *manu* reminds us of the importance of bodily strength in the story the poet unfolds. But he puts a nuance on the theme by a bow to Virgil at the opening of the paragraph. The only other appearance in Latin of the phrase *quin age et* occurs at *G.* 4.329 in a context we have touched on before.[90] There Aristaeus ironically urges his supposedly uncaring mother to chop down the flourishing orchards that he cherishes: *quin age et ipsa manu felicis erue silvas...* ('Come now and you yourself destroy our flourishing shrubs with your hand'). The allusion continues with the discrete change from *ipsa* to *ipse*. The sea-nymph Cyrene is replaced by the hero-god Hercules. But the passages have something else in common. The ruinous instrument that son imagines mother possibly employing, we recall, is a *valida bipennis*, a sturdy double-bladed axe, the very tool that Statius puts into the hands of the god as he goes about the task of reshaping the Surrentine coast (126). By reminding us again of the earlier moment Statius stresses how the tone of the section from the *Georgics* has been changed from negative to positive. Just as in the earlier contexts that we examined the axe was not to be used to destroy either inanimate objects or fighters in battle, so now we are in a situation where once more human strength is to be put to creative ends. After the effort to train nature is over, Hercules can turn his powerful talents to enjoying, maybe even to having a part in, the games honouring him in the setting that he has enhanced. The poet, in his turn, has recourse to the language of didactic, at a moment when it verges on epic, as he tells the tale.

Statius asks the god to take pleasure in the proceedings (*sacris*, 158), as if once again the games were also holy in and of themselves.[91] Now, with his geographer's eye, he lures his reader's vision away from Neapolitan detail to a more spacious sweep west, by means of its winds, the 'swift Zephyrs' (*volucres Zephyros*). But first we stop at *Libycas palaestras*, places of wrestling along the North African coast. The reference is to Hercules' victorious struggle with the giant Antaeus.[92] But he is on his way west, and so are we,

---

[89] Like the *tubae* announcing the games to come, the javelin (*telo*, 156) here becomes an instrument of peaceful competition not of war-making. See, again, Hor. *Saec.* 33 where the *telum* is Apollo's bow.

[90] The repetition is noted by Laguna Mariscal (1992) 181.

[91] Forms of the word *sacer* serve as one of the poem's thematic links. Besides 158, cf. also 82, 140, and 152 as well as *sacerdos* (46). Virgil uses the phrase *sacris... indulge* at *A.* 4.50–1 where Anna urges Dido to welcome Aeneas. The hint of eroticism in the allusion is taken up by Statius in what follows. It reminds us once more of the importance also of the fourth book of Virgil's epic to the later author.

[92] Among Latin authors Lucan tells the story of Hercules and Antaeus at greatest length (4.581–660). At 9.689–90, he moves from *Zephyro* to *Libyen* while detailing the exploits of Perseus.

140 THE POETIC WORLD OF STATIUS' *SILVAE*

via Statius, to the Gardens of the Hesperides whose golden apples it was the hero's eleventh labour to procure.

Propertius makes the connection between the two events in a poem that is essentially a *laus Italiae*. A traveller would prefer the world of Rome, claims the speaker, even were he to view: *Geryonis stabula et luctantum in puluere signa/Herculis Antaeique, Hesperidumque choros*...('...the stables of Geryon and marks in the dust of Hercules and Antaeus struggling, and the choruses of Hesperides...', 3.22.9–10). We are back for a moment in the world of physical valiancy and superhuman endeavour that characterizes the career of Hercules when he was fulfilling the tasks dictated by Eurystheus. But the reference to Propertius takes us from valorous deeds into the world of elegy, and Statius is quick to follow up on the suggestion. To seize the apples is one matter. To use them later as an erotic offering is another. The poet now not only pacifies his hero once more, he also turns him into the implicit wooer of Polla, as he represents him bestowing a traditional gift of one beloved upon another.[93]

We also return to the suggestiveness of the poem's opening line which, we remember, draws on the initial verse of Horace's fourth book of the *Carmina*: *intermissa, Venus, diu*...(*Carm.* 4.1.1) To strengthen the recollection Statius dignifies Polla with the adjective *venerabilis*.[94] We respect her as worthy of adoration like a divinity. But we hear in particular the resonance of the name of Venus, the goddess of love. Pollius' wife graces the event by her esteemed presence, but her comeliness is enough to have the hero proffer to her the fruits of one of his final labours, fruits that now seem almost to serve as the tokens of a suitor. Were she young again, the poet avers, Hercules would willingly be both her slave and her lover, as he was for Omphale. The sweetness (*dulce*, 157) that the hero-god might find in the athletic competitions is, after the space of three verses, attached to the grace of the young Polla (*dulce*, 161).[95] It is this characteristic that the poet would have us remember as he once more links the games, and Hercules, with the native elegance and charm of one of his chief admirers. And, in terms of genre, Statius yet again moves us away from epic's grand gestures into the realm of lyric and elegy:

---

[93] For the apple as a lover's offering, see Littlewood (1968) who is expanding on Foster (1899). For an earlier example, cf. Catul. 65.19–20 (*malum*...*gremio*).

[94] We also recall that the Muse Calliope is called *veneranda* (49).

[95] The phrase *dulce decus* is a reminiscence of Hor. *Carm.* 1.1.2, where the poet is affectionately complimenting his patron Maecenas.

A LABOUR OF LOVE (STATIUS' *SILVAE* 3.1) 141

> haec ego nascentes laetus bacchatus ad aras
> libamenta tuli.
>
> (Stat. Silv. 3.1.163–4)

I myself, drunken, in my happiness brought these offerings to the newborn altars.

The 'I' of the narrator now enters the poem directly for the second time. The first occurrence of *ego* was at line 61 where the speaker strongly positions himself at the house of *facundus Pollius* instead of at his own dwelling under the Alban hills. He now puts himself forward, for the first and only time, as the author of the poem itself. He was happy, under the influence of the god of wine, when, at the newborn altars, he brought *haec libamenta*, presumably this very poem that we are reading, as his offering.[96] The bibacious speaking voice thus assumes the role of sacrificant, pouring forth the wine of stately language as the gift of his imagination to glorify the god at his time of renaissance on the coast of Italy.

A few hexameters earlier Statius sent us back to Propertius as aid to our understanding. Here again he has the third book of poems by the elegist in mind as he writes, and once more it serves as a resource for assisting us in the appreciation of his own accomplishment. Statius takes advantage of a moment when ordinarily subjective erotic elegy largely assumes the guise of a brilliant hymn, addressed, appropriately here, to Bacchus. We come in a few lines before its conclusion as the speaking 'I' summarizes his own undertaking:

> ante fores templi cratere antistes et auro
> libatum[97] fundens in tua sacra merum,
> haec ego non humili referam memoranda coturno,
> qualis Pindarico spiritus ore tonat.
>
> (Prop. 3.17.37–40)

Before the doors of the temple, as a priest pouring from a golden jug an offering of wine for your rites, I myself will put forward with a proud buskin these words to remember, a breath such as thundered from Pindar's mouth.

---

[96] Laguna Mariscal (1992) 185 rightly calls attention to Horace's use of *bacchabor* (*Carm.* 2.7.27) of his own song-making. We also remember the metaphorical description of the poetic wine he offers Maecenas (*Carm.* 1.20.2–3): 'which I myself sealed, stored in a Greek jar…' (*Graeca quod ego ipse testa/conditum levi*…). The allusion to Horace in turn may help confirm *ipse*, the reading of *M*, at line 164. Pollius has had a form of epiphany (89–116); see below, n. 98.

[97] I follow the reading *libatum* (Ω) to the emendation *libabit*.

142 THE POETIC WORLD OF STATIUS' *SILVAE*

Propertius' *libatum merum* has become the later poet's *libamenta* with which *haec ego*, also introducing an adjacent line, is now directly linked. Allusion to the earlier magniloquent author adds confirmation to Statius' role as priest-wordsmith, under the sway of Bacchus—and previous Roman poetry—but now standing before the entrance of Hercules' new shrine. This he honours with his own special vinous offering of a multifaceted poem as a liturgy, an outpouring from the imagination, in praise of the god and his resplendent, Surrentine setting.[98]

Hercules' Epiphany

> nunc ipse[99] in limine cerno
> solventem voces et talia dicta ferentem:
> 'macte animis opibusque meos imitate labores,
> qui rigidas rupes infecundaeque pudenda
> naturae deserta domas et vertis in usum
> lustra habitata feris foedeque latentia profers
> numina...'
>
> (Stat. Silv. 3.1.164–70)

Now I myself behold him on the threshold, releasing his voice and uttering such words (165): 'Hail to your enthusiasm and your resources, emulator of my labours, who tame rugged rocks and the shameful barrens of sterile nature and turn toward productivity the haunts dwelt in by beasts and bring forth deities hiding in shame...(170)'

The word *nunc* (164) takes us emphatically into the present moment at the same time as *ipse* lays stress on the speaker himself. With the exception of line 17, where the demonstrative pronoun is applied to *annus*, the poem's four preceding uses of *ipse* have all been applied to Hercules, enlivened before us. Here it is the speaker who, even after the preceding *ego*, is again drawn to our attention. Using the same verb, he takes us from his past

---

[98] The reader has been schooled, already from the preface of *Silv.* 3.1, to expect the association of ritual and poetry in what follows. For instance, at *praef.* 5 we hear, as Statius addresses Pollius, of the 'inner shrine of your eloquence' (*facundiae tuae penetrale*) that we are about to enter. At *praef.* 9 the poet describes this initial poem of his book as a *limen* for the others that follow, and at line 164 mention of the temple's threshold (*limine*) follows immediately upon the comparison of the poem's contents to *libamenta*. Finally, *praef.* 9–10 tell of Hercules Surrentinus 'whom I prayed to with these verses' (*quem...his uersibus adoravi*), taking us directly into a comparison of poetry with a ceremony of worship.

[99] At line 164, I follow *ipse*, the reading of *M*, rather than the change to *ipsum* (as Liberman does). Pollius has had an epiphany of the god (89–116). Now it is the poet-speaker's turn.

A LABOUR OF LOVE (STATIUS' *SILVAE* 3.1)   143

performance (*tuli*) to the immediacy of Hercules as the latter is about to speak (*dicta ferentem*, 165). Now it is the poet's turn to be featured as, on the temple's doorstep, he sees the god himself. The bard as priest gives himself the privilege of imagining an epiphany of Hercules and of quoting his very words.

If the phrase *cernere erat* (15) took us into the history of ekphrasis, the emphatic *cerno* (164) even more strongly suggests the poet's part in persuading us to envision an image of the god in person, appearing before his votary. What 'I discern' now takes further palpable shape in the landscape, transformed by Pollius, that Hercules conjures up for us as he addresses his follower. He begins with two compliments. His first words, *macte animis*, take us back to the second book of the *Silvae*, where it is Statius himself who addresses his patron: *macte animo quod Graia probas, quod Graia frequentas/arva...* ('Hail to your spirit: that you applaud things Greek, that you spend time in Greek lands...', 2.2.95–6).[100] Before beginning his survey of the changed prospect before him, Hercules reminds us that it is the quality of Greek artistry that remains a paragon for Pollius. Statius' patron is blessed because of intelligence, imagination, and depth of character as well as external wealth. But the god also pays him the tribute of implicitly comparing his accomplishment to one of the hero's own labours which in many instances consisted of ridding the world of the monstrous, the ugly, the frightening, the evil. Hercules will come to Surrentum in the guise of humanizing hero who supports Pollius in his role as beautifier and civilizer of land and people, of exteriors and interiors, of visual surroundings and moral values. It is the genius of Statius vividly to put before us this landscape before it undergoes amelioration. In so doing he is expanding on the hints that he had already given at lines 12–16. The rocks are *rigidas* which is to say preternaturally hard. But we also think, for instance, of Horace's *rigidi Getae* (*Carm.* 3.24.11),[101] the Getae as emblems of grimness and primitivism. The personified landscape needs to be freed from its savagery before being accepted as the sophisticated domicile of a great temple and its divinity. A similar ambiguity rests with the word *deserta*. That an example of what the language suggests was in Statius' mind, we need only think of the words of Achaimenides, abandoned by his colleagues, that Aeneas quotes, telling of

---

[100] The passage is also discussed by Bessone (2022b). With *animis opibusque* (166) and *macte animo*, cf. Hor. *Carm.* 4.4.60 (*opes animumque*) in a context concerned with the labours of Hercules; see also Laguna Mariscal (1992) 185.

[101] Cf. also Hor. *Ep.* 2.1.25 (*rigidis Sabinis*).

144 THE POETIC WORLD OF STATIUS' *SILVAE*

the time: *cum vitam in silvis inter deserta ferarum/lustra domosque traho*... ('when I eke out my life in woods amid the barren haunts and dwellings of beasts...', *A.* 3.646-7).[102] The dens of the animals are *deserta* not because they are uninhabited but because they typify what is wild and uncivilized. Given the implications of both *rigidas* and *deserta*, therefore, Pollius' property needed to be schooled and refined, with any rudeness eliminated, to become suited to receive the honour destined for it.

Another trait of the topography is its previous lack of fertility. But the word *lustra*, also in common with Virgil's text, adds a further dimension to Statius' characterization, a dimension already intimated in the word *infecundae*. *Lus tra* are the lairs of feral creatures but, from Plautus on, the word also has the connotation of dens where sexual vice is practiced.[103] Their presence might be the cause of sterility but it might also suggest why the locales themselves are also shameful (*pudenda*), and their resident divinities 'foully in hiding' as if, at least metaphorically, the quality of their ethical lives was not deserving of close scrutiny. In sum, the landscape that Pollius has now so handsomely domesticated was originally neither productive nor seductive to the eye nor spiritually enhancing. It would certainly not have suited a Polla who is both *nitida* (87) and *placida* (179), radiant and stylish as well as gentle. As he makes the landscape useful, its *dominus* also transfigures its indigenous divine inhabitants to be both luminous and presumably now also worthy of devotion along with the great god himself:

> quae tibi nunc meritorum praemia solvam?
> quas referam grates? Parcarum fila tenebo
> extendamque colus (duram scio vincere Mortem),
> avertam luctus et tristia damna vetabo
> teque nihil laesum viridi renovabo senecta
> concedamque diu iuvenes spectare nepotes,
> donec et hic sponsae maturus et illa marito
> rursus et ex illis soboles nova grexque protervus
> nunc umeris inreptet avi, nunc agmine blando
> certatim placidae concurrat ad oscula Pollae.
>
> (Stat. *Silv.* 3.1.170–9)

---

[102] For *lustra feris*, see also Virg. *G.* 2.471 (*lustra ferarum*).

[103] Cf. also the etymology of Servius (*ad A.* 1.607): 'we call *lustra* both the dens of wild beasts and, by antiphrasis, brothels because they are ill lit' (*lustra et ferarum cubilia et lupanaria per contrarium dicimus, quia parum inlustrantur*).

A LABOUR OF LOVE (STATIUS' *SILVAE* 3.1)   145

What rewards will I now offer you for your excellence? (170) What thanks will I return? I will clutch the threads of the Parcae and will stretch their distaffs (I know how to vanquish hard Death), I will turn grief aside and forbid sad losses and I will refresh you, maimed not in the least, with green old age and I will grant that you long gaze at your young grand-children (175) until he is ripe for a bride and she for a husband, and again their new offspring and eager brood will now wind around the shoulders of their grandfather, now as a gentle throng run in competition to the kisses of peaceful Polla.

Statius now has Hercules offer to reward Pollius for his services on his behalf, which is to say because of his good works for the god but also for his, and Pollius', environment. The offer is extraordinary, and it again brings to the fore the theme of temporality that is central to the poem. Hercules can stop, or at least restrain, the passage of time. He can control the threads and manoeuvre the spinning of the Parcae because he can master death. We thus move in the god's career, appropriately as the poem nears its conclusion, from his wrestling with Antaeus and his eleventh labour, the seizure of the apples of the Hesperides, to a reminder of his final task, the capture of Cerberus, three-headed hound who guards the realm of the dead, and the hauling of him to the world above.

So, as Hercules boasts, 'I know how to vanquish hard death' (*duram scio vincere Mortem*). Not only can he slow the work of the Fates, he can even overcome the figure who inexorably looms at the end of every human existence. Just as he can subdue obdurate nature in preparation for his temple, so he can even mollify the pitilessness of *Mors* herself.

Statius is thinking back to a moment in *Georgic* 3 that will help us place the poet's words, here and in what follows, in wider perspective:

> optima quaeque dies miseris mortalibus aevi
> prima fugit; subeunt morbi tristisque senectus
> et labor, et durae rapit inclementia mortis.

(Virg. G. 3.66–8)

For pitiable mortals the best days of our lives are the first to take flight. Diseases and sad old age and suffering take its place and the mercilessness of hard death does the snatching.

146 THE POETIC WORLD OF STATIUS' *SILVAE*

Death has no mercy, and the best of days are ever the first to flee, laments the speaker.[104] As we move from *mortalibus* to *mortis*, didactic Virgil expands our thinking about the inroads of time in the lives of animals so as to embrace all humankind as well, all, that is, who are subject to the almighty power of personified *dura Mors*. Statius in his turn narrows this broad perspective to dwell on Pollius alone and then his family. But the imagined compliment is on a grand scale.

For Pollius, Statius concentrates in particular on his old age and its potential. From the first line of the poem renovation, renewal (*renovat*) and rejuvenation have remained regularly in our thoughts. Now it is the turn of Pollius to be the focus of attention. The poet already shares in transmitting Hercules' magic by giving Pollius' *senecta* the attribute *viridis*, an adjective that is ordinarily associated with youth and its freshness. No harm is to come to his patron from the course of time. Rather the reverse of aging will occur: a return to life's springtime or, to follow the language more directly, the unimaginable combining of life's youth with old age.

Here, as so often, an allusion to Virgil deepens our appreciation of the context. Through the phrase *viridi senecta* Statius would have us recall the Augustan poet's description of Charon, sturdy ferryman of souls over the Styx: '... a god's old age is vigorous and green' (*cruda deo viridisque senectus*, A. 6.304).[105] We remember again, as does Charon himself in Virgil's epic, that Hercules entered the world of the dead but returned to the land of the living unscathed. Now it is in the poet's power to actuate a parallel between Charon and Pollius which suggests that the latter will not only enjoy a youthful senescence but may even share in aspects of divinity so as to remain ever fresh like the restored rites of Hercules that we hear of in the poem's initial hexameter.

Statius keeps the suggestiveness working as he turns to the descendants of Pollius. His grandchildren are *iuvenes* just like their supposedly aged grandsire, and he can long have the pleasure of looking at them (*spectare*), the way the 'green' (*virides*) Nereides view (*spectare*) the athletic events in Hercules' honour. But the poet's language also subtly intimates another aspect of the hero's magic: that the patriarch's gaze somehow has the potential

---

[104] With *duram Mortem*, cf. Virg. A. 10.791 where the singing 'I' will stave off 'the fate of hard death' (*mortis durae casum*), that is, will immortalize, the deeds of Lausus. Death and its conquering form a strong theme with Statius elegantly combining elements of lyric and epic, elegy and eulogy, as the poem reaches an end.

[105] In this instance both *cruda* and *viridis* look to youthfulness. Like Charon's, Pollius' ongoing senescence will be akin to the existence of a young man. The notion extends into the next line with *iuvenes nepotes* where *iuvenes* recalls *iuvenum* (44) and *iuvenem* (92).

A LABOUR OF LOVE (STATIUS' *SILVAE* 3.1)   147

to keep his progeny young. He will gain enjoyment from the prospect of their youth, but they will also remain young for as long as he watches them.

This 'newness' will continue on into yet another generation (*suboles nova*) who will enthusiastically approach their *avus* and his spouse, Polla. In his description of the merger of the two disparate generations Statius once again takes the opportunity to show how any potential for fruitless violence in Pollius' world gives way to visionary energy. Take the word *agmen*, for instance. It often has martial connotations and the poet used it at line 34 to describe 'your quiver's pitiless array' (*agmen...immite pharetrae*), the arrows of Hercules that have no forbearance. When we turn to Pollius' happy domicile *immite* yields to *blando* and the normal harshness of heroic endeavour is replaced by the gentleness of familial affection. Likewise, just as the spectre of Hercules, putting aside his battler's intensity, had earlier embraced Pollius with 'gentle arms' (*blandis...ulnis*, 90), so now a similar mildness is on display as her progeny greet *placidae Pollae*, Polla who is appropriately serene.

Statius had previously used the adjective *placidus* at line 139, to mark the trumpets (*placidae tubae*) which now introduce games instead of warring, and again at 149, to depict Limon which contained one of the dwellings of peace-loving Pollius. The associations continue here. The youngsters flock to their matriarch *certatim*, as if they were vying in a *certamen* (154), a private form of athletic contest with no negative connotations. The accompanying phrase, *concurrat ad*, is unexampled elsewhere but commentators are right to point to Virgil's use of the verb *concurritur* at *G*. 4.78 where it is used metaphorically for the clashing of bee swarms.[106] As with Statius' preceding use of *agmen*, the suggestion of military combat is carefully transformed into an example of salutary fervour, as her progeny rush not into bellicose contention but toward gentle Polla's kisses.

> 'nam templis numquam statuetur terminus aevi
> dum me flammigeri portabit machina caeli.
> nec mihi plus Nemee priscumque habitabitur Argos
> nec Tiburna domus solisque cubilia Gades.'
> sic ait, et tangens surgentem altaribus ignem
> populeaque movens albentia tempora silva
> et Styga et aetherii iuravit fulmina patris.
>
> (Stat. *Silv.* 3.1.180–6)

---

[106] See Laguna Mariscal (1992) 188, who refers also to Hor. *S*. 1.1.7 (likewise *concurritur*).

148   THE POETIC WORLD OF STATIUS' *SILVAE*

'For never will a limit of age be placed on the temple (180) so long as the fabric of the fire-bearing heavens shall carry me. Nor will Nemea or ancient Argos be more my homestead nor my dwelling in Tibur nor Gades, bedchamber of the sun'. Thus he speaks, and, touching the fire rising from the altar and nodding his brow, white with poplar foliage (185), he swore by the Styx and by the thunderbolts of his heavenly father.

Hercules' concluding words centre on his particular interest in his temple, and the *Georgics* still remain in Statius' mind as he writes. We continue in the world of bees:

> ergo ipsas quamvis angusti terminus aevi
> excipiat (neque enim plus septima ducitur aestas),
> at genus immortale manet, multosque per annos
> stat fortuna domus, et avi numerantur avorum.
>
> (Virg. G. 4.206–9)

Therefore, although the limit of a restricted age greets them (for it never is extended beyond the seventh summer), yet the race remains undying and the fortune of the group is steady for many years, and the grandsires of grandsires are counted.

The poet has just offered an example of a human *avus* (178) who, through a god's grace, can keep death's obduracy at bay. With the help of Virgil and didactic poetry we now turn for a moment to creatures of the natural world who gain a form of immortality as they count *avi avorum*, grandfathers of grandfathers. But, in his compliment to Hercules, and by extension Pollius, Statius now surpasses his predecessor's optimistic calendar. Though the *genus* of bees as a whole remains undying, its individual members never survive beyond seven summers. The same, however, will not be said for the god's new shrine on which he places no 'limit of time'. If Pollius' family, like the bees, will, through the god's benevolence, abide from generation to generation, the temple of Hercules will excel individual bees by remaining as ever-enduring as their race itself.[107] The edifice will remain permanent as long as the heavens hold Hercules, which means presumably for eternity.[108] He will also prefer it to other terrestrial places with which he is associated,

---

[107] With *aevi* (180), cf. *longaevum* (19) as well as Virg. G. 3.66, quoted earlier.

[108] The only other uses of the phrase *machina caeli* are by Statius himself (*Theb.* 7.812 and 8.310), but, as so often, he may be thinking of Virgil, specifically of A. 4.89 (*machina caelo*) where the building of Carthage is interrupted by Dido's sudden attraction to Aeneas. The

A LABOUR OF LOVE (STATIUS' *SILVAE* 3.1)   149

whether because of his labours (Nemea, Gades), his city of birth (Argos, neighbour of Tiryns), or an Italian town where he had a special place of worship (Tibur). Mention of the heavens returns our minds to the opening of the poem to which we will revert shortly. But an allusion to Horace in line 183 has a wider demarcating affect. The phrase *solis... cubilia Gades* recalls *Carm.* 4.15.16 where the poet defines the majesty of Rome, under Augustus, as extending to the sun's eastern rising 'from his Hesperian bedchamber' (*solis ab Hesperio cubili*).[109] As the concluding words of Hercules that act also as a last suggestion of the role the far west played in his heroic endeavours, they have special import. But their placement in Horace adds still further significance. We find them halfway through the poet's final ode, a eulogy that puts lyric on a par with Virgil's epic as a glorification of the emperor's Rome. For a reader of Statius, however, the allusion is a reminder that the opening word of his great poem— *intermissa*—directly echoes the initial word of the first poem of this same last book of Horace's *Carmina*. Statius thus brackets his own poem by means of reference to the opening and closing odes of his predecessor's final collection of lyrics.

In the course of our discussion we have traced several instances of the influence of Horace, especially the lyric Horace, on Statius' poem. This concluding act of ordering is a strong bow to the presence, also in *Silvae* 3.1, of the personal immediacy we feel in great lyric poetry as it responds to a variety of situations, whether they are private or public, specific or general. However grandiose be the essence of Statius' poem as a whole, as it expansively surveys the fabrication of the god's new dwelling, the allusion to Horace also reaffirms for us the poem's strong sense of intimacy, be it in Statius' several adumbrations of Hercules' inner thoughts, in the caring portrayals of Pollius and Polla, or simply in the incisive recounting of a convivial summer's day.

The creative artist, as so often the case elsewhere, does not here enter the poem at its conclusion that still remains strongly centred on the god himself as Statius has him 'seal' the poem with an oath sworn at the temple's altar. But the genius of Statius is very much at work with an adroit act of rhetorical circularity that further corroborates the unity of the whole. The flame that Hercules touches as he sanctions his promise draws our attention back to the flame that purifies the mortal hero in preparation for his rising upwards

---

queen's apparent loss of power and stableness, as a result, is replaced by Hercules' assurance of immortality.
[109] The verbal parallel is noted by Laguna Mariscal (1992) 189.

150   THE POETIC WORLD OF STATIUS' *SILVAE*

into the sphere of the gods:...*ceu taedis iterum lustratus honesti/ignis ab Oetaea conscenderis aethera flamma* (6-7). The initial fire, reaffirmed by *flamma* at line end, now reappears in the form of the fire at his altar of worship. And a reworking of the word *aethera*, the ether of heaven where the gods reside, reappears in the poem's final line as an attribute of Jupiter, Hercules' 'celestial father' (*aetherii patris*). This second reference back to the poem's initial hexameters further strengthens the bond between beginning and end and adds to our impression of full closure.[110]

A major notion that reappears pointedly in these final lines, and that further solidifies a sense of the poem's ensemble, is the interconnection between life and death, mortality and immortality, that runs through the poem and is associated with both Pollius and Hercules. It is on the latter that the final lines concentrate. Take, for example, the word *populea* to describe the elaborate crown that Hercules is wearing. Statius reminds us twice of *Aeneid* 8, the epic's book that was most on his mind as he wrote because of the conspicuous presence of Hercules in its storyline. We first hear of the poplar tree. King Evander has finished his account of the hero's vanquishing of the wicked giant Cacus on the future site of Rome:... *Herculea bicolor cum populus umbra/velavitque comas foliisque innexa pependit...* ('...when the twin-coloured poplar, its shade associated with Hercules, shrouded his locks and hung down, intertwined with leaves...', *A.* 8.276-7). The reference is picked up, with wording close to that of Statius, as the Salii join in the celebration: *tum Salii ad cantus incensa altaria circum/populeis adsunt evincti tempora ramis...* ('Then the Salii around the blazing altars are at hand for the singing, their brows bound with sprays of poplar...', *A.* 8.285-6). Statius would recall for us the labours of Hercules and in particular, through the lens of Virgil, have us view his dynamic presence on the Aventine, ridding this Arcadian world of the malevolent and the horrific.[111]

The word *bicolor* has a particular resonance that allows us to extend the vision that Statius suggests. In the first of his two comments on the connection between Hercules and the poplar, Servius (*ad A.* 8.276) connects the

---

[110] The poem's opening lines, as we saw, offer a précis of the life of Hercules, taking us from Tiryns (*Tirynthie*) to heaven, from birth to apotheosis. By his final reference to *aetherii patris*, Statius is furthering the suggestion of his hero's progression from human to god, from the pseudo-son of Amphitryon of Tiryns, and therefore apparently mortal, to the heavens and to the presence of Jupiter, his true begetter.

[111] Line 185 also may refer to Hor. *Carm.* 1.7.22-3 where Teucer 'is said to have put round his forehead a poplar garland moistened by Lyaeus [Bacchus]' (...*uda Lyaeo/tempora populea fertur vinxisse corona*...). The allusion anticipates, and confirms, the reference to *Carm.* 1.3 in the subsequent, final line. In both instances the presence of Hercules is in the background.

A LABOUR OF LOVE (STATIUS' *SILVAE* 3.1)   151

leaves of the tree, which are dark on one side and light on the other, with the labours of Hercules, which took place in our sublunar brightness with the salient exception of the harrowing of hell's darkness to seize Cerberus. In a still more detailed gloss, the commentator explains that the hero wore a poplar crown while embarked on his Underworld venture.[112] One side of this grew white from the sweat of his brow while the other was stained black because of its association with the nether regions.

Statius' context thus allows us to reaffirm the hero's previous associations with temporality in the widest sense. His intimacy with death allows him not only to transcend its grasp on his own existence but also to ameliorate its inflexible command over the lives of his human patron and the latter's family.[113] But Statius also carefully connects him with birth. We hear first of his *templis nascentibus* (28) where the poetic plural lends puissance to the mention of his shrine as it comes into being. Then, at line 163, we look particularly at the *nascentes aras* where the plural has us again ponder with special closeness an aspect of the building as a venue for adoration.

The career of Hercules has been before us from the poem's start where, we remember, already within its initial seven lines we journeyed in our mind's eye from the hero's birth at Tiryns to his ascension from the flames on Mt. Oeta toward glorification in heaven. Here in the poem's final hexameter, as a form of recapitulation, the demarcation is narrower but no less imposing. In Statius' wording of the hero's oath, we move from the Styx to Father Jupiter with his thunderbolts, from the territory of the deceased to the realm of the immortals. The fire on Hercules' altar may seem to rise upward at his touch but his own grand career, which we have been following throughout the preceding lines, has taken us not only from birth to death but, more extravagantly, from his mundane origins to his everlasting role as a deity.

In Virgil the choruses sing the *laudes Herculeas* (*A.* 8.287–8) as the ceremonies to the god reach their finale. Statius' poem, which owes so much to his predecessor, is essentially one long hymn of praise. We begin with a renewal of *sacra,* and we end, in a splendid example of ring-composition,

---

[112]   In his annotation of *Ecl.* 7.61, Servius observes that the double colour of the poplar bears witness to the double nature of Hercules' *labores*, some connected with the world above, some with the realm below.

[113]   For Hercules in the Underworld, see Virg. *A.* 6.123 and Charon's comment at 392–3 (cf. 801–3 where Virgil gives a brief tour of the territory the hero covers in the course of his labours). Once again, we note how Hercules is able not only to mollify recalcitrant nature but also to overcome the inexorable pressures of time.

152   THE POETIC WORLD OF STATIUS' *SILVAE*

first as Statius himself approaches the *aras* (163) with his own offering of poetry. Then, at the poem's finale, we find ourselves at the *altaribus* (184) where Hercules himself nods his head and swears by the Styx and the thunderbolts of his father, by the world of the dead, that he has broached while still living, and by the invincible power of heaven.

So we begin and end with reference to sacred rituals and share in the poem itself as part of the performance. And the pointed reference to *Aeneid* 8 puts its whole context also into play as we reach the close. It is appropriate that, at his poem's end, Statius pay homage to his greatest poetic model. We thus participate in two poetic ceremonies recreating actual rites in the hero-god's honour.

We have seen how allusions to the opening and closing lyrics of the fourth book of Horace's *Carmina* bring together the start and finish of a text that essentially remains a panegyric to Hercules. In conclusion, let me offer one final example of how a single ode, in which the god also makes a prominent appearance, remains forcefully in the background as a unifying agent of Statius' poem. I am thinking of *Carm.* 1.3, which we have looked at briefly before. The later poet calls attention to its importance in his final hexameter that, as we saw, takes us from Underworld to heaven, from death to the realm of the immortals: ... *et Styga et aetherii iuravit fulmina patris* (186). Horace ends his great diatribe against man's overweening ambitions with much the same language. We seek even the heavens in our folly, says the poet, and do not allow Jupiter to forego the employment of his thunderbolts as manifestation of his displeasure:

> caelum ipsum petimus stultitia neque
> per nostrum patimur scelus
> iracunda Iovem ponere fulmina.
>
> (Hor. *Carm.* 1.3.38–40)

In our folly we seek heaven itself nor, because of our wickedness, do we allow Jupiter to put aside his angry thunderbolts.

Reference to this other powerful finale is the climax of a series of allusions to Horace's ode that punctuate Statius' poem. The first, we recall, is to be found at line 32 where the phrase *fraudum...malarum* is anticipated by Horace at *Carm.* 1.3.28 as he tells of the *fraude mala* by which Prometheus stole fire, to the continuing hurt of the human race. We come upon another example of interaction at *Carm.* 1.3.36 where the words *Herculeus labor* fulfil two purposes. They recall for us the several occasions on which Statius

A LABOUR OF LOVE (STATIUS' *SILVAE* 3.1)   153

alludes to the god's descent into the world of the dead to perform his twelfth and final labour. At line 19 Horace has already demonstrated that ambitious man seemed fearless in the face of death while at lines 31–2 he openly blames death's quickened pace on our destructive aspirations.

Mention of the labour of Hercules also looks specifically at *Silv*. 3.1.116. There the phrase *Pergameus labor*, reminding us of the hero's share in building the walls of Troy, follows two lines after his direct instruction to Pollius to follow *Herculeis hortatibus* (114). Hercules' self-naming reinforces the necessary promptings to his worshiper. Finally, the words that open line 53, *incumbit terris*, are a bow to the similar phraseology—*terris incubuit*—that Horace adopts at line 31 to depict the wasting disease and troop of fevers that brood over the earth as a result of man's iniquitous intentions.

A pessimistic tone pervades Horace's powerful address to Virgil, his fellow master-poet and friend. The ode, as we saw, has often been taken as an allegorical cautionary tale to someone embarking on the seas of epic, where narrating the saga of Aeneas and of Rome's rise to power would make a host of diverse demands on his imagination. It is interesting and enlightening to watch how Statius in instance after instance has taken Horace's gloomy overview of man's history—in a lyric with adumbrations of the challenges of writing more expansive poetry—and changed it, in his own potent presentation, to more uplifting ends. *Carm*. 1.3 is a deeply personal lyric with powerful overtones of more comprehensive themes, in fact a poem akin to *Silv*. 3.1 itself. The forceful presence of Hercules is to be felt in both poems, but Statius stabilizes the now immortal hero in a temple situated within a human context of quality and warmth.

The evil deceit that here permeates Horace's delineation of human nature can gain no entry to the house of Pollius which is both blessed and ingenuous (*felix simplexque*, 32). The devastating plague that Horace imagines settling over the world because of man's wrongdoing is replaced by the blazing rays of the sun that lead not to possible retribution on the part of the gods but to a time of festivity on a warm summer's day. The labour of Hercules that results in his triumph over death, instead of standing, as it does in Horace, as an instance of man's rash venturing into forbidden territory, takes propitious form for Statius not only in the god's mighty preparations for the building of an edifice in his honour but in his personal intervention to postpone the inevitability of death in the lives of Pollius and his family. Lastly, the thunderbolts of Jupiter, whose use Horace sees as a manifestation of the god's anger against man's sinful behaviour, become, in Statius'

154   THE POETIC WORLD OF STATIUS' *SILVAE*

brilliant finale, a source of reassurance of the excellence of his godlike son's works and ways. They cap Hercules' singular career with the approval of heaven.

Refreshment and renewal, continuity and novelty, time's relentless flow, death and immortality, have been topics of importance throughout Statius' poem. At lines 66–7, we remember, Statius, in a direct act of esteem for Pollius, calls our attention to the *novos Pieridum flores intactaque carmina*, the 'fresh flowers of the Pierides and virginal songs' that are to be learned (*discens*) by the poet-guest as he gains nurture in the beneficial proximity of his patron. In conclusion we might reverse the flattery and ask what is special about Statius' own accomplishment. He has told us that his verses take the metaphoric form of *libamenta* (164), of wine to be poured during the celebratory rituals that honour the renewed as well as magnified reverence for Hercules. As part of the ceremony, he will inventively merge the liturgies of athletic competition, religious rites, and poetry-making in his offering.

Hercules' *sacra* will be restored, and Pollius' family will be assured of continuity. But part of this lasting quality will also stem from the endurance of the poem that expands on both points. What is novel about the 'flower' that the Muses have inspired our poet to grow? What is 'untouched' about his song so that it can seem at once deeply beholden to tradition and yet original?

One answer rests with a theme we have been following from the initial lines of the poem. The opening septet of verses forewarned us that what was to follow had the potential of epic grandeur about it. Yet the first word, *intermissa*, directly echoes the first word of Horace's fourth book of *Carmina*. Statius has thus set himself the task of telling, in the tradition of the *Iliad* and the *Aeneid*, the story of the new temple to Hercules at Surrentum, of the god's crucial part in its realization, of the human participants in his endeavours, including the poet in his own person, of the natural setting that is transformed in the process. But at the same time, he is acknowledging the presence of a strong lyric element in the makeup of what follows. Forceful narrative flow is regularly peppered with touches that call our attention to the individual, immediate aspects of events as they unfold. Hercules himself can even turn his bow into a lyre to accompany the muse Calliope as she sings the aetiology of the god's new residence. Statius suggests that he, as poet, will symbolically make use of both bow and lyre as he merges the heroic and the personal, the grand sweep of an important event in Surrentine history and the human elements that suffuse its evolution.

A LABOUR OF LOVE (STATIUS' *SILVAE* 3.1)   155

Other genres play equally strong roles in strengthening Statius' presentation as he summarizes and incorporates aspects of past poetry. We experience the power of didactic verse through the constant influence of Lucretius and especially of Virgil's *Georgics* upon the writing, for instance, in the former poet's discourse on originality and in the reminders on the part of the latter of time's ineluctable passage. Horatian satire makes an appearance as we trace the kaleidoscopic details of Diana's feast. Through reminiscences of Propertius, Statius makes use of elegy and its dynamic combination of the intimate and the social as it situates the private realm of eroticism in its larger Augustan context. Beyond all else, in the poem's exhilarating generic interplay, the single influence of Virgil looms largest. This is the case especially with Statius' constant homage to the earlier poet's language throughout his own narrative. His most detailed references, whether explicit or implicit, are to *Aeneid* 8 that, as we have often observed, tells of Hercules' exploits on the site of future Rome as well as of the manufacture of the shield of Aeneas. We have also seen Statius, for a variety of reasons, regularly advert to the story of Dido as it unfolds in the epic's first six books. But it is the poet's own brilliance both to engage ingeniously with the past and to create a masterful example of his own substantial gifts of the imagination.

4

Atedius Melior's Parrot
(Statius' *Silvae* 2.4)

Silvae 2.4, Statius' meditation on the death of the parrot of his patron Atedius Melior, follows in the long tradition of laments on the passing of cherished pets. It has an especially close exemplar in *Amores* 2.6 of Ovid, a poem whose shadow rightly looms over Statius' elegy and is likewise devoted to the loss of a parrot, on this occasion the plaything of the writer's beloved, Corinna. The intense complementarity between the two works has been much studied and I, as well, will refer to Ovid's accomplishment in the pages that follow.[1]

Statius first addresses the bird, delight of its master, underscoring primarily its recent loss as company at dinner. The bird's sounds are now engulfed in the amnesia and stillness of Lethe. (It is not only swans who celebrate death, the poet reminds us.) The plaything, Statius further tells us, left vacant a cage, grand in size and rich in various noises made by the creature itself or complementary to them. We then enjoy a catalogue of other avians to whom nature has allotted the gift of imitating human expressiveness. These particular species are asked to learn a *carmen*, which first compares the parrot favourably to other birds. It then takes note of the favourite as speaker and friend, as companion in sorrow (*queruli*) and happiness (*conviva*). The singers then directly address Atedius Melior, the *dominus* of the opening line, befriender of poets as well as admirer of pet birds. They end song and poem with the vision of a funeral ceremony laced with careful intimations of immortality.

---

[1] My critique is deeply indebted to the commentaries of Van Dam (1984), Newlands (2011a), and Vollmer (1898). There are valuable insights in the appreciations of *Silv.* 2.4, among others, by Dietrich (2002); Newlands (2005); Rühl (2006) 203–8; Kirichenko (2017); Kronenberg (2017); Gunderson (2021) 271–7. For specific treatments of the relationship between Ov. *Am.* 2.6 and *Silv.* 2.4, see Colton (1967), Myers (2002), and James (2006). Statius' poem is roughly half the length of Ovid's, so concision could be seen here as a form of intensification.

The Poetic World of Statius' Silvae. Michael C. J. Putnam, Edited by: Antony Augoustakis with Carole E. Newlands, Oxford University Press. © Michael C. J. Putnam 2023. DOI: 10.1093/oso/9780192869272.003.0005

ATEDIUS MELIOR'S PARROT (STATIUS' *SILVAE* 2.4)   157

Statius himself, like a supremely gifted form of *imitator*, works with his literary past to create something brilliantly new. We will first start by searching out some of the imaginative riches that his opening lines initiate us into. As we move from Ovid's elegiac couplets to dactylic hexameter for the meter of choice, we find ourselves immersed in a rich interplay of genres that does justice as herald of the many paradoxes which the poem confronts. It prepares the reader for the meditation on loss and creativity that is its essence.[2] Statius will have us ponder matters of death and life, oblivion and immortality, tradition, emulation and originality, nature, and culture, but at the poem's core he sets in motion a creative confrontation between sound and stillness, talk and silence, the spoken and the written. He asks us especially to ponder words themselves and their varied users and applications, starting with the imaginative employment of a variety of verse forms.

The Opening of the Poem

The implicit didacticism in what I am suggesting—that we are about to experience a poem deeply concerned with language per se, primarily where verbal utterance is concerned—is borne out by the opening hexameters themselves:

> Psittace, dux volucrum, domini facunda voluptas,
> humanae sollers imitator, psittace, linguae,
> quis tua tam subito praeclusit murmura fato?
>
> (Stat. *Silv.* 2.4.1–3)

Parrot, leader of birds, eloquent delight of your master, parrot, ingenious copier of the human tongue, who has shut out your murmurs through so sudden a doom?

The word *voluptas*, bringing the initial hexameter to a striking conclusion, is a clear reminder of several moments in Lucretius' *De Rerum Natura*. The most striking is the opening itself: *Aeneadum genetrix, hominum divumque voluptas,/alma Venus...* ('Mother of the sons of Aeneas, delight of men and

---

[2] The opening lines are as rich with figuration as they are with allusions. We find varied examples of repetition along with metonymy, and alliteration. The initial apostrophe itself poses a paradox. It rhetorically brings the parrot to life, as does the adjective *facunda*, while at the same time announcing its decease.

158   THE POETIC WORLD OF STATIUS' *SILVAE*

gods, nourishing Venus...', 1.1–2). Through the powerful parallel Statius suggests to the reader that the subsequent poem, though centred on an erotic tale, will have a strong instructive element about it. But Lucretius himself also references the line again at 6.94–5, where he addresses:...*callida Musa/Calliope, requies hominum divumque voluptas...* ('...skilled Muse Calliope, rest for men and delight of the gods...'). Alliteration closely connects *callida* with Calliope, clever craftsmanship with the 'beautiful voice' associated with the muse of epic, poetry of the grand, expansive gesture. This further bow to Lucretius therefore enhances Statius' suggestion that what follows will be concerned with poetry and poetry-making, with genres and their admixture, with tradition and novelty in expression, with eloquence, which is to say with spoken words and the nuances of statement.[3]

Horace and Propertius also play parts in our poet's multivalent design. In his opening verse Statius focuses our attention on the parrot by the initial apostrophe and by the concluding address to it as *voluptas*, a striking abstraction that also serves as a metonymy and announces that we are also to expect a poem concerned with sexuality. The implications of the adjective *facundus*, which enables the poet to personify the parrot, will also resonate in the lines that follow. The ancient etymologies of the word regularly derive from the notion of speaking well, of using words to carry both conviction and character at once.[4] And, as we have already noted, language and various of its manifestations will be a recurring subject in what follows.

If Lucretius helped us feel the force of *voluptas*, it is Horace who furthers our understanding of *facundus* and its implications.

> Mercuri, facunde nepos Atlantis,
> qui feros cultus hominum recentum

---

[3] Both allusions are noted by Van Dam (1984) 343 and Newlands (2011a) 180–1. Lucretius' further reference to *iucunda voluptas* (2.3), to the pleasure that men should not feel at someone else's misfortune, also deserves mention. The language of 2.172–4, where the power of nature is the subject, likewise attracted Statius' thoughts as he wrote his initial lines:...*ipsaque deducit dux vitae dia Voluptas/et res per Veneris blanditur saecla propagent,/ne genus occidat humanum...* ('...and she herself [*natura*], leader of life, divine pleasure, leads (men) on and seduces them through the arts of Venus to renew the tribes so that the race of man does not pass away'). Statius' references to *De Rerum Natura*, therefore, take us from Venus, with inherent bows to Rome and the erotic, to human pleasure, to the reproductive force of *natura*, and to Calliope as emblem of eloquence and poetic inspiration.

[4] See, e.g., Var. *L.* 6.52 (*ab hac eadem voce* [i.e. *fari*] *qui facile fantur facundi dicti*) and ps.-Acro on Hor. *Ars* 217 (*facundia est iucunda eloquentia, unde facundus id est fatu iucundus*). See further Maltby s.v. (220).

ATEDIUS MELIOR'S PARROT (STATIUS' *SILVAE* 2.4) 159

> voce formasti catus et decorae
> > more palaestrae,
> te canam, magni Iovis et deorum
> nuntium curvaeque lyrae parentem…

(Hor. Carm. 1.10.1–6)

Mercury, eloquent grandson of Atlas, who cleverly shaped the rude ways of early men with language and with the institution of the graceful wrestling-place, you I will sing, messenger of great Jupiter and of the gods (5) and begetter of the curved lyre…

In a hymnic eulogy, Horace brilliantly brings before us the combination of voice and song, of words and music, that characterizes the messenger-god's civilizing mission. The notion of language, expanded into his role as *nuntius* and graced by metonymy (*voce*), is complemented by the poet's song (*canam*) as it praises Mercury's attributes, primarily the lyre and the beautiful sounds its presence portends.[5]

But it is the word *facunde* that most invites our appreciation. Save for one earlier use by the poet himself,[6] this is the first appearance of the adjective in the initial line of a poem since that of Horace. It asks us to reflect on the structural similarities between the two verses, each with a vocative at the start and trisyllabic words, with similar sound patterns, to conclude. In particular, it readies us for a poem that meditates, as we have suggested, on the creative concurrence of speech and sound, words and music. If the reference to Lucretius forewarned us to anticipate elements of a didactic poem in what follows, Statius' bow to Horace introduces the genre of lyric to the mixture and alerts us to expect a solemn, but also warm, immediacy in what follows, a poem in which verbal expressiveness will play a vital part in helping our spirits to soar.

But it is perhaps the genre of subjective erotic elegy that most sets the tone for what follows. The opening of Propertius 1.10 offers a pertinent example:

> O iucunda quies primo cum testis amori
> > adfueram vestris conscius in lacrimis!
> o noctem meminisse mihi iucunda voluptas,
> > o quotiens votis illa vocanda meis,

---

[5] Horace repeats *voce* at line 11 in relation to Apollo. [6] We find *facundi* at *Silv*.1.3.1.

160   THE POETIC WORLD OF STATIUS' *SILVAE*

> cum te complexa morientem, Galle, puella
> vidimus et longa ducere verba mora.
>
> (Prop. 1.10.1–6)

O delightful repose when I had been present as witness to the start of your love, privy to your tears! O delightful pleasure for me to remember the night, O how often is it to be summoned in my prayers, when I saw you, Gallus, perishing in your girl's embrace (5) and prolonging your conversation with extended delay.

The double use of *iucunda*, on the second occasion with *voluptas* as the line's concluding word, is a clear inspiration for Statius. The later poet not only reminds us of Propertius, as he will of the elegist Tibullus shortly later. He also alludes to a poem addressed to Gallus and hence to the origin of the poetic form itself. The change from *iucunda* to the wittily similar *facunda* alerts the reader again that we are to have a poem about words and speech. But the accompanying language sets us strongly in the world of elegy, of poetry that touches our deepest emotions. The *dominus* is not only master of the house but also, in elegiac parlance, lover in the position of power in a relationship centred on *voluptas*. Like Lesbia's sparrow as depicted by Catullus in his second and third poems, the parrot of Melior is both plaything and love-object as well. As Statius would have it, it is beautiful to look at but also gratifying to hear.[7]

Both themes are further suggested in line 3. The word *fato*, for instance, reminds us that it is destiny's spoken dictum, from the verb *for*, that pronounces the doom of the beloved bird and its final separation from Melior. But the phrase *praeclusit murmura* returns us in a richly metaphoric manner to the world of elegy. For help in determining the multi-layered implications of the first word we can turn again to Lucretius who, at 1.321, speaks of particles so small that we cannot perceive them, which: . . . *invida praeclusit speciem natura videndi* ('. . . the grudging nature of our seeing has shut out from our vision'). In the world of elegy a word such as *praeclusit* suggests in particular the stance of the *exclusus amator*, the yearning lover kept at bay by the bolted door of his *inamorata*.[8] Here it is the inexorability of

---

[7] The poem's function as a lesson and the speaker's role as erotic tutor are further connecting links with *Silv.* 2.4.

[8] '[The] image seems to come from shutting a door in a person's face' (Leonard and Smith [1961] *ad loc.*). The curbing of words is particularly suggested in Statius' context where the exclusion of a lover is a central concern. Lucretius also uses forms of *praecludo* at 1.975, 3.524, 5.373.

ATEDIUS MELIOR'S PARROT (STATIUS' *SILVAE* 2.4)   161

death that has kept the bird-*voluptas* at a distance, now apparently forever. Vision of any sort is no longer possible.

Murmura adds to the suggestiveness of the context. Once more we are in the world of sound, whether voiced or suppressed. The noises of the parrot are no longer possible now that mortality has asserted its might. But, as Ovid illustrates on several occasions, the word also finds a place in amatory vocabulary. For instance, at *Ars* 3.795, he speaks of the 'seductive words and delightful murmurs' (*blandae voces iucundaque murmura*) that form part of the act of lovemaking. The *murmura* of the parrot thus illustrate also the erotic 'language' that the bird would ordinarily bring to bear in expressing affection to and for its *dominus*. If death 'precludes' access to the beloved's residence, then *murmura* metaphorically typify the utterances with which the precious creature, had its entry been granted, would have announced its affection, but which are now forever suppressed.[9]

The word *sollers* points toward the intricate artistry that Statius displays in these initial verses.[10] We have already seen reference to didactic, lyric, and elegiac verse. The phrase *humanae linguae* adds further depth. As mentioned earlier, Statius regularly points to Ovid's elegiac poem on the death of Corinna's parrot for observation and comparison. Here it is a different Ovid that he asks us to consider, the writer of an extraordinary epic, *Metamorphoses*. We find ourselves in the land of the Cimmerians at the 'dwelling of sluggish Sleep' (*ignavi domus... Somni*, *Met.* 11.593):

> ... non fera, non pecudes, non moti flamine rami
> humanaeve sonum reddunt convicia linguae.
>
> <div align="right">(Ov. <i>Met.</i> 11.600–1)</div>

> ... no beast utters a sound, no cattle, no branches rustled by a breeze, or no clamouring of the human tongue.

We will shortly hear of the *convicia* that once emanated from the parrot's cage. Here Statius calls attention to the bird's talent for mimicry by himself doubly imitating Ovid. He brackets the line by the same phrase as his model and he uses metonymy, where *humanae linguae* stands for the sounds as

---

[9] For *murmur* in connection with birds see *OLD* s.v. 1b. Further instances of the noun in erotically suggestive contexts can be found at Ov. *Ars* 2.466 (doves are the subject) and 723. On the verb *murmuro*, see Quint. *Inst.* 1.6.38. Repetition and onomatopoeia are key factors in the usage of both noun and verb.

[10] On the etymology of *sollers* (=*sollus ars*) see the detailed study by Maltby (1991) s.v. (573). The Horatian uses (*Carm.* 4.8.8 and *Ars* 407) are pertinent.

162   THE POETIC WORLD OF STATIUS' *SILVAE*

well as the words to which the favourite gives utterance, for further emphasis. Meanwhile we have imagined a journey to the land of Sleep as further confirmation of the atmosphere of mortality which now surrounds the dead pet.

The Parrot's Death

For a moment we still watch the bird as well as listen to its vocal talent, but that soon changes:

> hesternas, miserande, dapes moriturus inisti
> nobiscum, et gratae carpentem munera mensae
> errantemque toris mediae plus tempore noctis
> vidimus. adfatus etiam meditataque verba
> reddideras. at nunc aeterna silentia Lethes
> ille canorus habes. cedat Phaethontia vulgi
> fabula: non soli celebrant sua funera cycni.
>
> (Stat. *Silv.* 2.4.4–10)

Yesterday, pitiable one, about to die, you joined our meal, and we observed you picking at the gifts of the attractive table (5) and wandering among the couches until after midnight. You had even repeated speeches and words that you had practiced. But now you, that tuneful one, possess the everlasting silence of Lethe. Let the well-known tale of Phaethon give place. It is not only swans that memorialize their deaths (10).

As we watch the parrot in its final moments and bear witness to its skill as a student of words and their communication, Virgil enters the poem and as usual enhances its resonance.[11] Take, for instance, the sad vocative addressed to the dead pet as *miserande*, deserving of sympathy. An admirer of the Augustan master could conjure up several instances of the same pathetic salutation. At *A.* 6.882, for example, the narrator apostrophizes the future Marcellus as *miserande puer*, dead at too early an age. Later, at 10.825, we find Aeneas himself addressing the young Lausus, whom his sword-thrust has just killed, as, again, *miserande puer*. Last in the sequence comes Pallas, done to death by Turnus and, in Aeneas' own words, a further

---

[11] The striking directness of the adjective *hesternas* finds parallels at Catul. 50.1 and Prop. 2.29A.1, both initiating their verses in contexts of pronounced eroticism.

miserande puer (11.42).[12] The parallels serve to humanize the avian creature and, by particular reference to Virgil's masterpiece, to attribute to it a momentary tone of heroic glory worthy of inclusion in epic.[13]

Statius keeps the theme alive at line 9 with the extraordinary phraseology *ille canorus habes* applied to the parrot as it finds placement among the silence of the waters of forgetfulness. The rare juxtaposition of the so-called third-person demonstrative pronoun (*ille*) with the second person verb (*habes*) creates a tension that both distances us from the singer and draws us toward him.[14] Death separates him from us as he accepts his destiny in the Underworld but, through the poet's imagination, we also are guided to apprehend that experience as well.

The only instance in the *Aeneid* where Virgil offers a parallel occasion in which language at once tugs us near and pushes us away offers a similarity for our reading of Statius:

> 'hunc ego te, Euryale, aspicio? tune ille senectae
> sera meae requies, potuisti linquere solam,
> crudelis?...'
>
> (Virg. A. 9.481–3)

> 'Is this you, Euryalus, that I gaze on? Are you, that late solace of my old age, able to leave me by myself, cruel one?...'

The unusual reference of *hunc* to *te* serves the purpose of detaching what the youth's mother sees before her from the being that her vocative would ordinarily address. The parallel juxtaposition of *tu* with *ille*, and further with *sera requies*, serves a similar purpose. Both collocations turn life to death, a living being into a corpse, a creative abstraction (*requies*) into a symbol of enduring quietude.

---

[12] Cydon is saved, by the intervention of the sons of Phorcus, from becoming a further example of a newly slain young warrior who, in the narrator's judgment, is *miserande* (*A*. 10.327). Statius reiterates the gerundive (*miserande*) at line 23 where the *carmen* that the birds sing in honour of their deceased colleague is styled *miserandum*. The bird itself and the song of lamentation meld together. Virgil's only use of the phrase *at nunc* (8) occurs at *A*. 10.393 as Pallas kills Thymber.

[13] The influence of Horace also recurs at line 5 where the conjunction *gratae carpentem* serves as a reminder of the similar juxtaposition, *grata carpentis*, at *Carm*. 4.2.29. There, we recall, Horace compares himself to a bee, and Pindar to a swan, in an ode as deeply concerned with poetics as *Silv*. 2.4 with its many echoes of the Latin literary past. The word *errantem* (6) also adds to the erotic suggestiveness in the elegiac context that Statius has fashioned.

[14] In his comment on line 9, Van Dam (1984) 346 lists *A*. 9.481 among examples of the use of *ille* with a second person verb.

164   THE POETIC WORLD OF STATIUS' *SILVAE*

It is no accident that here again we have the loss of a youth in a martial setting familiar from Homer on but given a particularly poignant depiction by Virgil as mother mourns for a lost son. Some of this same grief seeps into Statius' narrative. The bird is to be pitied (*miserande*) in his sudden death, like a young warrior fallen in battle. But he is both here and there at once, distanced by the *ille* of mortality and yet present as a 'you' songster who can still act as possessor (*habes*), even if it be only an unremembering hush to which he lays claim.

In the same verse alliteration connects the gerundive *miserande* with the participle *moriturus*, sorrow with death. The latter, while announcing the bird's imminent demise, also furthers the connection with the *Aeneid*, which is to say with the majesty of epic. Virgil, for instance, uses the form *moritura* three times of the Carthaginian queen Dido as book 4 draws to a close with her suicide (*A.* 4.415, 519, and 604). The implicit regality of Melior's parrot, as well as the gloom caused by its decease, is suggested by the reflections in language. But there is a still closer parallel. At line 511 of the poem's second book Aeneas tells of how king Priam 'is carried, about to die, into the thick of his foes' (...*densos fertur moriturus in hostis*). The resonance is especially striking here because Statius' wording (... *dapes moriturus inisti*...) also brings its hexameter to a conclusion with a similar sonic pattern as well as with the prominent verbal echo of the future participle.[15]

Statius thus twice-over wittily blends Melior's pet with famous royal characters in the *Aeneid* whose deaths received special prominence in the narrative, Priam at the vicious hands of Pyrrhus, Dido through self-slaughter. It will not be long before he calls the Trojan king yet again to our mind. Before leaving the initial lines, however, a few more details of the poet's mastery deserve mention. The word *vidimus*, for instance, catches our notice for its position at a sense pause after enjambment. In this world of sound, we are made to attend events with our eyes as well as ears. Statius also asks us specifically to recollect lines that we quoted earlier as Propertius ponders Gallus' lovemaking:...*cum te complexa morientem, Galle, puella/ vidimus et longa ducere verba mora* (1.10.5–6). In the midst of linguistic gestures bestowing epic stature on his parrot, Statius reminds us that we are attending to a poem that also projects major aspects of elegy as well, at once merging erotic desire with mourning.

Statius concludes his introduction with a reference to the myth of Phaethon which will soon play a role in the lines that follow We will also

---

[15] We note also how assonance combines with chiastic structure to emphasize *dapes*.

ATEDIUS MELIOR'S PARROT (STATIUS' *SILVAE* 2.4) 165

have reasons in particular to pause on the symbolic connection of swans, which figure importantly in the Phaethon myth, with poets and poetry-making. We should take note here as well of how the poet brings his impressive opening lines strongly full circle through the word *fabula*. As Varro defines the noun in the plural: '*fabulae* receive their name from the same verb, *fari* [to speak]' (*ab eodem verbo fari fabulae... dictae, L.* 6.55). Through mention of the myth of Phaethon and birds closely linked with song, Statius returns our thoughts to the opening line and the *facunda voluptas*, the cleverness at speaking that helps characterize Melior's parrot as personification of pleasure. The creature is at once beautiful and rhetorically deft.

But, as we have seen, expressiveness and the innate eloquence that lend quality to mere speech take different turns in the verses that follow. They can become negative with the abrupt word *fato*, the declaration that pronounces doom for the beloved pet. They can appear positive as the speaker in his role as guest remembers the *adfatus* and *meditata verba*, the utterances and pondered language of humans that came naturally to a gifted denizen of the wild. The multifaceted, often etymologically based, progress from *facunda* to *fabula*, from eloquence to the good storytelling that thrives on it, thus offers the poet's own meditation on varying ways of vocal enunciation as a complement to the parrot and its articulateness and, as we have suggested, to the poet's own larger contemplation of challenges that come our way between noise and silence, talk and muteness, remembrance and oblivion, life and its loss.

The Parrot's Cage

Statius now turns to a topic completely bypassed by Ovid in his parallel poem, namely the parrot's cage:

> at tibi quanta domus rutila testudine fulgens
> conexusque ebori virgarum argenteus ordo
> argutumque tuo stridentia limina cornu
> et querulae iam sponte fores! vacat ille beatus
> carcer, et augusti nusquam convicia tecti.[16]
>
> <div align="right">(Stat. <i>Silv.</i> 2.4.11–15)</div>

---

[16] At line 15, in following the authority of *M* (as Liberman does), I depart from Courtney's reading of *angusti*.

166   THE POETIC WORLD OF STATIUS' *SILVAE*

But yours was a grand house, gleaming with ruddy tortoiseshell, and a silver range of bars interlinked with ivory, and a threshold shrieking shrilly from your beak and doors now complaining on their own! That happy prison is empty, the racket of that noble dwelling is no more (15).

As so often, an allusion helps us probe the poet's meaning. In the fourth poem of his *libellus*, embedded in the corpus of Tibullus, Lygdamus has a dream of Apollo appearing before him, ennobled by beauteous lyre and ready to sing:

> artis opus rarae, fulgens testudine et auro
> pendebat laeva garrula parte lyra.
> hanc primum veniens plectro modulatus eburno
> felices cantus ore sonante dedit...
>
> [Tib.] 3.4.37–40

From his left side was hanging his talkative lyre, a work of unusual skill, gleaming with tortoiseshell and gold. When first he came, strumming this with ivory quill, he gave forth happy songs from his resonant mouth.

Ordinarily *testudo*, the shell of a tortoise, stands as metonymy for the whole lyre itself, and it is thus used in Virgil and Horace.[17] By reminding us of Lygdamus' reference to the shining lyre of Apollo himself, Statius turns the parrot's cage both literally and metaphorically into something kindred. The tortoise-shell decoration of the song-god's lyre is paralleled with the actual ornamentation of the bird's 'house' as it gleams with shell and also with ivory, like Apollo's *plectrum*. But the presence of *testudo* also suggests, as critics rightly note, that the cage itself is metaphorically a type of resonant instrument on which the humanly gifted bird makes music, even as if he were surrogate for the immortal god of the lyre, Apollo himself.[18]

In commenting on lines 9–10 we noted how Statius asks us to remember the 'common' *fabula* of Phaethon and Cycnus, only implicitly to downgrade its quality vis-à-vis the parrot's tale. But in the lines that follow the poet at the same time asks a special alertness of his reader. At line 11, through the phrase *testudine fulgens*, Statius had us turn our attention to the poetry of Lygdamus and the past of Roman elegy. Now at line 12, in an astonishing twist, we look back also to Ovid, but not to the author of the elegy (*Am.* 2.6)

---

[17] See Virg. *G.* 4.464; Hor. *Carm.* 1.32.14, 3.11.3, 4.3.17; *Ars* 395.
[18] See, e.g., Newlands (2011a) 184. The cage could also be envisioned as a type of poem and the parrot as emblematizing the practice of intertextuality, with imitation and novelty complementing each other.

ATEDIUS MELIOR'S PARROT (STATIUS' *SILVAE* 2.4) 167

that serves as Statius' model. Rather we are reminded again of his epic masterpiece, the *Metamorphoses*. The phrase *virgarum argenteus ordo* finds its source at line 108 of that poem's second book where we examine the shimmering chariot of Phoebus, Apollo in his guise as god of the sun, with its axle, pole, and wheel-rims of gold and 'ring of silver spokes' (*radiorum argenteus ordo*). The literal construction of the parrot's cage, the struts that hold it together, is inspired by Ovid's detailing of the dazzling fabric of the Sun's car.

But Statius challenges us creatively in yet another way. At lines 9–10, he had singled out for apparent demeaning the myth of Phaethon and Cycnus, the very tale, as narrated by Ovid in *Metamorphoses* 2, that serves as source for one of the brilliant decorations of the parrot's enclosure. By earlier dismissing the interconnected stories of Phaethon and his lover, the poet in fact prepares the reader for the pointed allusion to it at line 12. Both literal and figurative factors are at work here. Statius would have us, through hyperbole, imagine a parallel brilliance between the bird's cage and the bright vehicle that carries Phoebus through the heavens. But the astonishing fabric of the poetry itself is also enhanced as epic joins elegy in intensifying the structuring of words and genres that creates the brief ekphrasis. The junctures of the cage are metaphorically fashioned from the junctures of poetry, in no small part drawn by Statius from his literary past.

Alliteration between *virgarum*, *argenteus*, and *argutum* helps us move from one aspect of the cage to another just as it revives the importance of the awareness of sound to the storyline and adds it to the sharpness of vision that the poet has just asked from us in words like *rutila* and *fulgens*. And now another great author, Virgil, is brought back, to join Ovid in enhancing the grandeur of the moment. *Argutum* further vivifies a detail in what we are meant to hear from the birdcage itself, the threshold set sharply screeching (*stridentia limina*) by the beak of the parrot itself. The language brings to bear the force of a particularly dramatic moment in the *Aeneid* as the poet describes the *Belli Portae* (*A*. 7.607), the Gates of War that the consul must burst open at the start of a conflict.[19] With their equally *stridentia limina*, they add rich, perhaps deliberately exaggerated, resonance to the force of the bird as it makes grating music from the metallic framework of its enclosure.

---

[19] Given the context he has given its adjacent allusion, Statius may also be suggesting that we think of the *cornu* of the parrot as on occasion kindred to the war trumpets which also help further initiate the conflict to come in Latium (*cornua*, *A*. 7.615). Cf. the similar situations at Catul. 64.263 and Lucr. 2.619. The hyperbole brings with it a touch of humour.

168   THE POETIC WORLD OF STATIUS' *SILVAE*

The grandeur suggested by *quanta* (11), the relative adjective that first defines the home (*domus*, 11) of the pet-lover (*dominus*, 1), gains enhanced authority by a further reminder of Virgil and his epic.[20] As we follow out Statius' configuration of this cage-mansion, we move from threshold (*limina*, 13) to doors (*fores*, 14) to roof (*tecti*, 15), the concluding word of the description that stands as a synecdoche for the whole abode as well.[21] Virgil on several occasions names the same specific details of construction, once in an order exactly parallel to the present, when, in the second book of the *Aeneid*, he has the poem's hero describe for Dido the palace of Priam around which a major portion of the book's action revolves. At 2.440–5, Aeneas takes our eye from its roofs (*tecta*, 440) to its threshold (*limen*, 441) to the expansive home (*domorum*, 445) they help define. Soon thereafter we are asked to imagine its doors (*fores*, 450) and yet again its rooftops (*tectis*, 451). Finally, as if our imaginations needed constant reminders of how focal the position of the aged king was as symbol of his city's power, Virgil has his protagonist tell his listener once again of the *limen* (453), *fores* (453), and *tectorum* (454) that were crucial to his palace's defence.[22]

Thus Statius joins a lengthy reference to the palace of Priam, in *Aeneid* 2, to the preceding allusion to Virgil's depiction of the screeching *Portae Belli* in the epic's seventh book as a further means of enhancing our appreciation of the manifold distinction of the parrot's cage. We visualize, through its parallels in the epic, the quality of the object itself (as well as the importance of its 'prisoner') but further value its role as a symbolic container of exemplary moments in some of Roman poetry's greatest achievements. The cage is an instrument on which the bird can make artful music. But because it is partially built on, and of, the poetic past, it is also made up of art. Its own creation sings through the writings of Virgil, of Ovid. It sings the history of song, gaining further glory as poet expands on poet.

The adjective *augusti* (15) carries special weight in such a context. And here again we can draw on Virgil for authoritative support. He employs the powerful epithet on three occasions.[23] The first occurs at *G.* 4.228, applied

---

[20] The opening words of the hexameter, *at tibi*, echo Virgil twice (*Ecl.* 4.18 and *A.* 2.535, in the words of king Priam), both in settings of importance for apprehending the evolution of *Silv.* 2.4.

[21] For the plural *limina* used as singular in poetry, see *OLD* s.v. 2.

[22] The near juxtaposition of *stridentia* and *fores* recalls Tib. 1.3, another earlier poem on Statius' mind as he wrote. I think here in particular of 1.3.72:...*stridet et aeratas excubat ante fores* ('[Cerberus] shrieks and broods before the bronze-clad doors'). We also find *domus...fores* (11–14) at 1.3.43.

[23] For detailed discussion of the three passages, see Thomas (1988) 188–9.

ATEDIUS MELIOR'S PARROT (STATIUS' *SILVAE* 2.4)   169

by the poet to the beehive (*sedem*). He thereby prompts us to meditate on the venerable qualities of apian life and in particular on the majestic aspects of their dwelling which enable it to serve as a model for human civil life. Virgil's other uses of the epithet are still more to the point. They occur in near conjunction in the seventh book of the *Aeneid* to describe the city ramparts (*augusta moenia*, A. 7.153) and noble dwelling (*tectum augustum*, A. 7.170) of the local king Picus, as he prepares to receive a delegation of Trojans, newly arrived on the coast of Latium.

Statius thus has Virgil share with Ovid a major part in the glorification of Melior's parrot and his cage. We are asked to embrace in our imaginations not only the latter poet's *Metamorphoses* but also both halves of the *Aeneid* as we move from Book 2 to Book 7, from Troy to the Italian coast, from Priam to Picus, and from one royal establishment to another, all in honour of a *psittacus* already possessed, through Ovid, of an illustrious poetic past. At *Silv.* 4.2.18, Statius himself varies the central phrase when he describes the palace of Domitian as a *tectum augustum*, likewise a noble dwelling, in this instance enormous and supported by a multitude of marble columns instead of a rank of silver rods.[24] The echo, however, suggests that in our imaginations we here further reinforce the imagined grandeur of the parrot's lodging by associating it even with the awe attached to an emperor's abode.

Statius adds to the generic complexity of his ekphrasis by leading us yet again into the world of elegy which adds its own singular energy in formulating both tone and content. At the poem's opening line with its concluding emphasis on *voluptas* he had suggested to his reader that matters amatory would never be far from the poem's surface and the immediately subsequent hexameters continued the theme. Reference to the myth of Phaethon and Cycnus at 9–10 added the world of story to the erotic content.[25] Then at lines 14–15 a specific lexical usage helps us enter an elegiac context that further refreshes the language of the initial verses.

Through Statius' word choice we ponder the associations of the adjective *querulae* with its cognate noun, *querel(l)ae*. Tibullus, for instance, can speak of the 'suppliant complaints' (*querellis supplicibus*) that Venus allots love poets along with sad weeping, and on another occasion of the 'complaints'

---

[24] See the discussion on pp. 192–3 in this volume.
[25] The story is told at Virg. *A.* 10.189–93 and Ovid *Met.* 2.367–80.

170   THE POETIC WORLD OF STATIUS' *SILVAE*

(*querellis*) that a suitor utters before the closed door of his mistress.[26] Here *querulae* has the effect of personifying the doors (*fores*) of the cage. They now make lament of their own accord, patently for the loss of the bird that they helped house. But the implication also remains that once upon a time their sorrow was but an echo of the mourning of the creature which, when closed, they contained within its cage. This in turn suggests that the grieving of the doors, spontaneous now, in time past resulted from their reflection of the bird's audible yearning to be freed from its enclosure, if only momentarily. As the source of *voluptas* it could then keep appropriate company with its beloved master in a manner such as the poet already described at lines 4–6, enjoying his company at dinner even as the night wore on.

We have earlier taken note of the companion word *convicia* (15) in connection with the noises ordinarily emanating from the human tongue, not to be heard in the Ovidian cave of Somnus. Here the cacophony serves as complement to the moaning (*querulae*) of the cage's entranceway. Now we turn from present to past, from the doors' instinctive expression of sorrow at the parrot's passing to the clamour with which its shrieks had once filled the abode. But Statius brilliantly keeps the elegiac context vivid for us. The bird, re-enlivened in poetry, keeps its dwelling resounding with racket, but, given the setting already suggested by *querulae*, these are no ordinary *convicia*, the insults that people hurl at someone they loathe, but rather more likely the reproofs that lovers are wont to shout at each other. For instance, Propertius twice speaks of the *convicia* that his mistress sends his way, and Ovid urges against their use by lovers.[27] In this context, where doors exhibit a sadness (*querulae*) that smacks of erotic yearning, *convicia*, too, carry a similar aura. The bird could have voiced its now missing *convicia* against the cage itself, for keeping him penned in and away from his beloved. The abuse could also be directed against Melior himself for the parallel reason that on occasion he held his pet at an unnecessary distance away when it yearned for the pleasure it found in the proximity of its *dominus*—a pleasure made impossible during the times when it was suffering imprisonment, presumably at the whim of its master.

---

[26] For further examples, see Tib. 1.4.71–2 and 1.2.9; cf. [Tib.] 3.4.75. Not unexpectedly we find the cognate verb *quereris* at Ov. *Am* 2.6.7 and *querela* will follow at line 8. The technical name of the sub-genre of elegy is *paraklausithyron*. For a full discussion see Copley (1956).

[27] Prop. 1.6.15 (Cynthia); 3.8.11 (an unnamed *mulier*). At *Rem.* 507, Ovid urges the spurned swain from shouting *convicia* at his mistress' house-door or, for good measure, from uttering complaints (*querellis*, 509) against the girl herself the next day.

ATEDIUS MELIOR'S PARROT (STATIUS' *SILVAE* 2.4)   171

Within the same cluster of lines, the adjective *beatus* stands out, first for its ironic relation to *carcer* (what kind of cell radiates happiness?), but also for its further associations with a lover's contentment.[28] Statius may well have us think of the single occasion where Virgil also places the adjective *beatus* at the conclusion of a hexameter, namely *Ecl.* 6.82 as the *beatus Eurotas*, Sparta's paradoxically happy river, listens to Apollo's songs of lamentation for the death of his youthful lover, Hyacinthus. The allusion would form a further link in the chain of references to this multifaceted divinity. Lines 9–10 took us to the myth of Phoebus-Apollo, his son Phaethon and the latter's lover, Cycnus. We followed, at line 11, with Lygdamus' allusion to Apollo as god of the lyre, and at line 12, with Ovid's help, turned our attention again to the disaster of Phaethon. In terms of genre, as we have seen from the poem's initial lines, the mixture of elements of elegy and of epic, of a lover's complaint with the grandeur of heroic spaces, gives the description of the cage a special thrust.

Birds in Mourning

At nearly the poem's half-way mark, Statius turns momentarily away from portraying one especially talented bird, recently deceased, and its extraordinary, sound-ridden enclosure, to catalogue a series of equally gifted avian beings who will now join in mourning their comrade:

> huc doctae stipentur aves quis nobile fandi
> ius natura dedit; plangat Phoebeius ales
> auditasque memor penitus demittere voces
> sturnus et Aonio versae certamine picae.
> quique refert iungens iterata vocabula perdix
> et quae Bistonio queritur soror orba cubili.
>
> (Stat. *Silv.* 2.4.16–21)

Let learned birds crowd hither to whom nature has granted the lordly right of speaking; let the bird of Phoebus make moan and the starling, whose memory can committedly absorb the words that it has heard, and magpies, transformed during an Aonian contest, and the partridge which echoes words it repeats in sequence and the bereft (20) sister who grieves in her Bistonian chamber.

---

[28] See, e.g., Catul. 45.25; Tib. 1.10.63; Prop. 2.15.2; Ov. *Her.* 20.61.

172   THE POETIC WORLD OF STATIUS' *SILVAE*

Statius calls attention to the mid-point of his consolation as if it were a new beginning, first, by returning our thoughts to the poem's initial line and expanding on its suggestiveness. The opening allusion to Lucretius' masterpiece, *De Rerum Natura*, now takes a concrete form in the actual appearance of *natura* (17) and in the illustration of the direct role that it plays in avian existence. The topic had already been touched upon in the initial hexameter through the adjective *facunda*, focusing on the eloquence with which Melior's feathered 'delight' had been conferred. We learned at the start that nature herself had bestowed this honourable right on the beloved pet. The speaker's didacticism, implicit earlier, now takes more elaborate form but once again it focusses on the act of utterance (*fandi*), on the exceptional ability of an animal to employ a major distinctive characteristic of mankind's intelligence. And the poet's purview moves from the general to the specific, from scholar birds (*doctae*) who have the power to imitate human speech, to a detailed catalogue of examples from eight different species who have this talent.[29] Once again sound and song, in this case, more specifically, the motley noises that emanate from a variety of birds as they miraculously utter human speech, will be a central topic.

Apollo, too, continues as a coalescing figure. Thus far in the poem we have seen him as god of music with his lyre, through Statius' careful bow to Lygdamus at line 11, and as the sun-god Phoebus, through reference to the spokes of his chariot (12), on this occasion with Ovid as intermediary. At line 9 the poet mentions the myth of Phaethon, Apollo's son, and reference to swans (*cycni*, 10) and to the beauty of their final lament asks us to focus in particular on Cycnus, lover of Phaethon with whose tale his is often appropriately joined. It is therefore fitting that the crow, the 'bird of Phoebus' (*Phoebeius ales*, 17), be the first in the list of birds granted the noble right of speaking human words.[30]

Next on the roster are magpies (*picae*), once daughters of Pieros who suffered mutation because of their daring to challenge the Muses to a

---

[29] Lines 16–17 strongly suggest the importance of knowledge as a concomitant to speaking well. This is the only preserved use of the phrase *nobile...ius*. The etymological connection of *nobile* with *nosco* furthers a link with *doctae* to attest to the birds' necessary education. The theme continues at 23 with the unique preserved example of the form *addiscite*.

[30] *Plangat* (17) humanizes the crow as it mourns. As commentators note (Van Dam [1984] 353 and Newlands [2011a] 186), the phrase *ales...Phoebeius* is used first by Ovid (*Met.* 2.544–5), when telling the tale of Coronis, also to characterize the crow (*corvus*, 353). *Voces* (18), attributed to the starling, is a vivid form of metonymy where voices stand for the words that the bird utters in imitation of human vocal expression. It may not be accidental that, as we saw, Statius adopts the phrase *argenteus ordo* (12) from line 108 of the same book of Ovid's epic where the chariot of Phoebus/Apollo is the object of our attention.

ATEDIUS MELIOR'S PARROT (STATIUS' *SILVAE* 2.4)   173

contest. (Ovid, again, tells the story, on this occasion in *Metamorphoses* 5.) Statius here allows the reader to conjure up the noise that magpies make, though Ovid's mention of *convicia* will linger with the later poet's readers.[31] The mere mention of *versae...picae*, however, serves to draw the force of the *Aeneid* back into the poetic picture. We are reminded of the ancient Latian king Picus:

> Picus, equum domitor, quem capta cupidine coniunx
> aurea percussum virga versumque venenis
> fecit avem Circe sparsitque coloribus alas.[32]
>
> (Virg. *A.* 7.189–91)

Picus, tamer of horses, whom his wife, Circe, seized by desire, made a bird, stricken by her golden wand and transformed by drugs, and dappled its wings with colours.

It is not long since Statius suggested, as we saw, a hyperbolic parallel between the 'august dwelling' (*augusti tecti*, 15) in which the parrot is confined and the *tectum augustum*, huge and exalted on one hundred columns, that serves as palace for Latinus (*A.* 7.170).[33] Through his mention of *picae* and their metamorphosis Statius keeps fresh in our minds not just the grandiose qualities of his own narrative techniques but also especially striking reminders of the opening of the second half of Virgil's masterpiece—an allusion to Picus' grand dwelling followed by a suggestive reference to another transformation in the magpie family that took place not only on Latin soil but to one of its ancient kings himself.

Next in the list of mourners comes the partridge and it, too, gains its position because of the sounds that it utters in imitation of human words. If the starling achieves notoriety because of the more general *voces* it articulates, the partridge deserves our attention from the *vocabula* to which it gives voice, in this case the individual words, in particular nouns, that it strings together in conjunction. Through the course of the poem, we have thus seen *verba* give way to *voces* that grant them expression, and these in turn yield to the *vocabula* that give nuance to the spoken language echoed by the avian brood.

---

[31] Ovid relates the myth at *Met.* 5.294–678. *Convicia* occurs at 676.
[32] The pun on *versae* and *versum* would not be lost on the poem's readers.
[33] Virgil sketches the relationship between Latinus and Picus at 7.45–9. Ovid elaborates on the story at *Met.* 14.320–96.

174   THE POETIC WORLD OF STATIUS' *SILVAE*

A rich literary history lies behind the single line 21, devoted to either sister Philomela or Procne, transformed into nightingale or swallow, and, by innuendo, to her relationship with Tereus, the Thracian ruler who becomes a hoopoe: *...et quae Bistonio queritur soror orba cubili.* Not unexpectedly, a major influence on Statius' poetics here is the Ovid of *Amores* 2.6, when he directly addresses the sister who is most likely the nightingale:

> quod scelus Ismarii quereris, Philomela, tyranni
> expleta est annis ista querela suis...
>
> (Ov. *Am.* 2.6.7–8)

Philomela, if you are lamenting the crime of the tyrant of Ismarus, that lament has been fulfilled by its stretch of years.

Forms of the verb *queritur* are central to each vignette of this story of woe, and Statius' single-line summary receives supplementary force by absorbing the further emphasis of the cognate *querela* that Ovid places in the second line of his brief sketch.

Equally striking is Statius' more elaborate reference to the myth in the pseudo-Virgilian *Culex* in which forms of *Bistonius* and *orbus* are to be found in close proximity:[34]

> Iam Pandionia miserandas prole puellas,
> quarum vox Ityn edit Ityn, quo Bistonius rex
> orbus epops maeret volucres evectus in auras.
>
> ([Virg.] *Culex* 251–3)

Now [I catch sight of] the pitiable girls, offspring of Pandion, whose voice utters *Itys, Itys,* while the Bistonian king, bereft of him, grieves as a hoopoe, wafted to the swift breezes.

Once again elegy is the central genre and lament its theme. But the figuration inherent in the hexameter's own deployment itself adds to the power of the poet's presentation. The intensity of assonance takes us from *quae* to *quer-,* from *Bi-* to *ba-* to a concluding *bi-,* and, most vividly, to five syllables virtually in a row ending in *r,* three of them, juxtaposed, consisting of *or.*

---

[34] That the gnat is telling of those it sees suffering in the Underworld adds here an element of tragedy to the generic mixture. That Statius knew the *Culex* is clear also from *Silv.* 1 *praef.* 7 and 2.7.73–4. On the dating of the poem, see also commentators on Suet. *Vita Lucani* 1; Mart. 8.55.20, 14.185.

The force of this extraordinary grouping of sonic units is left to the reader to hear and process, but the melodies that birdsong gives vent to in the act of mourning are doubtless meant to be experienced to some degree by reader-listeners. And in this individual line the complaints of three different birds are implicit.

The poem concludes with a poem within a poem as the speaker commands the contingent of birds to bring the funeral ceremony to an end by learning an additional *carmen* that gives expression to the throng's grief:

> ferte simul gemitus cognataque ducite flammis
> funera, et hoc cunctae miserandum addiscite carmen:
> 'occidit aeriae celeberrima gloria gentis
> psittacus, ille plagae viridis regnator Eoae,
> quem non gemmata volucris Iunonia cauda
> vinceret aspectu, gelidi non Phasidis ales
> nec quas umenti Numidae rapuere sub austro...'
>
> <div align="right">(Stat. <i>Silv.</i> 2.4.22–8)</div>

Together bring your moans and bear the corpse of your relative to the flames, and all as well learn this saddening song: 'The parrot, the most famous glory of the airborne race, is dead, that green ruler of the Eastern realm (25), whom Juno's flyer, with its bejewelled tail, would not surpass in appearance, nor the bird of chill Phasis, nor the ones that the Numidians, beneath the moist south wind, have snared...'

As often, Statius opens his new segment with an allusion to Virgil, on this occasion to the opening words of *G.* 1.11–12: *ferte simul Faunique pedem Dryadesque puellae:/munera vestra cano...* ('Advance forward together, Fauns and Dryad maidens: I sing of your gifts...').[35] The echo of Virgil's central masterpiece, and its education into the rural world, reminds us of Statius' prominent bow to Lucretius' *De Rerum Natura* in his opening verse and reaffirms the didactic tone that surfaces from time to time throughout the poem. In particular, we watch the move from *pedem* to *gemitus* and then, in the subsequent lines, from *cano* to *carmen*. A catalogue of divinities concerned with agriculture who will assist the poet in his artistic endeavour is replaced, first, by the groans of the avian ones who form the cortege of the

---

[35] A third, and final, appearance of the phrase in Latin is also in the work of Statius (*Theb.* 4.480). The sonic echo of *munera* in *funera*, at the start of the next line in Statius, helps confirm the allusion.

176   THE POETIC WORLD OF STATIUS' *SILVAE*

deceased parrot on its way to the funeral pyre, and then by the song that they are to chant en route, in his honour. Statius here reverses the tonality that he often adopts in his echoes of Virgil when he regularly changes sad to happy or, put more generally, negative to positive. On this occasion the opposite occurs. We move from a listing of supportive immortals, who both foster the rural world in all its complexity and inspire the bard as he sings its tale, to the *gemitus* of the parrot's mourners. In negotiating this change of theme, we also turn generically from didactic to elegiac poetry, from verse that teaches us the farmer's life to expressions of sorrow, especially of lovers' laments, as the pet's fellow fliers and, we soon learn, once again, its amatory *dominus*, join in lamenting the passing of someone adored. The birds happen to have, according to the evidence of the preceding lines, the skill both to learn and to reiterate tunefully the *carmen* presumably of the speaker himself, the song within the song about songfulness.

The embedded *carmen*, with its new roster of birds, deepens the reader's focus on sight as well as on sound associated with the gifted birds' ability to mimic human speech. As the poet directs our attention back to the *psittacus*, he carries our vision up into the heavens (*aeriae*) but particularizes it through the help of Virgil. The enormous honour due the parrot (*aeriae celeberrima gloria gentis*) is enhanced by reference to the moment in the sixth book of the *Aeneid* where Anchises, as he surveys for his son the ghosts of future Roman greats, points out the figure of Capys, future king of Alba Longa, *Troianae gloria gentis* (*A.* 6.767).[36] The groans of the birds return us to the world of elegy, but their distinctive qualities of singular greatness point us deservedly to epic and its accompanying grandeur.

Much the same holds true of the phrase that follows: *ille plagae viridis regnator Eoae*. Our vision now expands to embrace the whole realm of the dawn as the parrot is entitled the ruler of its green sphere. But the specificity of Troy, as referential point for the East, still remains with us, and again Virgil's epic is its source. The conjunction *regnator Eoae* takes us back to Aeneas' designation of king Priam to Dido as *regnatorem Asiae* (*A.* 2.557).[37] The several notices by which Virgil, through Statius' words, has already brought the Trojan ruler to our attention, whether oriented to the death of

---

[36] The echo is noted by Van Dam (1984) 359. The phrase *gloria gentis* brings each hexameter to a conclusion.

[37] Statius may be suggesting that we likewise hear an affinity with the phrase *resonante Eoa* from Catul. 11.3, also at line ending. If so, an element of lyric is again added to the poetic discourse. Cf. also Sen. *Oed.* 426 (*Eoae plaga vasta terrae*) which joins tragedy to the generic mixture.

the parrot or to the grandeur of his habitat while still active, here reach a climax as we enter the final stretch of the eulogy for the brilliant bird. Three additional colleagues complete the catalogue. First comes Juno's peacock with its bright tail to focus our inner eyes on what is immediately at hand to the sight. There follows the pheasant which Statius locates in two ways. We move past Troy eastward to Phasis on the Black Sea, where the chill temperature signals to our sense of touch. We then reverse direction back to north Africa, where we find ourselves with the Numidians hunting guinea fowl. Once again bodily sensation plays a part as we feel, at least in our imaginations, the dampness that the south wind suggests.

The Parrot and Caesar

Comparison with exotic birds, whether educed for us by geographical distance or variations of climate, is one means by which the poet keeps our eyes on the parrot. More crucial still is the turn Statius now takes as he summarizes the pet's particular role as greeter of Caesar and, yet more precious, as a friend to his cherished lord:

> ille salutator regum nomenque locutus
> Caesareum et queruli quondam vice functus amici,
> nunc conviva levis monstrataque reddere verba
> tam facilis, quo tu, Melior dilecte, recluso
> numquam solus eras.
>
> <div align="right">(Stat. <i>Silv.</i> 2.4.29–33)</div>

He, greeter of kings, who has spoken the name of Caesar and once upon a time performed the part of complaining friend (30), now a quick-witted fellow diner, and so nimble at giving back words brought to his attention. Beloved Melior, when he was released, you yourself were never alone.

As we draw near the conclusion, Statius reminds us once more of the bird's possession of man's gifts as a speaker. The creature addresses the emperor and repeats words that come his way. The poet also brings to a final climax the elegiac motif that passes through the poem. We have heard of the 'doors' (*fores*, 14) that 'complain' (*querulae*) on their own, now that the cage's lamenting denizen is gone. We have born witness to the avian sister who mourns (*queritur*, 21) for her lost son. We now have the *psittacus* playing the part of 'mourning friend' (*queruli amici*), of close human companion

178   THE POETIC WORLD OF STATIUS' *SILVAE*

who shares in the sadnesses of the 'master', whose pleasure he has been since the poem's initial line. Both *levis* and *facilis* seem deliberately untainted by any hint of fickleness or promiscuity that they might contain in an erotic context, the first underscoring the bird's role as a pleasant, quasi-human companion, the second as an adept mimic of man's speech.

The word *recluso* also serves a similar purpose.[38] By echoing *praeclusit* (3) it helps bring the poem full circle. But the word also offers a final elegiac touch. At the start of the poem the bird's murmurs 'are shut out' forever by death's closing doors. Here at the end we are reminded of a happier time when doors are open to the temporarily enclosed parrot-lover who, upon release from his cage, can bring *voluptas* to his *dominus*, not least as friend and fellow banqueter. While the parrot-partner lived, his keeper was never lonely.[39]

Line 32 incorporates perhaps the most extraordinary intertext in the poem, *Melior dilecte*. This is the work's only invocation, emphasized by the addition of *tu*, of Statius' friend and patron Atedius Melior, and all the more strongly marked for coming near its finale instead of as an opening salutation. It underscores the position of Melior as the beloved of both parrot and poet, and hints at their interrelationship. It also brings to a powerful conclusion the language of subjective erotic elegy that permeates the poem. But the address fulfils another immediate purpose. It is a direct reminder of the words *dilecte Maecenas*, Horace's apostrophe to his own special benefactor that serves as dedication of the concluding poem in his second collection of odes.[40] By drawing a close parallel between their two sponsor connoisseurs, Statius presumes that his readers will further, and yet more cogently, connect him with the earlier master and his corpus of lyrics, a link that we have already traced in the first line of the poem.

There is a further, suggestive affiliation between the two poems. The core 'plot' of Horace's powerful ode is the metamorphosis of the speaker into a swan, namely into a bird who stands as symbol for the deathlessness of the

[38] Cf. also Virgil's use of *recludere* at *A*. 7.617 in a context which Statius has already called to our attention at line 13.
[39] For *reclusit* in a specifically erotic context, see, e.g., Prop. 3.19.24. For *solus* (33), see Pichon (1966) 266.
[40] Hor. *Carm*. 2.20.7. Of the five appearances of the participle *dilecte* in classical Latin only these two modify proper names (which happen also to begin with the same letter of the alphabet). The considerable further lexical overlap between the two poems deserves separate treatment. I single out two details. First is the reflection of *tenui penna* (2.20.1–2) in *tenues plumae* (*Silv*. 2.4.35) and the stylistic parallels it implies. (Horace uses the word *plumae* at 2.20.12.) The second is the resonance of Horace's *canorus ales* (2.20.15–16) with both the verbal music and sense of *canorus habes* (*Silv*. 2.4.9).

ATEDIUS MELIOR'S PARROT (STATIUS' *SILVAE* 2.4)   179

poet's imagination, which is to say the immortality of his verse. Thus, if Melior is a contemporary version of Maecenas, a witty final exemplification of an Ovidian metamorphosis, then Statius becomes a type of Horace and his *Silvae* stands in good measure as a modern manifestation of the Augustan poet's *Carmina* in significance and quality. It can therefore lay equal claim to its own form of permanence. Statius' echo, at line 9, of the adjective *canorus*, to characterize his parrot, which Horace applies to himself as swan at *Carm.* 2.20.15, helps particularize the linkage.[41] And at the neighbouring line 10, we remember, he cogently reminds us of the legend of the swan in relation to the parrot's demise: ... *non soli celebrant sua funera cycni* ('It is not only swans that memorialize their deaths'). Statius may be writing about a parrot but by carefully connecting himself with the lyric poet in his role as immortal swan the later poet suggests a form of perpetuity for himself and an association between his parrot, a palpable individual but also the subject of artistic reinvention and Horace's symbolic bird. As he writes about the *psittacus*, Statius is continually probing the past, Ovid most prominently, to bring new creative impulse to his poetic present, turning obeisance into originality.[42] And Horace's representation of his own career and achievement also remains in his mind as paragon.

The Poem's Conclusion

But, as we near the poem's conclusion, Statius proposes an expansive modification in tone:

> ... at non inglorius umbris
> mittitur: Assyrio cineres adolentur amomo
> et tenues Arabum respirant gramine plumae
> Sicaniisque crocis, senio nec fessus inerti
> scandet odoratos phoenix felicior ignes.
>
> (Stat. *Silv.* 2.4.33–7)

---

[41] For the association of the adjective *canorus* with swans see commentators on Virg. *A.* 7.700 and, with birds in general, on *G.* 2.328 which may be inspired by Lucr. 1.256. *Canorus* is also a regular attribute of the lyre (cf. Virg. *A.* 6.120; Hor. *Carm.* 1.12.11).

[42] Gunderson (2021) 277 concludes that 'we see the typical Statian split between the thing enunciated and the subject who is doing the enunciating. The narrator will be eternal: all one has to do is to read back the words that the Master Poet put on the page, just as he told us to'.

180   THE POETIC WORLD OF STATIUS' *SILVAE*

But he is sent to the shades not without glory. His ashes are burned with Assyrian spice and his slender feathers breathe herbs of the Arabians (35) and Sicanian saffron, and, not wearied by sluggish old age, a happier phoenix, he will climb the perfumed flames.

Up to this point Statius' poem has served as a form of elegy for the passing of a pet parrot, who while living was a form of *voluptas* for Melior, its keeper. The procession of mourning has consisted of kindred avian spirits and its hymn reaches a climax and conclusion with a comparison between the parrot and a phoenix, mythical bird known for its ability to reproduce itself and therefore for its gift of a form of continuous longevity. Statius begins his precis of the ceremony on the funeral pyre with a view of the ashes themselves:...*Assyrio cineres adolentur amomo*...As so often, he asks us to examine his expressiveness through our remembrance of Virgil, this time the fourth *Eclogue*. There the earlier poet has us imagine the coming of a *puer* who will initiate an ideal new world: *occidet et serpens, et fallax herba veneni/occidet; Assyrium vulgo nascetur amomum* ('The snake, too, will die, and the deceitful poison herb will die; Assyrian spice will be born everywhere', *Ecl.* 4.24–5). So with splendid irony at the moment he has us watch the parrot's fiery disintegration, Statius also asks us to ponder a singular instance in Virgil of deaths followed by an extraordinary new beginning. We observe the coming into being of a boy, whose arrival announces the start of a fresh Golden Age typified by the universal presence of Assyrian spice. The parrot's decease in its own turn brings with it through poetry a time of birth and renewal that also implies the immortality of both the bird and the poetry that so handsomely tells its tale.

At line 35 Statius would also have us remember a moment in Propertius, where the poet has us appreciate the love-enhanced scents emanating from the hair of Cynthia:...*afflabunt tibi non Arabum de gramine odores,/sed quos ipse suis fecit Amor manibus* ('No perfumes from the herbs of the Arabians will waft on you but those which Love himself has made with his very hands', 2.29A.17–18).[43] In one of his magical alterations of tone, Statius takes us back into the world of elegy, where we have so often found ourselves in the course of the poem. But instead of especially emphasizing our sense of emotional loss, where we would most expect to experience it, as funeral and poem conclude together, the poet turns to elegy to enliven us with a happy recollection of Cynthia and erotic grace. We have on occasion

---

[43] The echo is noted by Newlands (2011a) 191.

ATEDIUS MELIOR'S PARROT (STATIUS' *SILVAE* 2.4) 181

seen how Statius will turn a negative situation in Virgil to a positive end. Here, as the poem draws to a conclusion, by specific reference to the elegist Propertius, Statius gives a heartening tone to the ordinarily melancholic sense found in the latter's verse. Death can have comforting, even cheering, aspects.

Statius carefully brings his work full circle with etymological wordplay that links *sollers* in the poem's second line with *inerti*, which brings its penultimate verse to a conclusion. The mastery that at the start of the poem distinguishes the bird's skill at imitating the sounds of the human voice, will not be lost even at the moment of its departure from life. This funeral ceremony will smack neither of tiredness nor of an old age from which the demands of time have precluded the continued presence of *ars*.[44] Statius underlines his point by singling out the ever-self-renewing phoenix for the final analogy between Melior's parrot and his avian colleagues. For the *psittacus* death will only be a momentary jolt on a continuing journey toward eternity.[45]

The Ovid of *Amores* 2.6 has been regularly in the background of Statius' mind as he tests his originality against the presentation of the same topic by the Augustan master. But it is with a dynamic, final bow to the latter's *Metamorphoses* that Statius chooses to end his poem. In the words of Pythagoras, as we also near the conclusion of Ovid's epic, we learn about the phoenix in language that the author of the *Silvae* would have us ponder again. Most birds, claims the philosopher, receive their start in life from some other entity. But one is different:

> una est quae reparet seque ipsa reseminet ales,
> Assyrii phoenica vocant. non fruge neque herbis,
> sed turis lacrimis et suco vivit amomi.
>
> (Ov. *Met.* 15.392–4)

There is one bird that itself renews and restores itself. The Assyrians call it the phoenix. It does not thrive on corn or on grasses but on the tears of incense and the juice of the spice-plant.

---

[44] For the stylistic connotations of *iners* see commentators on Cic. *Fin.* 2.115; Hor. *Ep.* 1.20.12.

[45] The word *scandet* deserves special attention. Aside from Liv. 3.68.7, the verb's only other appearance in classical Latin is at Hor. *Carm.* 3.30.9, where it is prominently placed in the final poem of the lyricist's third book. It may not be fortuitous that Statius asks us to ponder the subsequent concluding Horatian poem in connection with his conspicuous earlier mentions of *Carm.* 2.20, the final opus of Book 2. Poetic immortality remains a constant theme.

182 THE POETIC WORLD OF STATIUS' *SILVAE*

It is brilliantly appropriate that Statius turns to the poet of metamorphosis for his final analogy and that the change in question be founded on immutability.[46] Melior's parrot in death will find a parallel in the phoenix that is continually revivified even after turning to ashes. But this particular parrot is not an ordinary phoenix but one that is *felicior*, more fortunate that any other, as it climbs the pyre. It has been given a special form of immortality not in the palpable figure of an eternally refurbished bird but through the words of Statius as they capture its shape in timeless words fashioned for the imagination of readers to come.

---

[46] Ovid devotes *Met.*15.391–407 to a discussion of the phoenix. The name itself may also serve as a reminder of Homer's Phoenix, who is both aged (Statius' *senio* in line 36; cf. Hom. *Il.* 9.432) and a powerful orator, whose name would serve appropriately in the conclusion of a poem often concerned with eloquence. At *Her.* 3.129, Ovid equates his rhetorical skill with that of *facundus Ulixes*.

5

Domitian's Banquet (Statius' *Silvae* 4.2)

The Poem's Opening

Statius' extraordinary manifestation of thanks to Domitian in *Silvae* 4.2,[1] an outpouring of gratitude for the opportunity to attend a resplendent dinner at the emperor's new mansion on the Palatine, opens with a powerful rhetorical gesture. We are greeted by two brief similes which serve as analogical preparation for much of what follows. A regular device for the enhancement of epic, the conceit takes emphatic form by direct reference to perhaps the two greatest practitioners of the form before Statius, namely Virgil and Homer. We are about to enjoy the handsomely crafted description of a moment of formidable majesty:

> Regia Sidoniae convivia laudat Elissae
> qui magnum Aenean Laurentibus intulit arvis;
> Alcinoique dapes mansuro carmine monstrat
> aequore qui multo reducem consumpsit Vlixem…
>
> (Stat. Silv. 4.2.1–4)

He who brought great Aeneas to the fields of Laurentum praises the royal banquets of Sidonian Elissa, and he who wore down returning Ulysses with an abundance of sea displays the feasts of Alcinous in ever-enduring song…

Virgil is given pride of place, appropriately since his influence permeates the poem, with Dido serving as the first parallel to Statius' host. We find ourselves specifically at the conclusion of the first book of the *Aeneid* where

---

[1] I am particularly indebted to the commentary on *Silvae* 4 by Coleman (1988), a constant source of stimulus and enlightenment, and to the insightful pages on the poem by Newlands (2002), esp. 260–83. Important recent studies of the poem include Leberl (2004) 167–81; Rühl (2006) 334–41; Malamud (2007); Kreuz (2017) 226–76. The commentary by Vollmer remains a *sine qua non*.

The Poetic World of Statius' Silvae. Michael C. J. Putnam, Edited by: Antony Augoustakis with Carole E. Newlands, Oxford University Press. © Michael C. J. Putnam 2023. DOI: 10.1093/oso/9780192869272.003.0006

184   THE POETIC WORLD OF STATIUS' *SILVAE*

the queen of Carthage entertains Aeneas and his Trojan colleagues at a grand feast.[2] The Homeric parallel, drawn from *Odyssey* 8, places us at a banquet where Alcinous, king of the Phaeacians, entertains Ulysses before returning him to his homeland. Domitian and his guests, courtiers, and the great poet himself, are thus honoured by parallels from the heroic past whose traditions all are keeping alive in present-day Rome.

Some details of Statius' presentation are noteworthy. Mighty (*magnum*) Aeneas, subject of a grand poem, is singled out for his arrival in Latium.[3] It is not accidental that the verb the poet uses, *intulit*, appears in the present tense in the sixth line of the epic that bears his name where we hear of the gods that he would bring to Latium (*inferret... deos Latio*). The corresponding adjective in the poet's precis of Homer's Ulysses is *multo*, applied to the sea (*aequore*) whose abundance not only brought the hero many woes but also serves as a metaphor for the extensive epic that tells his tale.[4]

In these four lines, we should also take due note of Statius' nuanced use of verb tenses that prepare the reader for the multifaceted mentions of temporality that punctuate the verses that follow. Details of the adventures that characterize each hero are put in the past tense (*intulit, consumpsit*), but the two epics as works of literature thrive in the present (*laudat, monstrat*) and assure the memory of the deeds they narrate at the same time as they affirm the quality of their presentation. The excellence of Virgil's chef-d'oeuvre presumes its continuity, for us as it had for Statius, when it extols the festivities in Carthage, and the masterful *Odyssey* of Homer still verbally displays the Phaeacian feast for our lasting pleasure. The future, too, receives a prominent citation at line 3 where the poet employs assonance and alliteration to help confirm the lasting endurance of Homer's song (*mansuro carmine monstrat*) and by implication the music of his two Roman disciples.[5]

---

[2] Virgil associates Dido's *convivia* with *regali luxu* at *A.* 1.637–8. Her designation, *Sidonia Elissa*, is never used by the earlier poet and is doubly exotic. According to Servius (*ad A.* 1.340 and 4.335) Elissa was her original Phoenician name, so we twice cast our inner eye toward the eastern Mediterranean just as *Laurentibus* asks us to imagine Trojan Aeneas at last settled in Italy.

[3] Aeneas is called *magnus* only once in his poem (*A.* 10.159), with size metaphorically representing inner greatness. We find him *magnanimum* at 1.260 and 9.204.

[4] The phrase *aequore multo* is unique but here especially apt as a metaphor for the amplitude of a grand poem as well as descriptive of a major protagonist of its content. Statius uses the phrase *longo aequore* (*Theb.* 12.809) of a seafaring journey as metaphor for the crafting of an epic poem, his *Thebaid*, now coming to a conclusion. Coleman (1988) 85 duly refers to Hor. *Carm.* 4.15.3 where the poet fleetingly contemplates the writing of epic by embarking 'across the Etruscan Sea' (*Tyrrhenum per aequor*). Cf. Virg. *G.* 2.541–2 for a terrestrial parallel.

[5] *Monstravit* is the verb chosen by Horace to illustrate Homer at work (*Ars* 74). It is appropriately cognate with *moneo* and *memini*. Statius turns Horace's past into the present as an

DOMITIAN'S BANQUET (STATIUS' *SILVAE* 4.2) 185

The genius behind the crafting of these hexameters now suddenly appears as a character in the very proceedings he is about to describe:

> ast ego, cui sacrae Caesar nova gaudia cenae
> nunc primum dominaque dedit non surgere mensa,
> qua celebrem mea vota lyra, quas solvere grates
> sufficiam?

(Stat. Silv. 4.2.5–8)

But I myself, to whom Caesar has now for the first time granted the fresh delights of his sacred dinner (5), as well as not to arise during the imperial repast, with what lyre am I to celebrate my answered prayers, what thanks may I have the capacity to render?

If Homer grants permanence through the magic of his *carmen*, it is the *lyra* of Statius that has the similar power to preserve Domitian's entertainment, and the larger world it puts on display, for time to come. The speaking 'I', which combines the dual roles of guest and creative writer, makes a dramatic entrance at the beginning of line 5 with the phrase *ast ego*. The poet-guest will now carve out his own imaginative territory, which is to say put himself forward as a rival to, but distinct from, Virgil and Homer. He does so, however, by exploiting a phrase (*ast ego*) that the former, his major poetic mentor in this poem and regularly elsewhere, uses twice in the *Aeneid* to dramatic affect. We find it at 1.46 and 7.308 where it is spoken by the goddess Juno. On each occasion, as we begin the first and second halves of the epic, she is lamenting her frustrated ambition to destroy the Trojans and pondering the destructive forces that she can summon to fulfil her evil goals. As she begins her monologues she reflects on her apparent powerlessness, even though she is the wife of Jupiter.

As so often in his allusions to his great predecessor, Statius turns a negative situation to more positive ends. Instead of anticipating war and its concomitant violence, the poet readies us for an act of celebration centred on the emperor and on the extent of his immediate circumstances. In place of a lament that she, the wife of the king of the gods, lacks the ability to carry out her nefarious designs, we find Statius announcing the joy with which he sat down to dinner 'with Jupiter' (*cum Iove*, 11). Adroit analogies between the

---

oblique gesture of self-praise. Just as the epics of Virgil and Homer live on in the late first century CE, so Statius' parallel poetic endeavours may expect the same longevity.

186   THE POETIC WORLD OF STATIUS' *SILVAE*

sovereign of Rome and the lord of Olympus will punctuate the paean that follows.

The implication that Domitian is worthy of divinization is subtly present in the words that immediately follow the poet's self-placement. In the preface of this book of the *Silvae* (*praef.* 6–7), he speaks of the 'most holy banquet' (*sacratissimis epulis*) which will be the subject of its second offering.[6] The adjective first appears in the poem itself at line 5 (*sacrae*) where it technically modifies *cenae* and serves as a reminder of the earlier mention of *epulis*. But its adjacency to, and evident similarity with, the word *Caesar* lends to the emperor already at his first mention an aura of divinity upon which Statius will offer a series of riffs as the poem progresses.

The phrase *celebrem lyra* introduces another figure who will play a prominent part in our on-going discussion. The only other occasion in classical Latin poetry where a form of the verb *celebrare* is juxtaposed with *lyra* occurs in the opening lines of Horace's *Carm.* 1.12, also in an interrogative setting:

> Quem virum aut heroa lyra vel acri
> tibia sumis celebrare, Clio?
> quem deum?
>
> (Hor. *Carm.* 1.12.1–3)

What man or hero do you accept to celebrate with lyre or shrill pipe, Clio? What god?

The allusion announces one of the other great influences on the work that follows, the poet Horace, and especially his *Carmina*, so that lyric elements often join with epic to further enrich Statius' achievement.[7] But there is a particular point to the reference back to the earlier genius here. Horace's great ode goes on to catalogue a series of heroic mortals or gods worthy of his homage, culminating in the figure of another great Caesar (51–2) who took the name Augustus in the year 27 BCE. In the poem's course we also have varied mentions of Jupiter, Athena, Bacchus, Apollo, Hercules, and Pollux, all of whom play roles in Statius' *laudatio*, with the majority serving

---

[6] Cf. also *sacro nectare* (54) of the drink of the gods and *sacra* (64) on the holiness of Domitian's feast.

[7] *Lyra* can also have special associations with epic. Statius twice uses *lyra* when comparing himself to Virgil. At *Silv.* 1.3.100 he refers to the earlier master's *lyra maiore* in relation to his own and at *Theb.* 10.446 his is the *inferiore lyra* where the author of the *Aeneid* is concerned; see the discussion of 1.3 in pp. 11–44 in this volume.

DOMITIAN'S BANQUET (STATIUS' *SILVAE* 4.2)   187

as analogies for the excellence of the emperor himself. But, as we shall see, the poem is also, in particular, dotted with vicarious references to Rome's first emperor, all of which redound to the credit of the present incumbent of that title. As a result, the allusion to Horace not only enhances Domitian's authority as sole ruler of Rome, with a past worthy of emulation, but further suggests that he is deserving to be ranked not only with heroes apt for divinization for their terrestrial accomplishments but also, again, alongside even the king of the gods himself for an appropriate parallel.

The phrase *solvere gratis* (7) serves as a further reminder of the conclusion of the first book of the *Aeneid*, as Aeneas announces to Dido that it is not in his power 'to pay proper thanks' (*grates persolvere dignas*, 600) for her beneficence toward the Trojans. And by reference back to Virgil's epic Statius fixes our attention further on the high standard that he must set himself when dealing with Domitian:

> …non, si pariter mihi vertice laeto
> nectat odoratas et Smyrna et Mantua lauros,
> digna loquar.
>
> (Stat. *Silv.* 4.2.8–10)

…not if both Smyrna and Mantua were to bind my rejoicing head with fragrant laurel would my utterance be worthy (10).

Homer re-enters the poem via a witty wordplay linking his supposed birthplace, Smyrna, the myrrh understood in its nomenclature, and the sweet-smelling laurels granted for epic renown. Mention of Mantua, in turn, reaffirms the constant inspiration of that city's brilliant offspring behind the verses before us. And the word *loquar* by itself suggests that we acknowledge again the influence of Horace, here and in what follows. Two passages seem especially apt. At *Carm.* 3.25.18, the poet proclaims, 'nothing mortal will I utter' (*nil mortale loquar*) when the core of the poem has been his ambition to set Augustus Caesar among the stars and 'in the council of Jupiter' (*consilio Iovis*). And in a later poem, focused on the emperor's return to Rome, he adds his own voice to the jubilation, 'if I will utter anything worth listening to' (*si quid loquar audiendum*, *Carm.* 4.2.45).[8] As he had three lines earlier, Statius here seizes the opportunity, through allusion back to the great craftsman of lyric during the Augustan age, to further

---

[8] Cf. also *Carm.* 4.9.1–4, and what follows, where *loquor* appears prominently (4).

188   THE POETIC WORLD OF STATIUS' *SILVAE*

glorify Domitian, and vicariously himself, by associating the emperor with his illustrious predecessor.[9]

We move now from poetic heritage to the event itself which takes place in a form of a terrestrial empyrean:

> ...mediis videor discumbere in astris
> cum Iove et Iliaca porrectum sumere dextra
> immortale merum. steriles transmisimus annos;
> haec aevi mihi prima dies, hic limina vitae.
>
> <div align="right">(Stat. <i>Silv.</i> 4.2.10–13)</div>

...I seem to recline with Jupiter in the midst of stars (10) and to accept deathless wine proffered from Ilian hand. We have passed through infertile years; this is the initial day of my life span, this is the threshold of my existence.

We enter a world where vision will play an important part in instructing the reader. The word *discumbere,* for instance, reminds us again of the end of the first book of the *Aeneid* through its two appearances during Virgil's description of Dido's banquet (*A.* 1.700 and 708) as he places her guests reclining at table.[10] Statius now imagines himself, as we already saw, in the company of someone suitable for a comparison with the lord of the gods, in a setting worthy to be likened to heaven and its stars. From Ganymede he receives immortal nectar which for a poet suggests, yet again, that his writing will join the works of Virgil and Homer and achieve a continued state of immediacy even as time presses on.

And contemplation of poetry's temporality modulates into a brief meditation on the life of the wordsmith himself. An infertile stretch of time is behind him as he anticipates a fresh beginning to his work, the start of a new period of inspired writing. Two allusions to Virgil help us appreciate the affirmative nature of the poet's prediction. For general terms Statius turns our thoughts to one of the more pessimistic passages in the *Georgics:*

---

[9] The phrase *mea vota* (7) also furthers the implication of Domitian's divinity. Whether the words suggest an offering of tribute from speaker to honouree or an expression of gratitude for favours received, or a combination of both, they presume the god-like quality of their destination.

[10] For Domitian and the nuances of the phrase *discumbere in astris,* see Vessey (1983).

DOMITIAN'S BANQUET (STATIUS' *SILVAE* 4.2) 189

> optima quaeque dies miseris mortalibus aevi
> prima fugit; subeunt morbi tristisque senectus
> et labor, et durae rapit inclementia mortis.
>
> <div align="right">(Virg. <i>G.</i> 3.66–8)</div>

For poor mortals the best days of our lives are ever the first to flee; diseases and sad old age and suffering ensue, and the ungentleness of hard death snatches us away.

The poet who drinks imperishable wine now carefully recalls Virgil's words for us only, as so often, to transmute a gloomy situation or pronouncement into a happier realm. Here Statius turns our minds away from our own mortality and the remorseless of death toward anticipating a new era for his career. He would have us ponder his future creativity, not our impermanence.

Statius may also be suggesting that we think back to a particularly fraught moment in the *Aeneid*, the untimely death of the young warrior Pallas for whom the poet breaks his narrative flow to address directly: *o dolor atque decus magnum rediture parenti,/haec te prima dies bello dedit, haec eadem aufert* ('O, about to return to your father as a grief and great glory, you this first day gave to war, this same day takes you away', *A.* 10.507–8). Through the similarity of language Statius announces his birth, not his demise, the start of a joyous period of inspiration, not a reminder of the limitation that time puts on our lives.

This renaissance of the imagination, this new influx of creative energy, take initial form in a succinct but magnificent gesture:

> tene ego, regnator terrarum orbisque subacti
> magne parens, te, spes hominum, te, cura deorum,
> cerno iacens?
>
> <div align="right">(Stat. <i>Silv.</i> 4.2.14–16)</div>

You, ruler of the lands and great parent of the world subdued, you, hope of mankind, you, ward of the gods (15), do I behold, lying here?

The poet's first new surge of spiritual elan brings with it a brief but forceful entry of a new genre into the celebratory poetic mix. We have already seen Statius have recourse to epic and lyric in his *laudatio* of the emperor and his own special moment of glory. He now adds an abbreviated example of

190 THE POETIC WORLD OF STATIUS' SILVAE

hymn as culmination of the initial segment of the poem.[11] The repetitions of *te* are intermingled with the speaker's 'I' to help form a litany of prayer, uniting creative artist and object of veneration. The word *cerno*, in particular, has a supportive reference, taking us back to *Silvae* 3.1 where, at line 164, the poet announces that he has had an epiphany of Hercules on the doorstep of his new temple: 'Now I see himself on the threshold' (*nunc ipsum in limine cerno*, 164).[12] Beholding the sovereign at his feast has a parallel impact on the speaker.

But it is the magic fostered by repetition, a salient feature of the hymnic genre, that is especially effective here. It confirms—what the poet's references to Virgil and Horace had already connoted—that Domitian should be treated as a god among humans. He remains fully deserving of the worship the poet had already suggested should be his, by the literary connections his initial verses had established between him and, first, Jupiter, monarch of the gods, then Augustus Caesar, premier Roman model for his host to emulate. It is not often that a poet has a chance not only to imply that his sponsor is worthy of apotheosis while still alive but also to address him directly through the creative form most suitable for exemplifying in verse the veneration of which he is worthy. Meanwhile we are strongly reminded, as we have been from the eulogy's opening hexameters, of the power of poetry, of poetry as power.

Statius mixes old and new elements in the finale to this segment of the poem:

> ...datur haec iuxta, datur ora tueri
> vina inter mensasque, et non adsurgere fas est?
>
> <div align="right">(Stat. <i>Silv.</i> 4.2.16–17)</div>

Is it granted, is it granted, to behold this face from nearby, amid the wines and the courses, and is it lawful not to rise?

---

[11] As noted by Coleman (1988) 88 and Newlands (2002) 272. The designation *regnator* also continues the direct association of Domitian with Jupiter. (For Virgil's uses of the title, see *A.* 2.779, 4.269, 7.558, 10.437). Domitian is a force of nature as well as a power controlling nature for the better. The phrase *magne parens* sends the reader back to Virg. *G.* 2.173–4: *salve, magna parens frugum, Saturnia tellus,/magna virum*... ('Hail, great mother of crops, land of Saturn, great mother of men...'). At *G.* 2.170 Augustus is addressed as *maxime Caesar* (Augustus is called Caesar also at 3.16, 47–8, and 4.560). The compliment to the poet's patron would not have been lost on an ancient reader. On recent re-evaluations of Domitian in Flavian literature, see the essays in Augoustakis, Buckley, and Stocks (2019).

[12] See pp. 142–3 in this volume.

DOMITIAN'S BANQUET (STATIUS' *SILVAE* 4.2) 191

The repetition of *datur* furthers the hymnic context of glories recited, but the ekphrastic phrase, *haec ora*, with its pronounced deictic, asks us to turn from hearing to seeing.[13] Imagining ourselves, like Statius, as guests at the feast, we are to look directly, in our mind's eye, at the godlike figure, presiding over the event, whose praises we have just read. At *A.* 1.494 Virgil accomplishes something similar by summoning us to join his hero in viewing 'these marvels' (*haec miranda*), the paintings of scenes from the Trojan war on Dido's temple to Juno. Here Statius invites us to look specifically at the face of Domitian almost as if it were a piece of sculpture, a bust of the emperor, with one art form joining another in abetting the act of memorialization.

A direct quotation from Virgil's epic heightens the intensity of the moment. With the phrase *datur ora tueri* Statius draws our attention back to one of the most dramatic moments in the *Aeneid* where Anchises catches sight of his son, Aeneas, who has made his way through the world of the dead to find his father in the fields of Elysium. The latter accosts the approaching hero:

> 'venisti tandem, tuaque expectata parenti
> vicit iter durum pietas? datur ora tueri,
> nate, tua et notas audire et reddere voces?'
>
> (Virg. *A.* 6.687–9)

'Have you come at last, and has your devotion to duty, foreseen by your father, overcome the difficult journey? Is it granted to behold your face, son, and to hear and to return familiar voices?'

After a hymnic exaltation of his host, Statius reminds us yet again of the epic magnificence of the dinner itself, but the specifics are also worthy of our careful notice. Through his spacious allusion Statius turns Domitian into an Aeneas-like figure, a warrior whose *pietas* conquers death as he loyally seeks out the shade of his father. The poet-guest in his turn becomes a type of Anchises, marvelling at the example of excellence on which he is allowed to fix his attention.

As this episode comes to an end we thus find confirmation of aspects of Statius' suggestiveness in the poem's opening couplet. The author sees

---

[13] Sight is, naturally enough, a major topic of the poem. Cf., e.g., *videor* (10), *species* (30), *visibus* (31), *spectare* (40), *conspectum* (45).

192   THE POETIC WORLD OF STATIUS' *SILVAE*

himself as a Virgil figure with the power not only to bring Aeneas into the Laurentian fields but also to immortalize his saga with a eulogy that maintains a continuous present.[14] As he had partially at the start, Aeneas now again serves as an analogy for Domitian with all the honour that the affiliation implies, for him and for his poet as well.

In the opening seventeen lines of his *silva*, Statius has offered largely a rumination on various aspects of temporality. This has taken us from the notion of the permanence of epic, with Virgil and Homer serving as exemplars, to the poet's own specific accomplishment. After imagining his drinking at Domitian's table, the deathless wine served to the immortals, Statius ponders his own imminent rebirth as a poet whose first accomplishment is a hymn addressed to his host, an implicit hero-god in the making, through the speaker's own deftness. There is only the passing mention of location as the poet envisions himself reclining in the midst of the stars as if he and his fellow guests were also gods, at ease in some celestial habitat.

The Space

At line 18, with sudden intensity, Statius modulates from time to space as his central concern. He has created a god. Now he has to house him suitably:

> Tectum augustum, ingens, non centum insigne columnis
> sed quantae superos caelumque Atlante remisso
> sustentare queant.
>
> (Stat. *Silv.* 4.2.18–20)

A majestic edifice, huge, remarkable not for a hundred columns but for as many as might support the gods above and the heavens, with Atlas let free (20).

At this moment of transition Statius claims our attention with an extraordinary allusion to Virgil, one of the most conspicuous in his corpus of writing because it constitutes a direct act of rivalry between the two poets as well as deepens the reader's respect for Statius' accomplishment. He transports us again to the seventh book of the *Aeneid*, here to the arrival

---

[14] Virgil did not just tell of Aeneas' arrival in the fields of the Laurentes. He carried (*intulit*) him there through the magic potential of epic verse. His only use of this form of the verb *infero* occurs at *A.* 11.36 where Aeneas arrives at the funeral of Pallas.

DOMITIAN'S BANQUET (STATIUS' *SILVAE* 4.2) 193

of the Trojan emissaries at the palace of king Latinus. The building claims its own concise ekphrasis: *tectum augustum, ingens, centum sublime columnis/urbe fuit summa, Laurentis regia Pici,/horrendum silvis et religione parentem* ('A majestic edifice, huge, lofty with one hundred columns, stood at the top of the city, the palace of Laurentian Picus, awe-inspiring for its grove and for the devotion of generations', *A.* 7.170–2).[15] Domitian's palace has in common with Picus' royal residence the fact that it is both due proper reverence and enormous in size. The word *augustum* in particular works its magic in ways both general and particular. While venerable in itself, the mansion is a reminder that the Palatine also served as location for the grand mansion of an earlier Caesar who bore the epithet Augustus.[16]

But the word *non* sets up a sudden distinction between the two poets which is also to say between the two dwellings they are depicting. The description of Picus' edifice harbours the implication that it sets a pattern for another 'august' dwelling in the distant Roman future. As republic turns to empire the city's first sole ruler in this new dispensation needs a residence worthy of his special stature. But even Augustus' mansion is limited by comparison to that which Statius' patron will build. By deprecating the grandeur of Picus' palace, and thereby diminishing the impressive pedigree that is attached to it through the adjective *augustus*, Statius heightens the stateliness that accrues to the new palace of Domitian. In the poet's hyperbole, its columns will hold up a new, earthly 'heaven' (*caelum*) deserving to be equated with the heavens that, as the myth would have it, were once shouldered by Atlas.

A further reversion to ekphrasis adds emphasis to the poet's grand gesture:

> … stupet hoc vicina Tonantis
> regia, teque pari laetantur sede locatum
> numina (nec magnum properes escendere caelum)…
>
> (Stat. *Silv.* 4.2.20–2)

The neighbouring palace of the Thunderer marvels at this (20) and the gods rejoice that you are settled in a similar dwelling (nor should you hurry to ascend to the mighty heavens).

---

[15] See also the allusion in *Silv.* 2.4 discussed in pp. 168–9 in this volume.

[16] At *Orig.* 9.3.16 Isidore discusses the connection between Augustus and *augeo*, reasoning that the emperors 'increased the republic by fostering its growth' (… *augerent rempublicam amplificando*).

194 THE POETIC WORLD OF STATIUS' *SILVAE*

The personified 'palace' of thundering Jupiter, looking in amazement at Domitian's mansion (*stupet hoc*), is a further reminder of Aeneas standing in awe at Dido's pictures of Troy's history (*haec...miranda.../dum stupet, A.* 1.494–5). In particular the deictic *hoc* draws us directly here into the event itself as we join Jupiter's temple on the Capitolium in marvelling at the new mansion of Domitian on the Palatine, across the valley of the Forum Romanum. The immediacy of 'this' vision is abetted by the presence of 'you' (*te*), Domitian, who, through the suggestiveness of the poet's language, becomes parallel with the king of the gods just as the latter's dwelling admires the emperor's similar creation on an adjacent hill.[17]

In this context the phrase *nec magnum properes escendere caelum* claims our particular attention. It is a standard topic of panegyric that the subject of praise, implicitly considered divine, should not hasten to leave his terrestrial domain, which would mean the end of his mortal existence and therefore of his beneficent presence among mankind. This compliment seems particularly pertinent to Domitian who is in the process of creating a form of *caelum*, as we saw, in Rome for the world to admire.[18] Here again reference to Horace helps deepen our understanding of Statius' meaning. The second poem in his first collection of odes (*Carm.* 1.2) is dedicated to Augustus. Its striking final word is Caesar, and its core theme is the immortality of the new emperor. Whatever aspect of divinity you choose to take, begs the poet, may you long remain with us! Even if you assume the semblance of Mercury, Horace prays: *serus in caelum redeas diuque/laetus intersis populo Quirini...* ('...may you be slow in returning to heaven and for a long time may you rejoice in being part of the people of Quirinus...', *Carm.* 1.2.45–6).We have already noted several occasions through which Statius underscores the potential apotheosis of Domitian by reference to Horace and in particular to occasions where the great lyricist sings the praises of Augustus, praises equally à propos for his own quasi-omnipotent sovereign whose prestige they enhance. The context brings out the ironic wit of the passage. Since the deity, Domitian, has already manufactured his *caelum* in the midst of Rome, there need be no worry that he hasten upward to a *magnum caelum* elsewhere. He may infer from the poet's words that the emperor's sacred presence will achieve a form of permanence.

---

[17] It is likely that Statius is referring to the splendid temple of Jupiter Capitolinus that looms over the Forum from the west. But he might also have us remember the smaller temple of Jupiter Tonans, not far from the larger shrine, not least because it was vowed by Augustus in 26 and dedicated by him in 22 BCE (Suet. *Aug.* 29.3).

[18] Cf. 19 (*caelum*) and 31 (*caeli*).

DOMITIAN'S BANQUET (STATIUS' *SILVAE* 4.2)   195

The poet has interspersed the opening of his ekphrastic look at the mansion of Domitian with concern over the passage of time, especially in the life of the emperor himself. He now focusses more strictly on space as he attends to the building itself:

> tanta patet moles effusaeque impetus aulae
> liberior campi multumque amplexus operti
> aetheros, et tantum domino minor; ille penates
> implet et ingenti genio iuvat. aemulus illic
> mons Libys Iliacusque nitet, <tum> multa Syene
> et Chios et glaucae certantia Doridi saxa
> Lunaque portandis tantum suffecta columnis.
>
> (Stat. *Silv.* 4.2.23–9)

Such a mass opens out and the thrust of the spreading hall, more open than a plain's extent and embracing much of the enclosed sky, and less only than its master; he fills the house (25) and strengthens it with his mighty spirit. There, in rivalry, gleams the Libyan mountain and the Ilian, along with Syene in abundance and Chios and rocks vying with grey-green Doris and Luna, substituted only to carry the columns.

Statius elucidates the capaciousness, as well as the beauty, of the royal edifice from several angles.[19] Our eyes follow analogies, both horizontal and vertical, that he draws from a vast stretch of land, from the heavens contained above, and vicariously from the world of water. We follow a geographical spread that embraces Africa, the Aegean Sea and the west coast of Italy.[20] Space receives particular emphasis as we watch the scope of the sky viewed above (*multum operti aetheros*) and the amount of stone quarried at

---

[19] Line 23 contains a vivid reference back to the *Aeneid* where the phrase *tanta...moles* serves as a reminder of *tantas moles* (*A.* 1.134), the enormous swirl of a hurricane that the winds have churned up against the Trojans. As regularly with Statius' bows to his great predecessor, we find a disquieting situation turned to formative ends. Catastrophic storm is transformed into grandiose palace, energy massed into destructive action yields to composed magnitude for our admiration. The word *moles* is glossed through hendiadys at *A.* 1.61 (*molemque et montis...altos*), adding to the sense of immensity.

[20] Line 8 contains the only appearance of the form *Doridi* in Latin poetry. So, as we survey this grand space, Doris, daughter of Oceanus and Thetis, strikingly represents the sea while Luna (mod. Luni), famous source of white marble near Carrara, suggests both the earth—a location in Italy famous for its bright stone—and the heavens, supplementing words like *astris* (10, 59) and *caelum* (19, 22, 31) that we have been tracing. As marble, Luna by metonymy supports Domitian's mighty abode. As moon goddess, she joins Ceres and Bacchus as an additional divinity at the service of the emperor and his estate. The description of Domitian's abode here is discussed in detail in Kreuz (2017) 239–65.

196   THE POETIC WORLD OF STATIUS' *SILVAE*

Syene (*multa Syene*), as if, in the poet's expansiveness, the mansion put on display much of the town itself. Our vision is further gratified by the gleam of marbles from Libya and Asia Minor and by the colours suggested by the sea's darkness as well as by the brightness that the name Luna intimates.

One prominent example of size deserves separate mention, the appropriately named Domitian himself, master (*domino*, 25) of the house whose scope and artistry are being set out for our approbation. At Statius' climactic moment of greatest hyperbole, we learn that the palace is dwarfed only by the emperor himself. At the start of the description the poet bade us scrutinize a *tectum augustum ingens,* where the etymological connection between the first adjective and the verb *augeo* urges us to admire both the majesty and the extensiveness of the mansion. At its core we take note of the phrase *ingenti genio*, the nobleness of inner quality native to the edifice's builder as reflected in its external glories. The deictic *ille*, the distancing pronoun that helps pinpoint this magnificence of which we should be in awe, is echoed immediately in the adverb *illic* that takes our eye to mountains in north Africa and the Troad. They rival each other in their amplitude and in their radiance, but, through the pull of Statius' word deployment, they also reflect the emperor's own inherent impressiveness and nobility.[21]

In the midst of all this visual nourishment the poet has not forgotten his earlier focus on temporality and on how time's passage affects the poem's protagonists. Let us look again, but from another lexicographical point of view, at a phrase that we have just reviewed in connection with the emperor: *penates...ingenti genio iuvat*. Assonance links *ingenti* and *genio* but the adjective and noun are also related by ancient students of word origins who rightly associate *genius* with the idea of birth.[22] As we attend to the grandiosity of Domitian's new *domus* Statius would have us also again keep in mind the magnitude of his own innate quality. The word *iuvat* adds a further appropriate touch to the acclaim. In this case early etymologists connect the verb with *iuvenis*, which is to say with youthfulness.[23] The intensity of the emperor's spiritual gift is complemented by the notion that it remains

---

[21] *Mons* (27) is an example of synecdoche where the whole stands for the part, the mountain for the marble cut from its surface. The hyperbole suits the enormity of the setting. The emphasis on size leads easily to *multa Syene.* Here metonymy is the operative figure: the city stands for marble quarried in its precincts. Hyperbole again adds to the power of the exposition. Not just its quarries but the whole town itself helps represent the palace's spatial grandeur. As he sets forth the scale of this monumentality, Statius has us attend to size, shape, and quantified amounts of material as well as to visual attributes such as brightness and colour.

[22] For details, see Maltby (1991) s.v. *gens* and *ingens* (256, 304).

[23] For further examples, see Maltby (1991) s.v. *iuvenis* (320).

DOMITIAN'S BANQUET (STATIUS' *SILVAE* 4.2) 197

untouched by time. Once again, his potential apotheosis is supported by a clear intimation of immortality.

Statius concludes the core of his ekphrastic moment by focusing our attention on vision before returning to the feast and its participants:

> longa supra species: fessis vix culmina prendas
> visibus auratique putes laquearia caeli.
> hic cum Romuleos proceres trabeataque Caesar
> agmina mille simul iussit discumbere mensis,
> ipsa sinus accincta Ceres Bacchusque laborat
> sufficere. aetherii felix sic orbita fluxit
> Triptolemi, sic vitifero sub palmite nudos
> umbravit colles et sobria rura Lyaeus.
>
> (Stat. *Silv.* 4.2.30–7)

The view above is extensive: you might scarcely take in (30) the roof with your exhausted sight, and you might consider it the ceiling of a gilded heaven. Here, when Caesar ordered Romulus' princes and the *trabea*-robed ranks to recline together at a thousand tables, Ceres herself, with her dress girt up, and Bacchus toil to bring satisfaction. The bountiful path of Triptolemus in the sky above flowed thus (35), thus Lyaeus, under vine-bearing tendril, shaded naked hills and sober countryside.

Etymology and assonance combine to help us make the transition from line 29 to 30. According to one ancient definition: 'columns are so-called because they hold up roofs' (*columnae dictae, quod culmina sustineant*).[24] Once again the enormity of Domitian's palace becomes apparent through the distance that Statius asks our eyes, tired from the effort, to travel as we measure the height of the columns from floor to housetop, reaching what appears to be a ceiling like a gold-edged heaven.

The poet stresses the sight by having further recourse to the specific vocabulary of ekphrasis to which he first called attention at line 20 where the personified temple of Jupiter Tonans is in awe of 'this' sight of Domitian's edifice on the Palatine. We noted a parallel there with *A.* 1.494–5 as Aeneas stands in awe at 'these' marvellous paintings (*haec miranda stupet*) of events

---

[24] Maltby (1991) s.v. *columna* (142). The word also appears at 18 and 38, where it is used for the only time with the meaning 'table-leg' (*TLL* iii.1738.62–30). The repetition, so soon after Statius' first two uses, has the effect of exaggerating the size of the supports. For a moment, the legs seem parallel to the marble columns in grandeur, adding to the magnificence of the whole.

198   THE POETIC WORLD OF STATIUS' *SILVAE*

at Troy. Statius now puts to use another characteristic of ekphrasis of which Virgil takes triple advantage in *Aeneid* 8. While Aeneas there marvels at the shield which Vulcan has crafted for him, Virgil draws his audience into enjoying individual scenes by making 'you', the reader as viewer, a palpable part of the event itself. Along with Aeneas 'you could behold' (*aspiceres*, 650) Porsenna in all his emotionality; 'you could see' (*videres*, 676) Leucate all aglow with the panoply of war in preparation for the conflict of Actium, and 'you could believe' (*credas*, 691) that the Cyclades had gotten loose, so large were the battleships.

Statius' first example, *prendas*, stands out for being the only use that we have of this form of the verb. Its force is enhanced by assonance with a further instance, *putes*, in the subsequent line.[25] Both together have the effect of strengthening our position as imagined viewers of the scene itself. We are like guests at the emperor's bountiful table, or even like the emperor himself, the major 'you' of the poem hitherto. We are astonished, ourselves, at the striking vistas that mentally open before us. Finally, we must remember that, unlike Dido's frescoes and Vulcan's shield, it is a palpable work of extraordinary architecture that is in process before our astonished eyes, not a product of the wordsmith's imagination. Ekphrasis here conjures up the immediately tangible, not the writer's dream. We are witnessing a singular portrait of an actual space of true grandeur in which we are instructed to imagine ourselves dining, not just a poet's dream of an artifact, however rich its symbolic value.

Virgil is not forgotten as the scene progresses. The phrase *iussit discumbere mensis* asks us to remember the moment in the first book of the *Aeneid* where the Carthaginians, summoned to Dido's banquet, are 'ordered to recline on the embroidered couches' (*toris iussi discumbere pictis*, 708). Statius would thus have us recall the initial lines of the present poem and the tradition that he is emulating. But, unlike events in the plot line that begins to evolve for Virgil's unfortunate protagonists, we continue to be 'here' (*hic*), enjoying Domitian's feast along with his guests.

---

[25] In both construction and lexical usage, line 31 bears a remarkable similarity to *A.* 8.25, where Aeneas' darting thoughts are compared to a light flashing upward off a bronze bowl:...*iamque sub auras/erigitur summique ferit laquearia tecti* ('...and now [the light] rises up toward the heavens and strikes the ceiling-panels of the topmost roof', *A.* 8.24–5). Once again Statius expertly connects 'you', Domitian, in particular, as well as individual guests and readers, with Aeneas and the world of the *Aeneid*. And Statius' earlier *tectum* (based on *A.* 7.170) is turned hyperbolically into *caeli*, following the lead of 19 and 22.

DOMITIAN'S BANQUET (STATIUS' *SILVAE* 4.2) 199

We are privileged to witness an epiphany (*ipsa*) of Ceres, goddess of grain as well as of Bacchus, god of wine, as they individually work (*laborat*) at waiting on the participants.[26] Once more we think of a Virgilian meal, this time when the Arcadian king Evander offers food to Aeneas and his fellow Trojans. Chosen youths and a priest:...*onerant...canistris/dona laboratae Cereris, Bacchumque ministrant* ('...pile in baskets the gifts of Ceres that they had toiled over and serve Bacchus', *A.* 8.180–1). Virgil's use of metonymy turns the goddess into well-crafted loaves made from the grain over which she presides as patron while Bacchus becomes his very wine itself.[27] Statius offers a remarkable variation on this already impressive figuration by turning the divinities back into themselves. But they now also appear in person, gods at the service of another incipient divinity as they grace a meal presumably by offering the best examples of the food and drink for which they are emblematic.[28]

Their splendour is further marked by the associations which follow, of Ceres-Demeter, with her favourite, Triptolemus, disseminator of corn, and of Bacchus with another incarnation of himself, Lyaeus, 'the releaser', who clothes the hills and the ordinarily temperate landscape with pleasure-inducing vines.[29] The former, whose grain we imagine flowing earthward, catches our attention through the poet's double exploitation of hypallage. The personified *orbita*, Triptolemus' celestial path, is *felix*, fertile like the

---

[26] Coleman (1988) 93 points out the emphatic position in which Statius places *sufficere* and the reminiscence with *A.* 9.803, with both uses suggesting the toil involved. In Book 9 we have a concatenation of Turnus, Saturnia Juno, and Iris, as the king of the gods delegates the latter to forbid his wife-sister from interfering in the terrestrial battles by lending support to Aeneas' chief antagonist as he attacks the Trojan ramparts. As often, therefore, we find in the later poet an auspicious scene replacing one of implicit violence in the earlier master. In Virgil Jupiter is driven to send down his messenger to Juno to demand that she desist from abetting the conflict in Italy. In Statius the king of the gods is implicitly present in the figure of Domitian who presides over a banquet at which two Olympic divinities are at hand to provide not fresh energy for bellicose ferocity but supplies for an event notable for civility and the suppression of the appurtenances of war.

[27] For the implicit metonymy, as well as for another bow to Dido's dinner, cf. *A.* 1.701–2.

[28] After entertaining the Trojans at dinner, Evander regales his guests with the saga of Hercules on the Aventine. The reminder may well be meant to anticipate the equation of Domitian with Hercules at 50–1.

[29] Statius' phraseology at line 37 is beholden to Virg. *Ecl.* 7.58: *Liber pampineas invidit collibus umbras...* ('Liber has begrudged the hills the shade of his vine-shoots'). As often, Statius takes an adverse moment in Virgil and turns it to something uplifting. In the pastoral poem Liber (Bacchus, 'the freer') takes away his protective, beautifying cover from the hills. Statius, by contrast, has the god clothe them with dense vineyards for all to enjoy the results. The varied personifications implicit in *nudos colles* and *sobria rura* serve to extend the god's hegemony even over the inanimate. For the association of Bacchus with hills, see Mynors (1990) on Virg. *G.* 2.110–13.

200 THE POETIC WORLD OF STATIUS' *SILVAE*

hero himself as its benefits pour down on humankind and on the overlord of Rome in particular. And it is Triptolemus himself, not his orbit, who is *aetherius*, fostering men's lives from a well-deserved position in the sky.

Bacchus, who appears as Lyaeus, the god with the potential to set us free from our concerns, has his notable features in Statius' portrayal. He envelops naked hills with his vines, an exploit which has the consequent effect of luring into his sphere of influence the ordinarily moderate countryside. But the phrase *vitifero palmite* gives him special potency.[30] Such is his influence that the tendril itself produces the vine, that the part helps generate the whole as the god goes about his task of shrouding the landscape with plants whose produce, among other gifts, will enhance the dinner parties of the mighty.

The Host

By concentrating our attention on the two gods in attendance Statius prepares us to turn away from the banquet and its magnificent setting back to the host himself, the prime object of his applause:

> sed mihi non epulas Indisque innixa columnis
> robora Maurorum famulasque ex ordine turmas,
> ipsum, ipsum cupido tantum spectare vacavit
> tranquillum vultu sed maiestate serena
> mulcentem radios submittentemque modeste
> fortunae vexilla suae; tamen ore nitebat
> dissimulatus honos. talem quoque barbarus hostis
> posset et ignotae conspectum agnoscere gentes.
> <div align="right">(Stat. <i>Silv.</i> 4.2.38–45)</div>

But for me in my eagerness there was leisure to gaze not at the feast and at the Moorish wood supported on Indian columns and the ordered ranks of servants, only on himself, himself, calm in his features (40) but soothing its radiance with peaceful grandeur and modestly lowering the banners of his success; yet the glory he disguised kept gleaming on his countenance.

---

[30] In adopting the adjective *vitifero* here, the reading of *M*, I differ from Courtney, followed by Coleman, who emends to *uvifero*.

DOMITIAN'S BANQUET (STATIUS' *SILVAE* 4.2)   201

Even a barbarian foe and unknown tribes would have been able to recognize such a man on sight (45).

The speaker's 'I', which has not been present in the poem's narrative since line 16, now returns with particular emphasis. In between we have been attending to the palace's splendid furnishings and to the banquet itself.[31] With *mihi* Statius casts our thoughts back to the hymn-like language with which he had addressed Domitian at lines 14–17 as he looks directly on his features. The clear implications of the emperor's godliness are now reenforced by the cogent repetition of the demonstrative *ipsum*. At line 34 the poet used *ipsa* to sustain the epiphany of the goddess Ceres, who in actuality is toiling at a dinner which offers the wares she blesses. The double use of *ipsum* at line 40 not only reflects the poet's astonishment as he watches his host, but it also intimates that the object of his observation may surpass even the goddess of grain in displaying attributes of divinity for his many invitees to admire and even worship.[32]

The implication is confirmed and aggrandized in the verses that follow. The language, especially of line 41, sends us to Lucretius' description of the gods who, indifferent to the affairs of men, 'in the quiet of peace' (*tranquilla pace*) pass 'a life of calm' (*vitam serenam*, 2.1093–4).[33] Here also a reminiscence from Virgil serves both to comment on and to enhance Statius' text. For the Augustan poet, writing a generation after his Epicurean predecessor, the gods are deeply involved with human history. One deity in particular stands out as we read this segment of the later poet's rendering of thanksgiving. We find ourselves at a moment in the first book of the *Aeneid* when Venus, distraught with the unfortunate turn her son's saga is taking, appeals to her father, the king of the gods, for understanding and help. Statius would have us remember Jupiter's demeanour as he prepares to give her a reply: *olli subridens hominum sator atque deorum/vultu, quo caelum tempestatesque*

---

[31] The language of line 39 (*famulas... ex ordine turmas*) serves to have us still keep in mind Dido's dinner for the Trojans: *quinquaginta intus famulae, quibus ordine/longam cura penum struere...* ('...there are within fifty servant-maids whose duty was to arrange in order the long feast', *A.* 1.703–4). Virgil there is probably thinking of the fifty slave women in the service of Alcinous (Hom. *Od.* 7.103), a reminder of Homer's epic and its setting, before the banquet to which Statius alluded in lines 3–4. So Statius, through the reference to servers, would have us think back to the feasts of both Alcinous and Dido, for a variety of reasons.

[32] This is the only example of an adjacent repetition of *ipsum* in Latin, and asyndeton adds to the intensity of the gesture as our eyes fix on the features of the emperor. The series of plurals in lines 38–9 now yields pointedly to the individuality of the extraordinary figure who presides over the affair.

[33] Cf. also Lucr. 3.292–3 on the human mind when calm and at peace.

202 THE POETIC WORLD OF STATIUS' *SILVAE*

serenat,/oscula libavit natae ('Smiling on her with the countenance by which he brings calm to the heavens and to its storms, he gently kissed his daughter...' *A.* 1.254-6). In suggesting that we turn in our imaginations from Lucretius' indifferent divinities to a god who controls our weather with his glance, we move not only from the general to the particular but to an authority who exerts his power to bring quiet and repose to our world by mollifying the elemental forces inherent in nature.[34]

The overall compliment to Domitian, that he is the terrestrial equivalent of the lord of the Olympic gods who brings quiet to whatever might roil our ambient world, is enormous.[35] And Statius furthers the tribute in what follows. Like Jupiter, god of the elements, the emperor can ameliorate the force of his rays. He can also lower his banners in a display of temperateness.[36] He has vast power at his command, but he knows how to wield it both appropriately and with restraint (*modeste*). Modesty prevails over any manifestation of hubris.[37]

Virgil again may help us further gloss the poet's tribute. At line 18, in a strong gesture of affinity, Statius, we remember, has us recall the earlier author's account of the palace of Latinus in Book 7 of the *Aeneid*. That depiction ends with a lengthy display of likenesses of men wounded while fighting for their fatherland and of the many types of armour available to them:

[34] Virgil uses similar language at *A.* 4.476-7 where Dido, fully a prey to furies, hides her impending suicide in conversation with her sister:...*maestam dictis adgressa sororem/consilium vultu tegit ac spem fronte serenat*...('...addressing her sorrowful sister, she masks her plan on her countenance and brings the calm of hope to her brow...'). If Statius would have us ponder this occasion as well, he follows his regular procedure and turns a fateful moment in the earlier poet to positive ends. Dido's pretence at serenity turns out well in the case of the true tranquillity of Domitian-Jupiter.

[35] Cf. Virgil's uses of *mulceo* at *A.* 1.66 and 153. The first centres on the god Aeolus who has ability to soothe his destructive winds. The second finds Neptune, later in the same opening scene, calming their violence like a man of piety quieting a raging mob. Domitian-Jupiter keeps under wise control the flashing vitality that emanates from his brow. The god who governs water has been transmuted into the lord of the sky. Suetonius (*Aug.* 94.6) helps us expand the context. He notes that Augustus' father dreamed that his son appeared to him carrying Jupiter's thunderbolt and sporting a *radiata corona*.

[36] If the word *radios* looks to Jovian meteorological power, *vexilla* are metaphoric for military might and therefore are associated with Mars. The double trope anticipates the direct comparisons of Domitian with Mars (Gradivus) and, once more, Jupiter (*dux superum*) which initiate and conclude the catalogue at 46–56 of analogies between the emperor and superhuman exemplars.

[37] With *submittentem* we might compare Virgil two uses of the verb's past participle to describe Juno in uncharacteristic moments of apparent meekness. At *A.* 10.611 we find her *summissa* toward her omnipotent spouse, and at 12.807 she gazes upon him *summisso vultu*. The adverb *modeste* would suggest that in the case of Domitian appearances are not deceptive.

DOMITIAN'S BANQUET (STATIUS' *SILVAE* 4.2)   203

> multaque praeterea sacris in postibus arma,
> captivi pendent currus curvaeque secures
> et cristae capitum et portarum ingentia claustra
> spiculaque clipeique ereptaque rostra carinis.
>
> (Virg. A. 7.183–6)

And many weapons besides hang on the sacred doors, captive chariots and curved axes and helmet crests and massive bars of gates, and javelins and shields and beaks wrenched from ships.

The difference between Domitian and the ancient model with which Statius suggests a parallel is purposefully incisive. Latinus and his forebears have devoted themselves to warfare and take pride in displaying the evidence of their successful militarism for visitors to appreciate and esteem. The emperor, by contrast, lets his banners sink so that the very lack of ostentation will suggest to the onlooker the unremarked availability of plentiful martial might to be used with discretion and sagacity. Subsequent verses will offer us evidence. At the moment, the poet would have us think that our royal focus of attention gleams like the marbles that embellish his palace (*nitet*, 27) and that the glow of his inborn nobility cannot be veiled even by a becoming unpretentiousness. The Jovian aspects of Domitian shine through, whatever his pretense at masking his splendour.[38]

At the conclusion of his direct portrait of the emperor Statius plays brilliantly on the root -*nosc*: even peoples who are, not to say ignorant of us, but even unknown to us (*ignotae*), would perceive (*agnoscere*) his superiority when gazing upon him.[39] Sight becomes insight, vision deepens into knowledge. But there is a particularity that lends special point to the wordplay. It is a 'barbarian foe', someone both unschooled and antagonistic to Rome, who suffers the revelation. Perhaps this form of epiphany is sufficient for the enemy to realize the quality of its opponent and limit the extent of any potential armed conflict.

Statius further bolsters his implications of divine status for Domitian with a series of five comparisons of him with gods and demigods. The first likens him to Mars:

---

[38] This example of *dissimulatio* is to be contrasted with the behaviour of which Dido accuses Aeneas (*A*. 4.305). Cf. also 4.291 where the hero indirectly suggests the same conduct to his allies.

[39] The common root meaning is pointed out by Coleman (1988) 97.

204 THE POETIC WORLD OF STATIUS' *SILVAE*

> non aliter gelida Rhodopes in valle recumbit
> dimissis Gradivus equis...
>
> (Stat. *Silv.* 4.2.46–7)

In no other manner does Gradivus, with his horses unharnessed, recline in a chill valley of Rhodope.

Given the preceding implications of the emperor's prudence in advertising his military capability, it is a brilliant gesture on the poet's part to put first a similarity between his luminary and the Roman god of war but display him in a posture of rest. His horses, symbol of strength and power, have been put to pasture, and he, the Strider into battle, lies quietly in a mountain valley.[40] We will return to the verb *recumbit* later. Suffice it to note here its similarity with *discumbere* which Statius has used twice earlier (10, 33) to describe guests reclining at ease at the regal dinner, first the poet himself, then the thousand peers, senators and equestrians, who take advantage of his largesse. Domitian Mars may be famous for his military prowess, but he also knows how to display it unobtrusively as well as when and how to relax from his aggressive endeavours.[41]

Three further, equally brief, analogies follow in quick succession:

> ...sic lubrica ponit
> membra Therapnaea resolutus gymnade Pollux,
> sic iacet ad Gangen Indis ululantibus Euhan,
> sic gravis Alcides post horrida iussa reversus
> gaudebat strato latus adclinare leoni.
>
> (Stat. *Silv.* 4.2.47–51)

Thus Pollux lays down his slippery limbs, at ease from wrestling at Therapnae, thus Euhan lies by the Ganges as the Indians howl, thus grim Alcides, returned after his dread commands (50), was rejoicing to lean his side against the lion coverlet.

---

[40] For a detailed examination of the connection between *Gradivus* and the verb *gradior* see Maltby (1991) s.v. (262). The touch of wit is noted by Coleman (1988) 98. The Strider, who has been using horses, is now at rest, his battling days over for the present. With *dimissis equis* cf. *Atlante remisso* (19)—a moment of relaxation in Atlas' burdened existence? Virgil's two mentions of the god's title are to be found at *A.* 3.35 and 10.542.

[41] With *gelida Rhodopes in valle*, cf. *gelidis convallibus Haemi* (Virg. *G.* 2.488), equally in Thrace, where the poet would like to find a quiet resting place. It may not be coincidental that there are adjacent references to Sparta in each instance.

DOMITIAN'S BANQUET (STATIUS' *SILVAE* 4.2)   205

As our eye moves south from Thrace to Sparta, our orientation changes from god, resting after warfare, to human hero, Pollux, made one of the gods through the efforts of his immortal father, Jupiter, relaxed after a bout of wrestling.[42] We then turn back to an immortal, Bacchus, in repose at the Ganges, presumably after his eastern military campaigns. The grand river, yowling worshipers and a cult title of the divinity himself are meshed together in a magnificent hexameter whose sonic expressiveness captures an ecstatic moment in space and time.[43]

Next follows Hercules, a hero turned demigod, like Pollux, and first in the list to be allotted two full lines. The name Alcides stresses his human side, but mention of the 'orders' laid upon him by Eurystheus reminds us of the fabled labours whose accomplishment led to his apotheosis. The moment of relaxation that he can now enjoy sparkles with the poet's wit. By metonymy the Nemean lion, whom the hero strangled to death, has become its pelt against which he now reclines, and which remains one of his two great emblems. The past participle of the verb *sterno, strato*, serves as bridge for the figuration. Its initial meaning here is 'to lay low', the way the hero dealt with his animal opponent. But the word also means 'stretched out' like a piece of cloth. The beast has been done to death and then skinned, and it is against this remnant, raised to the level of symbol, that Hercules can happily take his rest, like Domitian and his reposing guests.

The phrase *horrida iussa* deserves separate study. The only other use of the word pair in Latin poetry is put by Virgil into the mouth of Dido as she describes to Aeneas the commands from heaven that send her quondam lover on his fated way toward Italy (4.378). The word *horrida* resonates widely, depending on celestial source and earthly receivers. To Aeneas the orders may seem both awesome and daunting, but we mostly think of their dread effect on the queen of Carthage herself that leads ultimately to self-slaughter. As so often with Statius' bows to his great predecessor, he takes an unfortunate episode and gives it a favourable turn. Hercules has come back to Tiryns, having brought to a successful conclusion the hazardous tasks

---

[42] As often, there is a contrasting Virgilian passage to Statius' *lubrica membra*. At *A.* 7.353 the snake hurled at Amata by the Fury Allecto 'slithers slippery along her limbs' (*membris lubricus errat*).

[43] *Indis ululantibus* may serve as a reminder of *Indis columnis* (38). If so, Statius offers an association of Domitian with Bacchus just as he has earlier with Jupiter. With his brilliantly onomatopoetic verse the poet helps reconstruct the hymnic chorus itself.

206 THE POETIC WORLD OF STATIUS' *SILVAE*

imposed upon him. His return posits a recurrence of better fortune, and at least a season of quiet when his latest exploits can be implicitly celebrated.[44]

In the concluding place of honour, we find the king of the heavens himself, preceded by a reminder that the speaking 'I' is creating these lines about a royal 'you' whose countenance has been a frequent object of our attention. The poem regularly intertwines the two:

> parva loquor necdum aequo tuos, Germanice, vultus:
> talis, ubi Oceani finem mensasque revisit
> Aethiopum sacro diffusus nectare vultus,
> dux superum secreta iubet dare carmina Musas
> et Pallenaeos Phoebum laudare triumphos.

> (Stat. *Silv.* 4.2.52–6)

I speak in a scanty way nor yet do I equal your features, Germanicus: such as the leader of the heaven-dwellers, when he revisits Ocean's boundary and the tables of the Aethiopes, his face suffused with holy nectar, orders the Muses to perform private songs (55) and Phoebus to praise the triumphs at Pallene.

Parva loquor is a reminder of *non ... digna loquar* (8–10) and of Statius' tacit emulation of Virgil that runs through the poem. The emphatic repetition of *vultus* at the line endings of 52 and 54 fixes our eyes on the emperor's features and refers us back to line 41 where the context of *vultu* returned our thoughts to Jupiter in *Aeneid* 1. The uses of *Oceani* and *Aethiopum* in adjacent lines recalls the similar collocation at *A.* 4.480–1, further bolstering the epic quality of the dinner and its setting.[45] Jupiter-Domitian would seem to order the songs presented by the Muses, newly minted for the occasion, to be kept confidential.[46] But the subject matter of Apollo's presentation is

---

[44] Statius may also be punning on *reversus*. Upon his return home, dreadful orders accomplished, Hercules can also move from serious matters (an implication of *gravis*) to pleasurable ones (*gaudebat*), as intense physical activity yields to relaxation, and a lion who has been a ferocious opponent becomes a pelt for the hero to rest his side against. (*Reversus* is one of four words in an eight line stretch beginning with *re-*. They suggest both action and its termination.) With *latus* in the present context, cf. Horace's reference to his soldier-friend Pompeius and 'his flank tired from long campaigning' (*longa ... fessum militia latus, Carm.* 2.7.18).

[45] Dido there is speaking, in pretence, to her sister about possible uses of magic to solve her difficulties.

[46] For the varied nuances of *carmina secreta*, see Man. 5.334–5; Luc. 1.599; Mart. 1.66.5. On the one hand, they have not been published yet. On the other, they may have an element even of mysticism about them that speaks of fresh inspiration. The reminder of *mansuro carmine* (3) imagines their lastingness and quality.

DOMITIAN'S BANQUET (STATIUS' *SILVAE* 4.2)   207

different, the triumphs at Pallene, which is to say a *Gigantomachia*, extolling the victories of the enlightened Olympic divinities over the brutish Giants. In an environment where military accomplishments are deliberately underplayed, they can at least be part of an evening's entertainment. The epic praise that Phoebus offers (*laudare*) keeps company with the praises (*laudat*, 1) that Virgil presents to Dido and her *convivia*. When the chief hero is Jupiter, the subject matter has the consequence of further confirming the poem's frequent linkage of the emperor himself with the supreme ruler of the gods. And once again Statius carefully brings the poem full circle.

As often, reference back to Horace will help us further elucidate and substantiate Statius' notions. I am thinking of occasions where the poet also catalogues figures of outstanding nobility in his heritage. For instance, the third of the sequence of odes that opens his third book of *Carmina* offers a particularly pertinent example. After a mention of thundering Jupiter (6), the poet lists mortals deified because of the integrity characterizing their notable conduct:

> hac arte Pollux et vagus Hercules
> enisus arces attigit igneas
>   quos inter Augustus recumbens
>   purpureo bibet ore nectar.
> hac te merentem, Bacche pater, tuae
> vexere tigres indocili iugum
>   collo trahentes; hac Quirinus
>   Martis equis Acheronta fugit...

(Hor. Carm. 3.3.9–16)

Through this virtue Pollux and roaming Hercules after a struggle attained the fiery heights. Reclining in their company Augustus will drink nectar with crimson lips. Through this, father Bacchus, as you deserved, your tigers bore you aloft, tugging their yoke with untutored neck, through this Quirinus fled Acheron by the horses of Mars...

In both lists, of heroes who have become gods, we have in common Pollux and Hercules with whom the god Bacchus could also be associated because of his substantial gifts to humankind. In-between, in Horace we have Augustus whose potential as a future god the poet honours. His portrayal is absorbed by Statius in several ways. He reclines (*recumbens*) like Mars relaxing (*recumbit*), warfare over for the moment, and after his divinization

208   THE POETIC WORLD OF STATIUS' *SILVAE*

he will drink nectar (*nectar*) the way Jupiter imbibes it along with the Aethiopes, 'his face suffused with holy nectar' (*sacro diffusus nectare vultus*).

The compliment to Domitian here is conspicuous. As we have seen, already at lines 41–2 the emperor is implicitly linked to the king of the gods and the connection is directly made through the simile at 53–6. The comparison with Pollux, Bacchus and Hercules announces that the ruler of Rome is of sufficient stature to merit a place on Olympus. But the identification with Augustus, accomplished with the assistance of Horace, stands apart and suggests that he deserves an analogy with the first emperor of Rome who left behind an extraordinary legacy, and who, according to the great lyricist, will deserve apotheosis as a result. We are in a new Augustan age of which, not by chance, Statius is a preeminent literary figure.[47]

The Poem's Conclusion

In the course of his five vivid analogies for Domitian among gods and glorified heroes, Statius has taken us on a wide geographical tour ranging from Thrace and Sparta to the Aethiopes, imagined to be located in the remote west. Our eye helps extend the grandeur that accrues to the emperor accordingly. We now turn back to time as a central concern of the eulogy:

> di tibi (namque animas saepe exaudire minores
> dicuntur) patriae bis terque exire senectae
> adnuerint fines.
>
> (Stat. *Silv.* 4.2.57–9)

May the gods (for they are often said to give ear to lesser souls) grant that you twice and thrice surpass the bounds of your father's old age.

The boundary (*finem*) of the far distant ocean is replaced by grand limits (*fines*) of human time that the poet, modestly considering his virtuosity that of a 'lesser soul' to aid the efficacy of his entreaty, asks the gods on behalf of

---

[47] Other Horatian catalogues valuable in interpreting Statius' list can be found in *Carm.* 1.12, 4.5, and 4.8 (where Jupiter, Hercules, the Tyndaridae, and Liber are among the named, worthy of the poet's *laus*), and in *Ep.* 2.1.4–5. Augustus Caesar is a regular component. He is also the central figure of *Carm.* 3.25, an ode written under the influence of Bacchus which, among other echoes, mentions Rhodope in its course. Horace himself may be drawing on a similar grouping to be found at Cic. *N. D.* 2.24.62.

DOMITIAN'S BANQUET (STATIUS' *SILVAE* 4.2) 209

the patron.[48] Statius introduces his prayer with a careful allusion to the *Aeneid*. Virgil's only use of the phrase *di tibi* occurs at the start of line 603 of the epic's initial book where Aeneas apostrophizes Dido prior to beseeching the gods to justly reward her sympathetic handling of the suffering Trojans. His eulogy leads shortly to the banquet, mention of which receives place of prominence at the opening lines of the present *eucharisticon*. Domitian is again Dido, gratifying his multitudinous constituency with a sumptuous repast. Statius therefore allots himself a dual role. He is an Aeneas, guest at the event, offering a moment of prayer in thanksgiving for his kindly treatment by his host. But, as we expand the bow to the poem's initial hexameters, he is also a Virgil, recounting in verse his response to the present adventure and making use of the language, and frame of reference, of his great predecessor in the process.

There is much to be done in this personal history, extended by the goodwill of the gods:

> ... rata numina miseris astris
> templaque des habitesque domos. saepe annua pandas
> limina, saepe novo Ianum lictore salutes,
> saepe coronatis iteres quinquennia lustris.
>
> (Stat. *Silv.* 4.2.59–62)

May you send consecrated divinities to the stars, may you bestow temples and dwell in houses. May you often open the gates of the year (60), may you often greet Ianus with a new lictor, may you often repeat the quinquennial celebrations with garlanded lustrations.

In the poet's prayer, may the emperor send duly sanctioned gods to the heavens and establish places of worship to the deserving dead but himself live on as a figure sharing in the dwellings of earthlings.[49] Yearly periods

---

[48] With *exaudire* cf. Virg. *A.* 11.157–8 (*exaudita...vota*), Evander's unanswered prayers at the death of Pallas. The only other preserved use of the form *adnuerint* in classical Latin literature occurs at *A.* 11.20, also at the opening of a hexameter, where Aeneas is exhorting his troops.

[49] The combination of ABAB order, abetted by alliteration, chiasmus (pointed out by Coleman [1988] 100), and sense pause, puts special stress on the word *domos* in line 60. We have been looking at a unique *dominus* of a unique *domus*. Long may he remain lord of his mansion on the Palatine instead of hurrying to a different destination due him as an immortal! There are just two other uses of the form *habites* in Latin literature, and the only one in verse occurs at Ov. *Tr.* 5.2.51–2, where the poet addresses Augustus: *sic habites terras et te desideret aether./sic ad pacta tibi sidera tardus eas* ('So may you dwell on earth and may the heavens yearn for you, so may you be slow in making your way to the stars promised you'). Once more

210   THE POETIC WORLD OF STATIUS' *SILVAE*

and stretches of five years will dot the time frame.[50] Statius confirms his point by employing one of his favourite rhetorical devices, repetition, here exploited to an extraordinary degree. Within the space of six hexameters, he offers us four instances of the word *saepe*. Iteration here performs a quasi-liturgical function bordering on magic. The presumption is that continued verbal insistence will help turn hope into fact, dream into reality. The heightened tone also prepares readers for Statius' return to the hymnic form which brings the poem to a climactic conclusion:

> qua mihi felices epulas mensaeque dedisti
> sacra tuae, talis longo post tempore venit
> lux mihi, Troianae qualis sub collibus Albae,
> cum modo Germanas acies, modo Daca sonantem
> proelia Palladio tua me manus induit auro.
>
> (Stat. *Silv.* 4.2.63–7)

The day you granted me the auspicious feast and the blessings of your table, thus it came to me, after a long passage of time, as when, beneath the hills of Trojan Alba (65), your hand crowned me with Pallas' gold as I was singing, now of German wars, now of Dacian battles.

One of the striking lexical features of these final verses is the unremitting association of the first and second persons, between poet and prince. Beginning at line 57 with *tibi*, we progress to *mihi, tuae, tua*, and *me*. They in fact merge at the final juxtaposition as the emperor's hand clothes the singing bard with an aureate crown to honour his poetic performance and to be honoured in the process. *Tua manus* surrounds *me*.

We examined an earlier example of this interaction between pronouns and their adjectives at lines 13–17 where Statius first adopts the characteristics of a hymn in the celebration of his host. The clear example of ring-composition helps serve a unifying purpose with genre as its basis. At the start of the poem Statius places us strongly in an epic setting analogical to

---

we have a specific reference to Augustus in relation to the theme of a dilatory return to heaven. (In this regard we have earlier called attention to Hor. *Carm.* 1.2.45 and 3.3.11–12.) Yet again Statius takes a difficult or sad situation and alters its tone. In *Tr.* 5.2 the exiled poet is begging the omnipotent leader for mercy and in particular for a change of setting. Statius, by contrast, is pleading for longevity for his lord and a continuance of his present prosperous circumstances. His prayer is to the gods on behalf of the emperor, not, as in the case of the earlier author, to the emperor on the poet's own behalf.

[50] Five years is explicit in *quinquennia*, implicit in *lustris*.

DOMITIAN'S BANQUET (STATIUS' *SILVAE* 4.2)   211

similar situations in Virgil and Homer. As we move into the poem's central section, Statius employs a hymnic structure to draw us near the personal quality of his central subject. The order is reversed at the poem's conclusion as we move from the celebration of the emperor's humanity, and of his interplay with the poet-speaker himself, to his epic accomplishments as victor against German tribes and in Dacia.[51] Virgil and his Dido lead in conclusion to Statius' exaltation of the soldierly quality of Domitian. And Apollo's singing a *Gigantomachia* to Jupiter-Domitian is an appropriate reminder of epic along the way.

A Virgilian reference helps reinforce the poet's point. The phrase *epulas mensaeque* has two counterparts in the first book of the *Aeneid*. At line 216 the newly landed Trojans, exhausted, are yearning for their missing companions: *postquam exempta fames epulis mensaeque remotae*...('after hunger was banished by the feast and tables were removed...', *A.* 1.216). Then, later in the same book, we find ourselves at a lull during the grand banquet that Dido offered to her unexpected guests: *postquam prima quies epulis mensaeque remotae*... ('after an initial calm came to the feast and the tables were removed...', 1.723). As he brings his own narrative to an end, Statius carefully reminds us of its beginning. Domitian's grand repast finds again its epic parallels in the Trojans enjoying their first meal after reaching safety on the shores of Africa and above all in the *convivia* of Dido which were the subject of our poem's opening hexameters. Once more Domitian is the counterpart of the magnificent queen of Carthage and Statius takes the place of his illustrious predecessor, Virgil, as the singer of the tale.

The doubling of generic interplay, therefore, adds to the force of the ring-composition that, as we have noted, strongly unifies the whole. At the poem's start we are immediately drawn into the world of epic by reference to Virgil and Homer. Statius then selects attributes of the hymn to serve as transition into the body of the text and the *laudes* of the emperor and his setting. The conclusion powerfully reverses this order. Mention of Domitian's *sacra* and of the blessings that the gods have bestowed upon him introduces a final moment where epic again holds sway. The poet himself comes stage front to sing not the mythic tales of a Ulysses or an Aeneas but the modern history of the emperor's wars and battles. We end appropriately with the gold by which the subject of his performance rewards the poet's achievements.

---

[51] *Germanas* is a reminder of the apostrophe of Domitian as *Germanice* (52). This in turn recalls the conquests of Julius Caesar Germanicus (15 BCE—19 CE) earlier in the century.

212   THE POETIC WORLD OF STATIUS' *SILVAE*

The phrase *longo post tempore venit* stands out for several reasons. We find the only other instance in Latin letters where this exact language occurs during the first *Eclogue* of Virgil where the shepherd Tityrus tells of his good luck:

> Libertas, quae sera tamen respexit inertem,
> candidior postquam tondenti barba cadebat,
> respexit tamen et longo post tempore venit...
>
> (Virg. *Ecl.* 1.27–9)

Freedom, though in my laziness she looked at me late, after my beard fell whiter from the clippers, nevertheless looked at me and came after a long time...

The source of this freedom is to be found in the city of Rome and its deliverer is a young god, a clear allegory for the youthful Octavian, still some years before he accepted the title of Augustus.[52] A parallel phrase is used later in the poem by the soon to be exiled shepherd Meliboeus who wonders if he will ever see his paternal lands 'after a long time' (*longo post tempore*, 67). At the moment, they will be in the hands of a Roman veteran called, with some irony, a godless, barbarian soldier (*impius... miles... barbarus*, 70–1). Virgil thus presents us, in the course of the poem, with a meditation on two faces of Roman might: the one offers freedom, the other takes it away. Statius compliments Domitian by suggesting a parallel between him and the young Augustus with the distinction that the emperor deals not with the horrors of civil conflict but with wars in defence of Rome's border territories. The *barbarus miles*, the Roman soldier who exiles the shepherd from his inherited acreage, is replaced by distant warriors who instigate 'German wars' (*Germanas acies*) and 'Dacian battles' (*Daca proelia*) against which all of Rome must contend.

In a way Statius, as regularly, gives Virgil a happy ending for the plight of Meliboeus. *Libertas* did come to Tityrus, thanks to a youthful Roman *deus*. For Statius *libertas* becomes *lux*, the light of day come yet again, when feasting serves as a reminder of an earlier celebration as Statius sang of Domitian at the Alban Games.[53] The presumption is that now a Meliboeus would never lose his property and that Tityran freedom would be assured by a new

---

[52] Newlands (2002) 281–2 insightfully discusses the allusion. There is another parallel at *A.* 6.406 (*longo post tempore*), used in connection with the golden bough.

[53] For the Alban Games and their performances, see Hardie (2003).

DOMITIAN'S BANQUET (STATIUS' *SILVAE* 4.2) 213

young god who holds sway in Rome. The brightness of the day reflects the brilliance that the emperor showers on his environment as he 'soothes' the Jovian *radii* that emanate from his brow (42).

Looking in summary at the poem's last fifteen lines, we find that emphasis on place (46–56) is followed by detailed evocation of time (57–62). This in turn yields to a combination of specific locales and occasions to bring the poem to a focused conclusion. The present event—an auspicious banquet and the table's rites—indoors, on the Palatine Hill, is paralleled with another equally particular moment and place, a long time before the present affair, on a special day (*lux*) and at a precise location beneath the hills southeast of the metropolis, when the poet was crowned at the Alban Games while singing of Domitian's military prowess. The emperor is at the centre of both events, sponsoring the dinner and presiding over the awards. But, then, the poet is also an essential figure. It is he who self-effacingly ranks himself among *animas minores* as he appeals for his host's extended longevity. But it is also he who creates the whole, which is to say whose facility to immortalize has been on display for sixty impressive verses.

Ring-composition strengthens the whole. The creation of poetic song, of whatever genre—and lyric as well as hymn have entered our discussion—takes us from the beginning (*lyra*, 7) to the end (*sonantem*, 66), with a glance back to Apollo and the Muses and their performances at Jupiter's festival (55–6). At the poem's start Virgil is immortalizing Aeneas, at Dido's banquet, and Homer Ulysses, at the feast of Alcinous. At the conclusion, as capstone to his own banquet poem, Statius becomes the now prized singer of tales. Equally unnamed, like Virgil and Homer, he is immortalizing himself while ennobling Domitian. Just as he is on a par with the earlier masters of epic, so, through his good offices, Domitian becomes a modern equivalent of the classical heroes.

One gesture on Statius' part deserves final emphasis. The reflections of the first book of the *Aeneid* in these ultimate lines, and especially of line 63, to Dido's banquet, bring the poem full circle with the assistance of Virgil's plot and language. We pause within a sweeping history of heroic challenges for a moment of quiet and celebration. The powerful reference to the earlier poet's first *Eclogue* at line 64 serves as further bonding agent between the two virtuosi and their imaginations. Virgil's poem is in essence a meditation, in pastoral form, on two aspects of Roman power with a determining moment of praise for a young god among men who can secure the continuity of a shepherd's *libertas*. By alluding to both initial pastoral and later epic Statius puts the cycle of Virgil's rich career

214   THE POETIC WORLD OF STATIUS' *SILVAE*

before us to facilitate our understanding of his own shorter sequence. The resulting honour to Domitian is multivalent. He is a divinity, with an extraordinary terrestrial setting, who can facilitate the lives of those within his sphere of dominion. He is a Dido, lord of his lands who can put on a grand ritual feast to celebrate those worthy of honour. He is also an Aeneas, in the process of achieving his own place in history. But he is also lucky enough to have his own contemporary Virgil to enshrine the whole for future admiration and contemplation.

6
Reading Travel (Statius' *Silvae* 3.2)

The second poem of Statius' third book of the *Silvae*, addressed to Maecius Celer upon his departure to take up a military position in the Roman province of Syria, is the most elaborate example of a *propemptikon*, a poem of farewell, that we have preserved from classical literature.[1] Perhaps for reason of this very spaciousness it has attracted its share of denigration from critics.[2] But I think of it as akin to a symphony like the eighth of Anton Bruckner. Only by examining closely the complexity of its expanse, only by tracing with care its many strands of imaginative exposition, as they evolve and interweave, can we do justice to the range and depth of the whole.

We will find the standard themes of a *propemptikon* developed in an idiosyncratic way: farewell to the beloved, for instance, best wishes for a safe journey, apologies for not being a proper comrade, acknowledgment of the bravery that it takes for a terrestrial creature to embark upon the sea, and curses upon the individual who dared devise the vehicle which made such a foolhardy venture possible. At the same time, we find hope that the trip will prove successful, in spite of the hazards involved, and that the voyager will enjoy his destination and come back unharmed so that both the traveller, who has been missed, and the faithful friend awaiting his return, can compare the details of their biographies during the period of absence.

---

[1] For a list of classical *propemptica* and the pages on which they are discussed, see Cairns (2007) 284–5 (*Silv.* 3.2 is mentioned at 11, 16, 21–2, 27, 115–16, 128, 142, 158, 162–3, 233–4. For ancient commentary on the form, see Menander Rhetor, 395.1–399.10. Russell and Wilson (1981) 303–8 with notes). Quinn (1963) 239–73 has a long discussion with detailed examples ('Persistence of a Theme: The *Propempticon*'). For *propemptica* in general in relation to *Silv.* 3.2, see Newmyer (1979) 34–7 and Gibson (2006) 177–9. In his close examination of the poem, Hardie (1983) 156–64 looks in particular at the influence exerted by Horace (*Ep.* 1, *Carm.* 1.3) and Ovid (*Am.* 2.11) on Statius. Recent interpretations of the poem include Rühl (2006) 264–71; Manolaraki (2013) 184–219; Gunderson (2021) 238–9; Newlands (2021).

[2] Nisbet and Hubbard (1970), for example, in their introduction to Hor. *Carm* 1.3, speak of Statius' 'facile effusion in honour of Maecius Celer' (42) as part of a discussion of themes common to *propemptica*. See also Quinn (1963) 241 n. 2: 'Statius comes nearest to this [i.e., "a *bon voyage* poem pure and simple"]: his poem is a protracted exercise on the conventional clichés with little personal involvement or thematic originality'.

The Poetic World of Statius' Silvae. Michael C. J. Putnam, Edited by: Antony Augoustakis with Carole E. Newlands, Oxford University Press. © Michael C. J. Putnam 2023. DOI: 10.1093/oso/9780192869272.003.0007

216   THE POETIC WORLD OF STATIUS' *SILVAE*

As his narrative evolves, we will discover Statius making use of the several Roman writers who have preceded him in mastering examples of the genre. The work of the elegists Tibullus, Propertius, and Ovid is, not unexpectedly, of particular importance as we trace influences, as is that of the lyricists Catullus and Horace. But it is Virgil, especially as writer of the *Aeneid*, who figures most prominently in the intellectual background of Statius' poem. For his epic, as does Celer's voyage, embraces a series of emotional journeys within the one grand itinerary of the titular hero, in Aeneas' case from the embers of his home city to Carthage and thence to Italy which serves as entrance to the Underworld and as the site of future Rome and of the final warring that lays the groundwork for the glorious achievements to come.

The spate of references to Virgil's great masterpiece will play a major role in enriching his successor's own powerful accomplishment. But we will find that the art of allusion in general is a major weapon in Statius' poetic arsenal. By utilizing it as metaphor, the poet supplements and enhances his receiving text, in this case 3.2, by challenging, and often adapting, earlier models in a variety of genres aside from epic, not least elegy, lyric, and pastoral.

The Poem's Opening

In his opening address to the gods who protect seafarers Statius prepares his readers for much that follows:

> Di quibus audaces amor est servare carinas
> saevaque ventosi mulcere pericula ponti,
> sternite molle fretum placidumque advertite votis
> concilium, et lenis non obstrepat unda precanti.
>
> (Stat. Silv. 3.2.1–4)

Gods, whose love it is to watch over bold keels and soothe the fierce dangers of the windy sea, moderate the gentle deep and turn your assembly kindly to my entreaties, and let the smooth wave not roar against my prayer.

Audaces alerts us to a traditional theme of a *propemptikon* with the temerity of the adventurer, a regular topic, here transferred to the humanized ships themselves on which the word *carinas* has us focus. Their valour will later be appropriately shared with the inventor of seafaring vehicles who, 'intrepid in his skill' (*audax ingenii*, 64), urged man to leave his natural, 'solid earth' for the jeopardy that ocean threatens.[3]

As an entity the phrase *audaces carinas* stands out for its own individuality. It offers the initial use of several examples of synecdoche to describe the craft on which Celer will be sailing. The personification also adds powerfully to the figuration. Celer, not to speak of the first sailor, is courageous but so is the ship that takes him on his way, and the figuration adds intensity to the endeavour. So does allusion. Statius is making a specific bow to lines from a chorus in Seneca's *Medea*:

> quisquis audacis tetigit carinae
> nobiles remos nemorisque sacri
> Pelion densa spoliavit umbra,
> quisquis intravit scopulos vagantes
> et tot emensus pelagi labores
> barbara funem religavit ora...

(Sen. Med. 607–12)

Whoever manoeuvred the renowned oars of the bold ship and stripped Pelion of the thick shade of its holy grove, whoever entered the wandering rocks and, having traversed so many trials of the sea, tied his rope on a savage shore...

As he embarks on his own novel *propemptikon*, with its continuous overtones of epic, Statius would have us remember another initiatory moment, the *Argo*'s departure on a new heroic project with seafaring at its core.[4]

Amor is equally striking;[5] to dwell here, at the start of the poem, on the idea of the love that gods have for ships, is to prepare us for the depth of emotionality to be discovered in the lines that follow. Some of this richness

---

[3] See also on line 75 (*audebant*) where the advent of sailing brought daring to the seas and their goddess. The boldness of humankind in general (*audax*, 25) and of Prometheus in particular (*audax*, 27) is a prominent feature in Horace's farewell poem to Virgil (*Carm.* 1.3) that we will turn to shortly.

[4] The literary history behind these lines extends backwards chronologically from Catullus 64 to Ennius' *Medea*. Catullus, for example, begins with mention of the crest of Pelion (*Peliaco vertice*, 1), notes man's daring (*ausi sunt*, 6), then turns to the *carina* itself (10) and the 'windy sea' (*ventosum aequor*, 12) through which the *Argo* will have to furrow a path for the first time. Ennius' fragment, too, starts with mention of the 'grove on Pelion' (*nemore Pelio*, fr. 208 Jocelyn). Is Statius perhaps alluding to Valerius Flaccus' *Argonautica* as well, which in turn alludes to Ennius, Catullus, Horace, and Seneca among others? See Davis (2016).

[5] We note the near adjacency of *serva* and *amorem* at Virg. *A.* 2.789, where Creusa is bidding adieu to her husband: *iamque vale et nati serva communis amorem* ('and now farewell and guard your love of the son we share'). This is the first of several occasions in *Silv.* 3.2 on which Statius calls our attention to the epic's second book.

218   THE POETIC WORLD OF STATIUS' *SILVAE*

comes from the constant presence of the Roman elegists behind Statius' words as they keep alive the earlier poets' world of passion cherished, foregone, and sometimes regained. We are readied for the clear affection of which the story line will tell between poet and patron, as the latter leaves behind a sorrowing friend who, like the gods at the start, follows his comrade with prayers (*votis*, 100) and anticipates his safe homecoming.

But the hexameter begins with a clarion call that resonates through all that follows. since the words *di quibus* also initiate three verses in Virgil's *Aeneid*, Statius alerts his readers to the fact that his canonical text will serve as a major stimulus to their understanding and appreciation of his own attainment. By asking us to survey Virgil's poem as we commence his own, Statius suggests that in 3.2 we have in store a tale to enjoy that in its own way partakes in aspects of epic sweep and that the *Aeneid* will keep us regular company as we study the unfolding tale ahead. The notion of travel, and of the varied passages that moving from novel place to place occasions, will be a mutual, essential unifying thread.

Virgil's three uses appear in *Aeneid* 2, 5, and 6. We find the first at line 352 of the second book as Aeneas recounts how he spurred on his men for one final, hopeless sally against the Greeks. The gods on whom the city depends for its well-being have departed and a fight to the death is the only remaining possibility. What the hero is in fact doing, as he tells his tale to Dido, is announcing the demise of Troy and with it his withdrawal for the vague, portentous trek toward Rome. This includes a problematical sojourn with the Carthaginian queen that is already in progress.

We will see Dido making several appearances in the lines that follow and Statius will also direct us to another prominent figure of *Aeneid* 2, the wooden horse. But it is mainly on the idea of travel that we dwell—on Aeneas setting out on the road to Rome, but, more specifically, on Celer heading to Egypt, Syria, and back, and on the challenges as well as the opportunities that the undertaking entails.

Virgil presents the second appearance of the phrase *di quibus* at *A*. 5.235, where Cloanthus appeals to the gods who have dominion over the sea to help him in his final spurt toward a win in the rowing competition, part of the games given in honour of Aeneas' father, Anchises. We find ourselves experiencing a parodic version of Aeneas' real journey that recommences sombrely at the end of the book with the death of his helmsman Palinurus off the coast of Italy.

Once more we sense a parallel with Celer's itinerary and its difficulties. Statius re-enforces their complementarity by a series of echoes from text to text. In particular 5.239–40, which follow shortly and visualize for us a reaction to Cloanthus' earlier prayer (*...eum...imis sub fluctibus audiit omnis/Nereidum Phorcique chorus Panopeaque virgo...*, 'under the depths of the waves the whole band of Nereides and of Phorcus, and the virgin Panopea, gave ear to him...') is recalled by Statius at line 13 where on behalf of Celer he salutes: *vos quoque, caeruleum Phorci, Nereides, agmen...* ('you also, nereides, sea-blue cohort of Phorcus...'). And, as *Aeneid* 5 draws to a close, Virgil draws attention to the throng of sea deities who attend Aeneas' fleet as it embarks from Sicily. Lines 824–5 mention Phorcus again along with Triton, who will appear at Statius' line 35, Glaucus, at line 37, and Palaemon at 39.[6]

The third and final occurrence of *di quibus* occurs at line 264 of the *Aeneid*'s sixth book. There the poem's narrator, in the first person, calls on the gods of the domain of spirits to approve his revelations of the realm below. in other words, he is introducing us to a singular progress of Aeneas within his grander enterprise, namely to visit his father among the dead. We are to witness a descent that only a handful of mortal notables have undertaken and survived. In the case of Statius, we thus bear continued witness to the heroism of Celer's marine endeavour.

But the poet is also heralding a series of itineraries that have death as well as valorous achievement as their finale. We will shortly see the poet Horace brought before us to add his own *exempla*. And, before the poem draws to an end, we will follow the careers of Alexander, from military champion to interment in a mausoleum in Alexandria, and of Cleopatra. After her defeat at Actium she escaped with her lover, Antony, back to her native Egypt to endure suicide followed by burial in the same city. In conclusion, Statius turns to his own grand project, the *Thebaid*, and specifically to the *busta*, the funeral pyres, that form such a prominent feature of its finale as the battling comes to an end, the dead are mourned at appropriate rites, and the ship that symbolizes the poet's own epic voyage of creativity comes safely home to port.[7] We will trace this final endeavour discreetly on display within the present poem itself.

One more figure, adumbrated only in these lines but growing in prominence as the poem progresses, is Dido. She too is preparing for self-slaughter when

[6] Cf. also *Phorci chorus* at *Silv.* 2.2.19.
[7] For interpretations of the conclusion of the *Thebaid*, see, e.g., Braund (1996); Hardie (1993) 46–8; Augoustakis (2010) 75–91; Putnam (2016).

220   THE POETIC WORLD OF STATIUS' *SILVAE*

she calls on the sun, Hecate, and the avenging Furies and, at the end, on her own gods, to listen to her prayers:

> '...et dirae ultrices et di morientis Elissae,
> accipite haec, meritumque malis advertite numen
> et nostras audite preces'.
>
> (Virg. *A.* 4.610–12)

'...and avenging Furies and gods of dying Elissa: attend to this, and turn your power, which I deserve, toward my wrongs and give ear to my prayers'.

The double commands, including the repetition of *advertite*, to specific divinities in a context where the act of prayer is also crucial, suggest that we overhear Virgil's suffering lover as we listen to Statius' own pleas on behalf of Celer. But, as often with his allusiveness, the later poet varies his model. In Dido's case, she is calling for divine assistance in cursing her absconding, in her eyes faithless, suitor as he sails away. As earlier lines make clear, shipwreck is part of her malediction but, even if he makes it to his destination, misery, she wishes, will ever be Aeneas' lot![8] By adducing the parallel Statius makes clear the depth of his emotional feeling for Celer and the importance of seeing to a fitting conclusion his foreign commitments unscathed and of returning safely. And to this end he turns negative to positive, curse to entreaty, in the hope of securing an act of preservation rather than of destruction.[9] Statius becomes a Dido figure who now blesses his dear friend upon his departure instead of imprecating him.[10]

---

[8] See *A.* 4.382–3 (*mediis...scopulis*) for shipwreck at sea as part of Dido's prayer, and, even if he makes it to land, suffering is to be Aeneas' destiny, she wills!

[9] There is also a large overlap between these lines and Virg. *Ecl.* 9.56–8: *causando nostros in longum ducis amores./et nunc omne tibi stratum silet aequor et omnes,/aspice, ventosi ceciderunt murmuris aurae* ('By your conversation you put my yearning at a distance. and now the whole level plain lies silent for you, and, look, all the breezes of the roaring wind have died down'). *Amores* picks up *amor* as *sternite* does *stratum. Ventosi* is repeated in the same position in the hexameter, and *silet* finds a parallel in *non obstrepat.* Cf. also Virg. *A.* 5.763 (*placidi straverunt aequora venti*). The source of its inspiration (Theocr. *Id.* 2.38) suggests that the sea is meant in the passage from *Ecl.* 9. Reference to *Ecl.* 9 also anticipates the several allusions to its kindred *Ecl.* 1 in the lines that follow.

[10] The vocabulary of lines 2–3 deserves special attention. The personification of *pericula* adds further menace to the threats of the sea. *Mulcere*, the central word in a nicely balanced line, sends us back to Virg. *A.* 1.66 where the same verb is used of Aeolus' authority to soothe the violence of the winds that are also personified. We will turn later to the adjective *saevus. Molle* (3) is often a stylistic word. It is used by Propertius at 1.7.19 (*mollem versum*) where the

READING TRAVEL (STATIUS' *SILVAE* 3.2)   221

Statius next calls on a specific divinity, the premier god of the sea:

> grande tuo rarumque damus, Neptune, profundo
> depositum; iuvenis dubio committitur alto
> Maecius atque animae partem super aequora nostrae
> maiorem transferre parat.

(Stat. Silv. 3.2.5–8)

Neptune, we grant to your depths an important and special (5) ward; the youth Maecius is given over to your untrustworthy deep and prepares to carry the greater part of our soul across the seas.

Again we are assured of Statius' affection for his patron and again he uses a complex means of expressing it. This time the poet Horace is the guiding spirit in the background and two of his great lyrics play separate parts.[11] The first is *Carmen* 1.3, his farewell to Virgil, his contemporary poet and friend, embarking on a crossing to Greece. He apostrophizes the ship that carries such a precious cargo:

> ... navis, quae tibi creditum
> >debes Vergilium, finibus Atticis
> reddas incolumem precor,
> >et serves animae dimidium meae.

(Hor. Carm. 1.3.5–8)

... O ship, who owe back Vergilius entrusted to you, restore him intact, I pray, to the bounds of Attica and preserve the half of my soul.

---

poet's elegies are contrasted to Ponticus' epic on Thebes. He styles his second book, of what he here calls *amores*, a *mollis liber* (2.1.1–2). A gentle sea, then, is an object of personal prayer to replace the potential (epic) violence in store. (In his note on *A.* 1.66, Servius suggests a connection between *mulcere* and *mollire*.) The only other use of the phrase *molle fretum* in classical Latin is by Ovid (*Met.* 14.558) of the sea in which swim Aeneas' ships after becoming water nymphs. *Placidum* and *lenis* are also stylistic words. Both are used together by Cicero (*Or.* 2.43) to describe mildness of speech as is *lenis* by Quintilian (*Inst.* 9.4.127). If the reading is correct (and we assume the same for line 4 here), then Propertius (1.9.12) also uses the adjective (*lenia*) to designate songs (*carmina*) that *amor* requests. Once more human feeling is paramount in the expression.

[11] As regularly, Virgil is also in the background. The phrase *dubio committitur alto* recalls the moment in *A.* 11.560 when Metabus, after praying to Diana, is about to hurl across the river his child Camilla 'who now is entrusted to the treacherous breezes' (*quae nunc dubiis committitur auris*).

222 THE POETIC WORLD OF STATIUS' *SILVAE*

With economic metaphors and other language in common, especially the recollection of *animae dimidium meae* in *animae partem nostrae maiorem*, Statius would have us welcome the power of Horace's *propemptikon* into his own farewell. Celer on his way to the east becomes a type of Virgil, cherished by his fellow creator, on his potentially dangerous way to a nearer destination.[12]

But if Horace would have us also imagine his colleague launched on the precarious progress of composing the *Aeneid*, as many critics surmise, correctly in my view, then Statius is succinctly illustrating for us another strand of thought running through his own narrative.[13] Celer's passage is also an epic saga with its trials, passing satisfactions, and goals, near and far, to be implemented. During the course of his own poem, as we noted earlier, Statius does not allow us to forget that he himself has been writing the *Thebaid*, whose bark, he says at the epic's conclusion, 'has deserved its harbour after its lengthy time at sea' (*...longo meruit ratis aequore portum*, *Theb.* 12.809). For Horace, Virgil as well as departing on an actual journey is also figuratively fulfilling what Statius' Celer is essaying literally, and Statius, the poet, borrows from his great predecessor a suggestion of deep personal warmth that the ode provides so specially. Epic grandeur and lyric immediacy combine to set the tone for the unique excerpt from the *Silvae* in progress.[14]

The second Horatian lyric that resonates in Statius' lines is *Carmen* 2.17. Addressed to his friend and patron, Maecenas, it is concerned with the latter's worry that the two will be separated at death:

> cur me querelis exanimas tuis?
> nec dis amicum est nec mihi te prius
>   obire, Maecenas, mearum
>   grande decus columenque rerum.

---

[12] We should not forget that Celer is traveling on a commercial grain ship, so what is essentially an abstract figure in Horace becomes more literal. In this connection Martelli (2009) is particularly valuable in showing that the varying treatments of Statius' poetry by literary critics and by social historians should be complementary and of mutual value, not divisive. For Statius a grain ship has both practical and intellectual importance. It carries an annual harvest from Egypt to Italy but, through the poet's imagination, it is also transmuted into a vehicle of epic. The practical and the cultural ways of reading enhance each other in the course of Statius' elucidation of Celer's multifaceted experience.

[13] See among others, Elder (1952), Lockyer (1967), and Pucci (1992) with his bibliography in nn. 3–4.

[14] For the connection between Horace here and Statius, see Nisbet and Hubbard (1970) 48 (on *Carm.* 1.3.8); Hardie (1983) 158–64; and Cairns (2007) 233–4.

READING TRAVEL (STATIUS' *SILVAE* 3.2) 223

> a! te meae si partem animae rapit
> maturior vis, quid moror altera,
> nec carus aeque nec superstes
> integer?
>
> (Hor. *Carm.* 2.17.1–8)

Why do you deprive me of my soul with your complaints? It is not dear to the gods nor to me that you go to face death before me, Maecenas, great honour and keystone of my affairs. Ah, if some earlier force snatches away you, part of my soul, why should I, the other part, linger, neither beloved as much as before nor whole, if I survive?

Virgil has been replaced by Maecenas, poet friend by supportive benefactor, but the language remains similar, with Horace now punningly absorbing Maecenas' soul-destroying worries (*exanimas*) into the *anima* that is part of the poet's being. It is no accident that the name Maecenas reverberates in that of Maecius, each being trisyllabic with similar beginnings and endings.[15] And the echo brings with it a larger schema. The imaginative journey of a Virgil toward the invention of expansive poetry, the composition of epic, is replaced now by a more intimate, lyric subject, that of human individual or individuals—call them Horace and Maecenas—confronting the reality of death (the verb *obire* combines the ideas of motion toward and of encounter with), possibly alone, possibly, as here, with a trusted companion.

Thus, by the mediation of two great odes, Statius confirms two of his salient themes grouped under the over-arching topic of travel, namely the inspired enterprise before Virgil as he writes his sweeping national poem, and the private course toward death that Horace depicts for his patron who will also be his comrade on this inexorable march. Virgil is thus doubly present before us—as a major poetic influence on Statius' own poetic accomplishment and as reimagined by Horace, lyric genius observing his own talented colleague and the struggles that await his industry.

As we continue, Statius deftly takes us, in his prayer, on another itinerary. We turn from the supreme divinity of the sea to the heavens and to Castor and Pollux, designated *Oebalii fratres*, twin grandsons of the Spartan king,

---

[15] For further, even more exact, examples of Statius' use of Virgilian language to describe his own similarly named contemporaries, see Coleman on *Silv.* 4.4.8 (Vitorius Marcellus) and 4.4.20–1 (Gallus). Here context gives emphasis to the parallels in nomenclature.

224   THE POETIC WORLD OF STATIUS' *SILVAE*

Oebalius.[16] Their role is to protect the valued vessel and ward off the presence of their sister, Helen:

> ...Iliacae longe nimbosa sororis
> astra fugate, precor, totoque excludite caelo.
>
> <div align="right">(Stat. <i>Silv</i>. 3.2.11–12)</div>

Banish afar, I pray, the rain-filled star of your Ilian sister and shut her out from the whole heavens.

Helen herself is to be put in motion, away from the night sky during Celer's journey. But, by first placing us in Sparta and then characterizing the Dioscuri's sister as *Iliacae*, the poet takes us in our mind's eye on another fateful course, from Helen's home city to Troy, which is to say on the adulterous progress from west to east, with the deceiver Paris, that leads to the downfall of Troy (and, ultimately, to the creation of the *Iliad* by Homer).[17] It is no wonder that her star was considered ominous and that, in particular, our poet chose to mention her ill-boding heavenly representation only to presume that the naming will be apotropaic.[18] Her presence will, we trust, cast no shadow on Celer's immediate future.

Via mention of the Nereids and Doris' glassy caves, Statius now turns from matters of time to specifics of place.[19] We find ourselves soon at Baiae (*Baianos sinus*, 17) seeking out Celer's appropriately 'lofty ship' (*celsa ratis*, 19),[20] newly arrived from Egypt 'at Dicarchus' land' (*terris... Dicarcheis*, 21–2), which is to say to Puteoli (modern Pozzuoli), neighbouring Baiae, on the northern rim of the Bay of Naples.

Details catch the reader's ear. The shore at Baiae is *feta tepentibus undis* ('pregnant with warm waters', 17). Statius would have us remember Virgil's

---

[16] In his note on Virg. *G*. 4.125 (*sub Oebaliae... turribus arcis*), Servius makes one of the rare references to Statius in ancient literature (*... unde de Castore et Polluce ait Statius Oebalidae fratres*). See also commentators, on Juv. *Sat* 7.82–3; Coleman (1988).

[17] Since Paris' alternative name is Alexander, Statius may be preparing his readers for the appearance of another Alexander later in the poem. Such parallelism would find a counterpart in the connection Statius suggests between Phoenix, adviser to Achilles, and the bird of the same name.

[18] For the star of Helen, see Plin. *Nat*. 2.37.101 and Stat. *Theb*. 7.792–3, where Castor and Pollux are called *Therapnaei fratres*.

[19] The phrase *regni cessit fortuna secundi* (14) deserves special mention. Statius is thinking of Luc. 5.622, where Jupiter calls on his brother for help in rousing the sea-storm that Caesar endures (*... regnoque accessit terra secundo*). Laguna Mariscal (1992) 204 refers to Ov. *Met*. 5.368.

[20] The only other appearance of noun and adjective in classical literature is at Virg. *A*. 8.107, where we hear of the *celsas... rates* of Aeneas arriving at Pallanteum. As usual, the epic touch is appropriate.

READING TRAVEL (STATIUS' *SILVAE* 3.2)   225

description of the land of Aeolus as an area *feta furentibus Austris* ('pregnant with raging south winds', *A*. 1.51). The caves of Doris and the cave of Aeolus, which harbours the destructive blasts, would seem disparate entities, but the echo introduces a negative note, a hint of worry, at what should be Celer's felicitous embarkation. Virgil's parallel depiction of the wooden horse, that contributes to Troy's doom, as *feta armis* ('pregnant with weaponry', *A*. 2.238) furthers the negative tone.

As we turn to the boat itself, newly in port from Egypt, the mood seems to change.[21] The vessel itself is *gravis*, pregnant with an annual harvest of wheat. But this is also a word that Virgil uses to describe the wooden horse at *A*. 6.516, where Deiphobus tells how 'pregnant, it carried in its belly armed infantry' (*armatum peditem gravis attulit alvo*).[22] Perhaps, because destructive arms have yielded place to nourishing wheat, Statius may at first seem to be turning bad to good, ruinous into life-giving. But what follows suggests otherwise.

First, we watch the boat arrive, taking note of its primacy through the anaphora of *prima* (22–3). The accompanying verbs (*intulit*, *salutavit*, *sparsit*) are also scattered one on each line from 22–4 and help strongly to personify the craft itself. But it is to the context of the last that Statius would have us attend:... *et margine dextro/sparsit Tyrrhenae Mareotica vina Minervae* ('...and from its right gunwale it sprinkled Mareotic wine to Tyrrhenian Minerva', 23–4). One detail in this act of libation to the goddess, whose temple stood at the end of the peninsula of Surrentum, has a purposefully intertextual ring. We are reminded once again of Horace, this time of the great ode to Cleopatra, *Carmen* 1.37, where we find the Egyptian queen, 'drunk' (*ebria*, 12), with a mind that had been 'deranged by Mareotic' wine (*lymphatam Mareotico*, 14). We will return to the poem later. Here, as Celer sets out to Egypt on the way to Syria, we are asked for the first time to recall explicitly another, less pleasant, journey as the lover of Antony made her way, in defeat after the battle of Actium, also to Egypt and in her case to death.

From the boat itself and its activities, the poet turns to the sea goddesses and their various preparatory tasks. Once again Statius asks us to cast our mind back to a striking moment in his poetic inheritance. The speaker commands that their duties commence:

> huius utrumque latus molli praecingite gyro
> partitaeque vices vos stuppea tendite mali

---

[21] It should be noted that the phrase *trans aequora* (21) occurs before Statius only at Virg. *A*. 3.403.

[22] Statius uses the phrase *gravis intulit* at *Silv.* 2.1.54, also an ominous context.

226 THE POETIC WORLD OF STATIUS' *SILVAE*

> vincula, vos summis adnectite sipara velis,
> vos Zephyris aperite sinus...
>
> (Stat. Silv. 3.2.25–8)

Encircle each of her sides in a gentle ring (25) and, as apportioned tasks, do you stretch the hempen bonds of the mast, do you attach the topsail to the peak of the mainsail, do you spread the bellying canvas to the Zephyri.

The first appearance of the phrase *stuppea vincula* in preserved Latin literature occurs in Virgil (and we take note of the verbs *tendite* and *intendunt* likewise in common):[23]

> dividimus muros et moenia pandimus urbis.
> accingunt omnes operi pedibusque rotarum
> subiciunt lapsus et stuppea vincula collo
> intendunt...
>
> (Virg. A. 2.234–7)

We part the walls and lay open the battlements of the city. All gird themselves for the work and place rolling wheels under the feet and stretch hempen bonds about the neck.

We find ourselves in a similar situation to that in the *propemptikon*, with duties being shared for an important task at hand. This is also the third reference that we have traced back to the second book of the *Aeneid*. To be still more specific, the phrase *feta armis* appears in the hexameter immediately subsequent to the lines quoted above. We are asked to return not only to the fall of Troy but to a specific object crucial to the city's demise, the wooden horse, filled with the armed men whose release spells the start of her downfall.[24]

Two grand contrivances are brought together by the later poet's imagination, each fraught with peril. Passengers in the one actively bring about a city's doom. Those who are baggage in the other are passive slaves to the perils of seafaring, which is to say to the whimsy of the ocean's many

---

[23] The phrase is used in Luc. 10.493, during a passage that likewise clearly looks back to the second book of the *Aeneid*. Cf. also *Anth. Lat.* 112.1 for another instance.

[24] In Virgil the horse is regularly a symbol of violent energy, often connected with war. We think, for instance, of the horse's head, discovered at the site of Carthage (*A.* 1.444), the omen of the four horses that the Trojans see on landing in Italy (3.537–43), and the metaphorical language Virgil employs to describe Aeolus' destructive winds (see, e.g., 1.64). Cf. Serv. *ad A.* 2.15, where he describes the wooden horse as a *machinamentum bellicum*.

READING TRAVEL (STATIUS' *SILVAE* 3.2) 227

moods.[25] And once more personification helps enliven each wooden creature for us and draw further parallels between them. Both, for instance, have sides (*lateri*, A. 2.19, *latus*, 51, and line 25 above). Celer rejoices to climb aboard his transportation (*scandere gaudet*, 19), just as the horse ascends into the city of Troy (*scandit*, A. 2.237) and young boys and girls rejoice in touching the ropes that do the tugging (*gaudent*, 239).[26] So in double fashion we are brought into a world where grand wooden vehicles complement each other in treacherous situations for those involved, whether released from inside to do damage elsewhere or whether confined within and subject to menace from without.[27] And once again an ostensibly occasional poem is drawn into the realm of an epic tale and its provocative exploits.[28]

As the catalogue of sea-creatures continues we remain in the world of Virgilian poetry, first the *Georgics*, with mention of Proteus,[29] then the *Aeneid* through the names Triton, Glaucus, and Palaemon, from Book 5 of the epic, as we have seen. The middle creature gets special mention:

> ... et subitis qui perdidit inguina monstris[30]
> Glaucus, adhuc patriis quotiens adlabitur oris
> litoream blanda feriens Anthedona cauda.
>
> (Stat. *Silv.* 3.2.36–8)

... and Glaucus, whose groin was deformed by sudden portents, still striking Anthedon on the shore with affectionate tail, whenever he glides to his paternal coast.

The only appearances in classical Latin of the phrase *adlabitur oris* are here and at A. 6.2, where the fleet of Aeneas 'at last glides to the Euboean coast of Cumae' (*tandem Euboicis Cumarum adlabitur oris*). Two details add to the connection, one topographical, the other genealogical. Anthedon is a town in Boeotia on the Euboean gulf, not far from Chalcis, the mother city of

---

[25] We should of course remember that Celer is also in the process of bringing violence to Syria even as he helps cement Roman power.

[26] Virgil uses the word *funis* at A. 2.239 and 262; Statius uses it here at 54.

[27] See Rimell (2015), esp. 28–81, for Virgil specifically and for more general comments on empire and exploration as a penetrating, opening motion, common here to both Celer's ship and the wooden horse.

[28] The language of line 28 (*vos Zephyris aperite sinus*) may bring Virgil's *Georgics* (2.330–1) into play.

[29] Cf. *G.* 4.388 and four times thereafter.

[30] The words *inguina monstris* end a hexameter at Virg. *Ecl.* 6.75. The appropriate allusion describes Scylla bringing trouble to the boats of Ulysses. The line is varied at *Ciris* 60, and the phrase is adopted by Ovid of Nisus' Scylla (*Met.* 14.60).

228   THE POETIC WORLD OF STATIUS' *SILVAE*

Cumae. It happens also that the Sibyl, we soon learn, is the daughter of Glaucus (*Deiphobe Glauci*, 6.36). Thus poetic reference and matters of fact join in bringing the sixth book of the *Aeneid* again to our attention. Both location and crucial guide introduce us once more to a fateful enterprise as Virgil's hero risks entry into the location of the dead.

Though only part way through the poem, we have already followed the cue of the opening *di quibus* and traced examples of the vital presence of *Aeneid* 2, 5, and 6 in Statius' poem. We will return in a moment to the lines devoted to Palaemon. The litany of divinities connected with ocean travel ends with the ruler of the winds:

> et pater Aeolio frangit qui carcere ventos,
> cui varii flatus omnisque per aequora mundi
> spiritus at<que> hiemes nimbosaque nubila parent,
> artius obiecto Borean Eurumque Notumque
> monte premat...
>
> <div align="right">(Stat. <i>Silv.</i> 3.2.42–6)</div>

And may the father, who tempers the winds in their Aeolian prison, whom the differing breezes and every breath throughout the seas of the world and storms and rainy clouds obey, press down more tightly upon Boreas and Eurus and Notus (45) with the thrust of his mountain...

We are now back in the storyline of *Aeneid* 1 with almost a pastiche of Virgil's depiction of Aeolus' world and his winds whose storm Juno stirs up against Aeneas and his followers. At *A.* 1.53–4, for instance, we hear of the winds and their prison (*ventos...carcere*) and once again of the latter at 141 (*ventorum carcere*). The east wind and the south (*Eurusque Notusque*) are joined together at line 85.[31] Their mountain dungeon (*monte*) makes appearances at lines 55, 61, and 81, and the verb *premo* occurs twice when Virgil deals with the need for their control (54, 63).

Statius thus returns us with intensity to Virgil and to an event that nearly spelled doom for the Trojans. He reminds us not only of the overriding presence of the earlier poet in the background as he writes but also of a specific sea-voyage whose risks are of special prominence at the start of the poem and which set the mood for the many appearances of destructive fury that dot the subsequent chronicle.[32] Unlike Juno's command to Aeolus that

---

[31] Cf. also Tib. 1.5.35.

[32] It is with a purpose that Statius repeats the adjective *nimbosa* (45), applied now to Aeolus' storm-clouds, that he had given to Helen's star at line 11.

he unleash his violent charges, Statius' prayer to the lord of storms is apotropaic: may all winds except that from the west be confined and may Zephyrus speed Celer, who here assumes the quality of the ship, safely to the shores of Egypt:

> solus agat puppes summasque supernatet undas
> adsiduus pelago, donec tua turbine nullo
> laesa Paraetoniis adsignet carbasa ripis.
>
> (Stat. *Silv.* 3.2.47–9)

Let him alone impel the sterns and float above the tops of the waves, a constant presence on the sea, until he commits to the banks of Paraetonium your sails unharmed by any whirlwind.

The word *turbo* is used by Virgil three times (lines 45, 83, and 511) to describe the tornado that Aeolus stirs up against the goddess' potential victims.[33] Its appearance here serves as one final assurance that Celer will reach his first destination in safety without threat of Junonian violence.

I passed by the extraordinary lines addressed to Palaemon that break up the catalogue of divinities between Glaucus and Aeolus:

> tu tamen ante omnes diva cum matre, Palaemon,
> adnue, si vestras amor est mihi pandere Thebas
> nec cano degeneri Phoebeum Amphiona plectro.
>
> (Stat. *Silv.* 3.2.39–41)

Nevertheless ahead of all, Palaemon, with your goddess mother, nod approval, if it is my love to disclose your Thebes (40), nor do I sing of Phoebus' Amphion on any ignoble lyre.

We are suddenly witnessing an act of self-consciousness that deliberately breaks the pattern of thought uniting the previous and subsequent lines. By means of an aside in the form of an apostrophe to Palaemon that includes

---

[33] The phrase *summas undas* (47) is first used by Virgil, not unexpectedly, in *A.* 1.147. He is followed by Ovid, Manilius, and Lucan. For *turbine nullo*, cf. *Silv.* 1.3.41. The synecdoche of *carbasa* (49) is repeated at 100. It is used metapoetically to describe the writing of the *Thebaid* at *Silv.* 4.4.87–9, where the ship's sails are metaphoric for the epic itself, its production and contents: *nunc si forte meis quae sint exordia Musis/scire petis, iam Sidonios emensa labores/Thebais optato collegit carbasa portu . . .* ('now if by chance you seek to know what my muses are initiating, now the *Thebais*, having completed her Sidonian efforts, has furled her sails in the harbor she yearned for').

230   THE POETIC WORLD OF STATIUS' *SILVAE*

his mother, Ino,[34] we enter directly and powerfully into another dimension of our poem where *amor* is also crucial, that of poetry and poetry-making, where sea-voyage and crafting an epic about Thebes have their similarities.[35] But *cano* and *mihi* point us not to the present act of composition but to Statius' most extensive achievement, his epic on the history of Thebes.

Let us be more specific. To any student of Virgil, the word *cano* sends us back to the opening line of the *Aeneid*. Its appropriation here is an astonishing act of daring, confrontation, and, of course, in a deeper sense, allegiance. But Statius modulates readily from his mentor to his own epic, the *Thebaid*, and its publication. The language is markedly expressive. Instead of Troy and Rome, his song will be about Thebes and about Apollo's patronage of Amphion. The legendary builder of the walls of Thebes finds a modern counterpart in Statius as he reconstructs them through the power of his verse.[36]

The phrase *pandere Thebas* has a special expressiveness. On the one hand, it means to open Thebes to view, which is to say, to write an epic to be perused by all, one which details for the reader the legend by which the Boeotian city gained fame in the history of myth. For further uses of *pandere*, we think once more, for instance, of Virgil's third use of *di quibus*, in *Aeneid* 6, and the prayer that follows: *sit mihi fas audita loqui, sit lumine vestro/pandere res alta terra et caligine mersas* ('Through your divine power may I be allowed to say what I have heard, to reveal matters buried deep in the earth and darkness', *A.* 6.266–7). Still more à propos are words, to which we shall return, that Statius addresses to his father in a later poem:

> ... te nostra magistro
> Thebais urguebat priscorum exordia vatum;
> tu cantus stimulare meos, tu pandere facta
> heroum bellique modos positusque locorum
> monstrabas.

> (Stat. *Silv.* 5.3.233–7)

---

[34] Cf. also *Silv.* 2.1.180. Ino has been divinized which means that she has already fled Thebes to the safety of Corinth, a city that has associations with Pollius' estate at Surrentum (cf. *Silv.* 2.2.34–5, 3.1.16 and 115).

[35] Forms of the word *amor* appear in the poem at lines 1, 40, 81, and 99. With the first two, cf. the striking use of the noun by Statius at *Ach.* 1.5.

[36] It is no accident that the mention of the *Thebaid* here takes place in the course of a *propemptikon*, and that the epic itself concludes with the image of both poet and poem making it to port. Cf. *Silv.* 2.2.59–62.

With you as mentor our *Thebaid* bore close upon the works of bards of old. You yourself showed me how to spur on my songs, to disclose the deeds of heroes and the patterns of war and the sites of places.

Statius may even have in mind a command by which Virgil twice hails the Muses: *pandite nunc Helicona, deae, cantusque movete...*('Now open Helicon wide, goddesses, and set songs in motion...', *A.* 7.641 and 10.163). The physical affect for which Virgil prays—may the Muses unclose their mountain sanctuary to bring the poet inspiration—adds a further dimension to Statius' use of *pandere* here.[37] To spread Thebes wide (*pandere Thebas*) means not only to make its history available in verse to be recited or read but also, in a tangible sense, to open its gates. We have already seen the verb so used by Virgil as the Trojans open the fortifications of their city to the wooden horse (*moenia pandimus urbis, A.* 2.234). At the start of the book Troy's gates seem readied for the deadly invasion (*panduntur portae*, 27), and at 12.584, in similar language, the Latins debate the unbarring of their city to Trojan might (*pandere portas*).

The difference between publishing the *Thebaid* and opening the gates of the city, as Statius phrases it here, lies between sending out for general consumption a completed poem and entering the narrative itself near its finale. Statius here announces that Thebes has surrendered to the enemy by unclosing its gates to the attacking Seven. We will find shortly, at the conclusion of our poem, that it is in fact *busta*, pyres, that bring the *Thebaid* to an end and that it is the city itself over which the poet, again Amphion-like, has spent so much effort (*laboratas Thebas*, 143). At this moment earlier in the poem Statius seems akin to a reverse Amphion, breaching the walls that had been assembled through the magic music of his mythic ancestor. But, paradoxically, to destroy is to immortalize, to build a new and different Thebes of the imagination through the medium of words.

The apostrophe to Palaemon, with its self-reference but also with its bow to the opening of the *Aeneid* and, in particular, to the second book's narrative of the fall of Troy, its gates open to the enemy, tells us of an epic whose creation is nearly concluded. But it also serves as a reminder that we are in the process of absorbing a poem where both writing epic and detailing the

---

[37] *Pandere* is used of sails by Propertius (*pandere vela*, 2.21.14) but the same phrase takes on a metapoetic value because of its use by Quintilian to signify the idea of amplification (*Inst.* 6.1.52). Cf. Rimell (2015) 212: 'opening is epic's favourite spatial gesture...'

232   THE POETIC WORLD OF STATIUS' *SILVAE*

treacherous trials and heroic endeavours that are its standard contents are ever before us as part of our own process of understanding and enjoyment. Statius is varying both Virgil, in writing a new *Aeneid* that also tells of a city's capture, and Horace, in writing a *propemptikon* that, instead of making a latent acknowledgement of Virgil's challenging work in progress, tells of his own epic being composed on the fall of Thebes. And in so doing, to add to the complexity, he becomes a type of Horace referring to Virgil and thus doubly bowing to his poetic past by alluding not only to the epic tradition but also to a lyric that covertly embraces the composition of epic as one of its themes.

The Departure

We turn now from guardians of the boat to the moment of departure. The initial subject is Zephyrus, wind from the west:

> audimur. vocat ipse ratem nautasque morantes
> increpat. ecce meum timido iam frigore pectus
> labitur et nequeo, quamvis movet ominis horror,
> claudere suspensos oculorum in margine fletus.
> iamque ratem terris divisit fune soluto
> navita et angustum deiecit in aequora pontem
> saevus <et> e puppi longo clamore magister
> dissipat amplexus atque oscula fida revellit.
> nec longum cara licet in cervice morari.
> attamen in terras e plebe novissimus omni
> ibo, nec egrediar nisi iam <cedente> carina.
>
> (Stat. *Silv.* 3.2.50–60)

We are heard. Himself he calls the ship and chides the delaying sailors (50). See, my heart now collapses from fearful chill and, although dread of the omen disturbs, I am unable to close in the tears that hang on the edge of my eyes. And now with release of the rope a sailor has disengaged the ship from the land and dropped the narrow gangway into the water (55), and from the stern the savage helmsman with lengthy harangue divides embraces and tugs apart faithful kisses. nor is it permitted to delay at length on a beloved neck. Nevertheless, from the whole throng I will be the last to go ashore, and I will not withdraw until the ship now recedes (60).

READING TRAVEL (STATIUS' *SILVAE* 3.2)   233

The central figure in this scenario of leave-taking is the *magister* and since we are dealing with a plot that is both literal and figurative, he is at once the boat's captain but also, in metapoetical terms, the educator of both poet and audience, as we absorb and contemplate.[38]

But before we reach him we already enter the teacher's realm of poetic practice. Statius stresses the word *moror*, delay, by first applying it to the *nautas... morantes* as they linger over the moment of departure.[39] He repeats it (*morari*) when observing lovers lingering long on a fond neck. We observe private emotion on display, the palpable sorrows that come from the necessary relinquishment of someone held dear in order for him to participate in an impersonal, albeit grand and universal scheme, such as what Rome's imperial destiny might demand.

That the moment is metapoetic is suggested by some lines in Propertius: *non ego velifera tumidum mare findo carina:/tota sub exiguo flumine nostra mora est* ('I myself do not cleave the swollen sea on sail-bearing keel: our lingering is completely in the service of a small stream', Prop. 3.9.35–6). Not for him, the elegist continues, to tell, Statius-like, of the seven combats before the city of Cadmus or of battling, such as a Homer might sing, before the Scaean gates of Troy where the wooden horse won the day (37–42).[40] In Statius, then, delay suggests the difference between elegy, with its modest flow of fresh water, and the epic's swollen sea of opulent designs.

Within Statius' own work we might compare the use of *morae* at *Silv.* 2.2.13 (*sed iuvere morae*) to describe the poet's stay at the villa of Pollius Felix in Surrentum. The implication is that his residence with Pollius contrasts with his duty to remain committed to the 'sea' of epic, to 'our storm blasts' (*nostras procellas*, 142). This in turn suggests that 'delaying' at Surrentum is the equivalent of devoting oneself to less demanding literary forms such as writing *Silvae*.

---

[38] With the language of 55–6, cf. Virg. *A.* 1.114–16: *ipsius ante oculos ingens a vertice pontus/ in puppim ferit; excutitur pronusque magister/volvitur in caput* ('Before [Aeneas'] very eyes from high above a huge swell strikes against the stern; the helmsman is hurled off and rolled forward head first...'). In Statius the *magister* is in full control. For *longo clamore*, cf. *Theb.* 4.495.

[39] Statius' language here is a reminder of Virgil's Corycian old man (*G.* 4.138) 'chiding the late summer and the delaying Zephyrs' (*aestatem increpitans seram Zephyrosque morantis*). In Statius the wind itself, first mentioned at 46, is doing the rebuking. The Virgilian reference sharpens the personification and this intensity is picked up by the subsequent *ecce* where the deictic calls further attention to the presence of the first person. Compare also the later use of *ecce* at 78 after which *ego* enters strongly at 82. Cf. also (with Laguna Mariscal [1992] 213) Virg. *A.* 3.70 and Prop. 1.17.6).

[40] When read out loud line 36 juxtaposes *amor* and *mora*.

234   THE POETIC WORLD OF STATIUS' *SILVAE*

When Anna urges her sister Dido to yield to her feelings for her Trojan guest, her command is 'weave reasons for delay' (*causas... innecte morandi, A.* 4.51).[41] To delay, for Aeneas, would be to give in to personal feelings rather than to continue along the quasi-abstract itinerary toward Rome's foundation. This is to say, in poetic language, that he would retreat into the forbidden world of elegy's attractive, sheltered immediacies instead of pursuing his ambitious yet dispassionate progress as demanded by fate. As far as Statius is concerned, his time with Pollius intimates a momentary submission to the easy pleasure of writing occasional verse instead of continuing with the presumably more demanding vocation of writing epic.[42]

Though the physical representation of emotionality that Statius has us now observe has parallels in epic, and we will turn to an instance in a moment, it is toward the elegists that he would have us first look.[43] For instance, in the third poem of his first book, likewise dealing with a moment of departure, Tibullus makes it clear that to yield to weeping is considered an ill omen. The *sortes* are positive, yet his lady still remains tearful: *cuncta dabant reditus: tamen est deterrita nunquam/quin fleret nostras respiceretque vias* ('They all promised return, yet she did not refrain from weeping at my journey and from looking back', 1.3.13–14). The phrase *fune soluto* (54) is striking in this regard. Its only other use in Latin letters, and also at the conclusion of a hexameter line, is by Ovid at *Am.* 2.11.23 in his *propemptikon* to Corinna. It, too, serves as another direct reminder of the elegiac aspects of a sea-voyage. The words are aptly linked with the verb *divisit* because to separate ship from shore is to part lovers as well as to initiate a prejudice for the detached aspects of epic storytelling over the immediate, first-person emotionality of elegy.[44]

Nor do we lose sight of Dido as the narrative progresses because of a careful reminiscence at line 57 where, as we saw, the *magister* separates lovers (*dissipat amplexus atque oscula fida revellit*). Statius has us recall Venus' words to her son Cupid, who replaces the boy Ascanius as the

---

[41] In the fourth book of the *Aeneid* forms of *mora* appear at 407 and 569, of *moror* at 51, 235, 568, and 649. For further nuances to the word *mora*, see Reed (2016) *passim*. As we regularly see, elegiac events keep epic inexorability momentarily in abeyance.

[42] On the effort necessary to write the *Thebaid*, see *Silv.* 3.2.143; 3.5.35–6; 4.4.88–9; 4.7.2 (*heroos labores*) and 26; *Theb.* 12.809–12.

[43] For emotional contexts in which the phrase *frigore pectus* or its variants appear, see, e.g., Ov. *Her.* 12.142, 15.112, 19.192; *Fast.* 1.98 and 2.754.

[44] Propertius (2.33.5) replaces the sea with Isis whose worship is the cause for estrangement. She is the goddess who 'has so often separated yearning lovers' (*tam cupidos totiens divisit amantes*).

READING TRAVEL (STATIUS' *SILVAE* 3.2)   235

seduction of the Carthaginian queen proceeds apace. It will be at her celebratory banquet, says Venus to her offspring:...*cum dabit amplexus atque oscula dulcia figet*... ('...when she will offer [you] embraces and will impress sweet kisses...', *A.* 1.687).[45] Celer and Statius again draw to themselves analogies with Aeneas and Dido. The elegiac elements, therefore, continue to be double. They are prolonged within the story line itself, as bonds of affection are tested by distance, and they are also affirmed through literary history, from the elegists' first-person liaisons between poet and beloved, and from the larger, third-person narrative, with its tragic consequences, drawn from the opening half of Statius' great model.

Let us return to the word *magister* and its inferences. The *magister*, as manager of the boat and of the voyage itself, is also, as we have said, in metapoetic language, the teacher of both the poet and, ultimately, the audience. We have already remarked on the fact that Statius bestows this title on his father (*Silv.* 5.3.233) as maestro, as inspiring advocate who pressed his son toward emulation of past authors of genius.[46] It is also not unexpectedly the appellation that he later grants Virgil (*Silv.* 4.4.55), his *non pareil* example and guide.

This particular *magister* is purposefully *saevus*, echoing in his immediate behaviour the sea and its *saeva pericula* that we saw at the poem's start. He is a savage mariner not only because he confronts savage dangers but because he also breaks up loving couples. By demanding the boat's embarkation away from the shore and therefore from contact with humankind and its sympathies, he sets sail on the grandiose but threatening seas of epic, leaving behind the lingerings that inner feelings cause and the 'occasional' forms of poetry that give them voice.

The means by which the *magister* attracts attention is by sustained shouting (*longo clamore*, 3.2.55). This in turn catches the student's ear and eye because it is the unique occurrence of the phrase in Latin. And it, too, has metapoetic implications especially because of the proximate use of *longum* at line 58

---

[45] Laguna Mariscal (1992) 215 refers also to Virg. *A.* 8.568 where Evander bids farewell to his son Pallas: '...never would I myself now be torn from your sweet embrace...' (...*non ego nunc dulci amplexu divellerer usquam*...). Both occasions deal with the departure of someone dear, each with tragic consequences. Elements of elegy are drawn from within the poem itself but in each case deepened by reference to the *Aeneid*, specifically to the sorrows of Dido and Evander. Virgil offers a macabre parody of such embraces in his description of the grasp in which Laocoön and his sons are clutched by the twin serpents at *A.* 2.205–20, with such words as *incumbunt, amplexus, amplexi, ligant, ceruicibus*, and *divellere*.

[46] At *Silv.* 5.3.127, Aeneas' helmsman Palinurus is named as *Phrygius magister*, a direct reminder of the *Aeneid* earlier in the same poem.

236   THE POETIC WORLD OF STATIUS' *SILVAE*

where lengthy tarrying, with arms around a dear-one's neck, is not allowed because of the exigencies of a schedule. The double use of adjective and adverb implies the difference between the extent of challenges to come, and the epic form in which they are couched, and the elegiac moment that precedes their inception, a moment that battens on delay but must be cut short, however heartfelt the feelings involved. The epic voice must squelch the tones of elegy and lyric if it is to maintain its pride of place among genres and if the presumably dispassionate transition to military duties and their implementation that it represent is to proceed without negative incident.

One other detail helps carry through this distinction. It is a narrow gangway (*angustum...pontem*) that the sailor hurls toward the sea as the boat leaves port. Once again, the adjective has metapoetic connotations which is to say, in this and most other cases, that it helps us delve into Statius' creative enterprise and displays the poet's involvement with the crafting of good writing, often through the challenging interaction of a series of genres. The phrase is used in a practical sense by Cicero, of bridges narrowed for purposes of unimpeded voting.[47] Here it serves a figurative purpose, namely to recollect a moment in Propertius where the elegist is thinking of his great Alexandrian forebear as he ponders the difference between his own work and the writing of epic, whether the topic be old or new:

> sed neque Phlegraeos Iovis Enceladique tumultus
>   intonet angusto pectore Callimachus,
> nec mea conveniunt duro praecordia versu
>   Caesaris in Phrygios condere nomen avos.
>
> (Prop. 2.1.39–42)

But neither would Callimachus from his narrow breast thunder the turmoil at Phlegra between Jupiter and Enceladus, nor does it suit my heart in unyielding verse to trace the name of Caesar to his Phrygian forebears.

---

[47] Cic. *Leg.* 3.17.38. Laguna Mariscal (1992) 214 refers to Virg. *A.* 10.288 (*pontibus*). We note also 10.654 (*ponte parato*). Cf. *A.* 10.287–8: *interea Aeneas socios de puppibus altis/pontibus exponit.* Translation and interpretation depend on which noun receives the adjective *altis* ('lofty'). Virgil earlier refers to the 'lofty bridges' (*pontibus altis*) of a wooden gangway (*A.* 9.530). Servius (*ad A.* 10.287), however, insists that the epithet belongs with *puppibus*, and the use of the phrase *altis puppibus* by Valerius Flaccus (8.362) supports his contention. But if we grant it to *pontibus* here, as *A.* 9.530 might suggest, then Statius' multivalent use of *angustum* is highlighted for its difference from one and possibly two appearances of *altus* in Virgil.

READING TRAVEL (STATIUS' *SILVAE* 3.2)   237

At 2.34.32 Propertius speaks of the 'dreams of unturgid Callimachus' (*non inflati somnia Callimachi*). The combination urges us to envision the style of the elegist as akin to his model—restrained, with proper controls applied to both content and expression. The elegist also describes his subject matter, in a symbolic way, by speaking of the 'narrow couch' (*angusto... lecto*, 1.8.33) on which he makes love to Cynthia, and he reuses the phrase at 2.1.45 to imagine in more general terms the bed on which love's battles take place. Disciplined discourse and straitened circumstances complement each other to typify the elegiac poet's works and ways.

In Statius' poem, therefore, the abandonment of the walkway that connected ship to shore, and lover to lover, intimates the disavowal of smaller, more intimate forms of verse in order to embrace the larger, more detached sweep of epic as Celer leaves his friend behind and Statius prepares to view the latter's exploits from the distance that epic would seem to warrant.[48]

That apparent remoteness immediately becomes part of the poem as Statius turns to an abstract meditation on one of the standard themes of a *propemptikon*, namely the cursing of the inventor of seafaring and the trials and tribulations that his discovery initiated:

> quis rude et abscisum miseris animantibus aequor
> fecit iter solidaeque pios telluris alumnos
> expulit in fluctus pelagoque immisit hianti,
> audax ingenii? nec enim temeraria virtus
> illa magis, summae gelidum quae Pelion Ossae
> iunxit anhelantemque iugis bis pressit Olympum.
> usque adeone parum lentas transire paludes
> stagnaque et angustos summittere pontibus amnes?
> imus in abruptum gentilesque undique terras
> fugimus exigua clausi trabe et aëre nudo.
>
> (Stat. *Silv.* 3.2.61–70)

---

[48] The addition of *cedente* to the manuscript tradition gains support from Catul. 64.249 where we join Ariadne 'sadly watching the ship as it fades away...' (*prospectans cedentem maesta carinam*...). Statius is conceived as an Ariadne beholding the vessel of Celer/Theseus recede into the distance. Put metapoetically, the disappearing bark of epic is transported away from the elegiac moment of loyal kisses. The in-fact faithless, vagrant elegiac lover is transmuted into the epic hero, off on his impersonal adventures of intrepid accomplishment. Laguna Mariscal (1992) 215 calls attention as well to Propertius 1.3.1 (*cedente carina*), also dealing with Ariadne abandoned by Theseus.

238   THE POETIC WORLD OF STATIUS' *SILVAE*

Who made the untried and sundered sea a route for pitiful mortals and drove the holy offspring of the firm earth into the waves and, intrepid in his skill, sent them into the gaping ocean? For that courage was not more rash which joined chill Pelion to the top of Ossa (65) and twice pressed panting Olympus under ridges.[49] Was it not sufficient to cross sluggish swamps and ponds and to place narrow streams under bridges? We make our way into the abyss, and we everywhere take flight from our native lands, closed in by a thin plank and the naked air (70).

The necessary boldness of sailors stems also from the boldness of the imagination of the inventor of boats for men to sail across the water.[50] It also involves impiety.[51] For creatures like humans, who should be devoted to the land, to assert command of the seas is hubristic enough in its claim, according to the poets, to elicit the wrath of the gods for an act of over-reaching.[52] And in this case the general notion may have special bearing. The first time that Celer is given his cognomen he is called 'noble offspring of Ausonia, powerful in arms' (*nobilis Ausoniae Celer armipotentis alumnus*, 20).[53] By setting out on a voyage overseas, the speaker adroitly implies, our protagonist is being lured away from ordinary behaviour into an immoral undertaking, one that might potentially bring down heaven's ire upon him.

---

[49] The Latin could also appropriately be translated metaphorically as 'yokes'.

[50] In his comment on line 61 (*rude...aequor*), Laguna Mariscal (1992) 217 fittingly refers to Catullus' striking metonymy for the sea at 64.11 (*rudem...Amphitriten*) as he tells of the *Argo* pursuing its famous initiatory voyage. Since Statius' poem deals so frequently with metapoetic aspects of writing, it is appropriate to observe here that *rudis* is the adjective that Statius applies to Ennius at *Silv.* 2.7.75 when he speaks of the 'untutored Muse of fierce Ennius' (*Musa rudis ferocis Enni*). Newlands (2011a) 241 rightly calls to our attention Ovid's judgment of the Republican poet (*Tr.* 2.424: *Ennius ingenio maximus, arte rudis*, 'Ennius, mightiest in talent, clumsy in artistry'). He in turn is thinking of Hor. *Ars* 410. Ennius is *rudis* not only because his craftsmanship is still unhoned by comparison with those who follow in his footsteps but also because his *Annales* was the first expansive epic in Latin and was written in dactylic hexameter, the metre of Homer. (Ennius' work covers the history of Rome from the fall of Troy until the early second century BCE. Naevius, his predecessor in the history of Latin literature, had produced only a monographic poem, devoted to the First Punic War and written in Saturnian verse.) He is appropriately *ferox* not only for dealing extensively with military matters but also, as a result of his primacy in writing full-scale epic in Latin, for sharing in the boldness that we have seen to be a necessary trait for a seafarer, especially for one setting across the waters for the first time.

[51] The only other use of the phrase *miseris animantibus* is by Statius himself (*Theb.* 3.552) where in his own voice he inveighs against those whom 'sick love' (*aeger amor*) possesses to know the future. In the Golden Age, he goes on to say, men had no need for horoscopy any more than they did for seafaring, according to the present poem.

[52] Nisbet and Hubbard (1970) 49 (on *Carm.* 1.3.12) catalogue in detail the influence of Horace on these lines. We should also note again the presence of the opening of Catullus 64, esp. 11–12, as the theme of separation and alienation continues.

[53] Cf. Statius *Ach.* 1.420.

READING TRAVEL (STATIUS' *SILVAE* 3.2)   239

The same kind of rashness, the poet continues, impelled the Giants, like Enceladus, and Titans to pile Pelion on Ossa in order to scale Olympus, home of the gods. As Propertius puts it in another Callimachean moment earlier in a poem we have already quoted: *non ego Titanas canerem, non Ossan Olympo/impositam, ut caeli Pelion esset iter* ('I would not sing of the Titans, nor of Ossa placed on Olympus, so that Pelion might be the route to heaven', 2.1.19–20). To embark on impious seafaring, especially to be its originator, finds its equivalent in the world of literature, at least as the elegiac poets have it, in writing a Gigantomachy, a study in egomania and irreverence,[54] which is to say, in yielding to a corrupt ambition that is ultimately self-defeating because it goes beyond a writer's necessary stipulation of moderation and judiciousness.[55]

Lines 67–8 employ the terminology of water to form a contrast with the sea upon which Celer has embarked, and once again the language is as figurative as it is literal. Taken at face value, swamps, lakes, and streams are all, as it were, fresh-water entities, which is to say landlocked. They form an integral part of what is literally our earthly existence and are differentiated from the open ocean onto which man's foolhardy ambitions thrust him. Mention of swamps (*paludes*) anticipates the attribute swampy (*paludosi*, 108) of the Nile, the major inland body of water to occupy us toward the end of the poem. That they are sluggish forms a careful contrast with Maecius Celer himself, the 'swift', whose hurrying away from home and its surroundings is a prominent theme of the poem.

Stagna serves a similar purpose. Here, too, we anticipate the Nile, formed into pools by means of mud (*stagnata luto*, 110). More specifically, Servius (*ad A.* 1.126) tells us that *stagnum* 'gets its name from water standing still' (*dicitur aqua stans*). so, again, inland bodies of water are distinguished from

---

[54] At line 62, Statius associates piety with those who are earth's nurslings. The impiety of seafaring is perhaps most strongly put by Horace at *Carm.* 1.3.23–5 (*impiae rates*), a poem that ends in accusing guilty, modern man of performing his own form of Gigantomachy by attempting to master an element not his own: *caelum ipsum petimus stultitia neque/per nostrum patimur scelus/iracunda Iovem ponere fulmina* ('in our stupidity we seek heaven itself and by our villainy we do not suffer Jupiter to put aside his angry thunderbolts', 38–40); on this line, see also pp. 152–3 in this volume on *Silv.* 3.1. See also Ovid's summary at *Met* 1.154–5.

[55] For a list of parallels, besides Propertius, in Homer, Virgil, the *Aetna*, Horace, Seneca, and especially Ovid, see Laguna Mariscal (1992) 218 (on 64b–66). The order of the mountains, with Pelion and Ossa at the end of one line and Olympus concluding the next, and the common presence of the verb *pressit*, propose that Statius had in mind particularly Sen. *Ag.* 338–9:... *stetit imposita Pelion Ossa,/pinifer ambos pressit Olympus* ('Pelion stood with Ossa placed on top, pine-bearing Olympus pressed on both'). The joint use of forms of *impono* at Prop. 2.1.20 (*impositam*) and Hor. *Carm.* 3.4.52 (*imposuisse*) suggests that both earlier passages also remain specifically in the background for Seneca and Statius.

240   THE POETIC WORLD OF STATIUS' SILVAE

the windy sea and its perils, and once more speeding Maecius is differentiated from the land- surrounded examples of motionless quietude that he is
leaving behind.

Finally, we have the narrow streams submitting to man's bridges. It is not
long since we have observed the sailor tossing into the water his boat's *pon-
tem*, its bridge to land and to the affections that the shore sustains. We have
traced the metapoetic aspects of its adjective, *angustum*. They remain potent
also here as Statius reiterates the epithet (*angustos*) to limn the streams that
the seafarer abandons. By embarking on the roiling, expansive waters of
epic pursuits, Celer is leaving behind the sequestered, delimited rivulets of
elegy's intimacy for more expansive, more demonstrable, at times more
menacing goals.[56]

Virgil may help us to deepen our understanding as 'we', now generalized,
venture into the abyss[57] and hasten in flight, confined to a slight plank and
the exposed air. The opening of his first *Eclogue* allows us to look from
another angle at the dichotomy we have been tracing. The shepherd
Meliboeus is addressing his fortunate colleague:

> Tityre, tu patulae recubans sub tegmine fagi
> silvestrem tenui Musam meditaris avena;
> nos patriae finis et dulcia linquimus arva;
> nos patriam fugimus: tu, Tityre, lentus in umbra
> formosam resonare doces Amaryllida silvas.
>
> (Virg. *Ecl.* 1.1–5)

Tityrus, you who are reclining under the protection of a spreading beech,
you ponder the muse of the woods on slender reed; we are leaving the
bounds of our fatherland and our sweet fields. We are going into exile
from our fatherland. You, Tityrus, at ease in the shade, you teach the
woods to resound 'beautiful Amaryllis'.

---

[56] The phrase *solidae telluris* (62) should enter the discussion here as part of the same sphere
of *lentas paludes* and *angustos amnes* that Celer will leave behind. As a stylistic word, *solidus*, to
quote the *OLD*, stands for what has 'substance, [is] solid, real, lasting...opp. [of] frivolous or
superficial'. As part of the creative process, to abandon slow swamps, narrow streams, and firm
earth for the risks of seafaring is akin to relinquishing the steadier, more self-controlled, more
supposedly personal genres such as elegy and lyric in favor of what could seem the facile factu-
ality of epic song. The theme is continued with the unique phrase *pelago hianti* in the subsequent line (63). Unlike the land in its compactness, the sea gapes open which is to say,
stylistically, and again I quote the definition from the *OLD*, 'to be disjointed, disconnected'.
[57] The phrase *in abruptum* (69) adds an overtone of epic. Virgil uses it at *A.* 3.422 to describe
Charybdis—and the reference helps us anticipate the whirlpool's mention here at 85—as well
as at 12.687 of a huge boulder (*mons*) rushing downward and rolling with it everything in its
path. We are suddenly catapulted into danger.

READING TRAVEL (STATIUS' *SILVAE* 3.2) 241

Virgil lures us into a poetic sphere kindred to that of Statius where content and stylistics complement each other. The slender pipe of Callimachean poetics (*tenui avena*) finds its counterpart in the narrow bridge and narrow streams that the later poet posits as segments of the human realm of man in his proper landscape. Tityrus, *lentus in umbra*, easily fits into a world of *lentas paludes*, swamps whose quality is their stillness.

And the storylines of each poem echo each other. The shepherds who are leaving their homeland as a consequence of the warfare afflicting Rome (*linquimus, fugimus*) correspond to the many, typified by Maecius Celer, who take to navigating the seas for whatever misguided reason (*imus, fugimus*). In the case of Virgil's stricken Meliboeus, circumstances compel him to flee from his dreamland of song and ease to the reality of the Afri, Scythia, the Oaxes, the Britanni (65–6).

Because of these parallels perhaps we may even allow Statius a certain irony here. If to cross the seas from one's homeland (*gentiles...terras* is Statius' version of Virgil's *patriae fines*) is seen as a form of exile, then possibly the Roman mission itself, the empire building and preserving to which Celer is committed, can be seen as a form of overreaching, of abandoning the natural for the unnatural. We could characterize it as an existence that leaches the individual, human element from the social contacts and professional career requirements that imperial Rome imposes on its servants. One difference between the two poems is thus salient. Meliboeus passively, bitterly, suffers the destructive encroachment of the city's power upon his serenity. in Virgil's provocative locution, it is an 'immoral, barbarian soldier' (*impius...miles... barbarus*, 70–1), emanating from the metropolis, that causes the shepherd's relegation. Celer, by contrast, actively supports its expansive aspirations.

By drawing Virgil's bucolic poetry into his poetic orbit Statius thus adds elements of pastoral to the presence of elegy that we have been tracing in the *propemptikon*. As the imagination's vehicle that centres on music and song practiced in a setting of idealized natural calm, it is an appropriate companion to elegy in also dealing closely with the feelings of people one for the other. Both together contrast with the epic endeavours of which voyaging is a dangerous part.

The complementary phrases, *exigua clausi trabe et aëre nudo*, expand these horizons still further. The use of synecdoche in the first gives stress to the adjective which in turn reminds us of its stylistic role.[58] Metapoetically

---

[58] Other examples of *trabs* as an instance of synecdoche can be found at Enn. *Sc.* 247 Vahlen; Catul. 4.3; Virg. *A.* 3.191 and perhaps 4.566; Hor. *Carm.* 1.1.13. Skutsch considers Enn. *Ann.* 616 Vahlen as spurious (*Spur.* 9). There is no parallel for the use of *exigua* here.

242   THE POETIC WORLD OF STATIUS' *SILVAE*

the ship is *exiguus* because, as a carrier of people who share deep feelings with those whom they are leaving and who presumably will welcome them back, it here represents the personal, intimate—which in generic language is to say the lyric and elegiac—aspect of seafaring.[59] As a vehicle for the emotionality of arrival and departure and for the worries connected with the intervening travel, it again epitomizes the work of Propertius and his colleagues, with Callimachean poetics once more on display.

Within the language of figuration, we turn from synecdoche to paradox with the second phrase.[60] How can air be naked and, furthermore, how can we be hemmed in by the invisible? It is we, as passengers, who are the vulnerable, defenseless folk, confined inside a 'beam' and yet, again paradoxically, at the mercy of the surrounding atmosphere. By a form of hypallage, we travellers, and not just the elemental universe, are the ones exposed to the air around us. In Virgil's poem of the destructive clash between imagination and reality and of the resulting relegations that we have just been looking at, it is no wonder that the word *nudus* appears three times. It is associated with twin kids, doomed because born 'on uncovered flint' (*silice in nuda*, 15), with the naked stone (*lapis nudus*, 47) that is Tityrus' heritage, and with an impossibility like seas stranding unsheltered fish (*nudos pisces*, 60). The emphatic powerlessness of the pastoral world in face of the effects of Roman might deployed is transferred to voyagers at the mercy of externals who are in this case also fulfilling the destiny of Rome in threatening circumstances.

Statius next has us visualize the reasons why we stand at risk and their history:

> inde furor ventis indignataeque procellae
> et caeli fremitus et fulmina plura Tonanti.
> ante rates pigro torpebant aequora somno
> nec spumare Thetis nec spargere nubila fluctus
> audebant.[61] visis tumuerunt puppibus undae,
> inque hominem surrexit hiems. tunc nubila Plias
> Oleniumque pecus, solito tunc peior Orion.
>
> (Stat. *Silv.* 3.2.71–7)

---

[59] As Propertius puts it (3.9.4), *non sunt apta meae grandia uela rati* ('large sails are not suited to my boat'). For *parva rati*, cf. also Ov. *Met.* 1.319.

[60] The only other use of the phrase *aëre nudo* in classical Latin is found at *Theb.* 9.529. *Theb.* 12.19 ends with *aëra nudum*. Paulinus of Nola ends *sub aëre nudo* (*Carm.* 28.33).

[61] I keep *audebant*, the reading of *M*, instead of *gaudebant* (Markland), to which it is frequently changed (which Courtney and Liberman follow).

READING TRAVEL (STATIUS' *SILVAE* 3.2)   243

The result was rage for the winds and resentful gales and the sky's roaring and the Thunderer's many lightning-bolts. Before ships the seas languished in sluggish sleep nor did Thetis dare to foam nor billows to spatter the clouds. Once they caught sight of ships, waves swelled (75), and tempest rose up against man. Then the Pleiad was cloudy and the Olenian goat, then Orion was worse than his usual.

Again, Statius would have us think of the winds in *Aeneid* 1, upset that their own violent nature is under check and readied to wreak Juno's vengeance against the Trojans: *illi indignantes magno cum murmure montis/circum claustra fremunt...* ('in their resentment with great rumbling of the mountain they roar around their barriers...', 55–6). and shortly later they are compared to an irate rabble which *furor* supports with arms (150). Virgil thus offers a singular example of nature's personified violence aroused by man that is absorbed into the generality of Statius' pronouncement. Until man's intervention, the open seas were like the inland waters that we travellers foolishly leave behind. Oceans, then stilled by lazy somnolence, were kindred to the *lentas paludes* and *stagna* that were our untroubled lot before dubious ambitions, and the resultant involvement with the wildness of the sea, took hold.[62]

Here, too, Virgil serves as helpful commentator, this time through his fourth *Eclogue*. People once led an ideal, peaceful existence, says the poet, and still could, if they were to allow a renewed Golden Age to dawn:

> pauca tamen suberunt priscae vestigia fraudis
> quae temptare Thetim ratibus, quae cingere muris
> oppida, quae iubeant telluri infindere sulcos.
>
> (Virg. *Ecl.* 4.31–3)

Nevertheless a few traces of our ancient deceit will remain which order men to make trial of Thetis in ships, to gird towns with walls, to cleave the ground with furrows.

Through the commonality of the rare metonymy of the Nereid Thetis, standing for the sea itself, and ships, with whose inauguration she is often

---

[62] It could be presumed that pastoral, for instance, or elegy came before epic which was only made possible by man's audacious pursuits, often involving some aspect of seafaring and its consequences. For a combination of *stagni* and *paludis*, see also Virg. *A*. 8.88.

244   THE POETIC WORLD OF STATIUS' *SILVAE*

associated,[63] Statius, eliciting help from Virgil, asks us to cast our minds back to the initiation of seafaring and to its negative results.

The verb *audebant* deserves special attention. As the poem's opening line adumbrates, daring is often associated with the initial sailors and all those who have followed in their path. Here Statius gives the notion a twist by denying any audacity to the sea before man originally set sail. Once man's boldness had sent him seaward, however, the deep (Thetis strongly figured) and its personified floods responded in kind and aroused their destructive energies against his ill-advised projects. As Statius perceives it, the nature of open seas remained akin to tranquil inland waters until we foolishly put them to the test and elicited an appropriately negative response.

After this sweeping diatribe, Statius returns from generic to specific, from global denunciation of man as a whole to two special individuals, the poem's speaker in his personal voice and the addressee as he grows more and more distant:

> iusta queror. fugit ecce vagas ratis acta per undas
> paulatim minor et longe servantia vincit
> lumina, tot gracili ligno complexa timores,
> teque[64] super reliquos, te, nostri pignus amoris,
> portatura, Celer. quo nunc ego pectore somnos
> quove[65] queam perferre dies?
>
> (Stat. *Silv.* 3.2.78–83)

My complaint is just. See, the boat flees, driven through the wandering waves, diminishing bit by bit, and defeats our eyes that watch it from a way off, embracing so many fears in her slender wood (80), about to carry you, above the rest, you, pledge of our love, Celer. With what heart may I myself now be able to endure times of sleep, or with what heart the days?

The speaking 'I' now adopts the tone of an elegiac lover as the universal notion of we humans being expatriated (*fugimus*), a situation to which

---

[63] Compare, out of many instances, Catul. 64.19–21 and its larger context. Statius turns to the metonymy again at *Silv.* 4.6.18 to describe pearls.

[64] I adopt *teque* (Markland, Liberman) instead of *quaque* (M) or *quaeque* (Politianus). For a defence of *quique*, see Courtney (1984) 336–7.

[65] At 82–3, I adopt *quo...quove* (Rossberg, Courtney, Liberman) for *quos...quosve* (M). With an eye to Dido, we should note here the parallel between the authorial address to her at A. 4.408 and Statius' apostrophe to Celer at line 82. (Both disyllabic names appear in the same position in the hexameter line.) In this case, Statius plays the double role of Virgil, addressing a character within his own story, and of himself as both author of the present poem and friend of Celer.

READING TRAVEL (STATIUS' *SILVAE* 3.2)   245

Virgil's shepherds are driven by Roman might, becomes Celer, in his particular flight (*fugit*) from Naples to Egypt, and the plethora of boats (*rates*, 73) that caused our original plight becomes focused on the special craft (*ratis*, 78) that carries Celer into the distance.[66] Once more the deictic *ecce* asks that we, too, watch closely with the person watching.

Statius focuses our attention on himself and on the event in several ways. As at line 51, where the heart and eyes of the speaker are also involved, the deictic *ecce* makes our act of observing all the more forceful, with rhetoric supplementing the importance of vision. Pay attention, says the speaker, as our eyes struggle with him to see what he strains to view. and, as the distance between them grows, Statius positions himself and his vanishing friend immediately before us, through apostrophe, through the repetition of *te*, and the iteration of *t* sounds in the word *portatura*, the only use of the form in classical Latin.

The elegiac tone centres especially on the words *pignus amoris*. The metaphor takes us back to Celer as *depositum* (6), as something valuable entrusted to Neptune for safe-keeping and safe return. It also serves as a reminder that Horace, in *Carmen* 1.3, his *propemptikon* to Virgil setting out for Greece, describes his poet friend as *creditum* (5), entrusted to his ship, to be given back with worth undiminished (*incolumem*, 7). The production of epic remains in the background of each reference.[67]

The phrase *pignus amoris* has more specific Virgilian reminders. It appears twice in the fifth book of the *Aeneid* (538 and 572). In the first it serves as the attribute of a mixing bowl given by Cisseus to Anchises, token of the bond of warmth and respect between them. The second, still more à propos, is reserved for a horse that Dido has given young Ascanius as a pledge of affection between them.

We have already on several occasions traced the presence of the Carthaginian queen though the poem and the aura of emotionality that reminiscence of her brings to any new context. Here the bow to Virgil is particularly affective because Statius immediately takes us directly to Dido and to her suffering upon the departure of her quondam lover, Aeneas. All nature is asleep but not she:

---

[66] *Servantia* (79) functions as a reminder of *servare* from the poem's initial hexameter. The observing gods at the start are now replaced by the watching, yearning 'I' which here strongly re-enters the poem. To follow a boat carefully into the distance with one's line of sight is also to betray the ongoing affection of someone, in this case human, who deeply cares about it and its passengers.

[67] For Celer, in particular, the use of commercial language is fitting since he is traveling on a vessel plying the seas for economic gain.

246 THE POETIC WORLD OF STATIUS' *SILVAE*

> at non infelix animi Phoenissa, neque umquam
> solvitur in somnos oculisve aut pectore noctem
> accipit: ingeminant curae rursusque resurgens
> saevit amor magnoque irarum fluctuat aestu.

(Virg. A. 4.529–32)

But not Phoenissa, wretched in her mind, nor does she ever relax into times of sleep nor receive night into her eyes or heart. Her sufferings redouble and her love, swelling up again, grows fierce and she surges on a mighty tide of angers.

As in the nod to *Aeneid* 4 that opens the poem, Statius again refigures himself as Dido while the departing Celer plays the role of Aeneas.[68]

The phrase *gracili ligno complexa timores* not only continues the elegiac tone but through it we also deepen aspects of stylistics with a figurative thrust that we have observed before. The metapoetic overtones of *gracilis* are clarified from the adjective's use by Virgil near the conclusion of his tenth *Eclogue*:

> haec sat erit, divae, vestrum cecinisse poetam,
> dum sedet et gracili fiscellam texit hibisco,
> Pierides: vos haec facietis maxima Gallo,
> Gallo, cuius amor tantum mihi crescit in horas
> quantum vere novo viridis se subicit alnus.

(Virg. Ecl. 10.70–4)

This will be enough, goddess Pierides, for your poet to have sung while he sits and weaves a basket of slender mallow. You will make this the greatest for Gallus, for Gallus, my love for whom grows hour by hour as much as a green alder shoots upward in the freshness of spring.

Gracili hibisco, as Virgil's great collection draws to a close, balances *tenui avena* that we have seen near its start, and the two enclosing phrases tell of a poetic grouping that thrives on a manner of expression that is both refined and tempered.[69]

---

[68] With *queam perferre* (83), cf. Dido's lament at *A*. 4.420 (*perferre...potero*).

[69] Servius' note on line 71 deserves mention here: *allegoricos autem significat se composuisse hunc libellum tenuissimo stilo* ('but put allegorically he means that he composed this little book in the thinnest of styles'). His commentator, by linking *gracilis* with *tenuis*, also helps us unify Virgil's collection of pastorals. At the same time, he makes it clear that both stylistic words are to be taken allegorically, which here is also to say metapoetically. See also *Culex* 1; Prop. 2.13.3; Ov. *Pont.* 2.5.25–6.

READING TRAVEL (STATIUS' *SILVAE* 3.2) 247

The phrase *gracili ligno* has no parallel elsewhere in Latin. It does, however, have a counterpart earlier here in the words *exigua trabe* (70). Both nouns serve as synecdoche for ship, and both are modified by attributes that carry a double message.[70] First they suggest the vulnerability of the vessel that is bearing Celer across the seas. Since it is an object slender and small, both it and its passengers are easily assailable by the multifaceted, negative powers that rule the ocean.

Second, since both adjectives reflect the language of style, we enter once again the sphere of metapoetics. Propertius, for example, speaks of his 'slender Muses' (*graciles... Musas*, 2.13.3), and Ovid can describe his final exilic masterpiece in falsely modest phrasing: *dum tamen in rebus temptamus carmina parvis,/materiae gracili sufficit ingenium* ('Nevertheless as long as i attempt songs on small things, my wit is adequate for the slender subject-matter,' *Pont.* 2.5.25–6). Statius therefore once again draws us into the intimate world of elegy where private emotions are paramount, regularly centred on absence, yearning and potential loss.

We now follow Celer on the details of his itinerary:

> ... quis cuncta pacenti
> nuntius, an facili te praetermiserit unda
> Lucani rabida ora maris, num torta Charybdis
> fluctuet aut Siculi populatrix virgo profundi,
> quos tibi currenti praeceps gerat Hadria mores?
> quae pax Carpathio, quali te subvehat aura
> Doris Agenorei furtis blandita iuvenci?
>
> (Stat. *Silv.* 3.2.83–9)

What message to me, in fear of everything? Has the ravening coast of Lucania's sea sent you past with compliant wave? Does whirled Charybdis (85) surge or the virgin ravager of the Sicilian deep? Does headstrong Hadria control its behaviour for you in your haste? What peace to the Carpathian? With what sort of breeze does Doris, who encouraged the thefts of Agenor's bullock, draw you along?

Statius takes us through the menaces of Celer's journey, down the west coast of Italy, through Charybdis and past Scylla,[71] east into the southern Adriatic

---

[70] In both cases the nouns are also reminders of Statius' 'ligneous' poetics; see Wray (2007).

[71] Aeneas avoids these notorious hazards on his journey to Italy. For other mentions, see *A.* 3.420–32 and 7.302. Celer's route was usual for grain ships heading east.

248   THE POETIC WORLD OF STATIUS' *SILVAE*

and then the Carpathian sea. With typical dexterity the poet's naming of 'Agenor's bullock' asks us to follow another journey, the route of Jupiter, in his animal disguise, making his way further east to Tyre, then west again, with abducted Europa on his back. (The rest of the mythic trip to Crete is left to our imaginations.) From the upper Mediterranean it was an easy lap for Celer south to Egypt which we suddenly reach, in another brilliant stroke, with the apostrophe to Isis at line 101 and the resultant immediacy that it engenders.

At *Thebaid* 1.180–8, the Carpathian sea is part of another, related itinerary. Statius has a Theban remark, in language similar to our lines in the *Silvae*, on alarming portents from his city's past:

> '...an inde vetus Thebis extenditur omen,
> ex quo Sidonii nequiquam blanda iuvenci
> pondera Carpathio iussus sale quaerere Cadmus
> exsul Hyanteos invenit regna per agros...?'
>
> (Stat. Theb. 1.180–3)

'Or does the ancient omen for Thebes endure from the time when Cadmus, ordered to search the Carpathian sea in vain for the Sidonian bullock's pleasant burden, as an exile found a kingdom in Hyantean fields...?'

Statius' references to the sea around the island of Carpathus and to Agenor, king of Tyre, thus put forward two mythic stories—the one taking Cadmus from Tyre to Thebes, the other Jupiter from Tyre to Crete—as epic precedents for Celer's modern voyage from Puteoli to Alexandria.

And once again Statius complicates, and expands, our understanding by adding another component to the poetic mix. The story of Jupiter and Europa is the central element, the story that substantiates the immediate plot, of one of Horace's most elaborate and powerful poems, *Carmen* 3.27. It, too, is a *propemptikon* addressed by the speaker to a certain Galatea in the hope that she will remember him and will travel safely through the threats that she may confront. May only good portents see her on her way!

As in the case of Statius for Celer, she too arouses fear on the part of the speaker whose prominent use of 'I' in this connection (*ego cui timebo*, 'for whom I myself will experience dread', 7) urges us also to equate ourselves with the poet, on this occasion Horace himself. The Adriatic is part of each journey (19) and Orion again looms as a threat (18). Present in both cases is the roaring (*fremitus*) of sky and sea (23). But it is the tale of Jupiter and his

READING TRAVEL (STATIUS' *SILVAE* 3.2) 249

beloved, mentioned in passing by Statius and elaborated to form the core of his ode by Horace, that joins the two poems and tugs the Augustan poet again into Statius' complex schema. Galatea refers to her 'infamous bullock' (*infamem iuvencum*, 45), and Venus later mentions Europa's 'hated bull' (*invisus taurus*, 72). And the literal act of thievery (*furtis*) mentioned by Statius, which is at the same time an act of amatory deceit in the language of the elegists, is adopted from Horace's categorization of the god-animal as *doloso* (25), given to treachery.

So once again Horace, especially Horace as a writer of two extraordinary *propemptica*, enters our poem. And with him comes the lyric voice, the voice of the speaker addressing a cherished 'you', in this case setting out on a worrisome path. It is no coincidence that between lines 81 and 90 of Statius' poem there appear six instances of the pronoun 'you' in the Latin, whether *te* or *tibi*. Celer's epic adventure, as Statius would have us perceive it, once again projects a deeply personal side which on this occasion draws especially on the tonality of an ode to enhance its expression.

From Celer's topographical moves we turn back to the speaker and what might have been his situation:

> sed merui questus. quid enim te castra petente
> non vel ad ignotos ibam comes impiger Indos
> Cimmeriumque chaos? starem prope bellica regis
> signa mei, seu tela manu seu frena teneres
> armatis seu iura dares, operumque tuorum,
> etsi non socius, certe mirator adessem.
> si quondam magno Phoenix reverendus Achilli
> litus ad Iliacum Thymbraeaque Pergama venit
> imbellis tumidoque nihil iuratus Atridae,
> cur nobis ignavus amor? sed pectore fido
> numquam abero longisque sequar tua carbasa votis.
>
> (Stat. *Silv.* 3.2.90–100)

But I have deserved complaints. For, when you were on the way to war (90), why did I not go as your eager comrade even to the unknown Indi and Cimmerian darkness? I would take a place near the martial standards of my patron, whether you were holding weapons or reins in your hand or were giving judgments to armed men, and, although not as a partner, I would certainly be at hand as an admirer of your activities (95). If, once upon a time, Phoenix, worthy to be respected by great Achilles, came to the shore of Ilium and Thymbraean Pergama, he unwarlike and in no way

250   THE POETIC WORLD OF STATIUS' *SILVAE*

under oath to the arrogant son of Atreus, why was our love slothful? But in my faithful heart I will never be apart, and I will follow your sails with prayers from afar (100).

We have earlier given ear to the speaker's just complaints (*iusta queror*, 78) against Celer's leave-taking, in particular, and more generally about the invention of sailing and the fury it aroused in the sea and its forces. We now turn to the reproaches that the speaker might hold against himself or even that he might consider Celer to be harbouring. Here the role of *comes* is crucial, exemplifying as it should both loyalty and affection.

Catullus sets the pattern. He addresses his only original poem in Sapphic metre to Furius and Aurelius who are to be his companions (*comites Catulli*, 11.1) on a wide-ranging geographical course that would take him and his thoughts away from the horrors of his affair with Lesbia. The poem has aspects of a reverse *propemptikon*. In place of someone bidding adieu to a departing friend, in Catullus' poem it is the speaker, through the mediation of his associates, who says goodbye to a malevolent figure staying behind. The first stop for Catullus, the Indi in the farthest distance (*extremos Indos*, 2), is mimicked in Statius' *ignotos Indos* and several other parallels prove that the later poet would wish us to think back to Catullus' great lyric.[72]

But it is the presence of the word *comes* that is critical here. Catullus imagines claiming the attendance of his presumed friends as they join in touring landscapes far away from home and its emotional trials.[73] Statius, by contrast, chastises himself for not accompanying his patron on his duti-ful progress, even if this means visiting people unknown because of their remoteness or a land whose darkness is said to resemble the realm of the dead. The first poem is essentially a curse to the creature being left behind. The second is at basis here an act of apology for not fulfilling one's duty as friend and debtor.

To visit *Cimmerium chaos*, an above-ground world of the dead, would place Statius as a modern Pirithous accompanying Theseus into the Underworld—the ultimate in faithful comradeship. The poet himself draws

---

[72] See also, for instance, *litus* (11.3; 3.2.97, at start of line); *Eoa* (11.3; 3.2.104, at line endings, 126); *unda* (11.4; 3.2.84, at line endings); *Nilus* (11.8; *Nili*, 3.2.108); *Caesar* (11.10; 3.2.128); *amorem* (11.21; 3.2.81, *amoris*, at line endings).

[73] Catullus 11 (*comites Catulli*, 1; *parati*, 14) anticipates Horace's language at *Carm.* 2.17.11–12 addressed to Maecenas (...*supremum/carpere iter comites parati*, '...comrades ready to press on along the final journey'). Catullus' passage away from treacherous love anticipates Horace's final movement toward death, and both play into Statius' concern with the dangers of sea travel and with the emotional implications of loss that they arouse.

READING TRAVEL (STATIUS' *SILVAE* 3.2) 251

a direct analogy from epic at lines 96–8. Were he to venture east with his patron he would be like the aged counselor Phoenix accompanying his protégé Achilles to Troy. He is unwarlike and lacking the anger of Agamemnon, swollen (*tumido*) like the seas that now trouble mankind's voyaging (*tumuerunt*, 75).[74] Even so he would have shared in a grand undertaking that now finds a precedent in the *Iliad*, prototype of Western epics.

Line 100 takes us again to Statius' constant source of inspiration, the *Aeneid*, on this occasion to two separate moments. The first occurs in *A*. 2. 620, where Aeneas tells of an epiphany of his mother Venus who announces: *numquam abero et tutum patrio te limine sistam* ('never will I leave you and I will place you safely on your father's threshold').[75] The goddess of love will remain faithfully by her son's side just as Statius, in his heart and in his prayers, will remain a close part of Celer's doings, a modern-day Aeneas about the affairs of a well-established Rome.

The second is more complex. We are now in Book 4 and once more a character is speaking to Aeneas. This time, however, the hero is not at hand and the words, from Dido, the abandoned lover, are meant to curse rather than console:

> '. . . sequar atris ignibus absens
> et, cum frigida mors anima seduxerit artus,
> omnibus umbra locis adero. dabis, improbe, poenas'.
>
> (Virg. *A*. 4.384–6)

'. . . Though absent I will pursue you with black flames and, when cold death will have separated limbs from soul, as a shade I will be present in every place. Shameless, you will pay the penalty'.

If we compare the two Virgilian allusions, *numquam abero*, from Book 2, is replaced by *absens* while pointedly reflecting *adero* as well. Through her divine power Venus can remain guarding her son through a difficult moment in his withdrawal from Troy. Dido, trusting in the potent affect of a malediction, lays claim to haunt Aeneas, even at a distance, with a negative potency parallel to what is positive about Venus' allegiance. However far

---

[74] *Tumidus* can refer to style of expression as well as to emotionality, in which case, as the *OLD* puts it (s.v. 6), it means 'affecting grandeur, high-flown, inflated'.

[75] I follow the reading *numquam* of the Virgilian manuscript M and Statius' manuscript M. For Virgil, P reads *nusquam* ('nowhere'), as do ζ for Statius. In either case the readings would be in common.

252 THE POETIC WORLD OF STATIUS' SILVAE

away (*absens*) from the object of her fury, she will still be constantly at hand (*adero*) to bring woe upon him.[76]

Isis

Within the *Aeneid*, Dido, here, is a macabre variation of the earlier Venus. Statius, as a character in his poem, is a version of a still-loving Dido, as it were proclaiming her continued loyalty to Celer from afar. In both allusions Celer plays the role of Aeneas while Statius is a Venus, ever invisibly abetting his friend by prayers, and not an absent Dido, ever damning him with black flames, as he follows out his destiny. Instead of behaving like Dido who accuses her inamorato of treachery (*perfide*, she shouts twice),[77] we now find in Statius a counterpart whose kisses are 'faithful' (*fida*, 57) and who, 'with his faithful heart' (*pectore fido*, 99), will be ever present in spirit at his patron's side. And suddenly, we find ourselves face-to-face with Isis:

> Isi, Phoroneis olim stabulata sub antris,
> nunc regina Phari numenque orientis anheli,
> excipe multisono puppem Mareotida sistro,
> ac iuvenem egregium, Latius cui ductor Eoa
> signa Palaestinasque dedit frenare cohortes,
> ipsa manu placida per limina festa sacrosque
> duc portus urbesque tuas.
>
> (Stat. *Silv.* 3.2.101–7)

Isis, once stabled in the caves of Phoroneus, now queen of Pharos and a divinity of the panting orient, receive the Mareotid ship with your many-sounding sistrum, and yourself with gentle hand lead the remarkable young man, to whom the Latian leader has imparted Eoan standards and the control of the cohorts of Palestine (105), through festive thresholds and holy harbours and your cities.

As a dramatic example of the numerous journeys that Statius would have us take throughout his poem, we find ourselves, on the way to an Eastern *militia*, newly arrived in Egypt ahead of Celer and asking the goddess for help and

---

[76] Cf. Virgil's use of *abesses* (681) for Anna to describe the loss of her sister. *Sequar* appears in Virgil only at *A.* 4.384.
[77] *A.* 4.305 and 355. At 373 and 597, she accuses him of lacking *fides*.

READING TRAVEL (STATIUS' *SILVAE* 3.2) 253

guidance.[78] The epiphanic aspect of the sudden vocative is furthered by the directness of the poet's command to her to appear in person (*ipsa*) and do as bidden. The figuration makes the absent present; what is there becomes here. The speaker in his wisdom is already aware of her omniscience and therefore of what Celer could learn from her. The apostrophe enhances the sense of immediacy for us as we share in Celer's voyage into a new material and intellectual world.

The goddess, too, has had a rather singular *curriculum vitae*, and the poet ushers us briefly through it, first chronologically, from then (*olim*) to now (*nunc*). Alliteration helps us also follow her journey topographically as we move from *Phoroneis* to *Phari*.[79] We begin in Greece, at Argos where Phoroneus was the son of Inachus and therefore brother of Io. Turned into a cow by Hera, she swam the Bosphorus and crossed to Egypt via the Ionian sea. There she resumed mortal form only to be transformed into the goddess Isis. Geographical transplantation, therefore, is paralleled in her story by double metamorphosis, first from woman to animal, then from subhuman to divine.

The near adjacency of *regina* and *sistrum* brings to mind another Egyptian queen, also associated with the ceremonial rattle, namely Cleopatra.[80] Here she is, for instance, as depicted on Aeneas' shield in the turmoil at the battle of Actium: *regina in mediis patrio vocat agmina sistro* ('in the midst the queen calls upon her troops with her ancestral *sistrum*', *A.* 8.696). Mention of the Mareotid boat reminds us that we have earlier seen Cleopatra through the alembic of Horace's imagination with the phrase *Mareotica vina* (24). Here Statius has exploited Virgil to assist us in recalling a crucial moment in her notorious career.[81] We will see him do so again shortly.

But first we turn to the 'brilliant youth' (*iuvenem egregium*), Celer, and the circumstances of his Egyptian sojourn. Again the phrase is Virgilian,

---

[78] For an alternate interpretation of the Egyptian segment of *Silv.* 3.2, see Manolaraki (2013), esp. 206–16. She views the details of Celer's intellectual itinerary as a 'normalization' (196) of the relationship between Egypt and Rome, a 'domesticating ideology' bent on taming the foreign and alien so as to cohere with Roman thinking.

[79] The form *stabulata* is unique in classical Latin; though for word and context, cf. Ov. *Met.* 13.822: *multas silva tegit, multae stabulantur in antris* ('the woods hide many [flocks], many are stabled in caves'). There may be an inherent pun on the verb's etymology from *sto*. Her housing as an animal at Argos was one stop, as it were, on Io/Isis' exotic series of metamorphoses.

[80] For the *sistrum* of Isis, also in association with Cleopatra, see Luc. 10.63 and its larger context that Statius knew well. Ovid mentions the *sistrum* on eight occasions.

[81] *Orientis anheli* (102) may also be a bow to Virgil's mention of *viris Orientis* at *A.* 8.687. The phrase itself is drawn closely from Virg. *G.* 1.250, repeated at *A.* 5.739.

254   THE POETIC WORLD OF STATIUS' *SILVAE*

used of Nisus, prize-winner in the footrace, another of the events to honour Anchises (*A.* 5.361).[82] But the manner of description is typical of Statius throughout his poem. Toponyms take us on Celer's journey for us. We move from Latium and its unnamed leader, Domitian, to Eoan standards, which is to say, to generalized Roman forces with their ensigns located in the East, and finally to Palestine and the specified cohorts stationed there.

We are initially watching Egypt and Pharos which can stand for the whole country or more precisely for the famous island near Alexandria and its neighbourhood.[83] Both the phrases *limina festa* and *sacros portus* are used uniquely here and both, with their stress on plurality, record the extensiveness of the goddess' worship in the area.[84] The first looks to shrines in which she was venerated. The second, in conjunction with a number of cities devoted to her (*urbes tuas*), takes us to one special detail of the Nile delta best explained by recourse to two appropriate passages in Ovid. The first is *Amores* 2.13, devoted to Corinna who is gravely ill. Isis, whose aid the speaker implores, is also addressed as here in the vocative (7).[85] We hear of Pharos and *sistra*, along with Canopus and Memphis, soon to appear in Statius' poem, and of a country: *quaque celer Nilus lato delapsus in alveo/per septem portus in maris exit aquas...* ('where the swift Nile, gliding in its broad channel, makes its way out into the waters of the sea through seven harbours', Ov. *Am.* 2.13.9–10).[86] The number is reiterated by the same poet at *Heroides* 14.107–8, where the context also concerns the metamorphosis of Io, beloved of Jupiter: *per septem Nilus portus emissus in aequor/exuit insana paelicis ora bove* ('The Nile, discharged into the sea through seven harbours, strips from the maddened cow the features of a mistress').[87] This survey of the expansiveness of devotion to Isis is centred on the poet's

---

[82] The phrase is varied, in the order of words only, at *A.* 6.861 and 12.275. Recollection of Nisus' swiftness of foot (see *A.* 5.319) is another way in which Statius plays on the name of Maecius Celer.

[83] The generality is suggested by the subsequent *Oriens* (102), the particularity by *Mareotida* (103).

[84] For *limina* in relation to some form of *templum*, see, e.g., Virg. *A.* 1.446–8, 4.199–202; Luc. 5.155; Sil. 1.102–3, 6.454, 11.81.

[85] Isis is also addressed in the vocative by Ovid at *Met.* 9.773. With Statius, these are the only such invocations in Latin, and both passages were clearly in the later poet's mind. Laguna Mariscal (1992), 230 notes the passages but not the common presence of apostrophe.

[86] The Ovidian passage will again keep Celer's name before Statius' readers.

[87] Catullus speaks of the Nile's outflow in a general manner (*septemgeminus... Nilus*, 11.7–8) and Virgil more specifically of *septemgemini... ostia Nili* (*A.* 6.800). Cf. also Ovid's variations at *Met.* 1.422–3 (*septemfluus... Nilus*), 5.187 (*septemplice Nilo*) and 324 (*septem discretus in ostia Nilus*), and 9.774 (*septem digestum in cornua Nilum*). It is worth consideration that Statius chooses a seven-mouthed river as a major component of his poetry here while his *magnum opus*, the *Thebaid*, centres on a city noted for its seven gates.

command *duc* (107). She is to lead her new protégé on a tour of territory special to her. The imperative recurs at line 117 and centres on the burial places of Alexander the Great and Cleopatra.[88] In between we turn to scholarly topics of a scientific, aetiological, or religious nature, with the Nile itself as a special focus of interest:

> ... te praeside noscat
> unde paludosi fecunda licentia Nili,
> cur vada desidant et ripa coerceat undas
> Cecropio stagnata luto, cur invida Memphis,
> curve Therapnaei lasciviat ora Canopi,
> cur servet Pharias Lethaeus ianitor aras,
> vilia cur magnos aequent animalia divos,
> quae sibi praesternat vivax altaria phoenix,
> quos dignetur agros aut quo se gurgite Nili
> mergat adoratus trepidis pastoribus Apis.
>
> (Stat. *Silv.* 3.2.107–16)

Under your guidance may he learn whence the enriching freedom of the swampy Nile, why its waters sink back and its bank, stilled by the mud of Cecrops, confines its waves, why Memphis is envious (110), or why the shore of Therapnaean Canopus is wanton, why Lethe's doorkeeper guards the altars of Pharos, why ordinary beasts are the equal of great gods, what altars the long-lived phoenix strews for himself, what fields Apis considers worthy or in what swirl of the Nile (115) he plunges, worshipped by awestruck shepherds.

The adjective *paludosi* looks back to the mention of *paludes* at line 67 and reminds us that we are again in the world of fresh, inland water and therefore of the poetic contrast that it forms with the open ocean.[89] And the point of interest is not the familiar puzzle of the origin of the great river itself but of what gives it the nourishment that through its annual flooding sustained the crops and animal life along its bounds.[90]

---

[88] The bracketing repetition of *duc* at 107 and 117, each at the start of a hexameter, is complemented by the reiteration of *Nili* at the line endings of 108 and 115.

[89] *Stagnata* also serves as a reminder of *stagna* (68) in the earlier passage. *Desidant* is a unique use of the form. The verb offers a smooth transition from *licentia* to *coerceat*, from untended luxuriance to its gradual taming.

[90] Had the source of the Nile been in Statius' mind we would expect him to have given us a verbal clue such as, for some examples, *fons* or *fontes* (Hor. *Carm.* 4.14.45; Sen. *Nat.* 4.1; Luc. 10.40; Plin. *Nat.* 5.10.51), *ora* (Luc. 10.214), or *caput* (Tib. 1.7.24, as part of a larger depiction of the Nile; Ov. *Met.* 2.255; Luc. 10.191; Sen. *Nat.* 6.8).

256   THE POETIC WORLD OF STATIUS' *SILVAE*

Here again poetic usage can broaden our inquiry. The only other recorded use of the phrase *fecunda licentia* occurs in the context of Ovid's *Amores*: *exit in immensum fecunda licentia vatum/obligat historica nec sua verba fide* ('the enriching freedom of poets comes forth to an enormous degree nor does it control its words by means of history's truth', Ov. *Am.* 3.12.41–2). The plenitude of the Nile, which has to be regulated, finds its source, as Statius would have it, in poets' abundant openness of invention that according to Ovid they fail to curb even in the face of tangible evidence against their utterance. In both cases we are dealing with creativity, whether that of our own imagination or of a river that makes its territory fruitful.[91] Both need constraint to be productive or, in the case of the river, to be kept from turning fecundity into destruction.

Again we can think in metapoetic terms. The abundant Nile is a ready metaphor for the opulence of poetry that in this particular instance can draw so much of its energy and scope from the various genres that served Statius for inspiration.[92] By eliciting a comparison with Ovid here, the later poet poses a challenge to his predecessor, for the next lines show that Statius is in fact seriously interested in antiquarian lore and in getting at the truth, whatever the question, whatever, in fact, the well-spring. Unlike the bards that the Augustan author takes to task, he will turn science into art and be honest in the telling.

A few details follow strands that we have already been tracing. *Cecropio luto*, for instance, is a recondite reference to the myth of Procne and, therefore, to another instance of metamorphosis, on this occasion of human into bird. We make a quick mental journey from Egypt to Athens. The phrase *Therapnaei Canopi* elicits a similar response. According to legend Canopus, the town along with the island in the Nile delta, was named after the helmsman of Menelaus.[93] Therapnae, its attribute in adjectival form, was a village near Sparta, of which Menelaus was king. It was the birthplace of Helen and of

---

[91] The metapoetic aspect of the word *licentia* is picked up in *lasciviat* (111), where the excessive behaviour of the city of Canopus is in question. It is used on several occasions by Quintilian of over-indulgent writers, most famously of the stylistic permissiveness of Ovid: 'Ovid is wont to lack discipline in the *Metamorphoses*' (*Ovidius lascivire in* Metamorphoses *insolet, Inst.* 4.1.77).

[92] Ps.-Longinus (35.4) mentions the Nile, along with the Danube and the Rhine, as an example of the extraordinary, the great and the beautiful, of *sublimitas*, in a word. With what may be a negative bow to Callimachus, he prefers its grandeur to 'small streams, clear and useful as they are'. See Worman (2015) 13. Seneca (*Nat.* 6.7.1) links the Nile, Danube, and Rhine together when discussing navigability.

[93] The origin of the name is first mentioned by Hecataeus (*FGrHist* 1 F 308).

READING TRAVEL (STATIUS' *SILVAE* 3.2)   257

her brothers Castor and Pollux.[94] We are thus led back, in a form of ring composition, to lines 10 and 11 where the *Oebalii fratres* and their sister, known for her notorious trip from Greece to Troy, are first mentioned. What is explicit near the poem's beginning is implicit as we draw to a close, and we have also completed in our minds another odyssey from Egypt, this time to the Peloponnese.

Between mention of Cecrops and Therapnae, as the second in a brisk row of five interrogative 'whys' (*cur*) for which 'causes' ($a\H{\iota}\tau\iota\alpha$) might be forthcoming, there remains a curiosity: *invida Memphis*. Why is this famous Egyptian city on the Nile 'envious' and what is important about stressing this negative quality in the present context?

One answer proposed by scholars is to posit a play on Statius' part of an etymology for the name Memphis based on the Greek word $\mu\acute{\epsilon}\mu\phi\omega\mu\alpha\iota$ ('to blame'). Such a meaning may be in the background but to deserve censure is different from being an object of envy. The former is essentially a negative characteristic that suggests guilt on the part of the focus of interest. The latter, by contrast, posits a reason for jealousy suffered by the onlooker.

A more appropriate interpretation of Memphis' envy, I would suggest, lies in reference to a figure whose role in the poem becomes essential as we proceed toward its conclusion, Alexander the Great. Mentions of Pharos, Mareotis, and Canopus have already directed the reader's attention to the Nile and its expansive delta. This in turn would bring to mind the city of Alexandria, founded by Alexander in 331 BCE and in the time of Statius perhaps the most important commercial port in the Mediterranean next to Rome and Puteoli itself.[95] Therefore, as a site of great political significance to the centre of the empire itself, it could be an object of envy to Memphis, inland some twenty miles south along the Nile.

But there may be a still more precise reason for Memphis to be envious of Alexandria. The latter was the seat of the Ptolemies after its founder's death (323). Moreover, Ptolemy I had initially brought the body of Alexander to Memphis for burial where it would have been a chief object of interest, not to say veneration. However, some years later, according to Pausanias (1.6.3 and 1.7.1), probably around 280, Ptolemy II Philadelphus transferred it to

---

[94] See *Silv.* 4.2.48, 4.8.53, 5.3.140, and, for Castor and Pollux, *Theb.* 7.793 (*Therapnaei fratres*). See above, n. 18.

[95] See, e.g., *Silv.* 3.5.75–6 (...*tecta Dicaearchi portusque et litora mundi/hospita*..., 'the houses of Dicaearchus and the harbour and the world-welcoming shores'). On the port's growing significance, see D'Arms (1974) *passim*.

258   THE POETIC WORLD OF STATIUS' *SILVAE*

Alexandria, thus robbing Memphis of a major attraction, not to speak of a source of authority.[96]

We may also glean some help in interpreting Statius here from a passage in Lucan where the priest Acoreus is speaking of interest in the source of the Nile:

> '...sed vincit adhuc natura latendi.
> summus Alexander regum, quem Memphis adorat,
> invidit Nilo, misitque per ultima terrae
> Aethiopum lectos...'
>
> (Luc. 10.271–4)

'...its innate ability to deceive has won the day up to now. Alexander, greatest of kings, whom Memphis worships, was jealous of the Nile, and sent chosen men through the farthest areas of the Aethiopes'.

Statius, I suggest, transfers Alexander's envy of the Nile to Memphis' envy of Alexandria. And Memphis' adoration of Alexander, where he was crowned pharaoh in 332 and later buried, becomes resentment when the city's centrality as an Egyptian power is displaced onto its northern rival which bears the great king's name and houses for display in a mausoleum the remains that had once belonged to Memphis.

The themes of metamorphosis, and the passage of time through life to death, continue in the list of topics centred on the great river itself (*Nili*, 108 and 115). First we have *Lethaeus ianitor*, Cerberus, canine guardian of the classical Underworld, now become Anubis, dog-shaped Egyptian divinity, worshipped at the country's altars. His mention forms an easy transition to the more general Egyptian notion of animals as gods, and we again remember the multivalent progress of Isis as she changes from Argive Io into a cow and, finally, into an Egyptian divinity. We then turn to the long-lived phoenix, a reminder of Achilles' ancient counsellor, *reverendus* Phoenix (96),

---

[96] For further details, see Saunders (2006) 33–79. My suggestion does not preclude one aspect of the etymological play that critics beginning with Vollmer (1898) 402 have suggested. The city that 'lays blame on' or 'finds fault with' someone or something could be doing so for the very reason of *invidia*. In this case envy would be a way of faulting the later Ptolemy for the transfer of Alexander's corpse, as well as of begrudging the city that bears his name for receiving and housing it, with the prestige that would automatically accrue. Vollmer considers that the rivalry in question lies between Memphis and Thebes.

READING TRAVEL (STATIUS' *SILVAE* 3.2) 259

but now returned, appropriately to the context, in the shape of a bird with altars of his own making.[97]

As we near the end of the list we have Apis, bull as god, closely associated with the theme of death and renewal and hence with the annual re-fertilization that came with the flooding of the Nile. Statius does not associate him with Memphis, the centre of his worship (at the Apieion), but with his river and especially with *pastores*, the tenders of the animals who were nourished by it. But he does remind us that, for this stretch of Celer's itinerary, we are dealing again with inland water, not with the treacheries of the open sea. Hence the appearance of reverent shepherds is not only a suitable addition to the topic of religious worship so prominent in these lines. It also serves as a reminder of the references to pastoral poetry that Statius has earlier put before us and especially of the contrast it often illustrates between peaceful retreats and the difficulties that lived experience thrusts in our way.

Iteration of the imperative *duc* leads to the extraordinary finale of Celer's Egyptian tour:

> duc et ad Emathios manes, ubi belliger urbis
> conditor Hyblaeo perfusus nectare durat,
> anguiferamque domum, blando qua mersa veneno
> Actias Ausonias fugit Cleopatra catenas.
>
> (Stat. *Silv.* 3.2.117–20)

Lead him also to Emathian ghosts where the warrior founder of the city endures, bathed in the nectar of Hybla, and the snake-bearing dwelling where Cleopatra of Actium, sunk in soothing poison, fled the chains of Ausonia (120).

We find ourselves at the moment of climax in Alexandria, visiting the gravesites of the city's founder and its famous queen.

Mention of Emathia fulfils several roles. By taking us to Macedonia, it initiates the start of Alexander's career and encapsulates its course from its beginning to his death—the first of several ways in which Statius will have us survey the sweep of the great hero's career both chronologically and

---

[97] Line 114 contains the only preserved appearance of the form *praesternat* in classical Latin. Ovid uses the phrase *vivax phoenix* at *Am.* 2.6.54 and offers an extended survey of the bird's behaviour at *Met.* 15.391–407. The story of the phoenix continues the theme of death and renewal that runs through these lines. As the masculine form of *Phoenissa*, the name may also serve as another reminder of Dido to whom Virgil allots the adjective on four occasions (*A.* 1.670 and 714, 4.529, 6.450).

260 THE POETIC WORLD OF STATIUS' *SILVAE*

topographically. The name Emathia would also serve as a poignant reminder of the battles at Pharsalus and Philippi during Rome's civil strife in the late Republic. The locations are vividly sketched by Virgil:

> ergo inter sese paribus concurrere telis
> Romanas acies iterum videre Philippi;
> nec fuit indignum superis bis sanguine nostro
> Emathiam et latos Haemi pinguescere campos.
>
> (Virg. G. 1.489–92)

Therefore, Philippi again saw Roman battlelines clashing together with matching weapons; and it was not shocking to the gods that twice Emathia and the broad plains of Haemus should grow rich with our blood.

Ovid, in a bow to the future Augustus, shares Virgil's sentiments:... *Pharsalia sentiet illum/Emathiique iterum madefient caede Philippi* ('...Pharsalus will experience him and Emathian Philippi will again grow sodden with slaughter', *Met.* 15.823–4). Perhaps most striking are the opening lines of Lucan's *De bello civili: Bella per Emathios plus quam civilia campos,/iusque datum sceleri canimus...* ('We sing of wars more than civil through the plains of Emathia and of right bestowed on crime...', 1.1–2). Through the initiation of Alexander's career Statius takes us on our own journey through space and time, once again to the north of Greece but with a specificity that, with the help of earlier authors, draws us back to another moment in Roman history. By allusion to two momentous battles, imagined by the poets to have occurred on the same spot, we also find ourselves in the midst of Roman civil warring that was to continue on from 48 and 42 BCE for nearly another dozen years.[98]

The poetic progress to what follows is therefore brilliantly seamless. By reference to the birth of Alexander, and vicariously to the plains of Thessaly, we reached the territory of the next-to-last movement in the Roman civil wars. We now turn to Cleopatra, whose noteworthy corpse is also on view to our tourist in Alexandria. Through her we enter the last act of that stage in Roman history, the sea battle fought in 31 BCE off Actium on the west

---

[98] The unusual phrase *Emathios manes* spans the life of Alexander in a nutshell, from birthplace to death spirit. While looking explicitly to the embalmed body of Alexander, it serves also as a reminder of the ghosts of those who died in the Roman civil battling. Emathia regularly stands for Pharsalus in Lucan (e.g., 4.256; 6.315, 332, 350, 580, 620, 820; 7.166, 191, 427, 683).

READING TRAVEL (STATIUS' *SILVAE* 3.2)   261

coast of Greece, a battle that not only ended an era of civil war, but which also brought Octavian, soon to be known as Augustus, to full, unchallenged power. *Anguiferam* (119) looks to Cleopatra's personal form of death as well as to the general symbolic association of snakes with mortality.[99] With the phrase *blando...mersa veneno* (119), as critics note,[100] Statius would have us return once again to Horace's ode on her demise (*Carm.* 1.37) where, after telling us of her addiction to Mareotic wine and then of her bravery in handling the lethal serpents, the poet adds how (27–8) 'she drank in the black poison through her body' (*atrum/corpore combiberet venenum*). In Statius' picture, black poison, like Mareotic in Horace's vision of an earlier moment of need, has become an alluring necessity, as if the thought of suicide were consoling. The liquid imagery in 'drinking-up' has now been exaggerated into *mersa*. Ironically she who had avoided death by drowning at Actium is now completely immersed in the ugly fluid just as Alexander's corpse is steeped seemingly forever in Sicilian honey.[101]

But it is line 120 that most claims our attention. First a word on the figuration. It is built around a chiasmus made up largely of proper names whose syllabic lengths in order go as follows: 3, 4, 2, 4, and 3. With *fugit* at the centre, we have a careful balance between two adjectives and two nouns arranged in aBaB order. Both pairs are connected by alliteration, while the delicate assonance between *Actias* and *catenas* serves further to unify the whole.

The wording itself is also impressive. *Actias*, for instance, is unique here in its meaning 'of Actium'. At *A.* 8.704, we hear of *Actius Apollo*, the favouring god who presides at Octavian's great victory over Antony and his Egyptian consort. *Actias*, applied to Cleopatra, serves a similar, but now negative, purpose. She is controlled by the battle, just as she is fashioned by Statius' language, so as to become Actian. The juxtaposition with the subsequent proper name, *Ausonias*, adds further puissance to its implications. We have earlier seen Ausonia described as *armipotens* (23). The fetters from

---

[99] For twin snakes as symbolic of death for Cleopatra, see Virg. *A.* 8.697, where the reference may well allude to the asps that she used for suicide. These are punningly described by Horace as *asperas serpentis* (*Carm.* 1.37.26–7).

[100] See, e.g., Laguna Mariscal (1992) 234 (on line 119).

[101] In a poem as filled with Horace as *Silv.* 3.2, it is not inconceivable that with the phrase *Hyblaeo perfusus nectare* Statius means to remind us of the youth in *Carm.* 1.5 who is *perfusus liquidis odoribus* (2) and about to suffer metaphorical shipwreck on the sea of love. (The ode's speaker offers thanks for evading doom by erotic drowning.) Alexander's corpse, mummified by a slathering of honey, in its own way escapes the reality of death's conclusiveness. Cf. also the use of *perfundi* at Hor. *Epod.* 13.9.

262 THE POETIC WORLD OF STATIUS' *SILVAE*

which Cleopatra is fleeing belong to a land powerful with weaponry. She may be claimed by Actium, but her resultant flight from 'Ausonian chains', which is to say from enslavement to Italy and from its potential to keep her captive and on display, becomes all the more brave and heroic as an outcome.

Yet Statius, by positioning Celer and his readers at these two crucial spots in Alexandria on a visitor's itinerary, brings to an end the journeys of Alexander and Cleopatra, as he already had that of Isis. The difference is that the latter becomes a goddess to be worshipped in a number of shrines. By contrast, Alexander and Cleopatra in death suffer no grand metamorphosis but only continuous display as mummified corpses, here to gratify the eyes of a touring Roman. We will turn in a moment to the story of Alexander. For Cleopatra it is sufficient to say that her own journey back from Greece to Egypt, though it meant escape from the clutches of Roman power, not only brought about the bitter conclusion to an extraordinary life but also created a form of immortality that comes from monumentalization. The word *durat* that Statius allots to his Macedonian general is the Egyptian queen's due as well.

Statius finishes off this segment of the poem by asking Isis to see the youth safely to his eastern destination with which he is already familiar:

> usque et in Assyrias sedes mandataque castra
> prosequere et Marti iuvenem, dea, trade Latino.
> nec novus hospes erit: puer his sudavit in arvis
> notus adhuc tantum maioris lumine clavi,
> iam tamen et turmas facili praevertere gyro
> fortis et eoas iaculo damnare sagittas.
>
> (Stat. *Silv.* 3.2.121–6)

And escort him all the way to his Assyrian dwellings and the camp charged to him and, goddess, hand over the youth to Latin Mars. He will not be a new guest. He sweated in these fields as a boy, known until now only for the shimmer of the broader stripe but nevertheless also strong at outmanoeuvring squadrons with his agile course (125) and at taking credit away from Eoan arrows by means of his javelin.

The Egyptian goddess is still with us, but by the magic of the deictic *his* we are suddenly transported, along with Celer, to his military duties in Syria. And from the Greco-Roman past, and the famous dead associated with it, we turn to the Latin present. *Marti Latino* reminds us that a 'Latian leader'

(*Latius ductor*, 104), the unnamed Domitian, has sent him on his tour of duty. Rome is still at war but the task before the successor of Augustus is not only to keep the peace at home but also by military might to conquer enemies harassing the empire's frontier and to control the subdued who remain recalcitrant.

Time passes in Celer's life, also, as we move from his earlier position as *puer* to his fresh responsibilities as a *iuvenis*.[102] The phrase *novus hospes* takes us back to that earlier period. It, and its context, also return us again to one of Statius' primary sources of inspiration, the *Aeneid*.[103] We find ourselves near the beginning of its fourth book as Dido exclaims to her sister on their prepossessing visitor:

> 'Anna soror, quae me suspensam insomnia terrent!
> quis novus hic nostris successit sedibus hospes,
> quem sese ore ferens, quam forti pectore et armis!'
>
> (Virg. *A.* 4.9–11)

> 'Anna, my sister, what dreams frighten me in my anxiety! Who is this singular guest who has entered our dwelling? What a self he carries in his features, how brave in heart and weaponry!'

Like Aeneas, Celer was once a *novus hospes* in the land to which he is returning. In his case the location is more general (*Assyrias sedes*), his position in Syria; in that of Aeneas it is the home of Dido and her sister (*nostris sedibus*). Both are known for their bravery. Celer is *fortis* because of his prowess at manoeuvring a chariot, and once again his swiftness is given a place of prominence. Aeneas stands out for 'bravery of heart' (*forti pectore*).

Statius thus offers us another in the series of reminders of *Aeneid* 4 and the figure of Dido. But in this instance the object of comparison is not the Carthaginian queen but her attractive visitor. The poet compliments Celer by suggesting obliquely a parallel between him and Aeneas, on his way to Italy and to the foundation of Rome. Celer, too, is travelling, but much history has passed and now he is journeying away from a well-established fatherland in order to help preserve its imperial destiny in a distant place.

---

[102] For Celer's characterization as *iuvenis*, see also 6 as well as 104.

[103] The only other appearance of the phrase in Latin poetry is at *Silv.* 1.5.60–1: *nec si Baianis veniat novus hospes ab oris/talia despiciet* ('Were a new visitor to come from Baiae's shores, he would not scorn such (as this)…'). In prose, we also have Cic. *Ver.* 2.2.94, Sen. *Dial.* 9.11.10, and Apul. *Met.* 1.10. Servius (*ad A.* 11.93) adopts the phrase to describe Aeneas.

264 THE POETIC WORLD OF STATIUS' *SILVAE*

The Poem's Conclusion

As the poem begins to draw to a close, Statius imagines Celer's return, and the poem turns from a *propemptikon*, wishing the traveller well, to a *prosphoneticon*, that is, a joyful greeting upon safe return from a time away:[104]

> ergo erit illa dies qua te maiora daturus
> Caesar ab emerito iubeat discedere bello.
> at nos hoc iterum stantes in litore vastos
> cernemus fluctus aliasque rogabimus auras.
> o tum quantus ego aut quanta votiva movebo
> plectra lyra, cum me magna cervice ligatum
> attolles umeris atque in mea pectora primum
> incumbes e puppe novus servataque reddes
> colloquia inque vicem medios narrabimus annos...
>
> (Stat. Silv. 3.2.127–35)

And so that day will come when Caesar, ready to offer you greater things, orders you to withdraw from your completed war service. But, standing once more on this shore, we will behold the endless waves and will ask for other breezes (130). O how grand will I be then or with how grand a lyre will I strike my quills in prayer when you will raise me, bound to your mighty neck, on your shoulders and, fresh from the boat, you will lean upon my chest and you will grant me the conversations you have stored up and in turn we will tell each other of the years in-between! (135)

Ovid again helps us at the start. He uses the initial phrase *ergo erit illa dies* of Gaius Caesar departing to fight the Parthians: *ergo erit illa dies, qua tu, pulcherrime rerum,/quattuor in niveis aureus ibis equis* ('And so that day will come when you, most beautiful of things, will progress golden, on four snow-white horses', Ov. *Ars* 1.213–14). Ovid anticipates a triumph for Gaius that never occurred because of his untimely death. But the compliment to Celer, and vicariously, to Domitian is clear. These are grand affairs in which Celer has a share.

Emerito bello speaks to Celer's own potential military valour and its just reward.[105] *At nos*, in turn, anticipates Statius' own position as he awaits the

---

[104] For a discussion of lines 127–43 as a *prosphonetikon*, see Cairns (2007) 162–3.

[105] At *Silv.* 3.5.7, while using the phrase *quattuor emeritis lustris* (i.e., twenty years of military service), Statius compares himself to Ulysses and, implicitly, war-service to the writing of

READING TRAVEL (STATIUS' *SILVAE* 3.2) 265

arrival of his friend.[106] The adjacent phrase *in litore vastos...fluctus* adds an epic tone to the proceedings. As we have seen to be the poet's regular practice, Statius turns to Virgil to help guide his readers. The context is again *Aeneid* 1 as the narrator tells of the tempest that the winds arouse when they 'roll endless billows to the shore' (*vastos volvunt ad litora fluctus*, 86).[107] So the poet furnishes an epic setting for the advent of the hero after a time of menacing activity and also posits himself, vividly through the strong deictic *o* followed by the emphatic *ego*,[108] his grand lyre in hand, as the equally grand bard whose prayers have been answered.[109]

Line 131, with its initial *o* followed by two exclamatory adjectives, returns us to Horace: *o qui complexus et gaudia quanta fuerunt!* ('O what embraces and what great joys there were!' *S.* 1.5.43). The scene documents a moment when Horace, on his journey to Brundisium, is reunited with his beloved fellow-poet Virgil. Statius thus adds the energy of his great poetic predecessor to conveying the depth of his emotion upon being re-joined by the returning Celer.[110]

And with imagined arrival Statius makes a by now familiar turn away from epic to elegy, from impersonal *gesta* accomplished at a distance to the emotional immediacy by which cherisher greets cherished upon his advent. The sheer physicality of response takes us purposefully back to earlier moments in the poem which reach a summary climax here and help round out the whole. *Cervice*, for instance, reminds us of the word's use at line 58, when lingering on a beloved neck was no longer allowed because of the exigencies of departure. The word *cervix* also serves to recall the use of *collum* in an elegant gem by Catullus. Here, too, we are in a situation involving absence and homecoming. The poet has received news of Veranius' arrival,

---

epic. Here Celer would be the Ulysses figure and his deeds would be the subject of epic. Cf. also *Silv.* 2.2.142 and Pollius' well-managed ship of life (*emeritam puppem*).

[106] Cf. once more Virgil's first *Eclogue* at lines 64–6 which have parallel beginnings followed by two verbs in the future tense: *ibimus* and *veniemus* in Virgil, *cernemus* and *rogabimus* in Statius. (The latter two form a unique pair.) In the earlier poet, we are dealing with a form of exile to foreign parts. In Statius, we share in the joy of a return from a time away in distant lands.

[107] Since Virgil's own source is Hom. *Od.* 5.296, Statius, as often, draws doubly on his epic heritage; see Van Dam (2006) *passim*.

[108] The juxtaposition *quantus ego* is unique in classical Latin as is the subsequent phrase *quanta lyra*.

[109] *Votiva* also takes us back into the poem, to Statius' initial prayers (*votis*, 3) to the gods and to the lengthy prayers (*longis votis*, 100) with which the speaking 'I' will follow his patron.

[110] Statius thus helps our thoughts turn back to his earlier allusion to *Carm.* 1.3. His own reunion with Celer brings with it a happy ending missing from Horace's *propemptikon* to Virgil.

266   THE POETIC WORLD OF STATIUS' *SILVAE*

and the depth of his emotion is manifest as he, like Statius, prepares to listen to his friend's tale of travels in Spain:[111]

> visam te incolumem audiamque Hiberum
> narrantem loca, facta, nationes,
> ut mos est tuus, applicansque collum
> iucundum os oculosque suaviabor.
>
> (Catul. 9.6–9)

I will look at you, safe and sound, and will listen to you telling of the places, deeds, tribes of the Hiberi, as is your wont, and leaning against your neck I will kiss your sweet mouth and eyes.

Pectora, likewise, looks back to the word's several previous appearances. The first is at line 51 where the speaker's heart (*pectus*) grows cold at the prospect of what is in store for his departing friend. We next directly enter his heart (*pectore*, 82, juxtaposed with *ego*) as he ponders the days and nights of worry ahead. In the third instance he tells of his 'faithful heart' (*pectore fido*, 99) because of which he will never truly be apart from his absent comrade.[112]

The phrase *e puppe novus* serves a similar purpose. *E puppe*, for instance, acts as a reminder of the earlier occurrence of the words at line 56 where the *magister* bids an end to all delays.[113] And for *novus* we think back to line 59 where the speaker will be the very last of the whole throng (*e plebe novissimus omni*) to step ashore, and therefore to leave his dear friend behind, as the ship prepares to sail away.[114]

In summary, taken as a group these self-references serve to leaven the epic aspects of Statius' unique *propemptikon*. The general, expansive overview of the hazards of travel by sea and the individual challenges confronting Celer as he makes his way to military service on behalf of Rome are counterbalanced, softened, and personalized by the immediacy which these elegiac and lyric moments of private, personal feeling bring to the text.

---

[111] For the telling of stories after the end of a sea voyage that has parted lovers, see also Ov. *Am.* 2.11.49–56.

[112] *Fido* in turn looks back to *oscula fida* (57).

[113] The form of the accompanying verb, *incumbes*, is a unique appearance. Forms of the word *puppis* have already appeared at 29, 47, 56, 75, and 103. The start of the voyage brings an end to the display of personal emotion. Its conclusion initiates a renewal of individual, personal sentiment.

[114] Cf. Ov. *Her.* 13.99 (Laodamia warning Protesilaus): *de navi novissimus exi* ('be the last to leave the ship').

READING TRAVEL (STATIUS' *SILVAE* 3.2) 267

Here, as often in the elegiac corpus itself, they are occasioned by departure and arrival, by the sadness of leave-taking and the joy of safe return.

Celer will be the first to speak:

> tu rapidum Euphraten et regia Bactra sacrasque
> antiquae Babylonis opes et Zeu<g>ma, Latinae
> pacis iter, qua dulce nemus florentis Idumes,
> quo pretiosa Tyros rubeat, quo purpura suco
> Sidoniis iterata cadis, ubi germine primum
> candida felices sudent opobalsama virgae.
>
> (Stat. *Silv.* 3.2.136–41)

You the rushing Euphrates and royal Bactra and the holy wealth of ancient Babylon and Zeugma, path of Latin peace, where the sweet woods of flourishing Idume, with what juice costly Tyre reddens, with what juice the purple twice dipped in Sidonian vats, where, first from the bud (140), the fertile branches sweat bright balsam.

The places that Statius singles out for the opening of Celer's narrative all have associations with Alexander the Great. He built the famous bridge of boats that crossed the Euphrates at Zeugma. Lucan (8.237) speaks of *Zeugma Pellaeum*, as if the city belonged to Alexander, and Pliny the Elder tells about the iron chain, still extant in his time, used as part of the bridge (*Nat.* 34.43.150).[115] During 329–327 BCE, he conquered Bactria, whose capital is Bactra.[116] He first entered Babylon in 331 and died there in 323. His corpse, originally meant for burial in Macedonia at Aegae, was co-opted by Ptolemy for original interment in Memphis, as we have seen.

For his final reference to Alexander the Great Statius thus connects major place names associated with him to Celer and his career, probably as military tribune stationed in Palestine.[117] To visit his grave is a mark of Celer's respect. For Statius to link him with Alexander and his heroic career is to

---

[115] See also *Nat.* 5.21.86, and Stat. *Silv.* 5.3.187 with context, for Zeugma's present political role. In a poem so concerned with metapoetics it would be surprising if Statius, out of the many possibilities, had not chosen Zeugma secondarily for its figurative sense as well as for its topographical and historical importance. As a figure of speech zeugma does not appear in classical Latin except in the commentators (once, first, in Asconius [*in Verr.* 1.18], then on several occasions in Porphyrio and Servius).

[116] For Bactra and the Euphrates, see Prop. 3.11.25–6, dealing with Semiramis of Babylon. The river is also mentioned on the shield of Aeneas (*A.* 8.726).

[117] Mention of Celer's 'great neck' (*magna cervice*, 132) may act as another small link between him and the personage to whom he will pay homage in due course.

268 THE POETIC WORLD OF STATIUS' *SILVAE*

make one last bow on his behalf to the epic tradition and, by implication, to honour his friend by imagining him as a modern successor to this grand inheritance.[118]

Mention of the River Euphrates in this context serves several purposes. It is, of course, a major point of demarcation between east and west or, as Statius says of Zeugma, with perhaps a touch of irony, part of the 'path of Latin peace' (*Latinae pacis iter*). This is to say that it brought to mind Rome's conquering of so much of the near east and of the need for military wherewithal and political wisdom to maintain the resultant control. Virgil famously names the Euphrates at *G.* 1.509 and 4.561, at the balancing conclusions of his poem's first and final books and in settings where Roman warfare is paramount.[119] He thus calls attention to an important topographical demarcation for Rome as it battles to preserve its gains,[120] but he does so metapoetically in a way that carefully demarcates the parameter of his own accomplishment.

In the context of *Silvae* 3.2, mention of the *rapidum Euphraten* can thus work in several directions. At *A.* 8.726, as depicted on the shield of Aeneas, Virgil describes the Euphrates as now 'gentler in its waves' (*mollior undis*). Statius' use of *rapidus*, by direct contrast with Virgil, suggests something in violent motion, grabbing what it can in its course, to allow the full etymology from *rapio*.[121] This in turn suggests that times have changed since the initiation of the *pax Augusta* at the battle of Actium and that the new *pax Latina*, if such indeed ever existed, needed constant, on the spot, vigilance to make it less a hope than a reality.[122]

As critics often note, the mention of the Euphrates, the 'great flow of the Assyrian river', at line 108 of Callimachus' second hymn, to Apollo, in a context that deals with poetic creativity, asks the reader to apply the lesson

---

[118] The literary references to the tomb of Alexander have their salient moments. The story of Octavian/Augustus' viewing the body, for instance, is well known (Suet. *Aug.* 18.1). Caligula stole and wore the hero's breastplate (Suet. *Cal.* 52). Lucan (9.153) has young Pompey speak of the 'shrine' (*adytis*) in which the corpse is placed, and in 10.14–52, Lucan details at length Caesar's viewing of the burial place (the word *adytis* appears again, at l.23). Lucan's language at 10.23–4, with its use of *manibus* and *duravit*, bears a similarity to Statius' at 117–18 (*manes...durat*).

[119] See Thomas and Scodel (1987) and Clauss (1988). More generally on the Euphrates as a demarcating figure see Newlands (2009), esp. 395.

[120] For the river's taming as a symbol of Roman domination, see Nisbet and Hubbard (1978) 137 and on *Carm.* 2.9.21–2.

[121] *Rapidus* thus also serves as contrast with the *stagna* of the Nile whose bank is *stagnata luto* (110) and whose stream is adored by shepherds (*pastoribus*) because it nourishes the flocks they feed.

[122] See Newlands (2009) 394–6.

READING TRAVEL (STATIUS' *SILVAE* 3.2)   269

of its initial declaration to the work of the great Alexandrian's later imitators. There, as the foundation statement of Callimachean poetics, the large stream of epic, with all the filth that it carries in its course, is contrasted with the smaller, purer brooks of more moderated poetic forms such as lyric (*Hymn* 2.105–14).

Let us take a start with Virgil's word *mollis*. The adjective appears twice earlier in the poem. The first is in the speaker's opening prayer to the gods that they 'strew a gentle sea' (*sternite molle fretum*, 3) for Celer as he goes on his way. The second looks to 'the gentle ring' (*molli gyro*) in which he begs the sea divinities to surround the vessel soon to depart. May the waters and their denizens be indulgent to Statius' dear patron as he journeys eastward! The elegiac quality of the voyage's initiation, as friend bids farewell to friend, gives place to the river's grasping quality as the poet turns for one last time to the epic implications of the risks inherent in Celer's travels and in the Roman martial activities that they anticipate.

As we turn to the metapoetic aspects of *rapidum*, Cicero offers initial help when discussing the rhetorical presentation of his cousin Gaius Visellius Varro, whose 'speaking was rushed and blinded by its speed' (*rapida et Celeritate caecata oratio, Brut.* 264).[123] On another occasion he complains in nearly Callimachean wording: 'For when the exposition is carried along like a rushing stream, although it grabs with it much of this and that, nevertheless there is nothing you might hold onto, nothing you might grasp, nor can you anywhere confine the rush of speech' (*cum enim fertur quasi torrens oratio, quamvis multa cuiusque modi rapiat, nihil tamen teneas, nihil apprehendas, nusquam orationem rapidam coerceas, Fin.* 2.3). The etymological play in which Cicero indulges by connecting *rapiat* and *rapidam* returns us to the rushing Euphrates and from there to the Callimachean strictures on over-extended modes of expression. Put another way, as someone associated with the *rapidus Euphrates*, Celer is also involved with the world of epic which we have seen run through the poem, and seafaring is its sustaining complement.

The adjective *rapidum* also helps confirm another contrast that we have been tracing. One of its opposites is *lentus*, a designation that we have seen earlier applied to swamps (*lentas paludes*, 67) and to Virgil's fortunate shepherd, at ease in the shade (*lentus in umbra*). It returns us to the realm of inland waters which here serve the place of Callimachus' limpid streams

---

[123] The orator's language confirms Statius' implicit association of (swift) Celer with the *rapidum Euphraten*.

270   THE POETIC WORLD OF STATIUS' *SILVAE*

that by distinction put into relief the grandiosity of epic magniloquence. Another item that shares in this concentration on reticence and refinement is *angustos amnes* (67), the narrow streams that are the neighbours of 'slow swamps' and equally at home in a poetics of control, disdaining rivers that sweep all before them.

And here the Nile, for all its implicit glory as the mainstay of its country, acts in counterpoint to Callimachus', and for the moment Celer's, Euphrates. We have seen how the attribute *paludosi* (108) serves to connect the majestic river not with epic over-abundance but with the quiet of fresh-water ponds and rivulets. Nature governs the energy that might in other circumstances prove ruinous.[124]

It is surely purposeful that the same verb that Statius uses to describe its bank keeping the Nile in place (*coerceat*, 109) was employed by Cicero (*coerceas*), in the passage we examined earlier from the *De finibus*, for the reining in of language that hurries along too quickly and, in the case of the large river, carries with it whatever is within reach. As Statius would have it, the Nile, while in certain respects parallel in scope and reputation to the Euphrates, claims kinship instead with the calm waters of lakes and streams. We are, for a moment at least, in the province of leisured tourism, not to speak of personal feeling, instead of the world of externals, vivified here in the hectic, competitive setting of Roman power. The first is captured, throughout the poem, poetically by the voices of elegy, lyric, and pastoral that Statius so nimbly puts before us in our imaginations as we follow Celer's very palpable voyage.

Statius' far briefer vignette has the poem's last words:

> ast ego devictis dederim quae busta Pelasgis
> quaeve laboratas claudat mihi pagina Thebas
>
> (Stat. *Silv.* 3.2.142–3)

But I myself the pyres which I gave to the subdued Pelasgians or the page that closes my toiled-over Thebes.

What Statius has accomplished during Celer's absence is appropriately 'I' centred: he has finished writing his extraordinary epic, the *Thebaid*. Celer has devoted the intervening time to externals, to the purposes of Rome.

---

[124] The harnessed grandeur of the Nile may in fact stand as an emblem of Statius' own present poem, confining epic expanse within the bounds of a more intimate poetic type.

READING TRAVEL (STATIUS' *SILVAE* 3.2) 271

Statius, by contrast, has crafted a masterpiece of the imagination, his splendid opus in the tradition of Homer and his beloved Virgil.

It is appropriate that our present poem conclude with reference to the end of the *Thebaid*, to the pyres (*busta*, 12.798) that the poet gave to the unburied dead and at which the great terminating scene of mourning takes place. In looking here at his own accomplishment—the word *ego* is duly prominent[125]—Statius is taking the role, and absorbing the power, of the Theseus that he creates within his poem, practicing *clementia* and authorizing full burial rites for the defeated who were slain.

It is also noteworthy that the poem's final word names the city of Thebes, not the poem about its history. Statius could have directly recalled his magnum opus, had he so chosen, and as he does, for instance, at *Silv.* 3.5.36 (*mea Thebais*) or 4.4.89 (*Thebais*).[126] Instead, by mentioning the city and not the poem, he calls attention to what he entitles, at *Silvae* 2.2.60–1, the 'Theban lyre' (*chelys Thebais*), the magical instrument by which Amphion saw into place the walls of the city.[127] And, at *Thebaid* 8.232–3, Thebans themselves tell of '...stones that creep to the Tyrian lyre and Amphion giving life to hard boulders...' (...*Tyriam reptantia saxa/ad chelyn et duras animantem Amphiona cautes*...).

At line 41 Statius has already designated himself *Phoebeum Amphiona* as if he too were a protégé of Apollo as he produced his admirable *exemplum* of poetic artistry. So at the end, by implication, Statius imagines himself as the original, wonder-working singer who literally constructed the walls of Thebes (*Thebae*) and not just the modern recreator in poetry of her famous history. *Laboratas* can thus be looked at in at least three ways.[128] It calls attention to the imaginative effort that went into the production of a great poem.[129] It tells of a city struggled over in battle for its leadership—the

---

[125] Cf. the equally forceful uses of *ego* at 82 and 131, and of *nos* at 129.

[126] See also *Silv.* 4.7.26 (*Thebais multa cruciata lima*), with its sources at Hor. *S.* 1.10.65–6 and *Ars* 291 (*limae labor*). On the relationship with Virgil that Statius summarizes at 4.7.25–8, see Hinds (1998) 93–4. The *Thebaid* itself is personified at *Theb.* 12.812. See also *Silv.* 1 *praef.* 6 (*Thebaide mea*) and 4 *praef.* 19 (*Thebaidos meae*). At *Silv.* 5.3.233–4, as we have seen, in a context honouring his father, Statius denotes the *Thebais* as *nostra* instead of *mea*, as if the poem's creation had been a joint effort of mentor and disciple.

[127] In the *Silvae*, Amphion also appears vicariously at 3.1.16 (*Tyrio plectro*) and 115 (*Amphionae arces*). See also *Theb.* 1.10; 2.454–5; 4.357 and 611; 7.456 and, vicariously, 665; 10.787 and 873.

[128] On the interpretation of *laboratas*, see further Newlands (2009) 393–6. A partial Virgilian parallel is to be found at *A.* 1.639 (*laboratas vestes*).

[129] For the *labor* that went into the creation of the epic cf. *Silv.* 3.5.35 (*longi laboris*) and 4.4.88 (*Sidonios labores*), as well as the more general statement at 4.7.25–8 which adds a comparison with Virgil.

272   THE POETIC WORLD OF STATIUS' *SILVAE*

essential subject-matter of the *Thebaid*. At the same time it views the author himself as a type of spiritual Amphion, generating from his mind the effortful *paginae* that tell the story so superbly.

We looked earlier at the many meanings of the verb *pandere*, particularly with the double-entendre that the verb suggests between the opening of the gates of Thebes and the publication of the poem about the city's saga, between the narrative story and the epic that details it. Similarly expansive meanings centre on the word *claudat*. Horace, for instance, uses the verb to denote the forming of words into poetry (*S.* 1.10.59, 2.1.28). Statius gives it especial stress by personifying *pagina*. The page or, if we interpret the word as a synecdoche, the many pages which make up the whole, has the power to bring the work to a close.[130]

But *claudat* has a sense that is especially à propos here. *Pandere* looks both to the end of war at Thebes and to the promulgation of its story. *Claudat*, likewise, suggests that the city can be safely sealed away, and the shutting of the gates suggests closure for the poem itself.[131] And with the completion of the *Thebaid* comes a series of fulfilments, not least for Maecius Celer. His voyage will be happily finished with the mutual telling of stories. Statius himself, as he says at the end of the *Thebaid*, has earned the quiet of his harbour after the long sea- travel of writing an epic (12.809).

Last of the satisfactions is the rounding-off of the present poem itself, a *propemptikon* formally but very much about a series of voyages both literal and figurative. These tell a wide variety of tales, be they about Aeneas or Isis, Alexander or Cleopatra, or Horace's Virgil off to Greece or Horace himself ready to face whatever destiny brings after death. They are also concerned metapoetically with the imagination's travel involved in producing great literature, in the long expedition that betokens the writing of epic, or in the emotionality of the individual participants that draws us into the more succinct realms of elegy, lyric and pastoral and sets into relief the grand events of the primary tale.

The initial words of the poem's penultimate verse lead us one last time in one of the most important directions that we have been following, namely toward Virgil. His first use of the phrase *ast ego* occurs at *Aeneid* 1.46, where

---

[130] The word *claudat* is appropriate for a codex just as *pandere* might suggest a scroll.
[131] Cf. the other uses of *claudo* at 53 (*claudere*) and 70 (*clausi*) and of the compound *excludite* at 12. Enclosure and release, in whatever form, is a pattern that Statius would have sensed in the opening scene of the *Aeneid* which is so influential on our present poem. See, e.g., *A.* 1.56 (*claustra*), 141 (*clauso carcere*), and, later, of the gates of War (*claudentur*, 294).

Juno is exclaiming on her powerless opposition to the Trojans.[132] It occurs again at 7.308, where once more the queen of the gods is ruing her own impotence against Aeneas. The words thus serve as demarcations for the first and second halves of the epic as we turn from tempest at sea to war on land.[133]

In Statius' hands, however, they remind us of the poem's opening words (*di quibus*) and of their several appearances in Virgil's epic. By taking us back to the start of his poem by means of a bow to his poetic model and mentor, Statius thus brings unity to his accomplishment in such a way that his own poetic voyage seems steadied by that of his great predecessor who set the pattern for so much to follow in the Western world of letters including his follower's own distinguished contributions.

---

[132] Chronologically, the first appearances that we have preserved of the phrase are at Hor. *Epod.* 15.24 and Liv. 10.19.18.

[133] It is interesting that Statius' two references to the impotence of Juno occur at the moment when the poet himself emphasizes his own authority. He is like his own creature Theseus. The Athenian establishes moral order in a war-weary world while the poet brings his own work to a judicious, yet dynamic conclusion.

Bibliography

Adams, J. N. (1982). *The Latin Sexual Vocabulary*. Baltimore, MD: The Johns Hopkins University Press.

Augoustakis, A. (2010). *Motherhood and the Other: Fashioning Female Power in Flavian Epic*. Oxford: Oxford University Press.

Augoustakis, A., Buckley, E., and Stocks, C. (2019). 'Undamning Domitian? Reassessing the Last Flavian *princeps*'. *ICS* 44.2: 233–452.

Bailey, C., ed. (2017). *De rerum natura libri sex. Vol. 3: Commentary, Books IV–VI, addenda, indexes*. Oxford: Oxford University Press.

Baumann, H. (2019). *Das Epos im Blick: Intertextualität und Rollenkonstruktionen in Martials Epigrammen und Statius' Silvae*. Berlin: Walter de Gruyter.

Bessone, F. (2022a). 'Grecia e Roma nell' *Achilleide*'. *RCCM* 64.1: 101–21.

Bessone, F. (2022b). 'The Hut and the Temple: Private Aetiology and Augustan Models in *Silvae* 3.1'. In A. Lóio, ed., *Editing and Commenting on the Silvae*, 197–225. Leiden: Brill.

Braund, S. (1996). 'Ending Epic: Statius, Theseus and a Merciful Release'. *PCPhS* 42: 1–23.

Brink, C. O., ed. (1985). *Horace on Poetry. Vol. 2: The Ars Poetica*. Cambridge: Cambridge University Press.

Cairns, F. (2007). *Generic Composition in Greek and Roman Poetry*. Rev. ed. Ann Arbor, MI: Michigan Classical Press.

Cancik, H. (1978). 'Tibur Vopisci: Statius, *Silvae* 1.3: Villa Tiburtina Manili Vopisci'. *Boreas* 1: 116–34.

Casali, S. (2020). 'Evander and the Invention of the Prehistory of Latium in Virgil's *Aeneid*'. In M. Aberson, M. C. Biela, M. Di Fazio, and M. Wullschleger, eds., *Nos sumus Romani qui fuerunt ante…: Memory of Roman Past*, 145–68. Bern: Peter Lang.

Cawsey, F. (1983). 'Statius, *Silvae* II.iv: More than an Ex-parrot?' *The Proceedings of the African Classical Associations* 17: 69–84.

Cheesman, C. (2009). 'Names in *-por* and Slave Naming in Republican Rome'. *CQ* 59: 511–31.

Chinn, C. (2022). *Visualizing the Poetry of Statius: An Intertextual Approach*. Leiden: Brill.

Clauss, J. (1988). 'Vergil and the Euphrates Revisited'. *AJPh* 109: 309–20.

Coleman, K., ed. (1988). *Statius, Silvae IV*. Oxford: Clarendon Press.

Coleman, K. (1999). 'Mythological Figures as Spokespersons in Statius' *Silvae*'. In F. De Angelis, and S. Muth, eds., *Im Spiegel des Mythos, Bilderwelt und Lebenswelt; Lo specchio del mito, immaginario e realtà*, 67–80. Wiesbaden: Reichert.

Colton, R. E. (1967). 'Parrot Poems' in Ovid and Statius,' *CB* 43: 71–8.

Copley, F. O. (1956). *Exclusus Amator: A Study in Latin Love Poetry*. Madison, WI: American Philological Association.

276 BIBLIOGRAPHY

Courtney, E. (1984). 'Criticism and Elucidations of the *Silvae* of Statius'. *TAPhA* 104: 327–41.

Courtney, E. (1987). 'Problems in Tibullus and Lygdamus'. *Maia* 21: 29–32.

Courtney, E, ed. (1990). *P. Papinii Stati Silvae*. Oxford: Clarendon Press.

Dalby, A. (2000). *Empires of Pleasure: Luxury and Indulgence in the Roman World*. London: Routledge.

D'Arms, J. (1974). 'Puteoli in the Second Century of the Roman Empire: A Social and Economic Study'. *JRS* 64: 104–24.

Davis, M. A. (2016). '*Ratis audax*: Valerius Flaccus' Bold Ship'. In A. Augoustakis, ed., *Oxford Readings in Flavian Epic*, 17–44. Oxford: Oxford University Press.

Dewar, M. (2002). '*Siquid habent veri vatum praesagia*: Ovid in the 1st–5th Centuries A.D.' In B. W. Boyd, ed., *Brill's Companion to Ovid*, 383–412. Leiden: Brill.

Dietrich, J. S. (2002). 'Dead Parrots Society'. *AJP* 123: 95–110.

Dupont, F. (1992). *Daily Life in Ancient Rome* (trans. C. Woodall). Oxford: Blackwell.

Econimo, F. (2020). *La Parola e gli Occhi: L'ekphrasis nella Tebaide di Stazio*. Pisa: Edizioni Della Normale.

Elder, J. P. (1952). 'Horace, *C.* i, 3'. *AJPh* 73: 140–58.

Ernout, A. and Meillet, A., eds. (1959). *Dictionnaire étymologique de la langue latine*. Paris: Klincksieck.

Esposito, P. (2019). 'Campanian Geography in Statius' *Silvae*'. In A. Augoustakis, and R. J. Littlewood, eds., *Campania in the Flavian Poetic Imagination*, 101–12. Oxford: Oxford University Press.

Evans, H. (1993). '*In Tiburtium usum*: Special Arrangements in the Roman Water System (Frontinus, *Aq.* 6.5)'. *AJA* 97: 447–55.

Faber, R. (2018). 'Intermediality and Ekphrasis in Latin Epic Poetry'. *G&R* 65: 1–14.

Fitzgerald, W. (2000). *Slavery and the Roman Literary Imagination*. Cambridge: Cambridge University Press.

Foster, B. O. (1899). 'Notes on the Symbolism of the Apple in Classical Antiquity'. *HSPh* 10: 39–55.

Garrod, H. P., ed. (1901). *Horati Flacci: Opera*. Oxford: Clarendon Press.

Gevartius, I. C. (1616). *P. Papinius Statius, opera omnia*. Leiden: Iacob Marcum.

Gibson, B. J. (2006). 'The *Silvae* and Epic'. In R. R. Nauta, H.-J. Van Dam, and J. J. L. Smolenaars, eds., *Flavian Poetry*, 106–83. Leiden: Brill.

Gunderson, E. (2021). *The Art of Complicity in Martial and Statius: The Epigrams, Silvae, and Domitianic Rome*. Oxford: Oxford University Press.

Hardie, A. (1983). *Statius and the Silvae: Poets, Patrons and Epideixis in the Graeco-Roman World*. Liverpool: F. Cairns.

Hardie, A. (2003). 'Poetry and Politics at the Games of Domitian'. In A. J. Boyle and W. J. Dominik, eds., *Flavian Rome: Culture, Image, Text*, 125–47. Leiden: Brill.

Hardie, P. R. (1993). *The Epic Successors of Virgil: A Study in the Dynamics of a Tradition*. Cambridge: Cambridge University Press.

Hardie, P. R. (2006). 'Statius' Ovidian Poetics and the Tree of Atedius Melior (*Silvae* 2.3)'. In R. R. Nauta, H.-J. Van Dam, and J. J. L. Smolenaars, eds., *Flavian Poetry*, 207–21. Leiden: Brill.

Harrison, S. J. (1995). 'Horace, Pindar, Iullus Antonius, and Augustus: *Odes* 4.2'. *In* S. J. Harrison, ed., *Homage to Horace: A Bimillenary Celebration*, 108–27. Oxford: Clarendon Press.

BIBLIOGRAPHY 277

Harrison, S. J. (2007). 'The Primal Voyage and the Ocean of Epos: Two Aspects of Metapoetic Imagery in Catullus, Virgil and Horace'. *Dictynna* 4 (https://doi.org/10.4000/dictynna.143, accessed on 31 May 2022).

Heyworth, S. J. (2011). 'Roman Topography and Latin Diction'. *PBSR* 79: 43–65.

Hinds, S. (1998). *Allusion and Intertext: Dynamics of Appropriation in Roman Poetry*. Cambridge: Cambridge University Press.

Hinds, S. (2001). 'Cinna, Statius, and "Immanent Literary History" in the Cultural Economy'. In J. Schwindt, ed., *L'histoire littéraire immanente dans la poésie latine*, 221–65. Geneva: Fondation Hardt.

James, P. (2006). 'Two Poetic and Parodic Parrots in Latin Literature'. In J. Courtney and P. James, eds., *The Role of the Parrot in Selected Texts from Ovid to Jean Rhys*, 1–32. Lewiston: Edwin Mellen Press.

Janan, M. (2020). 'The Father's Tragedy: Assessing Paternity in Statius, *Silvae* 2.1'. *TAPhA* 150: 181–230.

Kershner, S. M. (2006). *Self-Fashioning and Horatian Allusion in Statius' Silvae*. Ph.D. diss., State University of New York at Buffalo.

Kirichenko, A. (2017). '*Beatus carcer / tristis harena*: The Spaces of Statius' *Silvae*'. In V. Rimell and M. Asper, eds., *Imagining Empire: Political Space in Hellenistic and Roman Literature*, 167–88. Heidelberg: Universitätsverlag.

Kondratieff, E. (2014). 'Future City in the Heroic Past: Rome, Romans, and Landscapes in *Aeneid* 6–8'. In A. Kemezis, ed., *Urban Dreams and Realities in Antiquity: Remains and Representations of the Ancient City*, 165–228. Leiden: Brill.

Konstan, D. (2008). *A Life Worthy of the Gods: The Materialist Psychology of Epicurus*. Las Vegas, NV: Parmenides Publishing.

Kronenberg, L. J. (2017). 'A Petronian Parrot in a Neronian Cage: A New Reading of Statius' *Silvae* 2.4'. *CQ* 67: 558–72.

Kreuz, G. E. (2017). *Besonderer Ort, poetischer Blick: Untersuchungen zu Räumen und Bildern in Statius' Silven*. Göttingen: Vandenhoeck & Ruprecht.

Laguna Mariscal, G., ed. (1992). *Estacio, Silvas III*. Madrid: Fundación Pastor de estudios clásicos.

Lausberg, H. (1998). *Handbook of Literary Rhetoric: A Foundation for Literary Study*. Leiden: Brill.

Leberl, J. (2004). *Domitian und die Dichter: Poesie als Medium der Herrschaftsdarstellung*. Göttingen: Vandenhoeck & Ruprecht.

Leonard, W. E. and Smith, S. B., eds. (1961). *T. Lucreti Cari: De Rerum Natura: Libri Sex*. Madison, WI: The University of Wisconsin Press.

Littlewood, A. R. (1968). 'The Symbolism of the Apple in Greek and Roman Literature'. *HSPh* 72: 147–81.

Lockyer, C. W. (1967). 'Horace's Propemptikon and Vergil's Voyage'. *CW* 61: 42–5.

Malamud, M. (2007). 'A Spectacular Feast: *Silvae* 4.2'. *Arethusa* 40.2: 223–44.

Maltby, R. (1991). *A Lexicon of Ancient Latin Etymologies*. Leeds: Francis Cairns.

Mankin, D., ed. (1995). *Horace, Epodes*. Cambridge: Cambridge University Press.

Mann, E. (1926). 'Some Private Houses in Ancient Rome'. *CW* 19: 127–32.

Manolaraki, E. (2013). *Noscendi Nilum cupido: Imagining Egypt from Lucan to Philostratus*. Berlin: Walter de Gruyter.

Marshall, A. R. (2009). 'Statius and the *Veteres*: *Silvae* 1.3 and the Homeric House of Alcinous'. *Scholia* 18: 78–88.

278 BIBLIOGRAPHY

Marshall, A. R. (2011). '*Spectandi Voluptas*: Ecphrasis and Poetic Immortality in Statius *Silvae* 1.1'. *CJ* 106: 321–47.

Martelli, F. (2009). 'Plumbing Helicon: Poetic Property and the Material World of Statius' *Silvae*'. *MD* 62: 145–77.

Mayer, R., ed. (1994). *Horace, Epistles: Book I*. Cambridge: Cambridge University Press.

Montiglio, S. (2018). *The Myth of Hero and Leander: The History and Reception of an Enduring Greek Legend*. London: I. B. Tauris.

Morzadec, F. (2003). 'Métamorphoses du paysage d'Ovide à Stace: Le 'paysage ovidien' dans la *Silve* II, 3'. In E. Bury and P. Laurens, eds., *Lectures d'Ovide publiées à la mémoire de Jean-Pierre Néraudau*, 89–105. Paris: Belles Lettres.

Morzadec, F. (2009). *Les images du monde: Structure, écriture et esthétique du paysage dans les oeuvres de Stace et Silius Italicus*. Brussels: Latomus.

Myers, K. S. (2000). '*Miranda fides*: Poets and Patrons in Paradoxographical Landscapes in Statius' *Silvae*'. *MD* 44: 103–38.

Myers, K. S. (2002). '*Psittacus Redux*: Imitation and Literary Polemic in Statius, *Silvae* 2.4'. In J. F. Miller, C. Damon, and K. S. Myers, eds., *Vertis in Vsum: Studies in Honor of Edward Courtney*, 188–99. Munich: K. G. Saur.

Myers, K. S. (2005). '*Docta otia*: Garden Ownership and Configurations of Leisure in Statius and Pliny the Younger'. *Arethusa* 38: 103–29.

Mynors, R. A. B., ed. (1969). *P. Vergili Maronis opera*. Oxford: Oxford University Press.

Mynors, R. A. B., ed. (1990). *Virgil, Georgics*. Oxford: Clarendon Press.

Nelis, D. and Nelis-Clément, J. (2020). 'Rome and Away: Space and Structure in the First Book of the *Silvae* of Statius'. In L. E. Baumer, D. Nelis, and M. Royo, eds., *Lire la Ville 2: Fragments d'une archéologie littéraire de Rome à l'époque flavienne*, 177–201. Bordeaux: Ausonius.

Newlands, C. E. (1988). 'Horace and Statius at Tibur: an Interpretation of *Silvae* 1. 3'. *ICS* 13: 95–111.

Newlands, C. E. (1991). '*Silvae* 3. 1 and Statius' Poetic Temple'. *CQ* 41: 438–52.

Newlands, C. E. (2002). *Statius' Silvae and the Poetics of Empire*. Cambridge: Cambridge University Press.

Newlands, C. E. (2005). 'Animal Claqueurs: Statius *Silv.* 2.4 and 2.5'. In W. W. Batstone and G. Tissol, eds., *Defining Genre and Gender in Latin Literature*, 151–73. New York: Peter Lang.

Newlands, C. E. (2009). 'Statius' Self-conscious Poetics: Hexameter on Hexameter'. In W. J. Dominik, J. Garthwaite, and R. A. Roche, eds., *Writing Politics in Imperial Rome*, 387–404. Leiden: Brill.

Newlands, C. E., ed. (2011a). *Statius, Silvae: Book II*. Cambridge: Cambridge University Press.

Newlands, C. E. (2011b). 'Martial, *Epigrams* 9.61 and Statius, *Silvae* 2.3: Branches from the Same Tree'. *Scholia* 20: 93–111.

Newlands, C. E. (2012). *Statius, Poet Between Rome and Naples*. London: Bristol Classical Press.

Newlands, C. E. (2013). 'Architectural Ecphrasis in Roman Poetry'. In T. Papanghelis, S. Harrison, and S. Frangoulides, eds., *Generic Interfaces in Latin Literature: Encounters, Interactions and Transformations*, 55–78. Berlin: Walter de Gruyter.

BIBLIOGRAPHY 279

Newlands, C. E. (2017). 'The Early Reception of the *Silvae*: From Statius to Sidonius'. In F. Bessone and M. Fucecchi, eds., *The Literary Genres in the Flavian Age: Canons, Transformations, Reception*, 167–84. Berlin: Walter de Gruyter.

Newlands, C. E. (2021). 'Statius' *Propemptikon* and the Geopoetics of *Silvae* 3.2'. In M. Y. Myers and E. Zimmermann Damer, eds., *Travel, Geography, and Empire in Latin Poetry*, 134–56. London: Routledge.

Newlands, C. E. (2022). 'Sound and Reception in Statius' *Silvae*'. *RCCM* 64.1: 19–39.

Newmyer, S. T. (1979). *The Silvae of Statius: Structure and Theme*. Leiden: Brill.

Nisbet, R. G. M. (1978). '*Felicitas* at Surrentum (Statius, *Silvae* II. 2)'. *JRS* 68: 1–11.

Nisbet, R. G. M. and Hubbard, M., eds. (1970). *A Commentary on Horace, Odes Book I*. Oxford: Clarendon Press.

Nisbet, R. G. M. and Hubbard, M., eds. (1978). *A Commentary on Horace, Odes Book II*. Oxford: Clarendon Press.

Nisbet, R. G. M. and Hubbard, M., eds. (1991). *A Commentary on Horace, Odes Book II*. Oxford: Oxford University Press.

Nisbet, R. G. M. and Rudd, N., eds. (2004). *A Commentary on Horace, Odes Book III*. Oxford: Oxford University Press.

Oliensis, E. (1995). 'Life after Publication: Horace, "*Epistles*" 1.20'. *Arethusa* 28: 209–24.

Papaioannou, S. (2003). 'Civilizer and Leader: Vergil's Evander and his Role in the Origins of Rome'. *Mnemosyne* 56: 680–702.

Pease, A. S., ed. (1935). *Publi Vergili Maronis, Aeneidos: Liber quartus*. Cambridge, MA: Harvard University Press.

Pease, A. S., ed. (1958). *Cicero, De Natura Deorum libri III*. Cambridge, MA.: Harvard University Press.

Pederzani, O. (1995). *Il talamo, l'albero e lo Specchio: Saggio di commento a Stat. Silv.* I 2, II 3, III 4. Bari: Edipuglia.

Pichon, R. (1966). *Index Verborum Amatoriorum*. Hildesheim: Olms.

Pittà, A., ed. (2021). *P. Papinius Statius, Silvae liber I: I carmi di Domiziano. Vol. I: Introduzione al ciclo, epistola prefatoria, carme 1*. Florence: Felice le Monnier.

Pittà, A. (2022). 'Critica fra le righe: scelte lessicali pregnanti (nelle *Silvae*) e un problema testuale (in Petronio)', *RCCM* 64.1: 145–65.

Pucci, J. (1992). 'Horace and Virgilian Mimesis: A Re-reading of *Odes* 1.3'. *CW* 85: 659–73.

Purves, A., ed. (2017). *Touch and the Ancient Senses: The Senses in Antiquity*. London: Routledge.

Putnam, M. C. J. (1998). *Virgil's Epic Design: Ekphrasis in the Aeneid*. New Haven: Yale University Press.

Putnam, M. C. J. (2016). 'The sense of Two Endings: How Virgil and Statius Conclude'. *ICS* 41.1: 85–149.

Quinn, K. (1963). *Latin Explorations: Critical Studies in Roman Literature*. New York: Humanities Press.

Reed, J. (2016). '*Mora* in the *Aeneid*'. In P. Mitsis and I. Ziogas, eds., *Wordplay and Powerplay in Latin Poetry*, 87–105. Berlin: Walter de Gruyter.

Rimell, V. (2015). *The Closure of Space in Roman Poetics: Empire's Inward Turn*. Cambridge: Cambridge University Press.

280 BIBLIOGRAPHY

Rimell, V. (2018). 'Rome's Dire Straits: Claustrophobic Seas and *imperium sine fundo*'. In W. Fitzgerald and E. Spentzou, eds., *The Production of Space in Latin Literature*, 1–24. Oxford: Oxford University Press.

Rosati, G. (2019). '*Laudes Campaniae*: Myth and Fantasies of Power in Statius' *Silvae*'. In A. Augoustakis, and R. J. Littlewood, eds., *Campania in the Flavian Poetic Imagination*, 113–30. Oxford: Oxford University Press.

Rühl, M. (2006). *Literatur gewordener Augenblick: Die Silven des Statius im Kontext literarischer und sozialer Bedingungen von Dichtung*. Berlin: Walter de Gruyter.

Rühl, M. (2015). 'Creating the Distinguished Addressee: Literary Patronage in The Works of Statius'. In W. J. Dominik, C. E. Newlands, and K. Gervais, eds., *Brill's Companion to Statius*, 91–105. Leiden: Brill.

Russell, D. A. and Wilson, N. G., eds. and trans. (1981). *Menander Rhetor*. Oxford: Clarendon Press.

Saunders, N. J. (2006). *Alexander's Tomb*. New York: Basic Books.

Schulze, W. (1904). *Zur Geschichte lateinsicher Eigennamen*. Berlin: Weidmann.

Shackleton Bailey, D. R. and Parrott, C. A., eds. and trans. (2015). *Statius, Silvae*. Cambridge, MA: Harvard University Press.

Smith, J. M. (2007). 'Apostrophe, or the Lyric Art of Turning Away'. *Texas Studies in Literature and Language* 44: 411–37.

Spencer, D. (2010). *Roman Landscape: Culture and Identity*. Cambridge: Cambridge University Press.

Swetnam-Burland, M. (2015). *Egypt in Italy: Visions of Egypt in Roman Imperial Culture*. Cambridge: Cambridge University Press.

Taisne, A.-M. (1996). 'Échos épiques dans les *Silves* de Stace'. In F. Delarue et al., eds., *Epicedion: Hommage à P. Papinius Statius (Poitiers, 1996)*, 215–34. Poitiers: UFR langues littératures.

Tarrant, R. J., ed. (1976). *Seneca: Agamemnon*. Cambridge: Cambridge University Press.

Thomas, R. F., ed. (1988). *Virgil, Georgics*. 2 vols. Cambridge: Cambridge University Press.

Thomas, R. F. and Scodel, R. (1984). 'Vergil and the Euphrates'. *AJPh* 105: 115–21.

Van Dam, H.-J., ed. (1984). *P. Papinius Statius, Silvae Book II: A Commentary*. Leiden: Brill.

Van Dam, H.-J. (2006). 'Multiple Imitation of Epic Models in the *Silvae*'. In R. R. Nauta, H.-J. van Dam, and J. J. L. Smolenaars, eds., *Flavian Poetry*, 185–205. Leiden: Brill.

Van den Hout, M. P. J., ed. (1954). *M. Cornelii Frontonis, Epistulae*. Leiden: Brill.

Vessey, D. W. T. C. (1976). 'A Note on *latus*'. *LCM* 1: 39–40.

Vessey, D. W. T. C. (1981). 'Atedius Melior's Tree: Statius *Silvae* 2.3'. *CPh* 76: 46–52.

Vessey, D. W. T. C. (1983). '*Mediis discumbere in astris*'. *AC* 52: 206–20.

Vollmer, F., ed. (1898). *P. Papinii Statii Silvarum Libri*. Leipzig: Teubner.

White, P. (1975). 'The Friends of Martial, Statius, and Pliny, and the Dispersal of Patronage'. *HSPh* 79: 265–300.

Whitton, C., ed. (2013). *Pliny, Epistles: Book II*. Cambridge: Cambridge University Press.

Woodman, A. J. (1988). *Rhetoric in Classical Historiography*. London: Routledge.

Worman, N. (2015). *Landscape and the Spaces of Metaphor in Ancient Literary Theory and Criticism*. Cambridge: Cambridge University Press.

Wray, D. (2007). 'Wood: Statius' *Silvae* and the Poetics of Genius'. *Arethusa* 40: 127–43.

Zeiner, N. C. (2005). *Nothing Ordinary Here: Status as Creator of Distinction in the Silvae*. London: Routledge.

General Index

This index is selective and thus does not include common terms such as the Augustan age or Flavian age or recurrent topics in Statius' *Silvae* such as leisure and villas. Statius' relationship with the Augustan poets (e.g., Virgil, Horace, Propertius, Tibullus) is discussed throughout the volume, and we urge the reader to consult the extensive Index Locorum.

Abydos 23
Achaimenides 143–4
Achilles 90–1, 249, 251, 258
Actium 97, 100, 198, 225, 253, 259–62, 268
Aeneas 3–4, 6–7, 37, 48, 52, 73, 84, 86, 90, 95, 97–101, 107–8, 112, 115–16, 118, 129, 131, 133–4, 143, 153, 155, 157, 162, 164, 168, 176, 183–4, 187, 191–2, 194, 197–9, 205, 209, 211, 213–14, 216, 218–20, 227–8, 234–5, 245–6, 251–3, 263, 268, 272–3
Aeolus 225, 228–9
Agamemnon 90, 249, 251
Agenor 247–8
Alban games 7, 212–13
Albula 34
Alcinous 36–9, 184, 213
Alexander the Great
    burial place of 255, 257–62, 267, 272
Alexandria 248, 254, 257–60, 262, 269
Alexis 120
Alpheus, River 33, 41
Amphion 99–100, 229–30, 271–2
Anchises 115–16, 123, 176, 191, 218, 245, 254
Anio, River (Anien) 12, 14, 18, 20–4, 34, 40, 45
Anna Perenna 234, 263
Antaeus 139–40, 145
Antiphates 37, 39
Antium 36, 38
Anubis 258
Anxur 36, 38, 114
Apis 255, 259
Apollo 48, 68, 72, 75, 88, 127, 136, 166–7, 171–2, 186, 206–7, 211, 213, 230, 261, 268, 271
Appia, Via 114

Archemorus
    see under Opheltes
Ardea 36–8
Arethusa 33, 40, 57
Argiletum 98
Argos 101–2, 107, 147–9, 253
Aricia 35, 114
Aristaeus 130
artifacts
    in Statius' poetry 28–38
    asarota 30, 33
Ascanius 234–5, 245
Atedius Melior 5–7, 45–88
    parrot of 156–82
Auge 108
Aventine Hill 53, 55, 57–8, 109, 150

Babylon 267
Bacchus 61, 103, 141, 186, 197–200, 204–5, 207–8
Bactria 267
Baiae 36–8, 137, 224
Blaesus 76, 83–4, 86–8
Bosphorus 253
Brundisium 114, 265
Bruttium 24
Busiris 103

Cacus 53–6
    see also under Hercules
Cadmus 248
Caeles (Caelius) Vibenna 55
Caelian Hill 45, 53–5, 72
Caieta 36–9
Calliope 110–12, 130, 158
Camilla 130–1
Canopus 254–7
Capitoline Hill 53–5, 98–9, 194

284 GENERAL INDEX

Castor 223–4, 257
Catillus 42–3
Cecrops 255–7
Cerberus 145, 151, 255, 258
Ceres 197–9, 201
Chalcis 24, 227
Charon 146
Charybdis 40, 247
Circe 37, 39, 173
Cleopatra 9, 225, 253, 255, 259–62, 272
Cloanthus 218–19
Corinna
  parrot of 156–92
Corydon 120
Cumae 227–8
Cyclopes
  Brontes, Steropes, and Pyracmon
    132–3
Cycnus 166–7, 169, 171–2
Cyrene 139

Dacia 210–11
Daphnis 66, 76
Dares 108–9
Deiphobus 225
Delphi 136
Diana 35, 45, 57–61, 72, 113–14, 117–18, 136
Dicarchus 224
Dido 7, 9, 95, 106–7, 112, 117–18, 133–4,
    164, 168, 176, 183–4, 187, 191, 194, 198,
    205, 207, 209, 211, 213, 218–20, 234,
    245–6, 251–2, 263
Diomedes, king of Thrace 103
Dioscuri
  see under Castor, Pollux
Domitian
  and Alba Longa 114
  as god 183–214
  as new Augustus 9, 263
  banquet of 7, 183–214
  conquests of 210–11, 254
  palace of 169, 192–200
  see also under Statius

Egypt 252–63
ekphrasis
  in Statius' poetry 3, 13, 18, 26, 28, 32, 95,
    97, 99–101, 132, 134, 143, 167, 169, 193,
    195, 197–8
Elis 33, 136

Elysium 86
Emathia 259
enargeia 29–30
Entellus 108
Epicurus 40–1
epicureanism 79, 116, 201
Enceladus 131, 236, 239
Erato 111, 114
Etna, Mt. 33, 131–3
Euboea 24, 227
Euphrates, River 267–9
Euploea 137
Euripus 24
Europa 247–8
Eurotas, River 171
Euryalus 163
Eurydice 122
Eurystheus 100, 102, 205
Evander 52, 98, 109, 150, 199

Fauns 5, 41–2, 47–8, 51–2, 59, 81, 175
Formiae 36, 114
Fortuna 38

Gades 147–9
Gaius Caesar 264
Gallus, Cornelius 159–60, 246
Ganges, River 204–5
Ganymede 102, 188
Gaurus, Mt. 136
Germania 210–11
Geryon 108
Getae 143
Giants 207, 211, 239
  see also Enceladus
Glaucus 227, 229
Golden Age 243

Hebe 101–2
Hecate
  see under Diana
Helen 107, 224, 256–7
Hellespont 23–4, 32, 40
Hercules
  and Cacus 54–5, 150
  apotheosis/deification of 92, 149–51,
    205, 207–8
  Pollius' temple of 6, 89–155
  see also under Juno
Hermus, River 44

GENERAL INDEX   285

Hero 23–4, 41
Hesperides 140, 145
Hyacinthus 171

Idalium 12, 17
Ino 136, 229–30
Io
  see under Isis
Isis 252–63, 272
Isthmos 136

Janus 54–5
Juno
  and Hercules 100, 118, 126, 134
  temple of 3–4, 95, 99–100, 133–4, 191
Jupiter 38–9, 68, 102, 126, 136, 150, 185–6,
    190, 193–4, 197, 201–3, 206–7, 211, 213,
    236, 247–8, 254

Laocoön 119
landscape
  in Statius' poetry 17–28
Latinus 7, 173, 192–3, 202–3
Lausus 162
Leander 23–4, 32, 40–1
Lethe 156, 162, 255
Limon 137
Lucrinus, Lake 137
Lyaeus
  see under Bacchus

Maecenas 178–9, 222–3
Maecius Celer 8–9
  imperial travel of 215–73
Malea, Cape 40
Mantua 187
Marcellus 162
Marcia, Aqua 32–4, 40–1
Mars 55, 203–4, 207, 262
Manilius Vopiscus 3–4, 11–44
Meliboeus 5, 7, 70, 78, 80, 212, 240–1
Melicertes
  see under Palaemon
Memphis 254, 257–9, 267
Menelaus 256
Mercury 158–9f
Messina 24
Midas 43–4
Minerva 127, 132–4, 186
Misenus 137–8

Molorchus 103
Mulciber
  see under Vulcan

Naiads 30–1, 45, 47–8, 57–8, 61, 70, 73, 76
Naples
  see under Statius
Nemi 113
Nemea 15–16, 103, 136, 147–9
Neptune 21, 127, 221, 245
Nesis 137
Nile, River 239, 254–9, 270
Nisus 254
Numidians 175–7
nymphs 5, 24–7, 31–2, 35, 40, 45–7, 51–3,
    56–76, 88, 117, 124, 126, 139
  see also Arethusa, Cyrene, Pholoe

Odysseus 37, 39, 183–4, 211, 213
Oebalius 223–4
Oeta, Mt. 90–2, 102, 150–1
Olympus, Mt. 208, 237–9
Omphale 108, 140
Opheltes 136
Orion 242–3, 248
Orpheus 99, 122
Ortygia 33
Osiris 103
Ossa, Mt. 237–9

Pactolus, River 44
Palaemon 136, 229–32
Palatine Hill 183, 193–4, 197, 213
Pallas
  see under Minerva
Pallas, son of Evander 162–3, 189
Pallene 206–7
Pan 5, 35, 45–88
paraklausithuron 67, 73
parrot
  see also Atedius Melior, Corinna
Paris 107
Parnassus, Mt. 136
Parthenope 137–8
Pausilypum 137
Pelion, Mt. 237–9
Pelorus 24
Phaeacia 36, 184
Phaethon 164–7, 169, 171–2
Pharos 252, 254, 257

286 GENERAL INDEX

Pharsalus 260
Phasis, River 175–7
Philippi 260
Philomela 174
Phlegra 236
phoenix/Phoenix 181–2, 249, 251, 258
Pholoe 45–88
Phoroneus 252–3
Picus 169, 173, 193
Pindar 42–3
Pirithous 250
Pisa 15–16, 136
Polla 3, 6, 15, 89, 94, 120, 135, 138, 140,
    144–5, 147, 149
Pollius Felix 2–3, 6, 39, 89–155, 233–4
    see also Hercules
Pollux 186, 204–5, 207–8, 223–4, 257
Pompey 49
Praeneste 35
Procne 174, 256
Priam 84, 131, 164, 168, 176
Prometheus 104
propemptikon 8, 215–73
Proserpina 48
Proteus 227
Ptolemy I 257, 267
Ptolemy II 257
Puteoli 135–7, 224, 248, 257
Pyrrhus 131, 164
Pythagoras 181

Quirinal Hill 55
Quirinus
    see under Romulus

Remus 55, 97
Romulus 55, 97, 194, 207

Sabines 55
Scylla 247
sea-faring
    see under Maecius Celer
Sestos 23
Sibyl 48, 228
Sirens 115
    see also under Parthenope
Sirius 15–16, 112–13
Sleep (Somnus) 161–2, 170
Smyrna 187
Statius
    and Callimachean poetics 215–73
    and Domitian 183–214

and the Bay of Naples 1–10
    father of 230–1
    see also artifacts, ekphrasis, landscape,
      trees, wealth
Surrentum 39, 89–155, 225, 233
Syene 195–6
synaesthesia 11, 17–28, 47

Tagus, River 44
Tarquinius Priscus 55
Taygetus, Mt. 35
Telegonus 37, 39
Tereus 174
Thebes 99–100, 127, 229–33, 248,
    270–2
Therapnae 204, 255–7
Theseus 77, 250
Thespius 108
Thessaly 260
Thetis 242–4
Tibur 4, 11–12, 15–16, 19, 21, 27, 32, 34–6,
    38–44, 147–9
Tiburnus 34
Tiryns 91, 102, 147–9, 151, 205
Titans 239
Tithonus 84–5
Titus Tatius 55
Tityrus 70, 212, 240–2
trees
    in Statius' poetry 45–88
Triptolemus 197–200
Trivia
    see under Diana
Turnus 36–7, 67, 110, 130, 162
Tusculum 36–7
Tyre 248, 267

Ulysses
    see under Odysseus

Venus 16, 41, 86, 93, 137, 140, 201–2,
    234–5, 251–2
Vesuvius
    eruption of 3
voluptas/Voluptas 12, 16, 23, 41,
    157–60, 169–70
Vulcan 95, 100, 103, 129, 132–3, 198

wealth
    in Statius' poetry 28–38

Zeugma 267–8

Index Locorum

ANTHOLOGIA LATINA
  112.1 226 n. 23
APULEIUS
  Metamorphoses
    1.10 263 n. 103
    5.12.21 115 n. 47
BVCOLICA EINSIDLENSIA
  1.46 57 n. 27
CALLIMACHUS
  Hymn to Apollo
    105–14 268–9
CALPURNIUS SICULUS
  Eclogae
    4.37 34 n. 56
CATULLUS
  Carmina
    3.1 17 n. 18
    4.3 241 n. 58
    9.6–9 265–6
    11.1–2 250
    11.3–4 250 n. 72
    11.3 176 n. 37
    11.7–8 254 n. 87
    11.8 250 n. 72
    11.10 250 n. 72
    11.14 250 n. 73
    11.21 250 n. 72
    11.23–4 116 n. 48
    13.12 17 n. 18
    29 55 n. 19
    30.4 20 n. 27
    45.25 171 n. 28
    50.1 162 n. 11
    50.2 29 n. 46
    57 55 n. 19
    61.110–11 108 n. 38
    62.7 91 n. 2
    62.45 116 n. 48
    62.56 116 n. 48
    64.1–12 217 n. 4
    64.11–12 238 nn. 50, 52

    64.19–21 244 n. 63
    64.56 20 n. 27
    64.151 20 n. 27
    64.249 237 n. 48
    64.263 167 n. 19
    64.290 62 n. 39
    65.19–20 140 n. 93
    72.1 14 n. 8
    85 74 n. 63
    101.9 108 n. 37
CICERO
  Ad Atticum
    4.8a.3 42 n. 73
  Ad Familiares
    1.9.21 79 n. 68
  Brutus
    264 269
  De consulatu suo
    6.58 (*FPL*[4]) 13 n. 3
  De divinatione
    2.63 62 n. 39
  De finibus
    2.3 269
    2.115 181 n. 44
  De legibus
    3.17.38 236 n. 47
  De natura deorum
    2.24.62 208 n. 47
    3.41.10 91 n. 2
  De oratore
    1.1 79 n. 68
    1.7 62 n. 39
    2.43 221 n. 10
    2.63 26 n. 40
  De re publica
    2.18.33 55 n. 19
  In Verrem
    2.2.94 263 n. 103
  Orator
    27.93 53 n. 12
  Pro Sestio
    98 79 n. 68

288 INDEX LOCORUM

DIONYSIUS OF HALICARNASSUS
Roman Antiquities
  1.57.1 14 n. 7
  1.68.2 14 n. 7
ENNIUS
Scaenica
  247 (Vahlen) 241 n. 58
Spuria
  9 (Skutsch) 241 n. 58
Tragoediae
  208 (Jocelyn) 217 n. 4
FRONTO
Epistulae
  1.204.25–6 81
GELLIUS
Noctes Atticae
  2.18.3 19 n. 21
HECATAEUS
  1 F 308 (Jacoby) 256 n. 93
HESIOD
Theogony
  79 110 n. 40
HOMER
Iliad
  9.432 182 n. 46
Odyssey
  5.296 265 n. 107
  7.103 201 n. 31
  21.406–8 112 n. 44
HORACE
Ars poetica
  217 158 n. 4
  274 184 n. 5
  291 271 n. 126
  395 166 n. 17
  407 161 n. 10
  408–11 19 n. 22
  410 238 n. 50
Carmen Saeculare
  1 51 n. 9
  33 105 n. 29, 139 n. 89
  41 83 n. 79
  45–8 85
  57–60 83
Carmina
  1.1.2 140 n. 95
  1.1.13 241 n. 58

1.1.34 112 n. 43
1.2.45–6 194
1.2.45 210 n. 49
1.3.5–8 221, 245
1.3.19 153
1.3.23–5 239 n. 54
1.3.27–31 103–4
1.3.28 152
1.3.31–2 153
1.3.36 152
1.3.38–40 152, 239 n. 54
1.5.2 261 n. 101
1.7.12–14 32 n. 51, 36 n. 60
1.7.22–3 150 n. 111
1.10.1–6 158–9
1.12.1–3 186
1.12.11 179 n. 41
1.12.51–2 186
1.18.2 19 n. 23, 43
1.18.6 79
1.20.2–3 141 n. 96
1.23.9–10 16 n. 13
1.24.7 79
1.32.2 29 n. 46
1.32.7–8 117 n. 49
1.32.14 166 n. 17
1.33.5–7 65–6
1.37.12–14 225
1.37.26–8 261
2.5.10–17 61 n. 36, 66 n. 46
2.6.18–20 93 n. 6
2.7.18 206 n. 44
2.7.27 141 n. 96
2.9.21–2 268 n. 120
2.10.18–20 112 n. 43
2.11.13 62–3
2.15.4 63
2.16.1–2 40 n. 69
2.16.9–12 79
2.17.1–8 222–3
2.17.11–12 250 n. 73
2.20.1–2 178 n. 40
2.20.7 7, 178 n. 40
2.20.12 178 n. 40
2.20.15–16 178 n. 40, 179
3.3.9–16 207
3.3.11–12 210 n. 49
3.3.15–16 55 n. 16
3.4.21–4 37 n. 62

INDEX LOCORUM   289

3.4.52 239 n. 55
3.11.3 166 n. 17
3.15.7 66 n. 46
3.24.11 143
3.25.18 187
3.27.7 248
3.27.19 248
3.27.23 248
3.27.25 249
3.27.45 249
3.27.72 249
3.29.6–24 40 n. 70
3.29.63 40, 79
3.30.2 42 n. 72, 87 n. 83, 94 n. 8
3.30.6 87 n. 82
3.30.9 181 n. 45
3.30.10 87 n. 82
4.1.1 154
4.1.33 94
4.1.35–6 93 n. 7
4.2.29 163 n. 13
4.2.30–2 14 n. 10
4.2.45 187
4.3.17 166 n. 17
4.4.1 140
4.4.60 144 n. 100
4.8.8 161 n. 10
4.9.1–4 187
4.9.9 29 n. 46
4.9.37–41 83 n. 78
4.14.45 255 n. 90
4.15.3 184 n. 4
4.15.9 55 n. 15
4.15.16 149
Epistulae
1.3.21–2 98
1.20 42 n. 73
1.20.12 181 n. 44
2.1.4–5 208 n. 47
2.1.25 144 n. 101
Epodi
6.15 56 n. 20
7.17–20 55 n. 17
13.9 261 n. 101
15.24 273 n. 132
Sermones
1.1.7 147 n. 106
1.5.3–24 114
1.5.43 265

1.10.37 29 n. 46
1.10.44–5 119
1.10.59 272
1.10.65–6 271 n. 126
2.1.28 272

ILIAS LATINA
561 105 n. 28

ISIDORE
Etymologiae sive Origines
9.3.16 193 n. 16
9.5.21 13 n. 5
15.16.9–10 125 n. 62

JUVENAL
Saturae
7.82–3 224 n. 16

LIVY
Ab urbe condita
1.30.1 55 n. 19
1.45.1–7 58 n. 30
3.68.7 181 n. 45
10.19.18 273 n. 132

[LONGINUS]
On the sublime
35.4 256 n. 92

LUCAN
De bello civili
1.1–2 260
1.135–40 49
1.599 206 n. 46
4.256 260 n. 98
4.581–660 139 n. 92
5.155 254 n. 84
5.622 224 n. 19
6.315 260 n. 98
6.332 260 n. 98
6.350 260 n. 98
6.580 260 n. 98
6.620 260 n. 98
6.820 260 n. 98
7.166 260 n. 98
7.191 260 n. 98
7.427 260 n. 98
7.683 260 n. 98
8.237 267
9.153 268 n. 118
9.689–90 139 n. 92
10.14–52 268 n. 118

290 INDEX LOCORUM

LUCAN (*cont.*)
    10.40 255 n. 90
    10.63 253 n. 80
    10.191 255 n. 90
    10.214 255 n. 90
    10.271–4 258
    10.493 226 n. 23

LUCRETIUS
  De rerum natura
    1.1–2 16, 86, 157–8
    1.17 172
    1.19 17 n. 17
    1.256 179 n. 41
    1.321 160
    1.926–8 116
    1.975 160 n. 8
    2.3 158 n. 3
    2.172–4 158 n. 3
    2.619 167 n. 19
    2.1093–4 201
    3.292–3 201 n. 33
    3.524 160 n. 8
    3.1060–75 41
    5.373 160 n. 8
    5.1011 120
    6.94–5 158

MANILIUS
  Astronomica
    5.334–5 206 n. 46

MARTIAL
  Epigrammata
    1.3.12 42 n. 73
    1.66.5 206 n. 46
    4.54.8 50
    8.55.20 174 n. 34
    9.18.6 32 n. 52
    9.61 50
    9.61.16 62 n. 39
    12.94.8 29 n. 46
    14.185 174 n. 34

NONIUS
  De compendiosa doctrina
    230M = 341L 13 n. 5

OVID
  Amores
    1.8.78 74 n. 63
    2.6.7–8 170 n. 26, 174
    2.6.54 259 n. 97
    2.11.23 234
    2.11.49–56 266 n. 111

    2.13.7–10 254
    3.1.1 49–50
    3.12.41–2 256
  Ars amatoria
    1.213–14 264
    2.466 161 n. 9
    2.723 161 n. 9
    3.561 14 n. 9
    3.795 161
  Epistulae ex Ponto
    2.5.25–6 246 n. 69, 247
  Fasti
    1.98 234 n. 43
    1.201 121 n. 55
    1.423–30 57 n. 25
    2.6 29 n. 46
    2.273 66 n. 46
    2.754 234 n. 43
    4.662 27 n. 43
    6.805–6 19 n. 21
  Heroides
    3.129 182 n. 46
    12.142 234 n. 43
    13.99 266 n. 114
    14.107–8 254
    15.31–2 19 n. 21
    15.112 234 n. 43
    18.179–80 23 n. 34
    18.198 33 n. 54
    19.192 234 n. 43
    20.61 171 n. 28
  Metamorphoses
    1.154–5 239 n. 54
    1.319 242 n. 59
    1.422–3 254 n. 87
    1.699 61 n. 32
    2.105–10 7
    2.108 167, 172 n. 30
    2.255 255 n. 90
    2.367–80 169 n. 25
    2.544–53 172 n. 30
    2.776 43 n. 74
    3.23 58 n. 28
    3.185–94 58 n. 28
    5.187 254 n. 87
    5.294–678 173 n. 31
    5.324 254 n. 87
    5.368 224 n. 19
    5.638 33
    6.103 92 n. 4
    6.667–79 55 n. 18
    9.773 254 n. 85

9.774 254 n. 87
11.63 122
11.593 161
11.600–1 161
13.822 253 n. 79
14.60 227 n. 30
14.88 115 n. 47
14.320–96 173 n. 33
14.558 221 n. 10
15.391–407 181–2, 259 n. 97
15.823–4 260
Remedia amoris
35–6 74 n. 63
507–9 170 n. 27
Tristia
2.424 19 n. 22, 238 n. 50
5.2.51–2 209 n. 49
5.10.35 14 n. 9

PAULINUS OF NOLA
Carmina
28.33 242 n. 60

PAULUS DIACONUS
Epitoma Festi
p. 301 68 n. 53

PAUSANIAS
Description of Greece
1.6.3 257
1.7.1 257

PETRONIUS
Satyrica
131.8 62 n. 39

PLATO
Phaedrus
229a–b 62 n. 39
236e 62 n. 39

PLINY THE ELDER
Naturalis Historia
2.37.101 224 n. 18
5.10.51 255 n. 90
5.21.86 267 n. 115
7.10.47 13 n. 5
12.6–13 62 n. 39
34.43.150 267
36.60.184 30 n. 48
36.7.48 55 n. 19

PLINY THE YOUNGER
Epistulae
1.3.1 62 n. 39
2.10.3 42 n. 73

PROPERTIUS
Elegiae
1.3.1 237 n. 48
1.3.43–4 22 n. 31
1.6.15 170 n. 27
1.7.19 220 n. 10
1.8.33 237
1.9.12 221 n. 10
1.10.1–6 159–60, 164
1.13.22 66 n. 47
1.13.23–4 91 n. 2
1.17.6 233 n. 39
2.1.1–2 221 n. 10
2.1.19–20 239
2.1.39–42 236
2.1.45 237
2.2.85–93 125 n. 64
2.13.3 246 n. 69, 247
2.15.2 171 n. 28
2.21.14 231 n. 37
2.24.23 19 n. 22
2.29A.1 162 n. 11
2.29A.17–18 180
2.33.5 234 n. 44
2.34.2 237
2.34.65–6 37
3.3.1 34 n. 56
3.2.12 25 n. 38
3.8.11 170 n. 27
3.9.4 242 n. 59
3.9.35–42 233
3.11.25–6 267 n. 116
3.17.37–40 141–2
3.19.24 178 n. 39
3.22.24 32 n. 52
3.22.9–10 140
4.6.69–70 112 n. 43
4.7.81–6 36 n. 60

QUINTILIAN
Institutio Oratoria
1.4.25 13 n. 5
1.6.38 161 n. 9
4.1.77 256 n. 91
6.1.52 231 n. 37
8.6.23–7 53 n. 12
9.4.127 221 n. 10

SENECA THE YOUNGER
Agamemnon
338–9 239 n. 55
Dialogi
9.11.10 263 n. 103

292   INDEX LOCORUM

SENECA THE YOUNGER (*cont.*)
  Epistulae morales
    100 25–6
  Medea
    607–12 217
  Naturales quaestiones
    4.1 255 n. 90
    6.7.1 256 n. 92
    6.8 255 n. 90
  Oedipus
    426 176 n. 37
  Thyestes
    646 25 n. 38

[SENECA THE YOUNGER]
  Hercules Oetaeus
    1625 62 n. 37

SERVIUS
  Ad Aeneida
    1.28 102 n. 24
    1.66 221 n. 10
    1.126 49 n. 7, 239
    1.340 184 n. 2
    1.607 144 n. 103
    1.686 67 n. 49
    2.15 226 n. 24
    3.12 14 n. 7
    4.193 40 n. 67
    4.335 184 n. 2
    7. 47 48 n. 6
    8.276 68 n. 55, 150–1
    10.287 236 n. 47
    11.93 263 n. 103
  Ad Eclogas
    7. 61 68 n. 55
    10.71 246 n. 69
  Ad Georgica
    3.135–7 40 n. 67
    4.125 224 n. 16

SILIUS ITALICUS
  Punica
    1.102–3 254 n. 84
    6.454 254 n. 84
    11.81 254 n. 84

STATIUS
  Achilleis
    1.5 230 n. 35
    1.408 127 n. 65
    1.420 238 n. 53
  Silvae
    1 *praef.* 6 271 n. 126

1 *praef.* 7 174 n. 34
1 *praef.* 23–5 3
1 *praef.* 24–5 42
1 *praef.* 26 13 n. 4
1.2.61 17 n. 17
1.2.203–8 15 n. 12
1.2.238 116 n. 48
1.3.1–12 11–17
1.3.1 159 n. 6
1.3.13–23 17–21
1.3.24–33 22–4
1.3.34–46 24–8
1.3.41 229 n. 33
1.3.47–51 28–9
1.3.52–7 29–30
1.3.52 4
1.3.57–63 30–1
1.3.64–9 31–3
1.3.70–5 33–4
1.3.76–80 34–6
1.3.81–9 36–8
1.3.90–8 38–41
1.3.99–104 41–43
1.3.100 186 n. 7
1.3.105–10 43–4
1.5.26–7 32 n. 52
1.5.60–1 263 n. 103
2.1.54 225 n. 22
2.1.180 230 n. 34
2.2.10 121 n. 57
2.2.13 233
2.2.19 219 n. 6
2.2.28–9 39
2.2.34–5 230 n. 34
2.2.59–62 230 n. 36
2.2.60–1 271
2.2.81–2 31 n. 50
2.2.85–93 125 n. 63
2.2.95–6 143
2.2.131–2 40 n. 68
2.2.142 233, 265 n. 105
2.3.1–7 46–51
2.3.8–17 51–7
2.3.18–30 57–60
2.3.31–42 60–3
2.3.43–52 63–9
2.3.43–5 20 n. 26
2.3.53–61 69–74
2.3.62–71 74–83
2.3.69 5
2.3.72–7 83–8

INDEX LOCORUM 293

2.4.1–3 157–62
2.4.4–10 162–5
2.4.11–15 6, 165–71
2.4.16–21 171–5
2.4.22–8 175–7
2.4.29–32 177–9
2.4.32 7
2.4.33–7 179–82
2.7.73–4 174 n. 34
2.7.75 238 n. 50
3 *praef.* 5 142 n. 98
3 *praef.* 6–7 2
3 *praef.* 9–10 142 n. 98
3.1.1–7 90–94
3.1.8–11 94–6
3.1.12–22 96–101
3.1.15 6, 13 n. 3
3.1.16 230 n. 34, 271 n. 127
3.1.23–33 101–4
3.1.34–48 104–10
3.1.49–51 110–12
3.1.52–4 112–13
3.1.55–67 113–17
3.1.68–75 117–18
3.1.76–81 119–20
3.1.82–8 120–1
3.1.89–90 121–2
3.1.91–6 122–4
3.1.97–116 124–7
3.1.115 230 n. 34, 271 n. 127
3.1.117–29 127–32
3.1.117 16 n. 16
3.1.130–8 132–4
3.1.139–53 134–8
3.1.154–62 138–40
3.1.163–4 140–2
3.1.164 190
3.1.164–70 142–4
3.1.170–9 144–7
3.1.180–6 147–55
3.2.1–4 216–20
3.2.5–8 220–4
3.2.11–12 224
3.2.17–24 224–5
3.2.20 238
3.2.25–8 225–7
3.2.36–8 227–8
3.2.39–41 229–32
3.2.42–6 228–9
3.2.47–9 229
3.2.50–60 232–7

3.2.61–70 237–42
3.2.71–7 242–4
3.2.78–83 244–7
3.2.83–9 247–9
3.2.90–100 249–52
3.2.101–7 252–5
3.2.107–16 255–9
3.2.117–20 259–62
3.2.121–6 262–3
3.2.127–35 264–7
3.2.136–41 267–70
3.2.142–3 270–3
3.2.143 234 n. 42
3.5.7 264 n. 105
3.5.35–6 234 n. 42, 271
3.5.75–6 257 n. 95
4 *praef.* 6–7 186
4 *praef.* 19 271 n. 126
4.2.1–4 183–4
4.2.5–8 185–7
4.2.8–10 187–8
4.2.10–13 188–9
4.2.14–16 189–90
4.2.16–17 190–2
4.2.18–20 192–3
4.2.18 169
4.2.20–2 193–4
4.2.23–9 195–7
4.2.26 76 n. 66
4.2.30–7 197–200
4.2.38–45 200–3
4.2.46–7 203–4
4.2.47–51 204–6
4.2.48 257 n. 94
4.2.52–6 206–8
4.2.57–9 208–9
4.2.59–62 209–10
4.2.63–7 210–14
4.2.64 7
4.4.8 223 n. 15
4.4.15 12 n. 2
4.4.20–1 223 n. 15
4.4.55 235
4.4.87–9 229 n. 33
4.4.88–9 234 n. 42, 271
4.6.90 94 n. 10
4.7.2 234 n. 42
4.7.25–8 271 nn. 126, 129
4.7.26 234 n. 42
4.8.16–17 43 n. 74
4.8.53 257 n. 94

294 INDEX LOCORUM

STATIUS (*cont.*)
  5.3.127 235 n. 46
  5.3.140 257 n. 94
  5.3.187 267 n. 115
  5.3.233–7 230–1, 235
  5.3.233–4 271 n. 126
  Thebais
    1.10 271 n. 127
    1.145 94 n. 10
    1.180–8 248
    2.454–5 271 n. 127
    3.552 238 n. 51
    4.238–9 15 n. 12
    4.357 271 n. 127
    4.480 175 n. 35
    4.495 233 n. 38
    4.611 271 n. 127
    5.668 14 n. 9
    6.257 127 n. 65
    7.456 271 n. 127
    7.500 95 n. 12
    7.665 271 n. 127
    7.792–3 224 n. 18
    7.793 257 n. 94
    7.812 148 n. 108
    8.232–3 271
    8.310 148 n. 108
    9.529 242 n. 60
    10.446 186 n. 7
    10.787 271 n. 127
    10.873 271 n. 127
    12.19 242 n. 60
    12.482 77
    12.798 271
    12.809–12 234 n. 42
    12.809 184 n. 4, 222, 272
    12.812 271 n. 126

SUETONIUS
  Augustus
    18.1 268 n. 118
    22 55 n. 15
    29.3 194 n. 17
    94.6 202 n. 35
  Caligula
    52 268 n. 118
  Vita Lucani
    1 174 n. 34
  Vita Vergilii
    30 38 n. 63

TACITUS
  Annales
    4.64–5 55 n. 19

THEOCRITUS
  Idylls
    2.38 220 n. 9

TIBULLUS
  Elegiae
    1.2.9 170 n. 26
    1.3.13–14 234
    1.3.43 168 n. 22
    1.3.72 168 n. 22
    1.4.71–2 170 n. 26
    1.5.35 228 n. 31
    1.6.63 64
    1.7.24 255 n. 90
    1.7.49 102–3
    1.8.69 66 n. 46
    1.10.63 171 n. 28
    2.1.87–90 27 n. 43

[TIBULLUS]
  Elegiae
    3.3.16 25 n. 38
    3.4.37–40 166
    3.4.75 170 n. 26
    3.6.58 32 n. 52

VALERIUS FLACCUS
  Argonautica
    8.362 236 n. 47

VALERIUS MAXIMUS
  Facta et dicta memorabilia
    4.7. *praef.* 40 n. 67

VARRO
  De lingua Latina
    5.35 125 n. 62
    5.46 55 n. 19
    6.52 158 n. 4
    6.55 165

VIRGIL
  Aeneis
    1.6 184
    1.10 97 n. 14
    1.23 118
    1.34 95
    1.45 229
    1.46 114 n. 45, 185, 272–3
    1.51 225

INDEX LOCORUM 295

1.53–5 228
1.55–6 243
1.56 272 n. 131
1.61 195 n. 19, 228
1.63 228
1.64 226 n. 24
1.66 202 n. 35, 220 n. 10
1.81 228
1.83 229
1.85 228
1.114–16 233 n. 38
1.134 195 n. 19
1.141 228, 272 n. 131
1.142 21
1.147 229 n. 33
1.150 243
1.153 202 n. 35
1.216 211
1.254–6 201–2
1.260 184 n. 3
1.263–4 115
1.293–6 54 n. 14
1.294 272 n. 131
1.304 69 n. 53
1.441–92 3
1.444 226 n. 24
1.446–8 254 n. 84
1.454–6 100
1.455–6 133
1.494–5 99, 194, 197
1.494 191
1.499 58 n. 28
1.511 229
1.538 245
1.572 245
1.590 86
1.600 187
1.603 209
1.617 95 n. 12
1.637–8 184 n. 2
1.639 271 n. 128
1.648–52 106–7
1.670 259 n. 97
1.687 234–5
1.700 188
1.701–2 199 n. 27
1.703–4 201 n. 31
1.708 188, 198
1.714 259 n. 97

1.723 211
2.19 227
2.27 231
2.51 227
2.177 130 n. 73
2.205–20 235 n. 45
2.212 119
2.234–9 225–7, 231
2.262 227 n. 26
2.268 112
2.313 138 n. 88
2.352 218
2.440–54 168
2.448 25 n. 38
2.463 130 n. 74
2.479 131
2.511 164
2.535 168 n. 20
2.557 176
2.620 251
2.627 131
2.697 78 n. 69
2.779 190 n. 11
2.789 217 n. 5
3.35 204 n. 40
3.70 233 n. 39
3.191 241 n. 58
3.403 225 n. 21
3.420–32 247 n. 71
3.422 240 n. 57
3.537–43 226 n. 24
3.575 127 n. 67
3.582 131
3.646–7 144
3.694–6 33 n. 54
4.9–11 263
4.50–1 139 n. 91
4.51 234
4.69 58 n. 28
4.89 148 n. 108
4.160–72 117–18
4.199–202 254 n. 84
4.227 86
4.235 234 n. 41
4.269 190 n. 11
4.291 203 n. 38
4.305 203 n. 38, 252 n. 77
4.355 252 n. 77
4.373 252 n. 77

296 INDEX LOCORUM

VIRGIL (*cont.*)

4.378 205
4.382–3 220 n. 8
4.384–6 251
4.384 252 n. 76
4.407 234 n. 41
4.408 244 n. 65
4.415 164
4.420 246 n. 68
4.425 130 n. 73
4.441–6 62 n. 37
4.476–7 202 n. 34
4.480–1 206
4.519 164
4.529–32 246
4.529 259 n. 97
4.566 241 n. 58
4.568–9 234 n. 41
4.590 57 n. 26
4.597 252 n. 77
4.604 164
4.610–12 220
4.649 234 n. 41
5.113 138 n. 88
5.139 138 n. 88
5.150 131 n. 77
5.235 218
5.239–40 219
5.285 66 n. 46
5.319 254 n. 82
5.361 254
5.410 108
5.424 108
5.479 108
5.739 253 n. 81
5.755 92 n. 4
5.763 220 n. 9
5.824–5 219
5.864 115 n. 47
6.2 227
6.36 228
6.120 179 n. 41
6.123 151 n. 113
6.136–7 48
6.149–235 137 n. 86
6.204 69
6.233 138 n. 88
6.266–7 230
6.304 146
6.392–3 151 n. 113
6.403 97 n. 14

6.406 212 n. 52
6.450 259 n. 97
6.471 130 n. 71
6.516 225
6.553 130 n. 73
6.596 13 n. 3, 100 n. 22
6.681 67 n. 52
6.687–9 191
6.767 176
6.800 254 n. 87
6.801–3 151 n. 113
6.851–3 115
6.847–9 123
6.857 80 n. 72
6.861 254 n. 82
6.882 162
6.900 78 n. 69
7.37–41 111
7.45–9 173 n. 33
7.94 94 n. 10
7.153 169
7.157 92 n. 4
7.162 62 n. 37
7.170–2 193
7.170 169, 173, 198 n. 25
7.183–6 202–3
7.189–91 173
7.302 247 n. 71
7.308 114 n. 45, 185, 273
7.353 205 n. 42
7.362 61 n. 35
7.495 114 n. 45
7.558 190 n. 11
7.607 167
7.610 54
7.615 167 n. 19
7.617 178 n. 38
7.626 114 n. 46
7.628 138 n. 88
7.641 231
7.655–69 114 n. 45
7.662 94 n. 10
7.669 106 n. 31
7.672 43
7.700 179 n. 41
7.761–82 114
7.799–800 38 n. 64
7.810 55 n. 18
8.4 80 n. 72
8.24–5 198 n. 25
8.33 34 n. 55

INDEX LOCORUM   297

8.51 66 n. 46
8.88 243 n. 62
8.102 66 n. 46, 117 n. 49
8.107 224 n. 20
8.180–1 199
8.189 91 n. 3
8.191 100 n. 21
8.219–20 54
8.221 100 n. 21, 106 n. 30
8.227–8 94 n. 10
8.228 55
8.230 108
8.231 100 n. 21
8.237 100 n. 21
8.276–7 150
8.276 68
8.285–8 150–1
8.288–9 109
8.305 131 n. 77
8.314–16 52
8.347–8 98
8.362–5 52–3
8.383 86
8.418–20 132–3
8.418–19 127 n. 66
8.421 133 n. 81
8.425 133
8.435–6 133 n. 79
8.446 129
8.526 138 n. 88
8.568 235 n. 45
8.625–731 3
8.676 6, 13 n. 3, 97, 100, 198
8.687 253 n. 81
8.691 101, 198
8.696 253
8.697 261 n. 99
8.704 13 n. 3
8.726 267 n. 116, 268
8.728 129
8.730 97 n. 15
9.137 130
9.204 184 n. 3
9.408 121 n. 56
9.481–3 163
9.481 95 nn. 12 and 14
9.503 138 n. 88
9.525–7 110
9.530 236 n. 47
9.710 37
9.803 199 n. 26

10.159 184 n. 3
10.163 231
10.179 15 n. 12
10.189–93 169 n. 25
10.212 17 n. 19
10.279 127 n. 67
10.287–8 236 n. 47
10.327 163 n. 12
10.330 131 n. 77
10.345 62 n. 37
10.393 163 n. 12
10.427–8 130 n. 72
10.437 190 n. 11
10.507–8 189
10.542 204 n. 40
10.545 62 n. 37
10.611 202 n. 37
10.654 236 n. 47
10.774 61 n. 35
10.791 146 n. 104
10.825 162
11.20 209 n. 48
11.36 192 n. 14
11.42 162–3
11.157–8 209 n. 48
11.192 138 n. 88
11.424 138 n. 88
11.484 61 n. 35
11.560 221 n. 11
11.578 16 n. 15
11.651 130
12.70 67
12.275 254 n. 82
12.412 86
12.433 122 n. 59
12.584 231
12.687 240 n. 57
12.695 130 n. 74
12.708 76 n. 66
12.807 202 n. 37
12.849 102 n. 23
12.885 34 n. 55
12.897–8 78
Eclogae
1.1–5 240
1.1 117 n. 50
1.4 34 n. 56, 70
1.10 29 n. 46
1.15 242
1.27–9 212
1.47 242

298   INDEX LOCORUM

VIRGIL (*cont.*)
    1.53 78
    1.60 242
    1.64–6 265 n. 106
    1.65–6 241
    1.67 8, 212
    1.70–1 212, 241
    1.73 5, 80
    1.83 70
    2.29 120
    2.45 102 n. 25
    4.18 168 n. 20
    4.24–5 180
    4.31–3 243
    5.40 66
    5.74–5 76
    5.74 75 n. 64
    6.1 29 n. 46
    6.75 227 n. 30
    6.82 171
    7.6 117 n. 50
    7.9 102 n. 25
    7.47 117 n. 50
    7.58 199 n. 29
    7.61 151 n. 112
    8.30 91 n. 2
    9.39–41 102 n. 25
    9.56–8 220 n. 9
    10.1–5 33 n. 54
    10.71–3 107 n. 33
    10.70–4 246
    10.75–6 70
  Georgica
    1.10–11 48 n. 6
    1.11–12 175
    1.70 62 n. 38, 97
    1.105 62 n. 38
    1.126 78 n. 69
    1.250 253 n. 81
    1.464 80 n. 72
    1.489–92 260
    1.509 268
    2.18–19 75
    2.20–1 72 n. 58
    2.29 72 n. 57
    2.54 80 n. 75
    2.55–6 82
    2.70 63
    2.76 72 n. 57
    2.78 71 n. 57
    2.87 36 n. 60
    2.110–13 199 n. 29

    2.170–4 190 n. 11
    2.207–8 53 n. 13
    2.267 80 n. 75
    2.277 80 n. 75
    2.307 72 n. 57
    2.312–13 86–7
    2.328 179 n. 41
    2.330–1 227 n. 28
    2.471 144 n. 102
    2.473–4 98
    2.488–9 70
    2.488 204 n. 41
    2.490–4 13 n. 3
    2.494 53 n. 13
    2.507 81 n. 77
    2.541–2 184 n. 4
    3.4–5 103 n. 26
    3.16 190 n. 11
    3.19 103 n. 26
    3.66–8 145, 188–9
    3.66 148 n. 107
    3.180 15 n. 12
    3.213 130 n. 72
    3.258–63 23
    3.294 111
    3.331–4 71
    3.373 130 n. 72
    4.78 147
    4.119 36 n. 60
    4.138 233 n. 39
    4.145–6 62
    4.206–9 148
    4.228 168–9
    4.329 139
    4.331 130
    4.339 57
    4.352 57
    4.388 227 n. 29
    4.418–19 127 n. 66
    4.464 166 n. 17
    4.560 190 n. 11
    4.561 268
    4.565 29 n. 46

[VIRGIL]
  Ciris
    60 227 n. 30
  Culex
    1 246 n. 69
    123–4 62 n. 39
    251–3 174
  Elegiae in Maecenatem
    2.171 64 n. 42